DATE DUE		

Building a
Sustainable Society

Norton/Worldwatch Books

Lester R. Brown: *The Twenty-Ninth Day: Accommodating Human Needs and Numbers to the Earth's Resources*

Lester R. Brown: *Building a Sustainable Society*

Lester R. Brown, Christopher Flavin, and Colin Norman: *Running on Empty: The Future of the Automobile in an Oil-Short World*

Erik P. Eckholm: *Losing Ground: Environmental Stress and World Food Prospects*

Erik P. Eckholm: *The Picture of Health: Environmental Sources of Disease*

Denis Hayes: *Rays of Hope: The Transition to a Post-Petroleum World*

Kathleen Newland: *The Sisterhood of Man*

Colin Norman: *The God That Limps: Science and Technology in the Eighties*

Bruce Stokes: *Helping Ourselves: Local Solutions to Global Problems*

Building a Sustainable Society

Lester R. Brown

A WORLDWATCH INSTITUTE BOOK

W·W·NORTON & COMPANY
New York   London

Library of Congress Cataloging in Publication Data
Brown, Lester Russell, 1934–
Building a sustainable society.
"A Worldwatch Institute book."
Includes bibliographical references and index.
1. Economic policy. I. Worldwatch Institute.
II. Title.
HD82.B733 1981   338.9   81–11135
ISBN 0-393-01482-7   AACR2

W. W. Norton & Company, Inc. 500 Fifth Avenue, New York, N.Y. 10110
W. W. Norton & Company Ltd. 25 New Street Square, London EC4A 3NT

1 2 3 4 5 6 7 8 9 0

To Brian and Brenda—
and generations to come

Contents

Part II. The Path to Sustainability

Contents :ix

Preface

This book is not an isolated effort to discuss the sustainable society, but rather part of the continuing research program of the Worldwatch Institute. For those who regularly read the Worldwatch Papers, much of the material in the early chapters on converging demands will be familiar. The material is included here particularly for the sake of those readers abroad who do not have ready access to the Institute's other publications. Those familiar with the issues may want to go directly from the Introduction to Part II, concentrating on the two-thirds of the book that is prescriptive.

Although the issues addressed here are the same as those covered in the early years of Worldwatch, the perspective is far different. When the Institute began in early 1975, there was little appreciation of the firewood crisis that was emerging in the Third World. In Washington, the official position was that OPEC's 1973 increase in the price of oil was artificially high and that it would shortly return to a more normal level. There was scant acknowledgment of the extent of soil erosion, a problem now recognized as worldwide. It was still hoped that the leveling off of the world fish catch in the early seventies was but a temporary interruption in a long-term increase. At that time there was little understanding of the relationship between global deforestation, and lumber prices and the cost of housing. Double-digit global inflation was believed to be an aberration, a result of the unwarranted OPEC oil-price increase.

Now, in 1981, the perspective has changed. Awareness of these problems is far more widespread. Publication during the seventies of such studies as *The Limits to Growth*, *Mankind at the Turning Point*, *Soft Energy Paths*, and *Energy Future* drew attention to the forces that threaten to undermine the economy, such as environmental deterioration and oil-reserve depletion, and to the need to move in new directions. Nearly a decade of public discussion and debate of the issues was capped with the release of the U.S. goverment's *Global 2000 Report* in the summer of 1980. With this official recognition of the issues, the time has come to devise a response, to outline the steps to a sustainable society.

The picture of a sustainable society that is drawn here has of necessity been painted with a broad brush. It could not be otherwise if the analysis were to be confined to a single volume. The purpose is to describe the essential character of a sustainable society, to provide a sense of direction for planners and policymakers who are too busy to do all the reading and research needed to make decisions.

Although this book was written in the urban setting of Washington, D.C., and taps the vast flows of information from all over the world that converge in a major capital, it also was shaped by my own agricultural roots. The analysis of trends and events reflects not only a decade of farming during my high school and college years, but six months spent living in Indian villages and more than a decade of intensive involvement in world agricultural development while working with the U.S. Department of Agriculture.

As noted earlier, this book is not a fresh beginning. Nor is it the last word. Subsequent Worldwatch Papers and other books will elaborate on many of the issues raised here. A forthcoming Worldwatch book, for example, will elaborate on the subject of Chapter 9, "Renewable Energy: Turning to the Sun."

In an undertaking of this scale, an author is indebted not only to people who assisted directly with the book, but also to many writers and analysts for their intellectual contributions. Beyond this, I am heavily indebted to the United Nations Fund for Population Activities for the financial support for this project. Rafael Salas, who heads the fund, and Jyoti Singh, our project officer, have been a great help as the book evolved. In addition, there are many sources of financial support for the Institute above and beyond those that directly supported *Building A Sustainable Society.* All these debts are so numerous that I have devoted several pages to acknowledgments at the end of the book.

Building a
Sustainable Society

civilization suddenly collapsed. Within decades, the population fell to less than one-tenth of what it had been. An analysis of core samplings from two lake beds in the area hints at the reason for this abrupt decline. As population pressure increased, soil erosion gradually accelerated. The topsoil was being washed into the area's lakes, draining the cropland of its productivity and one of the world's early civilizations of its sustenance.

The members of the joint research team from the University of Chicago and the University of Florida who made these discoveries observe that population-induced environmental stresses had become intense during the centuries preceding collapse. They report that the area was almost wholly deforested by A.D. 250. Deforestation and mounting pressure on croplands then led to the loss of topsoil and the gradual decline of the land's productivity. In passing, the research team points out that the environmental havoc so discernible from our current perspective may not have been perceptible to the "managerial elite or their economic advisors."[2]

These new findings make us look twice at the root causes of the collapse of other early civilizations. The fall of the societies located in the Tigris and Euphrates River Basin had long been attributed to outside invaders. Yet more recent information indicates that the Mesopotamian civilizations, too, may have been the victims of cumulative environmental stresses that eventually reduced food supplies and undermined their economies.[3]

Located in an arid region, the Fertile Crescent civilization grew and flourished on the strength of the food supply that irrigation made possible. But because the irrigation systems had no drainage components, the underground water table gradually rose, and waterlogging and salting of the soil ensued. The land's productivity could not be sustained over the long term.

Like the lowlands of Guatemala, which once supported as

1

Introduction

One of the major centers of Mayan civilization recently made the news, a thousand years after its collapse. This belated attention came when *Science* carried a detailed article in late 1979 analyzing the society's long-term evolution and eventual downfall.[1] Using the latest techniques of paleo-ecological research, scientists determined that the number of Mayans in the lowlands of Guatemala had expanded continuously over 17 centuries, beginning about the time of Homeric Greece in 800 B.C. Doubling on the average of every 408 years, the population by A.D. 900 had reached five million with a density comparable to that of the most agriculturally intensive societies of today.

At this agricultural, cultural, and architectural peak, the

many people as the whole of contemporary Guatemala, the Tigris-Euphrates area may have been even more populous in early times than it is today. Similarly, North Africa was once the granary of the Roman Empire, but Libya and Algeria now import half of their grain from North America.[4]

If environmental stresses undermined earlier civilizations, whose population doubling times were measured in centuries, what is their impact now when population doubling time is measured in decades? Today, world population is expanding at nearly 2 percent per year, and in many countries the rate is 3 percent or more.[5] The ultimately disastrous rate of increase among the Mayans appears almost leisurely in comparison.

Does this comparison suggest that the Mayans' legacy is our own? That our "managerial elite" is blind to the environmental signs of our times? And what are these signs?

Surely, soil erosion is one. Even though world food output has more than doubled since 1950, that impressive increase has entailed land abuse so severe that fully one-fifth and perhaps as much as one-third of the world's cropland is losing topsoil at a rate that is undermining its long-term productivity.[6] In Washington, the Department of Agriculture reported in early 1981 that the inherent productivity of 34 percent of U.S. cropland is now falling because of the excessive loss of topsoil.[7] A widespread global phenomenon, soil erosion remains a problem that few countries have been able to address effectively.

The global cropland base is also threatened by the conversion of agricultural lands to other uses. In the mid-western United States, shopping centers stand where only a few years ago corn grew. West Germany is losing 1 percent of its agricultural land to urban encroachment every four years.[8] In southern China, factories are being built on land that for generations yielded two rice harvests annually.

Each year, urban sprawl, village expansion, and highway construction claim several million acres of prime cropland, while land hungry farmers push cultivation onto ever more fragile soils. We can now see, as perhaps the Mayans could not, the double-edged effect of population growth on the cropland base. Population increase simultaneously generates a demand for more cropland and creates pressure to convert the cropland to other uses. Wherever population growth is rapid, this double-edged effect can quickly lead societies into crises.

In addition to the threat from soil erosion, a second major threat is the unsustainable relationship that has developed between our contemporary civilization and the biological systems that support it. Our economic system depends heavily on forests, grasslands, and oceanic fisheries for lumber, firewood, paper, meat, milk, butter, cheese, leather, wool, seafood, and numerous lesser commodities. Together, these three natural biological systems provide not only most of the animal protein in our diet but energy and raw materials as well.

Unprecedented demand for these commodities, the products of postwar affluence and record population increases, now exceeds the carrying capacity of biological systems in many parts of the world. Overfishing, overgrazing, and deforestation have become widespread. As demand exceeds the sustainable yield of biological systems, we begin to consume the productive resource base itself, engaging in the biological equivalent of deficit financing.

The third clearly identifiable threat to contemporary civilization is the potential depletion of oil reserves before alternative energy sources are developed. Most of the readily accessible, remaining reserves of oil will be consumed within a few decades, but development of new sources of energy to power the economy is far behind schedule. We live in a petroleum culture that is fast running out of petroleum.

Each of the three threats to civilization—the erosion of soil, the deterioration of biological systems, and the rapid depletion of oil reserves—adversely affects food prospects. Environmental stresses that affect the food system threaten to undermine our contemporary global civilization as they did earlier, local ones. In the absence of immediate attention to these threats, the struggle to make it from one harvest to the next may become a global preoccupation.

Indeed, there are signs that the food problem may unfold during the eighties as dramatically as the energy problem did during the seventies. The parallels are disturbing. Just as countries everywhere had become addicted to imported oil by the early seventies, so they have become dependent on imported grain by the early eighties. Just as the world had come to depend heavily on the Middle East for oil, so it now depends overwhelmingly on North America for grain. The final parallel is perhaps the most disturbing. Just as Middle Eastern oil is being depleted, so too are North American soils. At the existing intensity of cultivation, every ton of grain exported leads to the loss of several tons of topsoil.

These stresses and strains are shaping the world economy of the early eighties. Inflation threatens to become uncontrollable. There is no immediately foreseeable limit on the price of oil. World food reserves are at a near record low. Mounting international debt threatens the viability of the international monetary system. Inflationary fears are shifting capital away from productive investment to speculation in gold, farmland, grain, oil, and real estate.

In the United States the response to the economic stresses is to talk about the need for reindustrialization. "Supply-side" economists argue that incentives to expand production will bring back the rapid growth, low inflation, and full employment of yesteryear. They believe that reduced taxes for corporate investors and accelerated investment depreciation schedules will do the trick. Unfortunately, these remedies deal with the symptoms of our problems, not their causes.

If economists persist in treating only the symptoms, there is little hope that civilization can be sustained. If we cannot arrest the excessive erosion of soil from our croplands, how can we feed ourselves in the years ahead? If we cannot preserve the natural biological systems that underpin the global economy, how can we preserve the economic system on which our livelihood depends? If we cannot conserve the remaining reserves of oil until alternative energy sources are developed, the fate that befell the Mayans eleven centuries ago may be ours as well.

What separates us from the Mayans, of course, is our understanding of our environment and our predicament. We know we are on an unsustainable path. The Mayans may not have recognized the threats to their society, but we see what threatens ours. We also know that there are no simple technological fixes. Wrong responses can themselves spawn new threats to civilization. Attempts to replace oil with nuclear power will lead to weapons proliferation, political instability, and possibly self-destruction. Excessive dependence on coal as a transition fuel could lead to a buildup in atmospheric carbon dioxide and changes in climate that would make it impossible for our grandchildren to feed themselves.

Intertwined though they are, each of these threats to society requires a different policy response. If soils are to be preserved, millions of farmers the world over will have to change their agricultural practices, in most cases abandoning quick-return practices for more sustainable ones. Protecting the biological support systems will require regulating the harvest and, it follows, regulating demand either through higher prices or rationing. To maintain a steady supply of safe energy, governments, corporations, and individuals will need to invest heavily in renewable energy resources. Creating a sustainable society will require fundamental economic and social changes, a wholesale alteration of economic priorities and population policies.

The magnitude of these changes is scarcely in question. Every facet of human existence—diet, employment, leisure, values, politics, and habits—will be touched. As the transition proceeds, new skills will be needed and old skills will become obsolete. Wind meterologists will replace petroleum geologists. Farmers will become energy producers as well as consumers.

Energy auditors, solar architects, foresters, and family planners will be in great demand. This need for new skills will thoroughly challenge the educational and training facilities of universities, corporations, and government agencies.

Population distribution will be altered as economic activity gravitates toward sources of renewable energy. Just as early industrial society evolved in close proximity to coal mines, new industrial centers will develop around concentrations of renewable energy—hydroelectric power sites, geothermal fields, wind farms, heavily forested regions, and regions of abundant sunlight. Geographically, economic activity will be more diffuse and less centralized, in keeping with the broad dispersal of renewable energy sources.

Of the many dimensions of the transition to a sustainable society, the most critical is time. Because we are at the turning point in resource management, the course of the transformation will be set well before the eighties end. Unlike the earlier energy transitions which were relatively leisurely, the shift from oil to sustainable sources of energy must be compressed into the next few decades.

Mounting worldwide inflationary pressures indicate that the transition is already behind schedule. Yet, despite rising food prices and the other signs of the lag, there is reason for hope. China has halved its population growth rate in less than a decade.[9] The United States reduced its daily oil imports over 30 percent within a two-year span.[10] Here and there, the transition to a sustainable society is getting under way.

Part I

Converging Demands

2

Eroding the Base of Civilization

Croplands are the foundation not only of agriculture but of civilization itself. When soils are eroded and crops are poorly nourished, people are often undernourished as well. Thus, the loss of soil is in some ways the most serious of the threats civilization faces. Degraded biological systems can usually recover if given the opportunity, but an inch of topsoil lost through erosion may take nature centuries to replace. Similarly, alternatives to oil can be developed, but there are no widely usable substitutes for soil in food production. Civilization can survive the exhaustion of oil reserves, but not the continuing wholesale loss of topsoil.

Since mid-century, pressures on the earth's croplands have

mounted. Growing populations demand more land not only for food production but for other purposes as well. Even as the need for cropland expands, more and more farmland is being put to nonagricultural uses. Worse, the most productive croplands are the most likely to be converted to nonfarm uses.

As the eighties unfold, humanity faces a worldwide shortage of productive cropland, acute land hunger in many countries, and escalating prices for farmland almost everywhere. In a world with no excess agricultural capacity, the continuing loss of prime farmland anywhere can drive food prices upward everywhere. For most people rising food prices are the most immediate, most disastrous face of inflation, fueling political instability with desperation.

The Historical Expansion of Cropland

Historically, the expansion of cultivation has been closely tied to population growth. Responding to population pressures, farmers moved from valley to valley and continent to continent, gradually extending the area under cultivation. Today, one-tenth of the earth's land surface is under the plow, and the promising settlement frontiers have all but vanished.

Over time, as the demand for food has pressed against local supplies, farmers have devised ingenious techniques such as irrigating, terracing, and fallowing for extending agriculture onto new lands. Irrigation enables farmers to grow crops where rainfall is low or unpredictable. Terracing permits the extension of agriculture onto steeply sloping land, even mountainsides. Centuries of laborious effort shaped the elaborate, often picturesque, systems of terraces in Japan, China, Nepal, Indonesia, and in the Andean highlands the Incas once inhabited.

In semiarid regions where rainfall cannot sustain continuous cultivation—such as the western Great Plains of North America, the Anatolian Plateau of Turkey, and the drylands of the

Soviet Union—alternate-year cropping has evolved. Under this system, land lies fallow every other year to accumulate moisture; all vegetative cover is destroyed during the fallow year, and the land is covered with a dust mulch that curbs the evaporation of water from the soil. Where fallowing leaves the soil vulnerable to wind erosion, fields are plowed in strips: alternate strips are cropped and fallowed, with the cropped strips serving as windbreaks for the fallow strips. Adopting such practices permitted wheat production to continue in the western Great Plains after the Dust Bowl years of the thirties.

In parts of sub-Saharan Africa, Brazil, the outer islands of Indonesia, and other tropical regions where more nutrients are stored in vegetation than in the soil, fallowing restores soil fertility. Stripped of the dense vegetative cover, soils in the humid tropics quickly lose their fertility. In response, tropical farmers have mastered shifting cultivation, whereby they clear land and crop it for three or four years, then systematically abandon it as crop yields decline; when, after 20 to 25 years, the exhausted soils have revived, "shifting cultivators" repeat the cycle.

These practices enabled farmers to move onto land where conventional agriculture would not survive. In doing so, they have greatly increased the earth's capacity to feed people. But now, under population-induced stress, these time-tested practices are being abandoned.

Some of these stresses have been monitored by agronomists but analyses of overall cropland area and productivity trends have until recently been sketchy because data have been sparse. An analysis of data for grains only, which occupy some 70 percent of the world's cropland, shows rising land productivity for the period from 1950 to 1980, accounting for close to four-fifths of the growth in the world grain supply. During this period, when the area planted to grain expanded by 152 million hectares, or some 25 percent, two spurts of rapid expansion occurred. (See Figure 2-1.) During the first, from 1951 to 1956,

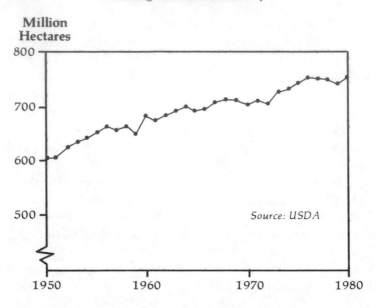

Figure 2-1. World Harvested Area of Cereals, 1950-80

fully half of the increase came from the extension of grain production onto the "Virgin Lands" of the Soviet Union. In the 16 years between 1956 and 1972, the area planted in cereals increased only 7 percent worldwide. During this period of excess production capacity, the United States idled some 20 million of its 140 million hectares (350 million acres) of cropland.[1]

The second spurt occurred from 1972 to 1976 in response to poor weather and short harvests. Some 50 million hectares were added to the world's harvested area of cereals in this four-year period. Overall, the area increase amounted to another 7 percent, at least one-third of the gain reflecting the return to production of U.S. cropland previously idled under government programs. A smaller share came from reducing the amount of land fallowed in the United States and the Soviet Union and from expanding the cultivated area in Argentina, Brazil, Nigeria, and other developing countries.[2]

When the food supply tightened a decade ago, the agricultural system had enough slack to allow the land planted to cereals to expand quickly. But that increase gives us no grounds to hope for another. Special circumstances obtained then: we had idled cropland to return to production. Now we do not.

Thinning Topsoil

Just as important to food production as the amount of land available to produce crops is its condition. Only inches deep (usually less than a foot) over much of the earth's surface, topsoil forms a fertile carpet over less productive subsoils. As the topsoil layer is lost, subsoil becomes part of the tillage layer, reducing the soil's organic matter, nutrient content, water-retention capacity, aeration, and other structural characteristics that make it ideal for plant growth.

Soil erosion is a natural process, one that occurs even on land in grass or in forests. But on land that is cleared and cropped, erosion often accelerates. Whenever the pace of erosion exceeds the natural rate of soil formation, what soil scientists call the tolerance or "T factor," the topsoil thins and eventually disappears, leaving only subsoil or even bare rock. New soil formed by natural processes commonly ranges from one to five tons per acre per year. Only when the soil erosion exceeds this does the land begin to lose its long-term productivity. When the topsoil can no longer adequately support crops, the land is abandoned. But the gradual loss of topsoil and the slow decline in inherent fertility that precedes abandonment may take many decades.

As the worldwide demand for food mounts, cultivation is being so intensified on some soils that excessive erosion and a gradual decline in inherent soil fertility are resulting. Elsewhere, cultivation is being extended onto less productive, erosion-prone soils. For most countries, the growing demand for food is internally generated, but for the United States the stresses on soils come from growing food deficits worldwide.

Within the United States, this mounting demand for food since mid-century, combined with the availability of cheap nitrogen fertilizer, has led farmers to abandon traditional rotations that included soil building pastures and hay, in favor of continuous planting of corn and other row crops. As a result, the overall gains in grain production since mid-century have been impressive, but the price paid in lost topsoil has been high. Fourteen years of data gathered at the Missouri Agricultural Experiment Station show land planted to a corn-wheat-clover rotation losing an average of 2.7 tons of topsoil per acre annually through erosion, whereas comparable land planted continuously to corn lost 19.7 tons per acre annually.[3] While the first loss is well within the tolerance range established by soil scientists, the latter leads to a progressive thinning of the topsoil layer and a steady decline in inherent land productivity. In Iowa alone, 260 million tons of soil is lost from cropland each year. According to the Iowa State University Experiment Station, that soil "simply cannot be replaced within our lifetime or those of our children. The eroded soil is gone, depleting the fertility of the land."[4]

Concern with these trends in the United States led in 1977 to the passage of the Soil and Water Resources Conservation Act, which called for a detailed survey of the state of U.S. soils. Soil scientists discovered "alarmingly high" rates of erosion by water in several states.[5] Tennessee, for example, was losing an average of 14.1 tons of topsoil per acre of cropland; Missouri, 11.4 tons; Mississippi, 10.9 tons; and Iowa, 9.9 tons. In the Great Plains, wind erosion was particularly severe, claiming an average of 14.9 tons per acre in Texas and 8.9 tons in Colorado.

Nationally, sheet and rill water erosion alone remove annually some two billion tons of topsoil from croplands—1.01 billion tons more than is formed each year.[6] Assuming 160 tons per acre inch of soil and a typical topsoil depth of 8 inches, this billion tons represented the loss of 781,000 acres of cropland equivalent per year.

Elsewhere in the world, the doubling of demand for food over the past generation has forced farmers onto dry and steep lands, which are inherently susceptible to erosion. In the Third World, record rates of population growth have forced farmers onto mountain soils, leaving them no time to construct terraces. Once the natural cover is removed, the topsoil quickly washes into adjacent valleys, where it silts streams, reservoirs, and canals.

In Andean Latin America, skewed land-ownership patterns can aggravate this problem. Wealthy ranchers use the relatively level valley floors for cattle grazing, forcing small landholders onto steep slopes to produce subsistence crops. This pattern leads to severe soil erosion on the slopes, which impairs the productivity of both the mountainsides and the valleys.

In dryland wheat producing areas, pressures to reduce the area in fallow can also sap the soil of moisture, as happened in the U.S. Great Plains during the Dust Bowl years and in the Soviet Virgin Lands during the sixties. Except where land can be irrigated, the natural constraints on cultivation under low rainfall conditions cannot be altered substantially.

Where fallowing and other restitutional agricultural practices have fallen by the way, compensatory measures can go only so far. In the Soviet Union, attempts to regain food self-sufficiency by investing heavily in agriculture are stymied because soils have lost some of their inherent productivity. Measuring extreme degradation of croplands in terms of gully formation, soil scientists at the Soil Erosion Laboratory at Moscow University have found that while only 2 percent of the south central Soviet Union shows severe gullying, as much as 50 percent of the land could follow suit as efforts to intensify agriculture proceed.[7] A parallel Soviet study of the present gully network in the Steppe and Forest Steppe regions in the European USSR found that gully formation has accelerated as "good land reserves became exhausted and sloping land began to be plowed."[8] In an analysis of Moscow's agricultural plans,

Harvard University's Thane Gustafson observes that the Soviet Government must now reckon with "50 years of neglect [that] have left a legacy of badly damaged soils."[9]

Even while soil erosion raises the demand in the Soviet Union for food imports, it reduces export capacity elsewhere. For example, Australia is experiencing serious soil erosion as it responds to the growing world demand for grain exports. Canberra-based soil scientist C. L. Watson reports that "some 50 percent of our existing agricultural and arid lands need ameliorative measures to just maintain present productivity."[10]

Neighboring Indonesia is falling prey to the same neglect. A report from the U.S. embassy in Jakarta indicates that soil erosion is bringing on an " 'ecological emergency' in Java, laying waste to land at an alarming rate, much faster than present reclamation programs can restore it."[11] Similar pressures are building in Pakistan's rainfed agricultural regions. An AID officer in the Punjab area reports the annual abandonment of several thousand hectares of cropland because of severe degradation caused by erosion.[12] In Nepal, the country's rivers now annually carry 240 million cubic meters of soil to India, making that country the recipient of what has been described as Nepal's "most precious export."[13]

In Ethiopia, according to U.S. AID Mission reports, "There is an environmental nightmare unfolding before our eyes. . . . It is the result of the acts of millions of Ethiopians struggling for survival: scratching the surface of eroded land and eroding it further; cutting down the trees for warmth and fuel and leaving the country denuded. . . . Over one billion—one billion—tons of topsoil flow from Ethiopia's highlands each year."[14] In South Africa, biologist John Hanks estimates that the province of Natal, incorporating Kwazulu, is losing 200 million tons of topsoil annually.[15] Far from complete, this litany of disasters merely suggests the scope and impact of soil erosion. A 1977 United Nations survey reported that almost one-fifth of the world's cropland is now being steadily degraded.[16]

Determining the precise effect of topsoil loss on cropland fertility is complicated since increasing fertilizer use can disguise declining natural productivity. However, Cornell University's David Pimentel has noted three U.S. studies showing that, other things being equal, corn yields decline by an average of "four bushels per acre for each inch of topsoil lost from a base of 12 inches of topsoil or less."[17]

Underscoring the gravity of the erosion threat is convincing evidence indicating that adopting erosion-control practices is in most cases not cost-effective for the farmer. An interdisciplinary team of agricultural scientists studied land in southern Iowa where erosion was excessive and calculated the projected near-term costs of erosion in terms of additional energy use, additional fertilizer use, and reduction in yields. They found that the costs of reducing soil erosion to a tolerable level came to three times the immediate economic benefits of doing so.[18] Unless governments share the cost of erosion control practices, a typical farmer with a narrow profit margin and with land suffering from excessive erosion would appear to have two choices: adopt the costly erosion control measures needed and face bankruptcy in the near term, or continue with business as usual until eventually the inherent productivity of the land falls to the point where it must be abandoned.

Another study undertaken by three agricultural scientists in neighboring Illinois attempted to determine whether terracing on sloping lands could be economically justified from the farmers' standpoint.[19] The team noted that 9.7 million acres of the state's cropland is sloping and that only 14 percent this acreage is adequately protected from erosion. After analyzing a number of soils common in Illinois, they concluded that "except in a few situations, the farmer will sacrifice income to control erosion by constructing terraces."

The tough choice confronting farmers in the U.S. midwest

must be made the world over. Differences in economic systems notwithstanding, the same basic pressures on the land are at work everywhere. In the interaction between the demands of the economic system and the tolerance of ecological systems, ideological boundaries count for little.

Spreading Deserts: The Human Hand

In semiarid regions where human and livestock populations are expanding at record rates, once useful land is turning to desert or desertlike terrain. According to reports prepared for the UN Conference on Desertification in 1977, some 630 million people, or one person of every seven, live in arid or semiarid areas.[20] An estimated 78 million people inhabit lands rendered useless by erosion, dune formation, changes in vegetation, and salt encrustation. For this group, desertification means the destruction of livelihood as well as land.

Agronomists who specialize in managing arid and semiarid croplands have long been aware of the mounting pressure on fragile arid soils and of their progressive deterioration. Not until the droughts of the late sixties and early seventies in Sahelian Africa, however, were the social consequences of desertification—starvation and dislocation—painfully apparent.

Fed by human abuses of the land—overgrazing, deforestation, and overplowing—the world's major deserts are all growing larger. As human and livestock populations increase, deserts or desertlike conditions are spreading in Africa, the Middle East, Iran, Afghanistan, and northwestern India. Although its southward spread gets more attention, the Sahara Desert is also marching relentlessly northward, squeezing the populations of North Africa against the Mediterranean. It is also expanding westward into Senegal and southeastward into the Sudan. Readings taken of the Sudan in 1958 and again in 1975 indicate the southeastern Sahara annexed some 90 to 100 kilometers during the 17-year period.[21] Brazilian ecologist J. Vasconcelos Sobrinho reports that the semiarid tip of Brazil's northeast is being desertified; similar conditions are developing in Argentinean states of La Rioja, San Luis, and La Pampa.[22]

The desert's insidious march has a particularly long history in the Middle East and Western Asia. The site of many early human civilizations, the arid landscape of this region has suffered millenia of imprudent cropping and soil erosion. Vast expanses have been transformed into deserts, capable of supporting fewer people than they did thousands of years ago. In the Middle East, even some rainfed farmlands are succumbing to desertification. Where cultivation has been pushed onto lands with extremely low and unpredictable rainfall, widespread desiccation has followed. According to Ibrahim Nahal, Professor of Forestry and Ecology at the University of Aleppo, improper cultivation in the rainfed agricultural zone of Syria, Jordan, and Iraq has led to a reduction in the yield of cereals, still the dietary staple.[23] Northwestern India is now the world's most densely populated arid zone, and quite possibly the dustiest. By extending cropping to submarginal lands, farmers there and elsewhere are creating potential "dust bowls."

The food outlook for desert countries is a matter of concern. Of 16 desert countries, per capita grain output has fallen over the past three decades in all but four.[24] Primarily by expanding irrigation, four countries (Iran, Libya, Senegal, and the Sudan) are able to offset the effects of land degradation. Among the remaining 12 countries, the drop in per capita grain output in Algeria, Iraq, Jordan, Lebanon, Mali, and Niger was precipitous—40 percent or more between 1950 and 1980.

While agricultural prospects and potentials differ among arid regions, desertification imperils food production wherever it occurs. It undercuts the benefits of agricultural investments even in countries that, judged by aggregate national statistics, appear to be making rapid agricultural gains. Populations in many arid regions have already reached the ecological danger point as the spread of desert-like conditions makes all too clear.

The Loss of Irrigated Land

Irrigated lands, which provide a disproportionately large share of the world's food, are also under seige. They are threatened both by ecological forces—waterlogging and salinity—and by economic forces that divert water to competing uses. In addition, some land is being irrigated by so-called "fossil water"—water from aquifers that can't be refilled or recharged. On balance, the world's irrigated acreage is still expanding since the area in new projects exceeds losses. But in some locales, irrigated acreage is shrinking.

Waterlogging and salinity occur whenever surface water from rivers or streams is diverted to irrigate land that has inadequate underground drainage. Increasing the natural underground water supply gradually raises the water table. When the table comes to within a few feet of the surface, the growth of deep-rooted crops is impaired. As it rises further, water begins to evaporate through the remaining few inches of soil, thereby concentrating the minerals and salt near the surface. Eventually, the concentrated salt inhibits plant growth. From an airplane, glistening white expanses of heavily salted land now incapable of supporting vegetation can be seen in Iraq, Pakistan, and other countries traditionally dependent on irrigation.

As old as irrigation itself, waterlogging and salinity helped undermine some of the earlier Middle Eastern civilizations. Although the designers of the earliest irrigation systems in the Tigris-Euphrates Valley did not understand subterranean hydrology well enough to prescribe corrective action, modern irrigation engineers do. Now the problem is the cost: by recent UN estimate, average salvage costs $650 per hectare.

Worldwide data compiled in a 1977 UN report indicate that

one-tenth of the world's total irrigated area is waterlogged—some 21 million hectares.[25] The productivity of this land has fallen by 20 percent, and almost as much land has been rendered less productive by salinization. Although fully half of the world's irrigation capacity has been developed since 1950, those gains are already being undermined by waterlogging and salinity. These modern experiences with irrigation mirror the experience of the early Mesopotamian civilization, though on a far larger scale. In the current agronomic literature of China, references to the problem abound. In the Nile River Valley, the more intensive irrigation made possible by the Aswan High Dam has upset the long-standing water balance, waterlogging and salting some Egyptian soils historically free of this problem. Many farms in the American southwest have drainage systems that remove the salt from irrigated fields, but some of that unwanted salt ends up in river waters that eventually irrigate Mexican crops.

Rehabilitating waterlogged soils takes time and prodigious amounts of capital—witness the heavy Soviet investments in the reclamation of agricultural lands. In Pakistan, a country almost entirely dependent on irrigation for food production, waterlogging and salinity affect the productivity of much of the land. In its Mona reclamation area, where irrigation began in 1901, close to 90 percent of the soils were waterlogged by the early sixties.[26] Thanks only to heavy investments in reclamation, much of it from foreign aid, the process has been reversed.

Besides the endemic problems irrigation is subject to, increasing urban and industrial demands for water in arid areas threaten the future of irrigated agriculture. Two cases in point are the Soviet Union's south central region and the U.S. Great Plains and southwest. Soviet efforts to regain food self-sufficiency rest heavily on attempts to expand irrigation, but ambitious plans and heavy capital commitments may fly in the face of reality if the water shortages predicted for the southern half of the country materialize. In Arizona the irrigated area in agriculturally important Maricopa County is shrinking steadily as water is diverted to the rapidly expanding Phoenix metropolitan area. Between the late fifties and the early seventies, the irrigated area fell from 224,000 to 177,900 hectares.[27] But even with reduced agricultural demands, groundwater levels have been dropping by some 10 to 20 feet per year.

California has similar problems, though on a larger scale. As a result of Los Angeles' thirst, irrigated valleys that were once lush green have now turned to dusty brown. Fields once among the most productive in the world have been abandoned. However wasteful and illogical, urban claims nearly always take precedence over farm demands for water, either because of economics, politics, or both.

In the southern Great Plains of the United States, irrigated agriculture is threatened by the depletion of the vast Ogallala aquifer, the waterbearing stratum which underlies the western plains from Nebraska south to Texas. The land atop this aquifer accounts for much of the growth in U.S. irrigated acreage since 1945. Many of the country's largest beef feedlots developed here because of a unique combination—a dry climate and plentiful supplies of grain sorghum, corn, and alfalfa grown on irrigated land. Unfortunately, the Ogallala aquifer is essentially nonrechargeable, so extensive irrigation in parts of Nebraska, Kansas, Colorado, Oklahoma, Texas, and New Mexico will be a relatively short-lived affair. A USDA study of 32 counties in the Texas panhandle estimates that by 1995 fuel price increases and water-table depletion will eliminate irrigation entirely in these countries, forcing a return to dryland farming.[28]

In the western United States, efforts to develop the extensive coal and oil-shale resources will divert still more water from agriculture. A Resources for the Future study of this region by Helen Ingram and her colleagues concludes that "water demands for energy development compound urban pressures upon irrigated agriculture. Every recipe for energy development has 'add water' in its instructions."[29] Ingram's analysis indicates that "a coal gasification plant in New Mexico or Arizona processing 24 million tons of coal per year to meet the energy needs of a million people would use about 300,000 acre-feet of water per year. A 10,000 megawatt coal-fired thermal electric power plant in the four corners region requires about 230,000 acre-feet of water per year."

While waterlogging and salinity have long been undermining irrigated land, the wholesale diversion of water from agriculture to cities and industries is more recent. It promises to become an even more hotly contested issue. In a *Science* article assessing the world food prospect, Neal Jensen of Cornell University predicted that "western U.S. irrigated agriculture faces gradual elimination as the pressures for higher priority water needs become more evident."[30] Even now, each new diversion of water from agriculture to other uses adds to the upward pressure on food prices.

Conversion of Cropland to Nonfarm Uses

Agriculture's principal competition for land comes from urban expansion, village expansion, energy production, and highway construction. In the United States, the world's leading food producer, nearly a million acres of prime cropland were converted to nonfarm uses each year between 1967 and 1977.[31] In the extreme case of Florida, source of half of the world's grapefruit and a quarter of its oranges, all the prime farmland will be put to other uses by the end of the century if the trend continues. In Virgina, 24 percent of the prime cropland would be lost; in California, 16 percent.[32]

Rural states are also feeling the squeeze. According to Allen Hidlebaugh of the National Agricultural Lands Study staff, "Even in America's agricultural heartland—the corn belt states—there is cause for concern. We anticipate a total 3.2 million acre prime farmland loss in Iowa, Illinois, Indiana,

Ohio, and Missouri combined. If present trends continue to the year 2000, the annual loss will equal 480 million bushels of corn—at $2.50 a bushel, a permanent loss of $1 billion a year, every year, by the century's end."[33]

Data on changing land use elsewhere confirm that the growth of cities is a leading source of cropland loss. A study of urban encroachment on Europe's grazing lands and croplands from 1960 to 1970 found that West Germany lost 1 percent of its agricultural land every four years. For France and the United Kingdom, it was nearly 2 percent for the decade.[34] For the Third World, information on land lost to rapid urbanization is sketchier. But UN demographers expect the world's urban population to expand from 1.81 billion in 1980 to 3.16 billion in 20 years.[35] If this projected increase created a need of only .04 hectares per person, then the world's cities would occupy an additional 54 million hectares of land by 2000. If 40 percent of this total is converted cropland, cities would consume an area equal to the cultivated area of France.[36]

Although this projected loss would amount to less than 2 percent of the world cropland, the impact on world food output is likely to be greater since cities are situated on the most fertile soils. A study of changing land-use patterns in Canada reports that "half of the farmland lost to urban expansion is coming from the best one-twentieth of our farmland."[37] But even if the best doesn't go first, the worldwide loss of 25 million hectares will mean the loss of enough food to feed some 84 million people.

Even outside of cities, habitats claim farmland. In the Third World, village growth extends into agricultural fields. Analyzing village growth in his native Bangladesh, Akef Quazi concludes that the amount of land occupied by the village correlates closely with the number of families in the village, in part because homes are "made of locally available materials, such as bamboo, thatch, and corrugated iron sheets, and, as such, are never strong enough to hold an upper story."[38]

Bangladesh's problem is also India's. Living space requirements of the 14 million Indians added to the population each
year are at least partly met by homes built on cropland surrounding the nation's cities and 600,000 villages.[39] Further
east, China is also losing cropland to cities and industry. USDA
China specialist Alva Erisman reports that "water control projects, urban growth, and the appropriation of agricultural land
for roads, railroads, airfields, industrial plants, and military uses
has removed good farmland from cultivation."[40] Dwight Perkins, China scholar at Harvard, makes the same point, noting
that the 10 percent growth in modern industry has been partly
at the expense of agricultural lands next to the city limits,
where most factories spring up.[41]

Rivaling urbanization as a claimant on cropland is energy
production. Hydroelectric dams can inundate vast stretches of
rich bottomland, even as they add to the irrigated area. An
electric generating plant can cover hundreds of hectares. More
often than not, oil refineries and storage tanks are built on
prime farmland along rivers and coastal plains.

Stripmining coal also reduces the cultivated area. Indeed, as
the world turns from oil to coal, energy producers are coming
into conflict with food producers. In the United States, where
coal production is projected to climb steadily, some of the most
accessible reserves of coal are by an accident of geography
directly beneath some of the nation's finest farmland.

A public interest group study entitled "Who's Mining the
Farm?" reports that "as of 1976, 81,981 hectares in 40 Illinois
counties have been affected by surface and deep mining of
coal."[42] In Congressional testimony, the zoning administrator
of Knox County, Illinois, indicated that stripmining threatened 284,000 acres of farmland in his county alone.[43] Given
the rich extensive resources of coal close to the surface in
Illinois, the potential for disrupting food production in the
heart of the corn belt appears great.

Where stripmining is already in full swing, hope lies in

revitalizing ravaged agricultural lands. But while mining companies are now required by law to restore land to its original productive state, doing so may be impossible in many situations. In 1977, USDA reported that "surface mining as practiced in much of the nation today either ruins farmland completely or reduces its production drastically."[44] Eager to convince the public that stripmining does not jeopardize farmland, coal companies and utilities have launched advertising campaigns aimed at deflecting attention from key issues. Jack Doyle of the Environmental Policy Center observes that "while coal companies and utilities are eager to show that stripmined farmland can be returned to agricultural use, they fail to address the question of yield. Will 'reclaimed' cropland and rangeland be able to yield what they did before mining— bushel-for-bushel and pound-for-pound?"[45] Even if the topsoil is carefully pushed aside before mining to be replaced afterwards, reinstating subsoil-drainage patterns is no easy matter.

If estimates of future cropland losses to urbanization are difficult to make, those of losses to the energy sector are even more so. But with or without hard statistics, we can see that to conserve energy is to conserve cropland. One offense to this obvious bit of wisdom is the automobile-centered transportation system that so voraciously consumes land. An enormous amount of U.S. cropland has been paved over for automobiles, millions of hectares of it just for parking spaces for the nation's 143 million licensed motor vehicles. But even this area pales in size when compared to that covered by streets, highways, filling stations, and other vehicle-service facilities. Added to auto-induced urban sprawl, these fixtures came at a high price, one too often paid at the supermarket.

How much cropland will be paved over, built on, stripmined, or flooded over in the remainder of this century is unknown, but if the projected growth in population and income should materialize, then urbanization, energy production, and transportation are certain to continue to encroach upon cropland. The threat posed by this continuing conversion of cropland to nonfarm uses is hard to exaggerate. As former U.S. Assistant Secretary of Agriculture M. Rupert Cutler observes, "When farmland goes, food goes. Asphalt is the land's last crop."[46]

The Cropland Prospect

The adequacy of the future cropland base will be influenced by numerous trends and forces, many of which will offset each other. All the trends discussed above—cropland conversion to nonfarm uses, excessive soil erosion, the addition of new land to the cropland base, the irrigation of new land, the diversion of irrigation water to nonfarm use, and the rate of cropland desertification and of desert reclamation—will interact and take their toll.

With most of the world's good agricultural land already under the plow, the potential for expanding cropland provides little ground for optimism. In North America, the conversion of cropland to nonfarm uses over the past three decades has been only partly offset by the reclamation of new land through irrigation projects or forest clearance.[47] In the absence of a concerted national effort to protect cropland from conversion to other uses, this net reduction in the cropland base may well continue.

In Western Europe, opportunities for developing new lands are negligible, while Eastern Europe has been hard pressed just to maintain its cultivated area over the last 15 years. In the Soviet Union, where farming has already been extended into marginal rainfall areas, further expansion will be limited.

In densely populated Asia, China has little unused land to bring under cultivation. Given China's already extensive irrigation works, the opportunities for multiple cropping more land are also limited. India's cropland base is expected to increase little, if at all, but multiple cropping could increase markedly if the full irrigation potential of the Gangetic Plain is developed. The one Asian region that could sustain increases both in cropland area and multiple cropping is the Mekong Valley and Delta, assuming political conditions permit its development.

In Africa, the one country with a healthy potential for expanding its cropland is the Sudan, since it has developed only part of the Nile waters reserved to it by treaty with Egypt. To the south the principal hope for more farmland lies in opening the Tsetse Fly belt to cultivation, provided that the disease-carrying fly can be eradicated.

In Latin America, croplands could be created by plowing up some grasslands, though doing so would reduce grazing capacity. In central Brazil, a belt of land—the Cerrado—bordering the southernmost regions of the Amazonian forest is now being brought under cultivation, though its inherent fertility is not exceptionally high. Within the Amazon basin, numerous isolated pockets of potentially productive cropland await development, but the investment in infrastructure required to exploit them could prove prohibitive. In 1970, Brazil launched with great fanfare the Transamazon Highway and an accompanying colonization scheme. The goal was to settle a million families along the highway by 1980, most of them from the drought-stricken, poverty-ridden northeast. As of 1980, only 7,000 families have been successfully settled, the government is phasing out its colonization scheme, and there are doubts that the highway will be completed.[48] Crop insects and disease, deteriorating soils, and costly road maintenance are contributing to the project's demise.

Although attempts to expand the globe's cultivated area will be numerous, both government efforts and the initiatives of individual farmers will be offset by ecological backsliding. Well before the end of the century, for example, the topsoil will be gone from recently opened hillside plots in the Andes, the highlands of east Africa, and the foothills and rugged valleys of the Himalayas, and these lands will have been abandoned. If comprehensive worldwide data were available on excessive soil erosion from cropland, and if this were then converted into cropland equivalent as was done earlier for the United States, it would likely show the loss of several million acres yearly.

Although land hunger has never been greater, the amount of cropland abandoned each year as economic pressures interact with ecological forces may also be at a record high. On balance, it is difficult to envisage an increase in the cropland base of much more than 10 percent by century's end. With projected population increases, this modest increase would leave us in the year 2000 with only .13 hectares of cereal land per person, well below the .17 hectares we each now have. (See Table 2-1.)

While the cropland base is likely to expand modestly over the next two decades, its inherent productivity seems certain to decline as a result of excessive erosion and marginal land additions. In most cases these losses will not be large enough to prevent future increases in yield per hectare, but they will slow the rate of gain. Satisfying the two-thirds increase in world food demand projected by the United Nations for the remainder of this century would require land productivity to accelerate sharply.

Responding effectively to the cropland threats that are associated with mounting food demands poses a dilemma for

Table 2-1. World Population and Area in Cereals, 1950 and 1980, with Projections to 2000

Year	Population	Area in Cereals	Area Per Person
	(billions)	(million hectares)	(hectares)
1950	2.51	601	.24
1980	4.42	758	.17
2000	6.20	828	.13

Source: United Nations, U.S. Department of Agriculture, and author's projections.

farmers and governmental planners alike. Both economic pressures and political instincts encourage a short-term focus but pressures to wring too much out of the land in the short run can destroy it over the long run. Preserving civilization's foundation requires redoubled efforts to protect cropland from erosion and from conversion to nonfarm uses. Staggering as the challenge may seem, countries have pulled back from disaster's edge before. In the United States, an earlier generation overcame the Dust Bowl threat, and China's longest march may have been on the road to agricultural recovery since 1949.

3

Biological Systems under Pressure

In the modern world it is easy to forget how dependent our economy is on its forests, grasslands, and fisheries. Although these natural systems provide food, feed, fuel, and a broad array of industrial raw materials, few economists think about the economy's biological underpinnings. The economist's desk may be piled high with references containing the latest statistical indicators on the health of the economy, but rare indeed is the reference in economic analysis to the health of the biological systems that support the economy.

This lapse is a serious one, for much is at stake. As the global economy expanded by some 4 percent per year during the decades following World War II, pressures on forests, grasslands, and fisheries began to mount, in many cases to unsustainable levels. Once the level of demand breaches the threshold of sustainability, additional demand can be satisfied only by consuming the productive resource base itself. In economic terms, this is the equivalent of consuming capital along with interest. When this happens, fisheries collapse, forests disappear, and grasslands become barren wastelands. Economic crises arise almost overnight.

Deforesting the Earth

We need only look about us to see the pervasive role of forest products in our lives. We use wood for lumber, fuel, and manufacturing. For the world's burgeoning white-collar labor force, paper is the essential feedstock. The world over, wood and wood products are used to construct buildings, to make furniture, to manufacture paper, plywood, fiberboard, and numerous other products.

In many Third World countries, wood is also the principal energy source. Surveys undertaken in Tanzania, Thailand, and elsewhere show village firewood consumption ranging from one to two tons per person annually. With an estimated 40 percent of the world's population using wood as the primary fuel, the drain on the world's forests is immense.

The demand for forest products expands at least as rapidly as world population. For housing, lumber demand reflects the size of world population, its annual increase, and the level of affluence. Each year some of the world's housing must be replaced as it ages and deteriorates, and each year 70 million additional people need housing. Together, these needs levy an ever growing claim on the world's forests.

The demand for forest products is on the rise everywhere. Where demand has come to exceed the sustainable yield of local forests, imports have risen or deforestation has occurred. At mid-century, roughly one quarter of the earth's land surface was covered by forests. By 1980 it was less than one-fifth.[1] (See Table 3-1.) Each year the earth's inhabitants, all users of wood products in one form or another, increase by the equivalent of the population of Mexico and Central America combined, and each year the forested area shrinks by an area the size of Hungary.[2]

Of the world's remaining closed forests (those with more than 20 percent tree cover), half are located in Latin America and the Soviet Union, each of which has 680 million hectares, or roughly a quarter of the world total. Most of the rest are in North America and Asia. While Africa's share of the remaining closed forest is only 6 percent, it does contain large areas of open forest—a combination of grass and trees where the latter cover less than 20 percent of the land area.

Although the economic role of forests is obvious, their ecological role is less well known. Among other functions, forests retain rainfall and permit it to percolate downward to recharge underground aquifers. When forest cover is stripped away, rain water runs off quickly instead of sinking in, so water tables fall and streamflows fluctuate unpredictably. The rapid runoff in

Table 3-1. The World's Forested Area by Region, Mid-Seventies

Region	Closed Forest	Closed Forest as Share of Land Area
	(million hectares)	(percent)
Latin America	680	33
USSR	680	30
North America	470	25
Asia	410	15
Africa	190	6
Europe	138	28
Oceania	89	10
World Total	2,657	20

Source: *Global 2000 Report* and Reidar Persson, "Need for a Continuous Assessment."

turn leads to soil erosion, which contributes to the sedimentation of streams and reservoirs. Combined, the effects of heavier runoff and rivers' reduced water-carrying capacity create floods and swell rivers so that they cut new channels through the countryside.

Born of deforestation in the Himalayas, floods in Pakistan, India, and Bangladesh are increasing in both frequency and severity. In 1973, Pakistan experienced a flood, the worst in its history, that destroyed much of the spring wheat crop in village storage as well as the standing crop in some areas. In 1974, extensive flooding in Bangladesh partly caused by progressive deforestation in the Nepalese and eastern Indian watersheds sharply reduced the rice harvest, and the ensuing famine claimed a third of a million lives.[3]

In November of 1978, a two-day rain led to enormous destruction in India. The World Environment Report, which linked the flood to deforestation, tabulated damages as "65,712 villages flooded, more than 2,000 drowned, 40,000 cattle washed away, and uncounted thousands of houses destroyed."[4] The crops lost in the two states of Uttar Pradesh and West Bengal were worth $750 million. In September of 1980, India was again hit by devastating floods. This time 978 people died in flood-related deaths.[5]

Hundreds of hydroelectric and irrigation reservoirs representing enormous investments are now losing capacity as deforestation takes its toll on the watersheds that feed them. Typical of these is the Ambuklao Dam in the Philippines. According to an Agency for International Development report, "The cutting of timber and the subsequent loss of water retention capacity of land surrounding the reservoir has resulted in massive silting of the reservoir, reducing its useful life from 60 to 32 years."[6] Another reservoir is in Cerron Grande in El Salvador. There, a $100 million capital commitment in a hydroelectric power project was based on a projected life expectancy of 100 years.[7] But as the watershed was deforested and as steep slopes were cleared for cultivation, erosion accelerated, reducing the reservoir's life expectancy to only 25 years.

The Panama Canal is also falling prey to the same forces.[8] Because of the strategic role of the Canal astride the world's shipping routes, most ships in the world fleet were built to negotiate its passage. But the Canal watershed is now being altered as timber is cut, land cleared for food crops, and forests opened up for grazing. If recent siltation rates continue without redress, the capacity of the Canal to handle shipping will be greatly reduced by the end of the century, and taking the shortcut that saves 10,000 miles will become the privilege of small craft.

While the world's aggregate forested area is shrinking, the losses have not been evenly distributed. In industrial Europe, North America, and Japan, the area in forest has stabilized. But this stability has been purchased in part from tropical countries, which are exporting wood in record volume. As forests continue to shrink, Third World countries will eventually be forced to restrict cutting. Then, importing countries will face difficult adjustments in the form of higher prices or rationing.

Even within some countries, the extent of deforestation varies by region. In the Soviet Union, for instance, the demand for wood has led to extensive deforestation in the European USSR, while vast forests in Siberia and other less accessible regions remain intact, even underutilized.

Like its effects, the causes of deforestation are numerous. Among them, efforts to expand crop and livestock production stand out. In Central America and Brazil, forest land is being cleared for grazing purposes, largely to produce beef destined for export. The cost of this conversion is high, particularly since tropical soils may not sustain grass for long.

In many Third World countries, firewood collection is a leading source of deforestation. In some cases, commercial timber harvesting by multinational companies that engage in clearcutting undermines the forest's reproductive system.

Whatever its cause, unchecked deforestation threatens to undermine the global economy at its ecological roots. Nor is it an easy problem for governments to deal with. Erik Eckholm summarized the situation in a Worldwatch Paper on reforestation: "Usually uncontrolled deforestation is a symptom of society's inability to get a grip on other fundamental development problems: agricultural stagnation, grossly unequal land tenure, rising unemployment, rapid population growth, and the incapacity to regulate private enterprise to protect the public interest."[9]

Deep Trouble in Oceanic Fisheries

Perhaps nothing better reflects the growing human appetite for protein since mid-century than the spectacular growth in the world's fish catch between 1950 and 1970. During this period, the catch more than tripled, expanding by some 5 percent yearly.[10] By 1970 the world catch totaled 68 million tons, including the inland fresh water catch and fish-farming, which together accounted for a tenth or more of the total. Throughout this period, the world's fisheries supplied more meat for human consumption than did its cattle herds.

Worldwide, the catch averaged 18 kilograms (fresh weight) per person in 1970, though people in some affluent industrial countries (such as Japan, Iceland, and Norway) were consuming easily twice the global per capita average while some landlocked Third World countries had fishless diets.[11] As population pressures built up in Japan beginning three generations ago, the Japanese set aside their limited arable lands for grain production and turned to the oceans for animal protein. Hence, their famous "fish and rice" diet was born. Similarly, the Soviet Union, faced with difficulties in expanding livestock output, turned to the oceans during the fifties for high quality protein. As a result, Soviet fish consumption per person is now double that in North America.[12]

Not all of the world's fish catch is consumed directly. Livestock, principally hogs and poultry, consume part of the fish catch as protein meal. (See Table 3-2.) Most species reserved for pigs, chickens, and other livestock are those that people don't relish, such as anchovies—but at some point livestock and people begin to compete for fish. Between 1950 and 1970, the share of the catch used for fishmeal increased from one-sixth to over one-third, a high point that coincided with the peak of the anchovy catch. Since 1974 the world fish catch appears to be leveling off at just over 50 million tons for food and some 21 million tons for fishmeal.

Overfishing has become the rule, not the exception, in oceanic fisheries, but it is often discovered after the fact—when the catch in a given fishery begins to decline precipitously. In the northwest Atlantic, the catch of cod, haddock, halibut, herring, and other much-savored species peaked in the late

Table 3-2. World Fish Catch, Food and Nonfood Uses, 1950–79

Year	Food	Fish Meal	Total
	(million metric tons)		
1950	18.1	3.0	21.1
1955	24.3	4.6	28.9
1960	31.4	8.6	40.0
1965	37.2	16.3	53.5
1970	42.6	25.5	68.1
1971	43.9	24.6	68.5
1972	45.0	19.2	64.2
1973	47.5	17.6	65.1
1974	48.9	20.6	69.5
1975	49.0	20.3	69.3
1976	50.7	22.1	72.8
1977	52.8	19.7	72.5
1978	52.8	21.0	73.8
1979 (prel.)	52.5	20.9	73.4

Source: Food and Agriculture Organization.

sixties. The catch of each has dropped substantially since then, with declines ranging from 40 percent for herring to over 90 percent for halibut. Fishing grounds in the northeast Atlantic, Europe's long-time source of table fish, are faring no better. According to British marine biologist D.H. Cushing, extensive overfishing has reduced the catch below the maximum sustainable yield in 27 of the region's 30 fisheries.[13]

Recently, overfishing has become commonplace in the waters of the Southern Hemisphere too. Abetted by a shift in the Humboldt current, overfishing led to a collapse of Peru's coastal anchovy fishery during the early seventies. The catch fell precipitously from a peak of 12 million tons to 2 million, where it has remained into the eighties.[14] The same pattern of rapid growth, overfishing, and abrupt decline also took hold in the Gulf of Thailand in the mid-seventies. Now some fisheries off China's coast have begun to decline as well.[15]

Oceanic fisheries everywhere have been plagued by the lack of central and effective management. Early efforts by the international community to create an international body with authority to manage fisheries failed. Instead, with the evolution of the concept of Exclusive Economic Zones came the extension by coastal states of offshore limits from the traditional 3 to 12 miles to 200 miles. This move to extend jurisdiction, a potential solution to the fisheries' problem, quickly acquired a momentum of its own. In 1969, a UN Food and Agriculture Organization (FAO) survey of 102 coastal states indicates only 15 nations claimed limits beyond 12 miles.[16] A decade later, a survey of 132 coastal states showed that 93 claimed jurisdiction beyond 12 miles, 78 of them claiming limits of 200 miles. By FAO estimates, some 99 percent of the world seafood catch is taken within 200 miles of land.

Under the doctrine of Exclusive Economic Zones, countries with technologically advanced fishing fleets lose their long-held advantage over coastal states. In 1979, the overall catch was essentially unchanged from 1978, but the Japanese fleet's catch fell by 7 percent while the Soviet Union's fell by 4 percent.[17] Within the European Economic Community, all countries except the Netherlands suffered a net decline.

In addition to overfishing, fisheries are also threatened by pollution. The U.S. government's *Global 2000 Report* notes that while attention focuses on oil spills or the discharge of toxic metals, the more important effects "stem from largely unnoticed and undetected chronic, low-level pollution."[18] Because the discharge of most pollutants into oceans does not generate public outcry, most people "consider the oceans as an important resource to be utilized in disposing of the wastes of man."[19] But even if this view were morally defensible, it does not hold up scientifically; the pollutants that initially threaten marine life will ultimately threaten human life.

Pollution is already eroding seafood stocks. In its 1979 report, the U.S. Council on Environmental Quality drew attention to the deterioration of the Chesapeake Bay, the country's largest estuary and one of the world's richest. There, in recent years the catch of oysters, shad, striped bass, and other prized sources of seafood has fallen off precipitously.[20] In France, prime oyster beds face extinction. In 1979, the Arcachon Bay off the Bordeaux coast failed to produce new oysters for the third successive year.[21] Since oysters need four years to mature, another year of failure could spell an end to this French culinary delight.

Other pollution-riddled areas include the Black and Azov Seas, which are surrounded by the Soviet Union, Turkey, Rumania, and Bulgaria. Dr. David Tolmazin, former head of the Marine Economy Department of the Ukranian Academy of Sciences in Odessa, writes that "the fishing industry of the Black and Azov Seas has suffered a disastrous decline over the past 20 years. The two sea basins once contained a large stock of valuable fish, but they are almost lifeless."[22] The original stock of some 50,000 to 100,000 tons of Black Sea mackerel has disappeared. At fault are the reduction of fresh water flow and the pollutants being dumped into the local rivers that feed the two seas.

Some hope for offsetting these declines rests in the potential for establishing new fisheries based on untraditional species such as kapelin and sprat in the northern Atlantic and pollock in the northern Pacific. Another possibility is making fuller use of underfished species. The blue whiting, the lantern fish, and squid are not fully exploited, for example, partly because of limited consumer appeal. Krill is another seldom-eaten, though abundant species that could become commercially important. The principal constraints on the development of krill—a small, shrimp-like Antarctic crustacean—are that it must be processed quickly and that it is found far from the world's population centers. Means must also be found to convert it into a palatable, commercially attractive product. In a 1979 report, the FAO noted that while "commercial pressures have already resulted in the development of methods for harvesting and processing krill . . . prospects for a mass market for krill products must be considered still some time away."[23]

While the nonfood portion of the world catch was dropping in the early seventies as the Peruvian anchovy fishery was collapsing, the food portion of the catch continued to show modest growth. As of the late seventies, however, the catch of traditional food species also appears to have leveled off, dampening the prospect for future increases. Whatever this drop portends, keeping fish on the menu will require disciplined management aimed at preventing overfishing and reducing marine pollution, particularly in coastal estuaries and inland streams where fish spawn.

Ever since science fiction writer Jules Verne first enticed the popular imagination into the deep sea, the expectation has been that when land-based food supplies became inadequate, food could be found or farmed in the oceans. But now, as U.S. National Marine Fishery Service specialist Carl Sindermann puts it, we must "sort out the myths from the realities. The

sorting process can be a sobering experience, particularly for
those who feel that somehow if famine stalks the land, the seas
will provide."[24]

Grasslands for Three Billion Ruminants

Once the plow has run its course, most of the unforested land
that remains is good for grazing only. Almost without exception, agricultural land too dry or too steeply sloping to sustain
cultivation is used to support livestock. Roughly double the
area in crops, the 23 percent of the earth's land surface (3.1
billion hectares) devoted to this purpose supports nearly three
billion domesticated ruminants.[25] Beef and dairy cattle together total some 1.21 billion while water buffalo, the other
large ruminant, total 131 million. The small ruminants are
dominated by some 1.03 billion sheep and 410 million goats.
Of these two equal sized groups, the large ruminants are far
more important economically for the world as a whole. Only
in the Mediterranean region and in New Zealand do the
smaller ruminants dominate the livestock industry.

Ruminants play an indispensable role in the world economy.
Unlike pigs, chickens, and people, whose diets consist primarily
of cereals and other concentrated food, ruminants are
equipped to digest roughage and to convert it into forms people
can use. In underlining the unique digestive capacity of ruminants to convert cellulose, livestock specialist Harlow J. Hodgson points out that cellulose is the world's most abundant
organic compound.[26] Capable of subsisting solely on grasses,
or even on foliage from shrubs and trees, livestock provide food
in the form of meat, milk, cheese, and butter. They also supply
other essential commodities—fuel, fertilizer, and industrial raw
materials such as leather, wool, and tallow. For hundreds of
millions of Third World villagers living in deforested areas,
cow dung has become the chief cooking fuel, while an estimated 40 percent of the world's farmers use cattle manure as

fertilizer.[27] The world's leather goods and footwear industries depend heavily on leather, and wool remains one of the world's high-quality textile fibers, modern synthetic fibers notwithstanding. In addition, close to one third of the world's cropland is tilled by draft animals who subsist almost entirely on forage.[28]

For sustenance, ruminants depend only in small part upon grain. Even in the United States, where feedlots are quite common, forage still amounts to 82 percent of all feed units consumed by beef cattle, 63 percent of the total consumed by dairy cattle, and 89 percent of that consumed by sheep and goats.[29] Elsewhere, the share of roughage in the ruminant diet is much higher. In India, for example, only 3 percent of the grain harvest goes to feed livestock.[30]

In many parts of the world, livestock, specifically ruminants, still dominate local economic activity. The national economies of Uruguay and New Zealand, for example, depend heavily on the livestock industry.[31] In parts of Africa, the nomadic populations still derive their livelihood almost entirely from their flocks and herds. Likewise, in the United States, beef cattle represent the leading source of farm income in some 21 states, while in nine other states the sale of dairy products tops the list.[32]

The relationship of national economies to livestock production underscores another economic fact of life: the 3.1 billion hectares of grass and rangeland used to support livestock is essentially a fixed resource. Ingenious farmers can sometimes raise the productivity of grasslands, and short-sighted ones reduce it through mismanagement, but the resource base itself cannot be appreciably expanded. Of the total grassland area, only some 8 percent has been improved, usually by reseeding with introduced varieties.[33] Occasionally, in such high rainfall areas as New Zealand or the United Kingdom, extensive application of fertilizer boosts grassland productivity.

From early Biblical days until recently, livestock numbers

have grown along with human population. After World War II, population growth interacting with rising incomes led to a vast increase in the demand for livestock products. Between 1950 and 1975, world beef consumption doubled.[34] Now, the expansion of herds and flocks is overtaxing the earth's grasslands, making it impossible for them to continue to expand apace with human numbers.

Pressure on grasslands may be most acute in the Biblical lands of the Middle East, where populations are now multiplying at record rates. Forage specialists figure that the rangelands of northern Iraq can safely sustain only 250,000 sheep without degradation—a far cry from the million or so currently eating away this resource base.[35] Likewise, Syria's ranges are currently carrying triple the number of grazing animals they can support over the long term. In the initial stage of such degradation, inferior plant species replace more useful varieties. Then, goats and camels take over pastures abandoned by sheep. Finally, as Syrian ecologist Ibrahim Nahal observes, "In the advanced stage of deterioration, the plant cover disappears as is apparent in many of the steppe zones in Syria, Jordan, Iraq, and the United Arab Emirates, where the rangelands have turned into semi-deserts covered with a layer of gravel or into semi-sand deserts."[36] A similar situation exists in Iran, where much of the vegetation has been destroyed by centuries of overgrazing. In the not-too distant future, Iran's oil will be gone and so too will its grasslands, a far older source of national wealth.

Grassland degradation is not limited to areas of ancient settlement, as recent analyses of U.S. grazing lands show. Reporting in 1975 on the 163 million acres of range it manages, the Bureau of Land Management (BLM) found half the area to be in only "fair" condition—meaning that the more valuable forage species had been depleted and replaced by less palatable plants or by bare ground.[37] Another 28 percent was in "poor" condition; stripped of much of its topsoil and vegetative cover, it produced only a fraction of its forage potential.

Five percent of all BLM-controlled land was deemed in "bad" condition: with most of its topsoil gone, it could support only a smattering of low-value plants. The 50 million acres of land in "poor" or "bad" condition, an area equal to that of the state of Utah, was damaged primarily by overgrazing.

One of the most dramatic and socially disruptive examples of desertification in the United States is that of the huge Navajo Indian reservation in northern Arizona and New Mexico. In one zone that range specialists calculated could safely support 16,000 sheep at most, some 11,500 Navajos with as many as 140,000 sheep were trying to wrest an existence.[38] Before a new stock-reduction program took effect in the mid-1970s their lot was growing increasingly difficult. In essence, families have been forced by economic dictates to pit short-term self-interest against respect for the tribe's patrimony. Yet, if herd reduction, grazing management, and reseeding can restore this zone to peak conditions, its carrying capacity could eventually rise above the current level by a factor of ten. The question is one of temporary restraint.

Farther to the south, in Chile's arid Coquimbo region, cacti have replaced shrubs on some overgrazed land, and on others native perennial plants have given way to less productive annuals. As these pastures decline in quality, sheep replace cattle and eventually goats replace sheep. A UN report on the Coquimbo region indicates that the region's inequitable land-tenure pattern, which concentrates large numbers of people in restricted areas, promotes ecologically unsound land use.[39] The large and sparsely populated estates of the wealthy have room for proper grazing rotations. The inadequate communal and personal holdings of the poor majority, overcrowded and increasingly degraded, do not.

A recent U.S. Department of Interior study, *Desertification in the United States*, measures the impact of grassland deterioration on food production.[40] Using data from a Texas study, it reports that "good" rangeland can yield 14 pounds of beef per acre per year, while semi-deteriorated (or "fair") lands yield only 11 pounds of beef per year, and severely degraded lands produce less than 9 pounds per acre per year.

Internationally, the pace of degradation leaves little time for farmers and consumers to adapt to the new conditions. Never before has world demand for livestock products doubled within a generation. Almost everywhere, efforts to expand livestock production to keep pace with demand is taking its toll on grasslands. In Africa, only the Tsetse Fly belt has been spared from overgrazing, and the severely overgrazed Indian subcontinent now supports the world's largest cattle herd.

Extending livestock production onto new territory, the natural response to the production crunch, has relieved market pressure only to exacerbate ecological stress. Brazil's attempt to encourage cattle ranching in the Amazon Basin through a massive program of financial and tax incentives illustrates the bind. In the opinion of ecologist Philip Fearnside, the conversion from forest to grassland will within a few years deplete soil nutrients and give full rein to weeds that compete with the range grasses that cattle eat.[41] Eventually, cattle yields will drop to low, probably uneconomic levels.

Between 1950 and 1976, world beef production more than doubled and mutton production increased by half. But since 1976, production has leveled off: in 1976, world production of beef and mutton totalled 54.9 million tons; in 1980, an estimated 54.2 million tons.[42] For the first time during the modern era, the growth in beef production has come to a halt, thereby raising questions about the prospects for resuming the long-term rise in consumption.

Per Capita Consumption Trends

Viewed in per capita terms, global resource trends are both illuminating and disturbing. They show the relationship between multiplying human numbers and the carrying capacity of the earth's life-support systems, a relationship that has received too little attention. But they also show that expanding human demands are becoming unsustainable.

Although averages obscure wide variation in individual consumption, they do help us put our resource use in a population perspective. As long as the per capita average is climbing, everyone has at least a theoretical chance of consuming more, but once the global average turns downward, if some people are to consume more, others must consume less. In such a situation, the unmet basic needs of the poor can be satisfied only if the affluent consume less. In a world where per capita resource supplies are shrinking, the questions of how the global supply of each resource is divided becomes a sticky international political issue.

Until world population reached the three billion mark in 1960, the yields of the three basic biological systems expanded more rapidly than population. At that point, however, the margin began to narrow. By the time population had moved beyond four billion (reached in 1976), the per capita production of wood, fish, beef, mutton, and wool was declining. While untapped capacity still exists here and there in each of these systems, per capita output in all is declining under current management and with current population growth rates.

Before 1964, world production of wood expanded more rapidly than population, but as forests began to shrink, expansion became more difficult. As a result, population growth outstripped forest production after 1964, leading to a decline of one tenth in the wood supply per person over the next 15 years. (See Table 3–3.) Small wonder that the prices of lumber and housing have risen the world over and that scarcities are unsettling the household economies of so many Third World villagers. Vast untapped forest resources do remain, but they are located in such remote sites as eastern Siberia, northern Canada, and the inner Amazon. For the fuel-starved villager in Ethiopia, they could as well be on the moon. And with oil

Table 3–3: World Production per Capita of Basic Biological
Resources, 1960–80

Year	Forests Wood (cubic meters)	Fisheries Fish (kilograms)	Grasslands Beef	Mutton (kilograms)	Wool
1960	—	13.2	9.32	1.88	.85
1961	.66	14.0	9.62	1.90	.84
1962	.65	14.9	9.85	1.89	.85
1963	.66	14.7	10.74	1.88	.83
1964	.67	16.1	10.06	1.84	.80
1965	.66	16.0	9.92	1.79	.78
1966	.66	16.8	10.20	1.77	.78
1967	.64	17.4	10.38	1.89	.78
1968	.64	18.0	10.67	1.89	.79
1969	.64	17.4	10.70	1.85	.78
1970	.64	18.5	10.60	1.87	.75
1971	.64	18.3	10.37	1.87	.73
1972	.63	16.8	10.56	1.88	.71
1973	.64	16.8	10.46	1.79	.66
1974	.63	17.7	10.97	1.73	.64
1975	.61	17.2	11.28	1.75	.66
1976	.62	17.7	11.58	1.78	.63
1977	.61	17.3	11.52	1.74	.62
1978	.61	17.3	11.36	1.73	.61
1979	.60	16.9	10.88	1.72	.60
1980 (prel.)	.60	16.1	10.53	1.74	.62

Note: Peak years are underlined.
Source: Food and Agriculture Organization.

prices driving up transport costs, these remote forest resources
are not likely to become much more accessible.

With fisheries, the critical point came in 1970, when world
population reached 3.6 billion. During the previous two
decades the fish catch had been growing at a record rate; but
since 1970, the fish catch per person has fallen by 13 percent,
or over 1 percent per year. Per capita, the catch of both table
fish and fish used for fishmeal have fallen.

With the output from grasslands, the production of mutton
and wool turned downwards even before the fish catch fell.
Hastened by the advent of synthetic fibers, these downturns
occurred in the early sixties, shortly after world population

reached three billion. With wool production becoming less profitable, so did sheep husbandry overall. Although world mutton production per person has been declining since 1961, the decline accelerated after 1972. Wool production per person, which peaked around 1960, has fallen by 27 percent since then. The production of beef, far more important than mutton production in global terms, continued to increase until 1976. But as world population hit four billion, beef production per person finally peaked. In four short years, it fell by 9 percent, indicating an absolute decline in world production since 1976.

One reason the world's beef herds continued to expand when sheep flocks had hit their limit is that more and more of the world's beef cattle were being "finished for market" in feedlots. This shifted some of the pressure from grasslands to corn fields. But now as mounting demands for grain drive prices upward, grain is not likely to be cheap enough again to use to relieve the pressure on grasslands.

Until recently, the reversal in per capita trends was obscured by the lack of worldwide data. But with better information, the trends are becoming only too clear. With human demand outstripping the sustainable yield of the natural biological systems that support the world economy, the output per person of virtually every major commodity produced by these systems appears to be declining. The implications of this decline will be felt everywhere and will occupy national political leaders for years to come.

Future Resource Trends

Projecting the yield of biological systems is not an easy task. But recent historical evidence does provide clues to the direction of the trends, if not their magnitude. A projection of the oceanic fish catch, which is influenced both by the inherent biological potential of the fisheries and by the human capacity to manage them wisely, illustrates the point. Calculating the yield potential requires precise information on each individual species, including that on age-group distribution, reproduction and maturation rates, and the species' relationship to other species in the oceanic food chain. Buoyed by the rapid expansion of the fish catch after World War II, some analysts projected a year 2000 catch as high as 300 million tons.[43] During the early seventies, however, projections fell to something around 100 million tons. More recently, the projections have become even more sober and conservative. The *Global 2000 Report* published in 1980, which drew heavily on analyses by the U.S. National Marine Fisheries Service, concluded that the generally accepted annual potential of 100 million metric tons of traditional marine species probably cannot be achieved *on a sustained basis.* [44] More likely, says *Global 2000*, the sustainable oceanic catch is close to the present catch of about 60 million metric tons.

One way of projecting the world fish harvest, oceanic and fresh water, is to assume that it will continue to fluctuate between 65 and 75 million tons over the next two decades as it has during the decade since 1970. Assuming an end-of-century catch of 70 million tons, the fish catch per person would fall by some 42 percent between 1970 and 2000. If severe protein shortages materialize, restraints on fishing could be lifted or violated. With stocks decimated, future catches would be smaller still.

More optimistically, we could assume that the management of fisheries will improve, that the few remaining underexploited stocks (such as those in the tropical fisheries around the Indonesian islands) will be fully developed, and that fish farming will double. Given these assumptions, a projected harvest of 85 million tons by the year 2000 is within reason. Such an increase would lead to a decline in the catch per person from 18.5 kilograms in 1970 to 13.7 kilograms in 2000—a drop of 30 percent. (See Figure 3–1.)

Any reasonable combination of assumptions concerning the future fish catch leads to the conclusion that the recent decline in the per capita fish supply will continue. If population grows

Kilograms

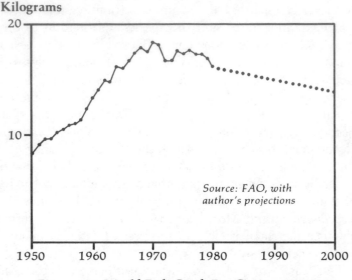

Figure 3-1. World Fish Catch Per Capita, 1950-80, With Projections to 2000

as expected, the key questions will be how much the catch per person declines, how it affects seafood prices, and who eats less fish.

Unfortunately, the figure showing a decline in the projected fish catch per person also probably describes the future per capita trends of beef, mutton, leather, wood, and other major commodities of biological origin over the remainder of this century—if the projected growth in world population materializes. Underlying each of these trends is some basic biology and brutal arithmetic: Production is constrained by sustainable yield, and that yield must be divided among an ever growing number.

Oil: The Safety Valve

During the last two decades, we have been sheltered from the full effects of the lag in output of commodities of biological origin and of the growing scarcity of new cropland by the extensive substitution of petroleum products for natural products. Gasoline and diesel fuels now used to power tractors and irrigation pumps have replaced draft animals and, to a lesser degree, human muscle power. Where agriculture has been mechanized, oil has in effect been substituted for the land once used to produce feed for draft animals. In the United States, some 60 million acres of cropland were released for other purposes between 1930 and 1960 as tractors replaced horses.[45]

To meet the continuously expanding demand for food, farmers lacking new land increase their yields by using petroleum in the form of fertilizer. Between 1950 and 1980, the world's farmers increased their use of energy-intensive chemical fertilizers nearly eightfold, from 15 million tons to over 114 million tons.[46] The use of pesticides, many of them produced from petrochemicals, also climbed markedly.[47]

Off the farm, too, synthetic materials from the petrochemical industry were substituted for natural materials following World War II. While per capita production of wool, cotton, and other natural fibers has leveled off or fallen, the use of synthetic fibers has climbed, partly because synthetics have cost relatively less and partly because many consumers prefer a blend of natural and synthetic fibers. In 1950, synthetic fibers accounted for only 1 percent of world fiber use, but by 1979 their share had climbed to an estimated 36 percent—compared with 47 percent for cotton, 5 percent for wool, and 12 percent for rayon, a fiber produced largely from wood pulp. Overall, fully one-third of the clothing and textiles the world's four billion consumers buy are now made of materials not found in nature.

With rubber, the substitution of synthetics produced by the petrochemical industry has progressed even farther. Although world production of natural rubber has kept pace with population growth since 1950, it has fallen far behind affluence-spurred demand. By 1978, synthetic rubber accounted for over two-thirds of the world's rubber supply.[48]

Plastics, also synthesized from petroleum, have been widely substituted for wood, paper, cardboard, and leather. In packaging alone, their use in the United States totaled 4 million tons in 1978, or some 18 kilograms per capita. Increasingly, they have been substituted for wood in the building, furniture, home appliance, and houseware industries.[49] In the Third World, kerosene has been substituted for firewood and charcoal as forests dwindle. Everywhere, synthetic detergents have replaced tallow-based soap. And as the leather supply lags farther and farther behind demand, the world's footwear and leather-goods industries have turned to imitation leathers.

This use of oil in the form of fertilizer and synthetic substitutes for natural materials has served as a safety valve, alleviating the pressure on natural systems. The potential for lessening pressure on natural systems has been keyed to the availability of oil and the evolution of a vast petrochemical industrial capacity. But as oil reserves dwindle, this safety valve will close, reversing the substitution process and putting even more pressure on croplands and the basic biological systems.

4

Twilight of the Age of Oil

Our age is often referred to as the nuclear age or the space age. Scientifically glamorous though these labels may be, it is petroleum that has shaped our time. The consumption of vast quantities of oil, some 60 million barrels a day, gives modern society its distinctive character.

Industrial economies turned to oil because it was convenient, abundant, and cheap. At its peak in 1973, oil and natural gas, its companion fuel, accounted for 67 percent of world commercial energy use.[1] Oil was the source of nearly all the world's transportation fuel and chemical feedstocks as well as much of the fuel for heating buildings and water, and for generating electricity. Production of this wondrously versatile fuel and feedstock multiplied fivefold between 1950 and 1973.[2] Within a generation, it reshaped the economic system. Yet, most of the readily accessible reserves of oil formed over hundreds of millions of years will be consumed within a single generation, spanning the years from 1960 to 1995.[3]

Supply disruptions and higher prices for oil have forced national leaders to reconsider the role of oil in their economies. The price of dependence on an exhaustible dwindling resource is being felt around the world and the short-term outlook for substitutes is not promising. Nuclear power, once regarded as petroleum's natural heir, has become less and less attractive as its numerous drawbacks come to light. Coal, the other fossil fuel, is ultimately as exhaustible as oil.

The Rise of Oil

The age of oil began in 1859 in Pennsylvania, when Captain E. L. Drake drilled the first oil well, but only within the last few decades has oil emerged as the dominant fuel. As recently as 1950, world production totaled only 3.8 billion barrels, a meager output by contemporary standards. By 1973, annual production topped 20 billion barrels.[4]

During those 23 oil-thirsty years, demand drove production upward by 7 percent annually. Each year, world oil production moved to a new high. World population grew at a record rate during this period, but the growth of oil production outpaced it handily, so oil production per person increased—from 1.5 barrels per year in 1950 to 5.3 barrels in 1973—mostly because consumption in the northern tier of industrial countries increased manyfold. (See Table 4-1.)

By 1961, the great postwar surge in oil and natural gas output had eclipsed the production of coal, which had been the principal source of commercial energy since the Industrial Revolution began.[5] By 1967, the production of oil alone had surpassed that of coal. By 1973, oil and natural gas together provided more than twice as much energy as did coal.

Table 4-1. World Oil Production, Total and Per Capita, 1950–80

Year	Population	Oil Production	Oil Production Per Capita
	(billion)	(billion barrels)	(barrels)
1950	2.51	3.8	1.5
1955	2.74	5.6	2.0
1960	3.03	7.7	2.5
1965	3.34	11.1	3.3
1970	3.68	16.7	4.5
1971	3.75	17.7	4.7
1972	3.82	18.6	4.9
1973	3.88	20.4	5.3
1974	3.96	20.5	5.2
1975	4.03	19.5	4.8
1976	4.11	20.9	5.1
1977	4.18	21.8	5.2
1978	4.26	22.0	5.2
1979	4.34	22.7	5.2
1980	4.42	21.7	4.9

Source: United Nations and U.S. Department of Energy.

The quarter century of extraordinary growth in production that made oil the world's primary fuel ended in late 1973 with the fourfold OPEC (Organization of Petroleum Exporting Countries) oil-price increase. During the years since, world oil production has increased less rapidly than population. In all probability, the 5.3 barrels per person produced in 1973 will be the historical high.

With per capita oil production on the wane, the next milestone will come when total production turns downward. Most projections do not show the onset of a gradual decline occurring before the early nineties, though recent evidence suggests that it could occur much sooner because of political decisions limiting production levels.[6] If it occurs before population growth halts, as now seems likely, oil output per person will plummet as a dwindling output is divided among a still-expanding world population.

Our Petroleum Culture

Oil has left an indelible imprint on virtually every facet of human existence and made our world one that our ancestors would scarcely recognize. A combination of demand-stimulating Keynesian economic policies and cheap oil fueled an unprecedented increase in the production of goods and services during the immediate postwar decades. Between 1950 and 1973, the world economy expanded at a record 4 percent per year, and the output of goods and services tripled in less than a generation.[7]

To some, the prevailing prices and policies seemed to indicate that rapid sustained economic growth had become part of the natural order. Economists, corporate executives, political leaders, and average citizens all assumed at least implicitly, if not explicitly, that such growth would continue indefinitely. Few realized how closely economic growth was tied to the abundance of cheap oil.

Not only did cheap oil underwrite unprecedented economic growth—it also sustained an explosive increase in human population. Growing supplies of liquid fuels and advancing technology permitted food production to expand more rapidly, and increased food production led to increased population. In some societies, population growth rates approached the biological maximum.

While the rapid growth in oil use greatly enhanced the earth's population-sustaining capacity, it also helped transform the world economy from a collection of essentially independent national economies into a closely knit international economic system. This transformation reflects three facts. First, oil reserves are concentrated in a few regions, whereas the demand for oil is universal. Second, oil is a highly transportable fuel. Third, as a liquid fuel oil has been central to the development of the international transportation network.

Because of its portability and its versatility as a fuel and a feedstock for the chemical industry, oil is widely used in almost all countries, most of which have little or no oil of their own. Japan and some of the industrial countries of Western Europe, for instance, have developed oil-based economies that are wholly dependent on foreign oil supplies. Prior to the oil age, most countries made do with indigenous energy resources; neither coal nor wood were ever exported in large quantities. Now oil has become the energy commodity with which national energy accounts are balanced.

As countries everywhere modernized, the uneven distribution of oil reserves spurred not only trade in oil but also trade in commodities to pay for oil. Since 1973 the soaring price of oil has further spurred oil-importing countries to launch vigorous export-expansion programs. Raw materials, industrial products, and agricultural commodities are sold for foreign exchange to import oil.

Oil has also been a force in the evolution of the modern international transportation system. International water-, air-, and land-transportation networks are fueled primarily with oil. Had nature never formed the oil trapped under the earth's surface, an integrated international economic system like ours might never have evolved. Oil proved ideal for powering ocean-going ships, and oil-fueled jets have helped create a global society.

More specifically, cheap oil led to the evolution of automobile-centered transportation systems in the Western industrial societies and precipitated a desire elsewhere to emulate these systems. In 1950, when world oil production amounted to less than four billion barrels, there were only 53 million automobiles on the road, four-fifths of them in North America and Europe.[8] By 1980, the world automobile fleet had multiplied to 325 million. In Western industrial societies, where the automobile culture is most deeply entrenched, the automobile has shaped life-styles as well as economies.

Automobile manufacturers, the world's largest industry, produced some 100,000 new vehicles each working day during the seventies.[9] The fate of the automobile industry and of industries that supply it with steel, rubber, glass, and parts is linked to the supply of liquid fuels. After three decades of rapid growth, world automobile production leveled off in the seventies along with oil production. With oil supplies dwindling, the demand for automobiles may never again reach the 1978 level of 31 million unless near-miraculous breakthroughs in mileage efficiency are made.

Along with social change and the integration of the world economy, cheap oil also encouraged the development of "throwaways." When oil was so cheap as to seem free, it was easier to throw things away than to reuse, recycle, or repair them. Without cheap energy with which to manufacture new goods, the concept of planned obsolescence would never have evolved.

On a country-by-country basis, the impact of oil has varied widely. In some countries, life-styles have been profoundly altered, and in others, barely touched. In the United States, the influence of liquid fossil fuels is visible everywhere. In contrast, parts of the rural Third World have scarcely been touched by oil's power. In India, for example, bullock carts, bicycles, and coal-powered trains still carry the bulk of passengers and freight.[10] Although the decline of oil will affect the structure of modern industrial economies far more than those of largely subsistence economies, the social impact on those living precariously close to the margin of survival will be far greater.

The Emergence of OPEC

Few things symbolize the changing oil outlook as much as the emergence of the powerful Organization of Petroleum Exporting Countries (OPEC). Although formed in 1960, it remained largely unknown until 1973. As recently as 1972, OPEC was an acronym known to few outside the oil industry, but since the 1973 oil price hike it has become a household word. Now it is widely recognized as one of the world's most influential organizations.

OPEC's 13 member countries are a diverse group containing 319 million people, or 7 percent of the world total. Six members are in the Middle East (Iran, Iraq, Kuwait, Qatar, Saudi Arabia, and the United Arab Emirates), two are in North Africa (Algeria and Libya), two are in sub-Saharan Africa (Gabon and Nigeria), two are in Latin America (Ecuador and Venezuela), and one (Indonesia) is in Asia. But these 13 geographically, culturally, and religiously diverse countries have a few things in common: exportable surpluses of oil, preindustrial infrastructures, and a keen desire for better prices for their oil. These three common interests have held this disparate group together in the face of great odds and frequent predictions of its demise.

OPEC's chief architect and founder, Juan Pablo Perez Alfonso, was a Venezuelan. The Minister of Mines and Hydrocarbons during the forties, Perez Alfonso grew deeply concerned with the wasteful use of oil and the prodigious speed at which oil reserves were being used up.[11] He developed the idea of an organization of petroleum exporting countries out of that concern.

Perez Alfonso was not an international political wheeler-dealer. Above all, he considered himself an ecologist. He gardened and raised flowers. He called the car a "cosmic curse" and thought the bicycle the worthier vehicle. The only car he owned, a 1936 Singer sports coupe, was parked on a pedestal in his garden, draped with tropical flowers and Venezuelan orchids. Although Perez Alfonso was a millionaire many times over, he lived in relative austerity in the suburbs of Caracas. He read by candlelight and reportedly asked all visitors to leave when darkness fell so that he would not waste electricity.

As the founder of OPEC saw it, his mission in life was to

stop the waste of valuable energy resources. When describing his early vision of OPEC, he said, "Most people see OPEC as a way to raise oil prices, but I see it as a way to lower the use of energy." Shortly before he died in late 1979, he referred to OPEC as the "leading ecology group in the world."[12]

While the idea for OPEC was conceived in 1946, it was not until 1960 that Perez Alfonso could convince several oil-exporting countries to join with Venezuela in a common pact.[13] The event that triggered the formation of OPEC was the international oil companies' attempt to reduce further the pittance they were paying countries for their oil. At a meeting in Baghdad, representatives from Venezuela, Saudi Arabia, Iran, and Kuwait established a minimum oil price of $1.80 a barrel.[14]

The first victory was a modest one. The OPEC members were unified enough to sustain the $1.80 floor price, but their inability collectively to limit production also limited their ability to further raise prices. Not until the early seventies, while the Suez Canal was closed, did Libya attempt to make the most of its high-quality oil and its geographic proximity to Europe by renegotiating a small price increase. After Libya succeeded, the Persian Gulf oil exporters pressed successfully for similar increases. The resultant leapfrogging series of price increases raised the oil price to $3.01 per barrel by October 1973.

The next key event in the evolution of OPEC's power was the 1973 Yom Kippur War, waged by Egypt and Syria against Israel. In support of Egypt and Syria, the Arab members of OPEC reduced exports to the Western industrial countries and embargoed all oil shipments to the United States and the Netherlands. At the same time, Iran tried auctioning oil to the highest bidder and discovered it could get as much as $17 a barrel. With this new understanding of the inelastic nature of the demand for oil, the OPEC countries decided in January of 1974 to raise the official price to $11.65 a barrel—a price many incorrectly predicted would not hold.

From 1974 to 1978, the OPEC oil price remained quite

stable, increasing gradually to $12.70 by 1978. (Adjusted for inflation, the real price of oil actually declined over this four-year span.) But OPEC used this time and its newly discovered power to whittle away the hold and span of the international oil companies by increasing the royalty charges per barrel and raising taxes.

As recently as 1972 the so-called "Seven Sisters"—Exxon, Mobil, Texaco, Gulf, Standard Oil of California, British Petroleum, and Royal Dutch Shell—had a virtual stranglehold on the world oil business. Not only did they own the oil fields, but they also set prices and made the production decisions, deciding how much oil each country would produce, where it would be shipped, and what its price would be. But all that changed as OPEC began to assert itself. Gradually, the governments of producing countries began assuming control over supply as well as price. Concessions to oil companies were replaced with long-term contracts. National oil companies such as Sonatrach in Algeria and Pertamina in Indonesia assumed more prominent roles vis à vis private firms. Several oil-exporting countries began refining operations in an effort to generate even larger oil incomes and to bring more of the production process under the control of the suppliers.

In late 1978, growing political unrest in Iran began to interrupt Iran's export of oil, creating shortages. Again taking their cues from the spot market as prices soared above $40 a barrel in early 1979, the OPEC countries began another round of price increases. By late June, the official OPEC price had climbed to $18 a barrel and the market showed no signs of collapse.

When OPEC members met in Caracas in late December of 1979, the system of unified pricing that had held up so well since 1960 began to break down in the face of bullish world demand. Agreement on a unified price proved impossible. Supported by Venezuela and Kuwait, Saudi Arabia had attempted to cap the price increase at $24 per barrel, but some members were not satisfied with that ceiling. By late spring of 1980, Algeria, Libya, and Nigeria had upped their prices to $35 a barrel.

Perez Alfonso had originally seen OPEC primarily as a means of conserving oil by raising oil prices. But in the end, OPEC was to create a new international order and to alter profoundly the economic and political relationship between the preindustrial oil-exporting countries and the rest of the world. During the late sixties and seventies, the developing countries had been pressing for a new international economic order, one that would improve both their international terms of trade and their access to investment capital and technology. While these countries, organized as the Group of 77, were calling for a new international economic order, the "Group of 13"—OPEC—was in fact implementing one. With its new-found ability to control the oil that fueled the world economy, it engineered history's greatest international transfer of wealth and power.

Among the developing countries, discussion of the need for a new international economic order centers on their deteriorating terms of trade with the industrial countries. However substantial that deterioration between 1950 and 1972, the terms of much of the trade between the preindustrial and industrial societies were abruptly altered by OPEC. Nowhere was this more evident than in the exchange of oil and grain between the OPEC countries and the United States (the world's leading oil importer and leading grain exporter). From 1950 to 1972, both the price of a bushel of wheat and that of a barrel of oil hovered around $1.80. (See Table 4-2.) Throughout this period, a bushel of wheat could be traded for a barrel of oil. But by 1980, it took six bushels of wheat to pay for a barrel of oil. Rarely, if ever, have the relative prices of two major commodities shifted so dramatically and so quickly.

The shift in the price relationship of oil and grain may signal the beginning of a long-term transformation in the relative

Table 4-2. The International Terms of Trade Between Wheat and Oil, 1950–80

Year	Wheat Price	Oil Price	Bushels of Wheat to Buy a Barrel of Oil
	(dollars per bushel)	(dollars per barrel)	
1950	1.91	1.71	1
1955	1.77	1.93	1
1960	1.58	1.50	1
1965	1.62	1.33	1
1970	1.50	1.30	1
1971	1.68	1.65	1
1972	1.90	1.90	1
1973	3.81	2.70	1
1974	4.90	9.76	2
1975	4.06	10.72	3
1976	3.62	11.51	3
1977	2.81	12.40	4
1978	3.48	12.70	4
1979	4.36	16.97	4
1980 (prel.)	4.70	30.50	6

Source: *International Financial Statistics,* International Monetary Fund; and author's estimate for 1980.

prices of nonrenewable resources (among which oil is by far the most important) and renewable ones. Although the price shift is most easily measured for major commodities such as grain, it also stands to affect the many agricultural commodities—tea, coffee, cocoa, bananas, cotton, and jute—sold to pay for imported oil. This shift in relative prices will bear heavily on the evolution of energy strategies. As fossil fuel prices rise, countries importing oil will find investment in renewable energy sources increasingly attractive.

OPEC has been held responsible for the double-digit global inflation, becoming a favorite scapegoat of politicians everywhere. Indeed, OPEC is primarily responsible for the shift in the relative market values of grain and oil and it has contributed to the economic stresses of recent years, playing out its self-interests even when poor countries were most hurt by its actions. Yet, its oil-pricing policy may be nonetheless socially constructive on the whole. With oil reserves shrinking, a socially responsible oil-pricing policy would be one that raised prices just fast enough to encourage conservation and the development of alternative energy sources at a rate that would minimize economic disruption in the transition to the post-petroleum era. As of 1981, one would be hard pressed to argue that the price of oil has risen fast enough to make this smooth transition possible. Although it is easy to criticize OPEC policy in the short run—especially the failure of cash-surplus OPEC countries to assist more aggressively the poorest countries whose development prospects have been devastated—OPEC's role in raising oil prices will almost certainly be vindicated over time. Historians may even express gratitude to Perez Alfonso and the OPEC leaders for having launched, albeit belatedly, the transition to a post-petroleum era.

The Decline of Oil

The climb in oil prices will inevitably accelerate as production falls off, as it is sure to do. At any given time, oil production is determined by a combination of physical conditions and by what might loosely be described as political influences. Among the physical conditions influencing oil production are the all-important reserves-to-production ratio and geographic accessibility.

M. King Hubbert, the geologist who quite accurately predicted in 1956 that U.S. oil production would peak around 1970, has also projected world oil production to peak somewhere just before the end of the century because of physical constraints.[15] In a more recent analysis, David H. Root and Emil B. Attanasi of the U.S. Geological Survey set the date at

1993.[16] Overall, production projections made in the mid and late seventies and based primarily on physical constraints show world oil production peaking sometime during the 1990s.[17]

Geologists take account of two types of oil reserves when they calculate oil-production prospects. "Proven reserves" are those known reserves of oil that can be recovered with existing technology and at current prices. "Ultimately recoverable reserves" (or "probable reserves"), a far larger category, includes expected new discoveries and allows for advances in extraction technologies. Proven reserves consist largely of oil that can be extracted easily using the natural pressure in oil-bearing geologic formations. In older oil fields, however, "secondary recovery" measures, whereby pressure in the oil-bearing structures is maintained by pumping water or gas into the structure, must be called into play. In Venezuela, the European part of the Soviet Union, and the United States, this recovery method is widely used, now accounting for some one-fourth to one-half of all oil production.[18] Tertiary recovery techniques involving the use of heat or chemicals to reduce the viscosity of oil can also be used, though they are not brought to bear until primary and secondary means fail to yield results since each of these techniques is progressively more costly and yields less net energy.

Naturally, estimates of proven reserves tend to be more precise than those of ultimately recoverable reserves. But some consensus is now forming around both. In early 1980, the editors of the *International Petroleum Encyclopedia*, consulting with both governments and oil companies, estimated proven world oil reserves at 641 billion barrels.[19] Estimates of ultimately recoverable reserves have tended to converge around 2000 billion barrels, or roughly three times proven reserves.[20]

Translated into per capita terms, these meganumbers become much more meaningful. Proven reserves of 600 billion barrels amount to 150 barrels for each of the world's four billion people, while recoverable reserves equal roughly 500 barrels per person. If the entire world were to consume oil at the U.S. rate of 30 barrels per person per year, the world's proven reserves of oil would be exhausted within five years. Ultimately recoverable reserves would last no more than another 13 years—less if all ultimately recoverable reserves do not materialize and population continues to grow.

Prior to 1973, oil production was constrained primarily by growth in demand and, in a few locales, by physical constraints. Since 1973, actual production has fallen well below the physical production potential, and accelerating inflation has helped widen the gap between the two. Uncertainty about the future value of money, particularly of the dollar, logically enough prompts oil-producing countries to keep as much of their wealth as possible in the form of oil underground. With oil prices on the rise, the advantages of conservation-oriented production policies in oil-exporting countries speak for themselves.

Also reducing oil output is concern over the disruptive effect of vast capital influxes on traditional pre-industrial societies. The problem grows more serious with each oil-price increase, witness the Iranian experience in 1979. In Iran, the wealth that accrued as export earnings climbed from less than $5 billion in 1973 to some $22 billion in 1974 became concentrated in a few hands, widening the gap between rich and poor and straining the country's social fabric intolerably. And Iran's case may not be unique. When asked about the overthrow of the Shah, a deputy minister of oil from an Arab country said, "The one thought that keeps coming back is that it could have happened to any of us."[21]

Mexico has already adopted policies that reflect this concern. Although the United States and other oil importers had initially assumed that Mexico would quickly join the ranks of the major petroleum exporters, occupying a position that matched the size of its newly discovered oil fields, the Mexican government is thinking otherwise. Officials of PEMEX, the state oil monopoly, have talked of stabilizing production when it reaches 2.7 billion barrels a day.[22] Mexican President Lopez Portillo believes that "output should be kept down to levels commensurate with the country's ability to absorb the resulting massive revenues."[23] The danger of a preindustrial society attempting to absorb massive amounts of capital, he says, is akin to that of indigestion from overeating.

At least as capable of influencing production policies as these other factors is the emergence in the world oil market of a "depletion psychology." When the amount of oil extracted surpasses the amount of new discoveries, proven reserves shrink and producing countries are forced to reckon with the day when their oil reserves are exhausted. The urge most such countries will feel to postpone the day when the wells go dry could steadily lower world oil production in the near term. To be sure, the market impact of a basically healthy fear of using up an irreplaceable resource is hard to gauge. But just as the changing market psychology drove prices far above the levels projected during the seventies, so the emergence of a depletion psychology could markedly reduce oil production below the levels commonly projected for the eighties and nineties.

Production in several major oil-producing countries has already dropped, both because reserves are dwindling and because producers are trying to stretch out remaining reserves. Oil production in Venezuela has fallen nearly 40 percent from its 1970 high of 3.7 million barrels per day.[24] Production in Libya peaked in the same year at 3.3 million barrels per day and now stands at 2 million barrels per day or less. Production peaked in the United States in 1970 and Canada in 1973. Other major producing countries experiencing more recent declines include Algeria, Iraq, Iran, and Kuwait. In politically unsettled Iran, production has fallen far below the mid-seventies level, to which it is unlikely to return.

This decline will, of course, be partially offset by production increases in China, Mexico, Norway, the United Kingdom, and other new producers. In China, future gains will depend heavily on the import of advanced drilling equipment from the West, especially that for exploiting offshore fields. Production in the United Kingdom's North Sea fields is expected to peak in 1982 or 1983 at about 3 million barrels a day.[25]

Several projections of world oil production made since 1975 by petroleum companies and private consultants indicate that world oil production will grow by some 15 to 35 percent between 1980 and 1990.[26] But these projections are based largely on assessments of physical conditions in the world's oil fields: They accord little weight to political forces or to the emergence of a strong depletion psychology. Because they are based largely on physical factors, the easiest of the three factors to analyze, these projections may lead to an unwarranted complacency.

Preliminary production reports for 1980, a recession year, indicate that world output fell below 22 billion barrels, some 4 percent below the all-time high of 22.7 billion barrels in 1979.[27] Although one year does not make a trend and although the Iraq-Iran war reduced output, the 1980 dip in oil output does demonstrate the potential for production declines as well as increases.

Given the strength of the production constraints reviewed here, a modest decline in output—to 20 billion barrels by 1990 and to 18 billion barrels at the end of the century—appears more likely than does a production increase. Even this modest decline means that per capita output would fall from roughly 5 barrels per person in 1980 to less than 3 barrels per person in the year 2000, assuming the projected growth in world population materializes. (See Figure 4-1.) With individual allotments reduced by some 43 percent, life-styles and energy-use patterns, particularly in heavily oil-dependent countries, will perforce change radically.

With world oil supply per person falling, a continuing rise in consumption in some countries could lead to an even more precipitous drop in the others. The saving grace is that the

Barrels

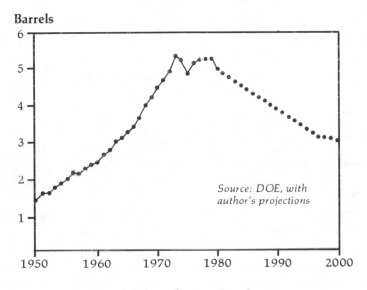

**Figure 4-1. World Oil Production Per Capita, 1950-80,
With Projections to 2000**

reverse is also true: If countries now consuming large amounts
of oil could reduce per capita consumption sharply, per person
consumption could still rise in some low-income countries. If
population growth could also be sharply reduced, that too
would enhance the prospects for raising consumption in the
countries where even now basic human needs are not being
met.

Giving Up on Nuclear Power

It has long been known that the age of oil would not last
forever, but during much of the postwar period when world oil
reserves were being depleted so rapidly, most people assumed
that nuclear power would provide vast amounts of cheap energy once the oil wells ran dry. Now most people think otherwise. At the end of 1980, some 255 nuclear reactors located in

over 20 countries were operating or at least had licenses to operate, but the vast expansion of nuclear capacity once planned is not materializing.[28]

Current difficulties with nuclear power came about in part because the energy source was misrepresented and in part because the risks and costs were not adequately analyzed at the beginning. Nuclear power also brings with it a host of special problems that do not afflict other power sources. A nuclear reactor can melt down, forcing the massive evacuation of people in the surrounding area. It produces dangerous, long-lived radioactive wastes. Reliance on nuclear power can lead to a proliferation of nuclear weapons among countries and raises the prospect of nuclear terrorism. At the same time, it is an inequitable source of energy, putting on those living nearest to a reactor a disproportionately large share of the risks associated with a meltdown.

As troubling as the prospect of weapons proliferation and long-lived wastes may be, the curtain could close on nuclear power for strictly economic reasons. The claim that reactors would generate "electricity too cheap to meter" is no longer made. As early as 1975, Donald Cook, chairman of the board of American Electric Power, the largest U.S. utility, was saying that "an erroneous conception of the economics of nuclear power" had sent U.S. utilities "down the wrong road."[29] Since then, few U.S. utilities have placed orders for reactors as other executives have come to share Cook's conclusions.

Between 1971 and 1978, the real costs of constructing a nuclear power plant rose nearly 14 percent per year, compared with less than 8 percent for coal-fired plants.[30] Incorporating the additional safety features now required in the wake of the Three Mile Island accident can only further erode nuclear power's economic feasibility. Indeed, Consolidated Edison of New York announced in late 1980 that it was permanently closing its Indian Point Number One plant because it would cost too much to make the 18-year-old reactor safe.[31]

Nowhere is the declining prospect for nuclear power more evident than in the United States, its leading producer. In 1972, the Atomic Energy Commission projected a nuclear-generating capacity by the end of the century of 1,010 giga-walts, (one gigawatt equals 1000 megawatts) roughly 1,000 large plants. (See Table 4-3.) When oil prices climbed sharply in late 1973, many thought that nuclear power would get a boost, but such has not been the case. By 1978, the Department of Energy, which encompassed the old AEC, reduced the projected figure to 410 gigawatts, less than half the level given only six years earlier. Three separate reports in 1980 reduced the 1978 projection by roughly half. Taking into account developments in late 1980 and early 1981, year 2000 consumption may not exceed 115 gigawatts—scarcely a tenth of that projected by the Atomic Energy Commission in 1972. Ironically, by 1980, firewood had eclipsed nuclear power in the

Table 4-3. Changing Projections of U.S. Nuclear Power Capacity, 1972–81[*]

Year of Forecast	By End 1980	By End 1985	By End 1990	By End 2000
	(gigawatts)			
1972 Atomic Energy Commission	130	268	460	1,010
1975 Atomic Industrial Forum	90	182	340	800
1978 Department of Energy	–	127	200	410
1980 Atomic Industrial Forum	56	104	138	257
Department of Energy	–	98	130	180
Nuclear Regulatory Commission	49	95	126	145
1981 Worldwatch Institute	49	85	120	115

[*]Where a range is projected the midpoint has been selected for this compilation.
Source: Nuclear Regulatory Commission, Atomic Industrial Forum, and Worldwatch Institute.

U.S. energy budget—and despite the $36 billion governmental subsidy given the latter.[32]

In its annual U.S. electrical industry forecast for 1981, *Electrical World* underlines the dire problems facing nuclear-generated electricity. In summary, it says, "The aggregation of extraordinary interest rates, unprecedented long-range inflation, federal ineffectiveness—or unwillingness—to create the necessary climate for a secure nuclear future, the prolonged financial decline of most utilities, and slackening growth have succeeded in doing what the most violently anti-nuclear groups have failed to do: They have, at least at the time being, shut off nuclear expansion beyond presently committed units."[33] Further, the industry journal projects no new reactor orders before 1985 or 1986 at the earliest. With Wall Street turning its back on the industry, with virtually no new plants ordered between 1975 and 1985, with numerous cancellations likely to follow the 18 plants cancelled in 1980, and with aging older plants faced with shutdown, U.S. nuclear-generating capacity will likely begin declining in the nineties.

A lack of reliable data for many other countries makes it somewhat more difficult to map the changing global outlook for nuclear power. But some of the same trends are evident. Several countries are abandoning plants in mid-construction as costs have gotten out of hand and as projections of electrical demand have dropped. West Germany is entering the sixth year of an unofficial but effective moratorium on nuclear power plant construction.[34] In neighboring Austria, a referendum held in 1978 led to a decision not to activate, at least for the time being, a large new nuclear-generating plant.[35] Other West European countries are also slowing their shift to nuclear power.[36] Such data as are available for Eastern Europe indicate a loss of momentum there as well.[37] Although the Soviet Union remains committed to nuclear power, plant construction there is lagging far behind schedule. Iran's nuclear program has come to a complete standstill, Brazil's once ambitious plans have been cut back, and South Korea dramatically downgraded its nuclear program in early 1981 in light of soaring costs and a projected slowdown in economic growth.[38] Even France, whose original program was so ambitious, has begun to de-emphasize the role of nuclear power in its long-term energy planning.

One telling sign of the worldwide disenchantment with nuclear power is the change in the ratio of cancellations to new orders. From early 1970 to late 1976, plans for some 270 plants were announced and only nine orders were cancelled.[39] From 1977 through 1980, 39 new plants were announced and 34 existing agreements were cancelled. In 1979, the last full year for which data are available, cancellations outnumbered announcements of new plants by 8 to 3. It was also the year when reactor safety became a major issue of public concern.

Until the accident at Three Mile Island in March 1979 nuclear proponents could argue that the chance of a meltdown was so small as to be dismissible but now that argument has lost all credence. The political effects of the partial meltdown may be felt throughout the world for years to come. At the time it occurred, 35,000 West Germans who were demonstrating against the opening of a nuclear waste-disposal site immediately saw its relevance to their protest. "We all live in Pennsylvania," they chanted, echoing John F. Kennedy's "Ich bin ein Berliner" of a half generation ago.[40] The risk of serious nuclear accidents is apparently higher than was earlier believed. In August 1980, the British science journal *Nature* reported that Czechoslovakia has had its own "Three Mile Island," an accident that led to the permanent closing of a nuclear power plant.[41]

Nuclear power is unique among power sources in that it produces a carcinogenic radioactive waste that remains dangerous for thousands of years, bequeathing risks to our children that will endure for more generations than have ever been encompassed in any geneaologist's family tree. With no permanent means of waste disposal yet available, the world nuclear waste problem literally grows larger day by day. Gus Speth, director of President Carter's Council on Environmental Quality, outlined the scale of the problem: "To date some 17,000 spent fuel assemblies, each containing large quantities of materials that are highly radioactive and will remain so for thousands of years, have accumulated as a result of commercial power reactor operations."[42] In addition to these wastes, most of which are stored temporarily in ponds at the reactor sites, Speth notes that over 140 million tons of uranium mill tailings, which are a source of low-level radioactive waste, are "strewn about the U.S. countryside." Just how much it costs to get rid of radioactive waste generated by nuclear power plants cannot be estimated because there is not yet an accepted procedure for doing so. Indeed, many geological engineers consider safe, permanent disposal an impossibility.

Early data developed by industry representatives on the costs of nuclear power also neglected the expense of decommissioning worn-out plants, which remain intensely radioactive for decades after they are shut down. Estimates of these costs have traditionally ranged from $50 to $100 million per plant.[43] After lengthy negotiations, the federal government has assumed responsibility for cleaning up the defunct West Valley Nuclear Fuel Processing Plant in New York State—and at a cost to taxpayers of some $225 million over the next nine years.[44]

Other neglected costs are only beginning to surface. A developer who bought 18 acres in Canonsburg, Pennsylvania, for an industrial park discovered 200,000 tons of uranium tailings buried at the site.[45] Because radioactivity issues from the tailings, the 12 buildings must now be razed, and the radioactive material excavated, decontaminated, and buried. The estimated cleanup bill of $20 million is to be underwritten chiefly by the federal government, with the Pennsylvania State Government paying 10 percent of the cost. With 25 such sites around the country, it will be years before taxpayers finish paying for the cleanup.

Beyond these general costs to society of nuclear power, disproportionately high financial risks accrue to people residing close to reactors. Although insurance companies will insure property against loss from hurricanes, earthquakes, and other catastrophes, they will not insure against a nuclear accident. Following the accident at Three Mile Island, the Federal Insurance Administration (FIA) tried to calculate the financial loss if there had been a meltdown and 800,000 people had to be permanently evacuated.[46] Assuming that no medical problems or deaths occurred, and without accounting for the loss of productive farmland within the region, FIA calculated that the loss would total at least $16.8 billion. Under the Price-Anderson Act, passed in 1957 to protect the nuclear industry, liabilities arising out of a nuclear accident cannot exceed $560 million. Under this arrangement, the typical homeowners in the Three Mile Island evacuation area could have collected only 3.3 percent of their $67,500 average loss.[47]

Nuclear reactors were until recently fueled only with uranium, but they can also use plutonium recovered from nuclear waste as fuel. Although this approach does help with the waste management problem, it also heightens the risk of weapons proliferation and nuclear terrorism. While uranium must be subjected to a complex treatment process before it can be used to fashion a bomb, plutonium can be used directly.

Victor Gilinsky, a member of the U.S. Nuclear Regulatory Commission, has chronicled the emerging concern with the potential shift to plutonium.[48] Originally, it was thought that the plutonium contained in spent fuel (and now accumulating in temporary storage facilities around the world) could be reprocessed and then recycled. Gilinsky points out that this was viewed as a "natural, legitimate, desirable, and even indispensable result of the exploitation of nuclear power for the generation of electricity." This policy, which made it difficult to contain the spread throughout the world of this explosive weapons-grade material, was first questioned seriously by the United States. In October 1976, President Ford declared that "the United States should no longer regard reprocessing of used nuclear fuel to produce plutonium as a necessary and inevitable step and that we should pursue reprocessing and recycling in the future only if they are found to be consistent with our international objectives."[49] Ford further said that if the choice came to that between proliferation and plutonium, "avoidance of proliferation must take precedence over economic interests."

In a plutonium-fueled economy, the risk of terrorism becomes all but uncontrollable and the specter of being held hostage by political radicals all too real. With millions of pounds of plutonium coursing through the international arteries of commerce and detailed technical information no farther away than a photocopier, designing a nuclear explosive device becomes undergraduate's play. Indeed, in late 1976 a Princeton undergraduate made headlines when he wrote a paper that contained accurate instructions for constructing a bomb.[50] In an age of hijackings, embassy invasions, and political assassinations, discounting the possibility of nuclear terrorism amounts to a misguided act of misplaced faith.

Taking the threat of nuclear terrorism seriously, the U.S. Government has formed a team to respond to nuclear bomb threats and other nuclear emergencies at a cost so far of $100 million.[51] The Nuclear Emergency Search Team (NEST), headquartered at Andrews Air Force Base and in the Nevada desert, responds to nuclear bomb threats of which there have been at least a score in recent years. The ability of such a group to eliminate the terrorist hazard is, however, doubtful. With sabotage or terrorism a genuine possibility, the pressures to take command either to forestall or manage an emergency could force political leaders to choose between safety on the one hand and freedom on the other. Confronted with possible annihilation, people might well voluntarily surrender individual liberty in exchange for a stronger guarantee of protection. Such a hard bargain could lead to unrelenting surveillance and repression.

As more information on nuclear energy becomes available, as nuclear economics becomes better understood, and as the political risks of using nuclear power come into sharper focus, more and more people are having second thoughts about nuclear energy's feasibility. Many of them have come to share the opinion of Harvard biologist George Wald: "The whole nuclear business . . . represents a disastrous turn for humanity."[52] The rising tide of concern has led to the formation of antinuclear groups throughout Western Europe, the United States, Canada, and Japan. In Brazil, the scientific community is expressing doubts about the practicality of nuclear power for Brazil.[53] In the Soviet Union, Nikolai Dollenzhal, a leading authority on nuclear power, has publicly questioned his government's decision to rely heavily on nuclear energy, particularly in the more densely populated regions.[54]

Nuclear power's now tenuous foothold was established because it was sold to the public as the only answer to humanity's future energy needs. But the public is wiser now, and far more attractive alternatives have emerged, as we shall later see. While phasing out nuclear power over the next couple of decades will require the courage it takes to own up to a mistake, it is not too late to cancel our order for a nuclear-powered society and a plutonium economy. Enough buyers are now wary.

Coal: The Stopgap

Coal was the world's leading commercial fuel from the early days of the Industrial Revolution until 1967 when it was displaced by oil. Coal was overtaken by oil not because coal production declined, but because petroleum output grew so rapidly. Although world coal production—estimated at 3.1 billion tons in 1980—is the energy equivalent of scarcely two-thirds of oil production, coal still enjoys a prominent position in the world energy budget.[55] More important, only coal can see us through from the petroleum culture to the solar culture that must evolve if our society is to endure.

The world over, coal is used to generate electricity, to produce steel, to develop process steam for industrial uses, to power trains, and to heat residential and commercial buildings. But patterns of use vary widely among countries. In the United States, nearly four-fifths of the coal consumed in 1980 was used to generate electricity, and virtually all of the remainder was used by industry.[56] Little coal is now used for residential and commercial heating, and it has lost its place in the American transportation system. In contrast, the world's three most populous countries—China, India, and the Soviet Union— have rail-based transportation systems that rely heavily on coal. And in China, one of the world's leading producers of coal, it is still widely used for heating, particularly in cities.[57]

One reason oil displaced coal during the postwar period is that it is easier to handle and transport. Unlike oil, coal has never been widely traded at the international level. Indeed, only 9 percent of the world's coal output crossed national borders in 1979, compared to 54 percent of world oil output.[58] Coal's growing importance derives not from any special attractions as a fuel but from its relative abundance compared to remaining reserves of oil and natural gas. But while vast quantities of coal are believed to underly the earth's surface, only 600 billion tons (or 136 tons per person for the 1980 world population) is considered economically recoverable.[59] These reserves are equal in energy content to 3,000 billion barrels of oil, or roughly five times the world's proven reserves of oil.

Fully four-fifths of the world's known coal reserves are concentrated in three regions—the Soviet Union and Eastern Europe, the United States, and China.[60] Most of the remaining reserves are in Western Europe, Australia, and India, while known reserves in all of Africa save for South Africa and in South America are quite limited. Because coal reserves are concentrated in large populous countries, in contrast with oil, the potential for international trade is much less.

Since 1950, world coal output has increased rather steadily, expanding from 1.5 billion metric tons annually to nearly 3 billion tons. Among the world's leading coal producers, the United States ranks first, producing well over 600 million tons per year.[61] The Soviet Union and China run a close second and third. In terms of exports, the United States, Poland, and Australia head the list. Current U.S. production is up from a modern low of 366 million tons in 1959.

As oil production dwindles, coal production is likely to expand to fill some of the gap. In particular, coal could be exploited more fully in electrical generation and synthetic fuels production. Many major oil-importing countries are now systematically converting electrical generating plants, retrofitting them to burn coal instead of oil. In the United States, the world's largest oil consumer, rising oil prices augmented by government-sponsored financial incentives are prompting utilities to switch from oil to coal. In Europe, the shift is also rapid. For example, West Germany has embarked on ambitious plans to replace oil with coal in electricity production and to convert coal into gasoline and chemical industry feedstocks.[62] In Japan, which imports both oil and coal, ten of the country's oil-fired generating plants were slated for conversion to coal in 1980 alone.[63]

World production of liquid fuels from coal promises to grow slowly during the late eighties and more rapidly during the nineties. So far, South Africa is the only country obtaining a significant share of its liquid fuels from coal. When the third South African Coal, Oil and Gas Corporation (SASOL) coal liquifaction plant comes on line, close to 40 percent of South Africa's liquid fuels will be derived from coal.[64] But the United

States, West Germany, and Japan are also vigorously research-
ing new technologies for converting coal into liquid fuel, as are
numerous international oil companies.

Given the various technological and cost uncertainties associated with the production and use of synthetic fuels derived
from coal, projections of coal to be used for liquid fuels vary
widely. *Coal: Bridge to the Future*, edited by Carroll Wilson
and his colleagues on the world coal study team, projects that
the demand for coal as a synthetic fuel feedstock in the industrial West and Japan will be between 74 million tons and 335
million tons in the year 2000.[65] The lower estimate assumes
that 15 large-scale synfuel plants (each with a production capacity of 50,000 barrels per day of oil equivalent) will be operating at century's end, while the higher estimate assumes 67 such
plants will be on line. Even allowing for some coal-liquefaction
operations elsewhere, coal's use in liquid fuels production two
decades from now is not likely to account for more than a tiny
fraction of total coal use.

The principal constraint on the future use of coal is likely
to be environmental degradation. Coal burning, whether for
generating electricity in the United States or heating homes in
urban China, generates toxic pollutants and raises atmospheric
carbon dioxide. The sulfur dioxide produced combines with
moisture in the atmosphere to produce acid rain, to which
fresh water lakes are especially vulnerable. Carried by the prevailing rains, acid precipitation damages lakes that are hundreds and even thousands of miles from the point of origin. In
Canada, where acid rain is delivered by the prevailing winds
from industrial regions in the United States, acid rain could
destroy fish in an estimated 50,000 lakes by the end of the
century.[66] Scandinavia is the recipient of acid rain from the
United Kingdom and Western Europe. In a study of 1,500
lakes in Norway, 70 percent of the highly acidified lakes (those
with a Ph below 4.3) were devoid of fish.[67] A survey of the
high-altitude lakes in the Adirondack Mountains of New York

found that in half of them acid deposits had eliminated fish.[68]

Acid rain also affects crops. Air pollution from coal burning and, to a lesser extent, oil combustion is already affecting crop production in many parts of the United States. Air pollution can damage crops directly and, through its effect on soils, indirectly. Crop damage attributable to air pollution has been reported in every one of New Jersey's 21 counties.[69] In California, experimental trials showed that ambient levels of air pollution reduced yields of alfalfa by 38 percent, lettuce by 42 percent, and sweet corn by 72 percent.[70] In Massachusetts, it reduced bean yields by 15 percent and tomato yields by 33 percent. Clearly, any long-term energy strategy must take into account acid rain's effect on fresh water fisheries and crop production.

Carbon dioxide build-up also poses a more serious problem with coal than with oil or natural gas because coal, with its higher carbon content, generates more carbon dioxide per unit of energy produced. Precisely how a continuing build-up of atmospheric carbon dioxide will affect climate is not known, but most meteorologists believe that it would bring a planet-wide warming.

Turning to coal as a transitional fuel is not without its risks, but none of them appear large when compared with those associated with nuclear power. The political winds clearly favor coal. Yet, it is an exhaustible resource, so those who invest in it now must later invest in energy alternatives as coal reserves dwindle.

Beyond the Age of Oil

No one knows exactly when the oil age will end, but the beginning of the end is already in sight. If oil production were constrained only by physical limits, output could climb much higher. But powerful economic, political, and psychological constraints are also at work. Oil prices already keep many countries from using as much oil as they once did, even as these same high prices have made investments in conservation measures profitable. At the same time, coal is being substituted for oil in electrical generation and other processes too vital to be left in jeopardy by an unstable oil market.

Political disruptions, particularly in the highly volatile Middle East, are also influencing production levels. Future conflicts involving oil-producing countries are almost inevitable, as are politically motivated oil-export embargoes. Add depletion psychology to political and economic imponderables and the uncertainty of predicting oil production's immediate future humbles even oil experts. Nevertheless, common sense suggests that production in the near-term should fall so as to extend petroleum's lifetime as long as possible. The key question seems to be whether the long-term decline in world oil output will be gradual and orderly or irregular and disruptive.

In per capita terms, the trend is clear. World oil consumption per person has unquestionably already begun its long-term and irreversible decline. (See Table 4-4.) From the high of 46 percent in 1973, oil's share of the global energy budget had fallen to 42 percent in 1980.

With that decline, coal's share has begun to increase. After falling from 63 percent of the total in 1950 to 31 percent in 1978, the coal share rebounded to 33 percent in 1980 and now promises to climb steadily. In comparison, roughly 20 years after the first nuclear power plant started to generate electricity, nuclear power's overall contribution finally reached 2 percent in 1975. Although a number of plants are still under construction, it now seems likely in many countries that economic and social pressures will keep this beleaguered source of power from growing much beyond the capacity now under construction.

Much has been made of the potential of nuclear fusion as a future source of power but unfortunately, the soaring construction costs that are sounding the death knell for nuclear

Table 4–4. Share of World Commercial Energy Use Supplied by
Fossil Fuels and Nuclear Power, 1950–80*

Year	Coal	Petroleum	Natural Gas	Nuclear Electricity	Total
			(percent)		
1950	63	27	10		100
1960	53	33	14		100
1970	36	44	20		100
1971	34	44	21	1	100
1972	33	45	21	1	100
1973	32	46	21	1	100
1974	32	46	21	1	100
1975	32	45	21	2	100
1976	32	45	21	2	100
1977	32	45	21	2	100
1978	31	45	21	3	100
1979	32	44	21	3	100
1980 (prel.)	33	42	22	3	100

*Renewable energy sources excluded because of a lack of historical data. Electricity
from all sources calculated in terms of coal required to produce equivalent amount.
Source: United Nations.

fission may be an even greater handicap for the more complex
fusion technology. By the time fusion power is technologically
developed enough to commercialize, it may already have become an economic white elephant, too costly ever to be seriously pursued. By that time, advances in wind power, photovoltaics, and other sources of electricity may make them far more
attractive economically.

A look at all sources of energy shows that world commercial
energy production expanded during the fifties and sixties at
roughly 5 percent per year. (See Table 4 5.) As the growth in
oil production slowed and leveled off during the seventies, the
growth in commercial energy production fell sharply, averaging
only 3 percent annually for the decade. In per capita terms, the
decline was even more dramatic, falling by nearly two-thirds
from the fifties to the seventies.

Table 4–5. Annual Growth in World Commercial Energy Use by
Decade, 1950–80*

Decade	Decade Rate	Annual Rate	Per Capita Annual Rate
		(percent)	
1950–60	70	5.4	3.7
1960–70	58	4.7	2.8
1970–80	36	3.1	1.3

*Includes coal, oil, natural gas, and nuclear power. Electricity from all sources cal-
culated in terms of coal required to produce equivalent amount.
Source: United Nations.

As the eighties begin, it seems clear that oil production will
not increase much more, if at all. Coal production is continuing
to increase but coal, like oil, is exhaustible. While coal can
bridge the gap to a sustainable society, it cannot itself be the
foundation of such a society. Countries that invest in a coal-
based economic system will inevitably face the costs of switching from coal to renewable energy sources. With this realization, and with each new report on the effects of acid rain and
each reminder of the potential climate alterations associated
with coal, the temptation to switch directly from oil to renewable energy sources will grow. Meanwhile, remaining coal reserves will help us buy a solar future, the only purchase worth
the last of our fossil fuel inheritance.

5

The Changing Food Prospect

Each threat to the sustainability of society—cropland degradation, the deterioration of basic biological systems, and the
depletion of our petroleum inventory—affects the food prospect. Anything that shrinks the cropland base or reduces its
inherent productivity makes eliminating hunger harder.
Overfishing and overgrazing directly affect the long-term food
supply, while deforestation affects it indirectly by accelerating
erosion and by forcing Third World villagers to burn cow dung
and crop residues for fuel.

As the oil outlook changes, so too does the food prospect.
The era of cheap oil that helped underwrite the explosive
growth in world food output during the century's third quarter

is now history. The depletion of oil reserves makes it more difficult to expand food production, even as the need to shift to alternative energy sources is setting up a new competition between the energy and food sectors for agricultural resources.

As these pressures converge, the worldwide effort to expand food production is losing momentum. The grain surpluses accumulated in food-exporting countries during the fifties and sixties have disappeared. Even though idled U.S. cropland recently has been returned to production, world food supplies are tightening and the slim margin between food production and population growth continues to narrow.

The Loss of Momentum

The middle of the twentieth century was a watershed in the evolution of world agriculture. From the beginning of agriculture until 1950 most increases in food output came from expanding the area under cultivation. Since then, most have come from raising yields on existing cropland. This drive to raise yields has made agriculture increasingly energy-intensive. Chemical fertilizers, irrigation, and mechanization—the primary means of expanding production—are all energy-intensive. In effect, as the frontiers disappeared, farmers learned to substitute energy for land.

The disappearance of frontiers notwithstanding, mid-century also marked the beginning of an unprecedented growth in food production. Between 1950 and 1971, the world's farmers increased grain production from 631 million tons to 1,237 million tons. (See Table 5-1.) In just 21 years, they nearly doubled output. In per capita terms, this period was also one of impressive progress. World cereal production per person climbed from 251 kilograms in 1950 to 330 kilograms in 1971, a gain of 31 percent. Diets improved measurably in many Third World countries, and consumption of livestock products climbed steadily throughout the industrial world.

Table 5–1. World Grain Production, Total and Per Capita, 1950–80

Year	Population	Grain Production	Grain Production Per Capita
	(billions)	(million metric tons)	(kilograms)
1950	2.51	631	251
1960	3.03	863	285
1970	3.68	1137	309
1971	3.75	1237	330
1972	3.82	1197	314
1973	3.88	1290	332
1974	3.96	1256	317
1975	4.03	1275	316
1976	4.11	1384	337
1977	4.18	1378	330
1978	4.26	1494	351
1979	4.34	1437	331
1980 (prel.)	4.42	1432	324

Source: U.S. Department of Agriculture and United Nations.

Since 1971, gains in output have barely kept pace with population growth; production per person has fluctuated widely but shown little real increase. Indeed, per capita grain production of 324 kilograms in 1980, an unusually poor harvest, was actually lower than the 330 kilograms of 1971. As food prices have climbed, diets have deteriorated in some Third World countries, especially among landless laborers and the urban poor. In some industrial societies, tightening grain supplies have led to a drop in per capita consumption of beef and other livestock products.

The long postwar period of food-price stability came to an end with the massive Soviet wheat purchase in 1972. The largest food-import deal in history, it signaled the beginning of a new era. Within months, the world price of wheat had doubled and famine had returned to the Indian subcontinent, Africa, and elsewhere after a quarter-century absence.

Shortfalls in harvests prevented until 1976 a rebuilding of the world food reserves depleted in 1972. With some uncommonly good harvests in the late seventies, the food situation then stabilized temporarily. But in 1980, a poor harvest in the Soviet Union and a mediocre one in the United States resulted in a drawdown of world food reserves to a near-record low. Inefficient agrarian structures, soil erosion, the conversion of prime cropland to nonfarm uses, the falling yield response to chemical fertilizers in the agriculturally advanced countries, and rising energy costs—all contributed to the slower growth in food output.

The North American Breadbasket

More and more countries in which grain production has not kept pace with demand have come to rely on North America's exportable surplus. (See Table 5-2.) Prior to World War II, Western Europe was the only grain-importing region. North America was not the only exporter nor even the leading one. During the late thirties, Latin American grain exports were nearly double those of North America, and Eastern Europe (including the Soviet Union) was exporting five million tons annually, the same amount as North America. All this has now changed beyond recognition. Asia has developed a massive

Table 5-2. The Changing Pattern of World Grain Trade*

Region	1934–38	1948–52	1960	1970	1980
	(million metric tons)				
North America	+ 5	+23	+39	+56	+131
Latin America	+ 9	+ 1	0	+ 4	− 10
Western Europe	−24	−22	−25	−30	− 16
E. Europe and USSR	+ 5	0	0	0	− 46
Africa	+ 1	0	− 2	− 5	− 15
Asia	+ 2	− 6	−17	−37	− 63
Australia and N. Z.	+ 3	+ 3	+ 6	+12	+ 19

*Plus sign indicates net exports; minus sign, net imports.
Source: Food and Agriculture Organization, U.S. Department of Agriculture, and author's estimates.

deficit. Africa, Latin America, and Eastern Europe all import food. Western Europe, consistently importing 15 to 30 million tons, has been the most stable element throughout the period. North America's emergence as the world's breadbasket began in the forties. The scale of exports expanded gradually during the fifties and sixties, but then more than doubled during the seventies as scores of countries began to lose the capacity to feed themselves.

This dramatic transformation of intercontinental food flows reflects wide differences in population growth, widely varying levels of agricultural management and, in many countries, a rate of soil erosion that is draining cropland of its fertility. As recently as 1950, for example, North America and Latin America had roughly equal populations—163 and 168 million, respectively. But while North America's population growth has tapered off substantially since then, Latin America's has escalated. Mexico, Venezuela, Peru, and Brazil all have population growth rates of close to 3 percent per year. Had North America's 1950 population expanded at 3 percent per year, it would have reached 395 million in 1980 (rather than the actual 248 million) and absorbed virtually all the region's exportable surplus, leaving it struggling to maintain self-sufficiency.

Today, over a hundred countries rely on North American grain. The worldwide movement of countries from export to import status is a much travelled one-way street. The reasons vary, but the tide is strong. No country has gone against it since World War II. Literally scores of countries have become food importers, but not one significant new exporter has emerged.

Not only are more countries joining the legions of importers, but the degree of reliance on outside supplies is growing. More and more nations, both industrial and developing, are importing more food than they produce. Among the countries that now import over half of their grain supply are Algeria, Belgium, Japan, Lebanon, Libya, Saudi Arabia, Senegal, Switzerland, and Venezuela. Other countries rapidly approaching primary dependence on imported foodstuffs include Costa Rica, Egypt, Portugal, South Korea, and Sri Lanka.[1]

For most countries, the need for imported food is more likely to increase than decrease. Agricultural mismanagement and inefficiency has taken its toll on food production, particularly in the Third World and the centrally planned economies of Eastern Europe. It is difficult, for example, to see how the Soviet Union can avoid importing even more grain in the near future. In the late thirties, the Soviet Union and Eastern Europe still had a regional export surplus of several million tons of grain yearly. But since then, the food balance has slowly shifted. Throughout the sixties, the Soviet Union teetered on the brink of food self-sufficiency, sometimes as exporter, sometimes as importer. But with Moscow's decision in 1972 to offset crop shortfalls by importing grain rather than by slaughtering the livestock herds, the Soviet Union emerged as a chronically food-deficit country. During the mid-seventies, grain imports averaged 9 million tons per year. Late in the decade, they were averaging some 20 million tons per year.[2] Even though U.S. grain shipments to the Soviet Union were restricted in January of 1980 following the Soviet invasion of Afghanistan, the Soviets began the new decade by importing 31 million tons of grain in its first year, more than any country in history.

Although the Soviet Union has the largest cropland area of any country, the inefficiency of its agricultural system represents a problem Moscow planners seem unable to solve. The factory-style organization of agriculture on the state farms and the size of the collectives weaken the key link between effort and reward for those who work the land. Consequently, production on Soviet agricultural collectives and giant state farms cannot approach that of the family-farm system that dominates West European and North American agriculture.

Other countries also face rapidly growing deficits. Egypt has little opportunity for expanding its agricultural base and yet its population is growing rapidly. According to the International

Food Policy Research Institute projections, Nigeria will have a food deficit of at least 17 million tons of grain in 1990 if recent trends continue. Mexican grain imports are growing by leaps and bounds, and unless Mexico loses an even larger fraction of its population through illegal migration to the United States, this trend is likely to continue.[3] The story is fundamentally the same in scores of countries.

Although the need for imported grain is projected to continue growing, the capacity of North America to respond to these demands may ultimately be overwhelmed. The disappearance of idled cropland, the growing use of U.S. grain in alcohol fuel distilleries, and the projected decline in irrigated acreage in key farm states will all make it more difficult to sustain the rapid growth in North American exports on which the world has none too wisely come to rely.

Behind this trade issue, a philosophical debate is beginning to emerge on the wisdom of mining soils in order to meet the ever growing world demand. Many agricultural analysts and environmentalists now argue that it makes little sense to sacrifice a resource that has been a source of economic strength since colonial days merely to buy a few billion barrels of oil. Others contend that the current generation of farmers has no right to engage in the agronomic equivalent of deficit financing and thus mortgage the future of generations to come. The current trend is fraught with risks both for those whose livelihoods depend on land being productive and for those in countries dependent on food imports that will dry up if the mining of soil continues. Even for the importers, lower imports and a reduction in pressure on North American soil resources in the short term would be better than losing the region's export capacity over the long run.

Growing Food Insecurity

From the late forties through the early seventies, the world enjoyed an unprecedented period of food security. Carryover stocks of grain, held largely by the principal exporters, and cropland idled under farm programs in the United States accounted for that security. Grain carry-over stocks—the grain in bins when the new harvest begins—were available for use when needed. Idled U.S. cropland could be brought back into production within a year. Together, these two reserves provided security for all mankind, a cushion against any imaginable disaster.

As recently as 1969, the amount of grain that either was held in storage or that could be produced within a season on idled U.S. cropland amounted to 91 days of world consumption. Following poor harvests in key producing countries in 1972 and 1974, world reserves fell to only 40 days. (See Table 5-3.) At this level, grain stocks constituted little more than pipeline supplies, barely enough to fill the supply line between the farmer and the ultimate consumer.

Table 5-3. Index of World Food Security, 1960–80

Year	Reserve Stocks of Grain	Grain Equiv. of Idled U.S. Cropland	Total Reserves	Reserves as Days of World Consumption
	(million metric tons)			(days)
1960	198	36	234	102
1965	143	70	213	80
1970	165	71	236	77
1971	183	46	229	73
1972	142	78	220	66
1973	147	25	172	51
1974	132	4	136	40
1975	138	3	141	40
1976	192	3	195	55
1977	191	1	192	51
1978	228	21	249	62
1979	191	15	206	51
1980	151	0	151	40

Source: Worldwatch Institute, derived from USDA data.

The world enters the eighties with only one of the two traditional reserves—carryover stocks of grain. For the first time in a generation, there is no cropland idled under U.S. farm programs. The loss of this reserve, which provided security for the entire world, may be permanent. Carryover stocks of grain in 1980 amounted to 40 days of consumption. In 1981, they are expected to fall further. Except for 1974 and 1975, when reserves fell to 40 days of consumption after bad weather reduced the harvest, food supplies have not been this low since World War II.

World food insecurity was exacerbated by the extension of agriculture onto marginal lands. While climate has changed little in recent years, the vulnerability to climatic anomalies is undoubtedly increasing. Meteorologist Kenneth Hare observes that "the Sahelian drought in Africa, for example, had several predecessors over the previous 500 years. What has changed is the vulnerability of the human economy."[4]

Global food insecurity mounts inexorably as agriculture is extended into marginal areas because the food economy is now global. Although the Soviet "Virgin Lands" are a major source of bread for Soviet tables, they are in an area of light and highly variable rainfall, subject to crop failure in one year of every three or four. When the decision was made in Moscow to offset these periodic shortfalls by increasing imports, the instability that had been confined to the Soviet food economy began to affect the supply and price of food for the entire world.

Soil erosion also contributes to food supply instability. When the organic matter in soil is reduced as a result of erosion, the soil's water-retention capacity declines so that the land becomes more vulnerable to short-term dry spells. A study by the U.S. Center for Environmental Assessment Services showed that eroded soils that had a yield 30 percent less than a non-eroded control plot also had a yield that was four times more variable.[5] Too often, efforts to expand output by extending cultivation onto marginal land increase harvest variability and global food insecurity.

Another source of world food insecurity is the dependence of the entire world on North America for food supplies. This unhealthy dependence has both meteorological and political dimensions since both the United States and Canada are affected by the same climatic cycles and since heavy dependence on any two countries for grain vests these countries with extraordinary political power. Both the United States and Canada already embargo the export of grain under certain conditions. The United States halted grain shipments to both the Soviet Union and Poland in the fall of 1975 because grain prices at home were rising too fast while Canada refused to license wheat exports in 1975 until it could more precisely determine the size of its harvest.[6]

Stripped of its reserves, the international community can no longer be counted on to respond effectively to crop shortages in poor countries. During the fifties and the sixties, the story was quite different. Then, the United States intervened unilaterally with food-aid shipments wherever famine threatened. For example, after consecutive monsoon failures in India in 1965 and 1966, the United States shipped a fifth of its wheat crop to that country two years in a row to avert famine.

The food scarcities and oscillating grain prices of the seventies affected all countries, but the poorest ones suffered most. One of the hardest hit was Bangladesh. With two poor harvests during the seventies, Bangladesh saw death rates climb sharply twice. An estimated 427,000 lives were lost in 1971/72 and another 330,000 in 1974/75.[7]

India too was hard hit during the seventies. After a weak monsoon and a poor harvest in 1972, the Indian Government discovered that the Soviet Union had tied up most of the world's exportable wheat supplies, leaving little for India to use to offset its poor harvest. Thus, the Indian Government sat by helplessly while food consumption fell and death rates climbed.

The increase in death rates above the previous year in the three poorest states of Uttar Pradesh, Bihar, and Orissa claimed an estimated 829,000 lives.[8] This loss of life in India alone far exceeded the total combat fatalities suffered in any war since World War II.

During the seventies, hunger also took a heavy toll in Africa, where a prolonged drought in the Sahel brought the deteriorating food situation into sharp focus. Senegal, Mauritania, Niger, Upper Volta, Chad, and Mali—all lost lives. No one knows exactly how many died of starvation and hunger-related disease, though Cornell nutritionist Michael Latham testified before the U.S. Congress that the number may have been in excess of 100,000.[9] Further east in Africa, the ecological deterioration of Ethiopia's food system was also made all too apparent by a drought that claimed an estimated 200,000 lives and brought Haile Selassie's 47-year reign to an end.[10] In Somalia, too, thousands died of severe malnutrition and disease in 1975; many of them perished after they reached relief camps.

Although grain stocks were partially rebuilt in the late seventies, after these calamities occurred in Africa and Asia, the global supply—demand balance remains delicate, as the sensitivity of commodity prices to weather reports indicates. Now, a poor harvest in a major producing country can set off a wave of global inflation. In poor countries, where rising food prices can push death rates upward, reduced harvests can have a demographic, as well as an economic, impact.

Following the grim experiences of the early seventies, the United Nations convened a World Food Conference in Rome in November 1974. In addition to the general agreement on a greater effort to expand world food output, there was also agreement on the need to create an international food reserve. After years of negotiation, little progress has been made. In late 1980 the United States passed the Food Security Act which finally establishes a modest food reserve with an initial input of four million tons, to assist countries experiencing severe food shortages. This aside, the international community has made little progress in building an effective international food reserve.

Land Productivity Trends

In a world where 70 million new residents are added each year and where little fertile land awaits the plow, land productivity is the key to the food prospect. From the beginning of agriculture until World War II, productivity edged upward only slowly, sometimes remaining static for long stretches. Rice yields in nineteenth century Japan, for instance, were only marginally higher than those obtained during the fourteenth century. U.S. corn yields during the 1930s were no higher than those during the 1860s, the first decade for which reliable yields estimates are available.

Following World War II, however, crop yields began to rise in a sustained, systematic fashion in virtually every industrial country. During the sixties, the introduction of the fertilizer-responsive varieties of wheat and rice enabled many Third World countries to raise food output per hectare too. Between mid-century and the early seventies the steady rise in cereal yield per hectare was one of the most predictable trends in the world economy, increasing at an average of 2.2 percent annually. Since 1970, however, the rate has fallen to 1.5 percent per year. (See Table 5-4.)

Table 5–4. World Production, Harvested Area, and Yield of Cereals, 1950–80

Year	Production	Area	Yield
	(million metric tons)	(million hectares)	(metric tons per hectare)
1950	631	601	1.05
1960	863	682	1.26
1970	1137	704	1.62
1980	1432	758	1.89

Source: U.S. Department of Agriculture.

Numerous factors appear responsible for the slower rate of yield increase. In the great majority of situations, the new cropland being brought under the plow is of lower quality than the land already in use. Often the marginal land added replaces the prime land that is continually being withdrawn for non-farm uses, leading to a reduction in land quality that is not evident from data on overall cropland area.

Also sapping farmland productivity is the reduction of fallow area in dryland farming regions. As world wheat prices rose between 1969 and 1974, U.S. summer fallow land dropped from 17 million hectares to 13 million.[11] This shrinkage led Kenneth Grant, then head of the Soil Conservation Service, to warn farmers that the other side of the lure of record wheat prices and short-term gains is the sacrifice of the land's long-term productivity.[12] The stresses are evident in other dryland farming regions as well. The U.S. Agricultural Attache in Moscow reported a strikingly similar reduction in fallow land in the Soviet Union from 17 million hectares to 12 million after the massive crop shortfall and heavy imports of 1972.[13]

In tropical and subtropical regions, where fallowing has evolved as a method of restoring fertility, mounting population pressures are forcing shifting cultivators to shorten rotation cycles and thus to undermine the land's productivity. For example, in Nigeria, where farming has been expanded onto marginal land and fallow cycles shortened, cereal yields have been falling since the early sixties. A World Bank study of Nigeria reports that "fallow periods under shifting cultivation have become too short to restore fertility in some areas."[14] In some locales, the original cropping cycle of 10 to 15 years has already been reduced to five.

While the shortening of fallow cycles is reducing land productivity in some countries, soil erosion is reducing it in others. One of the big unknowns facing agricultural analysts is how rapidly excessive soil erosion will reduce land productivity. If this erosion continues in the U.S. Corn Belt, the U.S. Department of Agriculture estimates that "potential corn and soybean yields would probably be reduced by 15 to 30 percent on some soils by the year 2030." A study of the erosion of Piedmont soils in Georgia showed a six-inch loss of topsoil reducing average yields 41 percent. A similar degree of erosion in West Tennessee led to a 42 percent drop in corn yields.[15]

Some agricultural scientists believe that inherent biological constraints will eventually restrict crop yield per hectare. One analyst of this issue, Louis Thompson, Associate Dean of Agriculture at Iowa State University, has plotted the average corn yields recorded on several experimental stations in Iowa from 1958 to 1972, as well as those achieved by the state's farmers.[16] In the late fifties, the gap between average yields on experimental plots and those on working farms was wide, but by the early seventies it had virtually disappeared. In effect, the backlog of technology has been largely used up, and Iowa farmers are literally looking over the shoulders of the agricultural scientists working the experimental plots.

An analysis of the long-term historical rise of wheat yields by Neal Jensen, professor of plant breeding at Cornell University, produced an even more sobering conclusion. Applying his findings to agriculture in general, he predicts that "the rate of productivity increase will become slower and will eventually become level."[17] Jensen believes that plant breeders and agronomists in the more advanced agricultural countries have already exploited most of the potential for raising yields.

While enormous opportunities for raising cropland productivity exist in some countries, the outlook for further dramatic worldwide increases appears less hopeful now than at mid-century. Soil erosion is lowering the inherent fertility of perhaps one-fifth of the world's cropland, while the backlog of new agricultural technologies in the agriculturally advanced countries is dwindling. Together, these two factors cast a formidable shadow over the prospect of a continuing rapid rise in land productivity.

Substituting Fertilizer for Land

When German chemist Justus von Liebig discovered in the 1840s that all the nutrients that crops remove from the soil could be replaced, he set the stage for the extensive substitution of chemical fertilizer for land as the frontiers closed. Since 1950, the expanding use of chemical fertilizer has been the principal source of growth in world food output. Increasing the use of irrigation, pesticides, and improved seeds has contributed to that growth, but without chemical fertilizer, world food output would likely fall by at least one-third.

The three basic plant nutrients that can readily be supplied to the soil as chemical fertilizers—nitrogen, phosphorus, and potassium—all require substantial amounts of energy to mine or synthesize and to transport. Particularly large amounts of energy are required to synthesize atmospheric nitrogen into stable compounds that can be used for fertilizer. Indeed, the use of chemical fertilizer epitomizes the growing energy intensity of food production in the late twentieth century. In 1950, the world's farmers applied some 14 million tons of chemical fertilizer to the soil. By 1980, they were using 113 million tons —an eightfold increase over a three-decade span. (See Figure 5-1.) At mid-century, worldwide fertilizer use averaged 5.6 kilograms per person, but by 1980, it had climbed to 25.6.

Crop yields increase predictably with each increment of chemical fertilizer—rapidly at first, then more slowly until they eventually level off. Understanding this fertilizer-response curve is key to understanding future food production prospects. Where fertilizer use is intensive, the response is already diminishing. In the Netherlands, Japan, the U.S. Corn Belt or elsewhere, where the use of chemical fertilizer is close to the saturation point, further increases simply will not appreciably increase yields. In such countries as India and Argentina, where fertilizer application rates are still low, the response to additional applications of fertilizer is high.

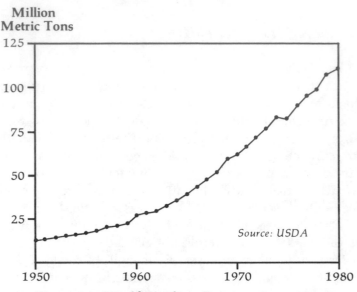

Figure 5-1. World Fertilizer Consumption, 1950-80

While future fertilizer requirements cannot be projected precisely, the amount of fertilizer required per capita to satisfy future food needs is certain to increase if population growth continues. As long as the cropland per person continues to shrink, the amount of fertilizer needed per person will rise. As a result, food production will become progressively more energy intensive, claiming a growing share of the world's scarce energy resources by the year 2000.

The Grain-Livestock Economy

Although most of the world's 1.4 billion ton annual grain harvest is consumed directly, a substantial share is consumed indirectly as livestock products. In the absence of religious restrictions on diet, the consumption of meat, milk, and eggs invariably rises with income. This whetted appetite for animal protein, in turn, translates into increases in grain fed to livestock. When world grain supplies are short, the competition between people and livestock for grain becomes acute.

Although corn and some other grains are used largely as feed and others, such as wheat, primarily as food, all grains can be used for either purpose—an important fact in view of recent per capita consumption patterns. As of 1979, annual grain use per capita ranged from roughly 160 kilograms in countries such as India and Kenya to just over 800 kilograms in the United States and the Soviet Union.[18] The high end of this scale quite literally represents the fat of the land. The lower end is determined by minimal survival requirements. If consumption drops below 160 kilograms per year (roughly a pound of grain per day), malnutrition becomes severe and mortality rates begin to climb.

As their incomes rise, people eventually consume more grain indirectly, in the form of livestock products, than directly as cereal, flour, and other food. In the United States, Canada, and other affluent countries, some three-fourths of the grain used is converted into livestock products. In India, China, and other countries where the grain supply per person barely sustains survival, no more than 3 percent of the available grain supply is converted into animal protein.[19] In Japan, the United Kingdom, and Brazil—the middle ground—roughly half the grain used is fed to livestock.

Despite rising affluence in industrial societies and among Third World elites, the share of the world grain harvest fed to livestock has remained remarkably stable in recent decades. In 1960, livestock and poultry consumed 255 million metric tons of grain, or roughly 31 percent of the 835 million tons consumed for food and feed. The overall numbers were larger in 1979—450 million tons of a 1.43 billion ton total—but the share, at 32 percent, was virtually unchanged. The balance held because the increases in the grain used for feed were offset by population growth, which increased that used for food. During the third quarter of this century, consumption of beef, pork, mutton, and poultry increased in almost all industrial countries. Among those with the highest annual consumption per person are the United States, France, and Poland. (See Table 5-5.) In sharp contrast, China, India, and other populous nations have few resources to spare for the production of animal protein.

While the amount of meat consumed is determined by income, the type of meat is influenced by population/land ratios. Those industrial countries that consume mostly beef have extensive grazing land—the United States, Canada, the Soviet Union, Australia, Argentina, and Brazil. In industrial countries that are more densely populated, such as those in both Western and Eastern Europe, pork dominates. Pork is also the dominant red meat in east Asian countries such as China and Japan.

The efficiency with which grain is converted into meat varies widely by country. For example, although per capita grain use is just over 800 kilograms (food and feed) in both the United States and the Soviet Union, those 800 kilograms provide each American consumer with 111 kilograms of meat and each

Table 5-5. Meat Consumption Per Capita in Selected Countries, 1978

Country	Beef & Veal	Pork	Mutton, Lamb & Goat	Poultry	Total
			(kilograms)		
USA	56	28	1	26	111
France	32	34	4	16	86
Poland	19	48	1	11	79
USSR	25	14	4	8	51
Brazil	18	7	—	7	32
Japan	5	12	2	10	29
China	2	15	1	3	21
Egypt	4	—	1	3	8
Nigeria	3	—	1	2	6
India	0.3	0.1	0.5	0.2	1.1

Source: U.S. Department of Agriculture, Food and Agriculture Organization, and author's estimates.

Soviet only 51 kilograms. The far better managed American farms get more than twice as much meat as Soviet farms do from a ton of grain.[20]

One way of increasing meat production when feed supplies are tight is to switch to those animals such as chicken that convert grain into meat most efficiently. This trend, now worldwide, helps explain why poultry production has outstripped that of other types of meat over the past decade or so. In the United States, where chicken was a Sunday dinner treat less than a generation ago, consumption has now climbed above 26 kilograms per person per year.

In spite of efforts to raise the efficiency of grain conversion into livestock products, competition between people and livestock for scarce grain supplies seems certain to intensify as pressures on the world's agricultural resource base increase. While the growing demand for animal protein has not so far raised the share of the grain harvest fed to livestock, it has generated an enormous demand for soybean meal for livestock rations. Since 1950, the world soybean harvest has multiplied fivefold, climbing from 18 million tons to 85 million.[21] In the United States, where the soybean was introduced from China, acreage in soybeans now rivals that in corn and wheat.

As rising affluence has converted the global appetite for livestock products into effective demand, the market for soybeans, an ideal protein complement to cereals in livestock and poultry rations, has grown rapidly. Growth has been particularly rapid since 1970 when the world fish catch leveled off. Between 1970 and 1980, the world soybean harvest doubled from 42 million tons to 85 million tons, with nearly all the increase being consumed by livestock.

While the Chinese harvest of nine million tons is used almost entirely for food, much of it as bean curd (tofu), most of the far larger U.S. and Brazilian soybean crops are used for feed, either domestically or when shipped abroad. An estimated two-thirds of the world harvest is now consumed as soybean meal, principally by livestock.[22]

What do these dietary patterns and trends say about the world food supply-demand equation? First, a vast potential for increased grain use for livestock feed exists in low-income countries if purchasing power permits. Second, in the event of a dire world food emergency, millions of tons of grain and soybeans could be diverted from feed to food use. Indeed, diverting only a quarter of the world soybean harvest from feed use to direct human consumption would provide five kilograms per year of a high protein food for everyone in the world. The key here, of course, is making the shift before food prices have risen high enough to push up mortality rates among the world's poor— something the market is unlikely to do on its own.

The New Food–Fuel Competition

As the eighties begin, the longstanding competition between food and feed is expanding to include fuel. In the past, the energy sector has supported the food sector, providing fuel for fertilizer and pesticide production, tillage, harvesting, crop drying, and numerous other farm-related processes. With energy subsidizing agriculture, the earth's population-sustaining capacity increased dramatically. But now, as the shortage of liquid fuels grows, energy producers are beginning to compete with food producers for limited agricultural resources.

In the rush to develop indigenous liquid fuels to replace imported oil, alcohol distilled from farm commodities has emerged as a short-run alternative. Several countries have already launched agriculturally based alcohol-fuel programs. Brazil, the United States, and the Philippines have major programs to convert agricultural commodities into alcohol for use as an automotive fuel, while Australia, New Zealand, and South Africa have programs either in operation or on the drawing board. For countries buffeted by soaring oil prices and fearful of supply disruptions, the prospect of an indigenous substitute for some of the imported oil is reassuring, but it means that automobiles now compete with people and livestock for the harvest.

Until recently, the claims of the poor and the affluent on the earth's agricultural resources have not diverged by more than a factor of five, the difference between an affluent diet rich in livestock products and a grain-based subsistence diet. If energy crops are figured in, however, the ratio increases dramatically since an automobile run on alcohol requires far more grain than a person does. Satisfying the annual food needs of a typical Third World consumer requires roughly one quarter of an acre of cropland, whereas the more affluent diet in an industrial society requires nearly an acre. By contrast, a typical American car fueled entirely by ethanol would require processing over seven tons of grain per year—the output from nine acres of average grain land.[23] In Western Europe, where cars are more fuel efficient and are driven less, the typical automobile could be run on a little over three tons of grain per year. These numbers are in a sense hypothetical because no country except Brazil is running automobiles exclusively on alcohol and because grain is by no means the only commodity from which alcohol can be made. Nonetheless, the figures do indicate how quickly alcohol fuel programs could absorb vast amounts of grain.

Providing gasohol (a 10 percent alcohol blend) for the typical U.S. car would each year require 1,460 pounds of grain, or slightly less grain than the average American annually consumes directly and indirectly as food. Accordingly, the cropland requirements of an American car owner who switches to grain-based gasohol would nearly double—rising from .9 to 1.7 acres. To the degree that the protein-rich by-product of the distillation process, distiller's dried grain, can be used successfully as livestock feed, the land requirement could be reduced. But if liquid fuel is used to produce and distill the grain, more land will be required to produce sufficient net amounts of liquid fuel. In the second case, headway toward reducing oil imports will be made two steps forward, one back.

Brazilian agricultural officials argue that energy crops will be produced in addition to rather than instead of food crops. In fact, though, energy crops compete not only for land but also for agricultural investment capital, water, fertilizer, farm-management skills, farm-to-market roads, agricultural credit, and technical advisory services. Only in a centrally planned economy, where all agricultural inputs are carefully controlled and clearly tagged for the production of either food or energy, could a major energy-crops program be launched without siphoning resources away from food production. Brazil's case is quite different. It may well reach its national goal of liquid fuel self-sufficiency by 1990 but have more hungry people than it does today.

The immediate consequences of the Brazilian energy-crops program may be more internal than external, but the more recently launched effort in the United States has broader ramifications. As more and more alcohol fuel distilleries are built in the United States to meet the official goal of producing two billion gallons of ethanol by the mid-eighties, the exportable surplus of grain will be reduced accordingly. The traditional buyers in the North American grain market—the flour millers, the feedlot operators, and the grain-importing countries—may be outbid by distillers, who are the beneficiaries of generous tax exemptions and other subsidies that can exceed a dollar per gallon.[24] As alcohol distilleries gradually replace oil refineries, more and more farmers in the United States and elsewhere will have to choose between producing food for people and fuel for automobiles. They are likely to produce whichever is the more profitable. In such a situation, the price of oil will eventually set the price of food.

For food-exporting countries, the immediate appeal of converting exportable food surpluses into alcohol fuel is undeniable. But in a world that has little if any excess food-production capacity, channelling foodstuffs into automotive fuel production will inevitably drive food prices upward. For the world's affluent, such rises in food prices may lead to belt tightening; but for the several hundred million people who are already spending most of their meager incomes on food, rising food prices will further narrow the thin margin of survival.

The Food Price Prospect

As the demand for food continues to press against the supply, inevitably real food prices will rise. The question no longer seems to be whether they will rise but how much. Since mid-century the growth in world grain production has unmistakably lost momentum. Expanding at well over 3 percent per year during the fifties, growth fell to just over 2 percent annually during the seventies.

In efforts to eliminate hunger, this loss of momentum is aggravated by the heavily skewed distribution of income both within and among countries. Incomes among the wealthier one-fifth of humanity are easily 20 times those of the poorest one-fifth. Similar ratios exist between the wealthiest and poorest fifths within societies where wealth is concentrated in a few hands, such as Iraq, Senegal, Brazil, Ecuador, and Mexico. Without effective efforts to redistribute income, meaningful progress in the eradication of hunger is unlikely.

The worldwide loss of agricultural momentum is serious in itself. But more serious are the gathering forces behind this loss. It is becoming ever more difficult to expand the cropland base, and soil erosion's toll on productivity is continuing unabated. Returns on the use of chemical fertilizer at the margin are also diminishing. Each of these forces promises to become an even stronger drag on the growth of food production during the eighties.

It is tempting to look to science and technology for help. But at the moment new agricultural technologies provide only small comfort. Hopes run high for increasing the photosynthetic efficiency of major crops and for developing cereals that can fix nitrogen. But these advances represent major feats of biological engineering, feats that cannot be taken for granted. If commercial nitrogen-fixing cereals become a reality, they will reduce energy requirements in agriculture but not necessarily increase output. Moreover, beyond these two possibilities there does not appear to be anything on the technological drawing board that could lead to quantum jumps in world food output. We cannot expect gains such as those made possible in postwar agriculture by the use of chemical fertilizer, improved seeds and irrigation.

Perhaps more than anything else, the price of food will be influenced by oil price rises. After the price of oil began its rapid climb in late 1973, it left the comparatively stable price of food far behind. But there are signs that food prices are beginning a long-term climb as well. Even as the price of liquid fuels required for farming rises, agriculture is being seen by more and more governments as a source of liquid fuels. With hundreds of large distilleries newly on line, under construction or in the planning stage, the diversion of agricultural resources to automotive fuel production could escalate rapidly. In 1980, Brazil devoted nearly one million hectares of cropland to the production of sugarcane for automotive fuel; the United States used some 80,000 hectares to produce grain that was converted into alcohol fuel; and the Philippines started marketing "alcogas" made from sugarcane.[25]

The sharp shift in the terms of trade between oil and grain tempts populous, oil-exporting countries that are having problems in agriculture to import more food. For these countries, which include the Soviet Union, Nigeria, Mexico, and China, the terms of exchange between oil and grain are exceedingly attractive, and they are rapidly expanding their food imports as the eighties begin. This extraordinary leverage in the world grain market is driving food prices upward far more rapidly than was possible when a barrel of oil and a bushel of wheat had the same value. In effect, the price of oil is gradually pulling the price of food upward in its wake.

This new relationship between the food and energy sectors makes food projections more complicated than ever before. The principal cushion now remaining in the world food economy is the grain that is fed to livestock. This grain could easily be made available for human consumption in times of shortage, though so far it has been diverted from livestock only when the price climbs to a level that induces widespread starvation.

The food price prospect inspires concern, not optimism. Just as the seventies dramatically underscored the new energy realities, the eighties promise to do the same for food. Indeed, rising food prices may become a more or less permanent feature of the economic landscape in the years ahead. Few, if any, economic indicators are as politically sensitive as food prices.

6

Emerging Economic
and Social Stresses

The third quarter of this century was a period of unprecedented economic expansion. Under the influence of Keynesian economics with its emphasis on demand stimulation, world economic growth averaged well over 4 percent per year, at least double the population growth rate.[1] A global economic growth rate of 4 percent per year would expand the global output of goods and services by 50 fold within a century. For anyone prepared to look ahead, the pressures on both nonrenewable and renewable resources that this would bring were obvious.

The first strong signal that this rapid growth era might not last forever came in 1972, when the massive Soviet purchase of wheat doubled the world wheat price within months. The second signal arrived soon after when OPEC abruptly quadrupled the price of oil in late 1973. Any remaining doubt as to whether the era was over ended in 1974: For the first time double-digit inflation invaded the world economy in peacetime, unemployment in the western industrial countries climbed to the highest levels since the Great Depression, and economic growth fell far below the postwar norm.

The question is why. It was not that the economists who sit at the elbows of the world's political leaders had suddenly lost their skills, but that the context in which those skills were applied had changed. In a matter of years, the relationship between the ever-expanding economic system and the natural systems and resources that support it had been fundamentally altered. The Soviets were blamed for the rise in world food prices and OPEC was roundly criticized for raising the world price of oil. But these actions simply mirrored the problem. They did not cause it.

As world population increased, mounting demands on some resources had become unsustainable. By the time the global population reached four billion in 1976, the per capita production of petroleum and of most major commodities of biological origin had already begun to decline. Accelerating inflation, rising unemployment, and slowing economic growth all testified to a new economic reality in which biological stresses and resource depletion registered in the marketplace.

Competing Demands

Historically, when one commodity became scarce another was quickly substituted for it. But substituting the plentiful for the scarce is no longer always an option. As Willis Harman of the Stanford Research Institute explains: "Because all of these interdependent factors are approaching planetary limits together, the solutions that resolved scarcity problems in the past —geographic expansion and technological advancement—do not promise the same sort of relief in the future."[2]

Demands on basic resource systems are now converging in

both industrial and preindustrial societies though the manifestations in each sometimes differ. The competition between the need for food and that for fuel, for example, takes different forms around the world. In Third World countries, where firewood demands have led to deforestation, villagers turn to dried cow dung for fuel, even though this use of precious animal wastes deprives soils of nutrients and humus. As soil fertility declines, the downward spiral acquires a momentum of its own, closing the poverty circle ever more tightly.

In the Indian subcontinent, China, and other Third World countries where even cow dung is scarce, villagers cook with crop residues and leaves. Desperate, they pull the roots of plants from the ground, dry them, and burn them for fuel. Here, too, the shortage of fuel aggravates that of food.

In other contexts, the food-energy competition wears other faces. In Central America, an expanding export-oriented beef industry contributes to deforestation. Responding to the growing world demand for beef, cattlemen on the Central American isthmus are converting forest land into grassland. One result is an emerging scarcity of firewood, the principal fuel not only for villagers, but for many urban dwellers as well.[3]

The unexpectedly rapid siltation of hydroelectric reservoirs in many Third World countries represents still another conflict, in this case between the food and firewood needs of people in the upper reaches of the watersheds that feed the reservoirs, and the downstream demand for electricity. The soil eroding from deforested land and overworked fields is reducing hydrogenerating capacity.

In the Soviet Union, competition between the food and energy sectors has taken a unique turn. Historically, multipurpose dams that provide both electricity and irrigation have been managed primarily by the energy ministry. But the growing internal food deficit is now leading to a shift in priorities that favors food production. Increasingly, dam reservoirs are being managed to maximize the water available for irrigation, but at a substantial sacrifice of electrical power. Thane Gustafson, Soviet scholar at Harvard, reports that hydropower output from the Dnieper River is being curtailed by 20 percent with further reductions a possibility and that "by the end of the century the capacity of the Volga hydropower units could be curtailed by as much as half."[4]

Competing demands for water can be felt in the United States too. At one time it was possible to use bodies of water such as the Chesapeake Bay both for food production and waste disposal, but as pollution levels have increased and fish catches have declined, it has become clear that some form of trade off is inevitable as populations expand.[5]

As demands on the earth's basic resources converge, political leaders will find themselves spending more and more time resolving the conflicting claims. For example, finding substitutes for the 22 billion barrels of oil used annually will add to the pressure on other resources, particularly land and water. Managing this new competition between the food and energy sectors promises to be particularly difficult politically.

Rereading Ricardo

The Law of Diminishing Returns was first articulated by David Ricardo, the nineteenth century English economist. He reasoned that at some point additional food could be produced only by extending cultivation onto less fertile land or by applying ever more labor and capital to land. In either case, returns would diminish.[6]

Initially based on calculations for wheat in the United Kingdom, Ricardo's formulation has a compelling logic. Yet, growth in food supplies or of overall economic output did not find its limits in Ricardo's day. For well over a century, the cultivated area continued to expand and advances in agricultural technology permitted grain yields to double or triple. For a while, the bounty of modern agriculture seemed to defy logic.

As the eighties begin, however, interest in Ricardo's analysis is reviving. Diminishing returns are beginning to affect the production of grain, oil, and other vital commodities. With the global economy growing at 4 percent annually or 50 fold per century, the shift at some point to resources of declining quality was inevitable. Technological advances leading to greater efficiency of resource use can offset declines in quality up to a point, but eventually even the most ingenious attempts to compensate for nature's limitations will fall short.

While Ricardo's concern with the diminishing quality of new land was initially unfounded, it is now being borne out. In countries as diverse as sparsely populated Canada and densely populated China, the quality of new land is far below that of settled lands. In Canada, where an estimated 233 hectares of cropland in the western provinces is required to replace each 100 hectares of Class I land lost to urban spread in the east, inherent cropland fertility is falling as cities annex new territory.[7] In China, the problem is even more severe. Lesley T. C. Kuo, a specialist on Chinese agriculture, reports that "the use of one acre of cultivated land for construction purposes must be offset by the reclamation of several acres of wasteland."[8] In Brazil, which since 1950 has nearly tripled the area planted to cereals, the pattern is much the same. The lower fertility of new land offsets heavy investments in fertilizer and the other mainstays of modern agriculture, leaving Brazil with a cereal yield per hectare that is no greater in 1980 than it was in 1950.[9]

Just as the quality of new cultivable land has declined, so too efforts to raise land productivity do not pay off as handsomely as they once did. The key here is the yield response to fertilizer. Between 1934–38, world grain production averaged 651 million tons per year and fertilizer consumption a rather modest 10 million tons. From then until 1950 fertilizer consumption increased by only 4 million tons. But as growth in the cultivated area slowed after 1950, fertilizer consumption began to grow by leaps and bounds. During the fifties, each additional million tons of fertilizer use was associated with an increase in the grain harvest of over 11 million tons. (See Table 6-1.) During the sixties, the response declined to 8.3 million tons of grain. For the seventies, the response was lower still—an additional million tons of fertilizer yielded only 6.8 million tons of additional grain. Because the grain/fertilizer response is falling, growth in fertilizer use will eventually slow as the cost of the additional fertilizer approaches the value of the additional grain it yields. Barring either a marked improvement in the capacity of cereals to utilize fertilizer or a sharp rise in food prices relative to those of fertilizer, growth in the use of this key agricultural input will begin to slow.

Efforts to expand the fish catch represent another clearcut case of diminishing returns. As stocks are depleted, fishermen compete for more distant waters. Even though the world fish catch has grown little since 1970, governments and corporations have continued to invest heavily in new fishing capacity. As a result, the catch per dollar invested has fallen precipitously.[10]

Table 6–1. World Grain Production and Fertilizer Use

Period	World Grain Production	Increment	World Fertilizer Use	Increment	Incremental Grain/Fertilizer Response Ratio
	(million metric tons)				
1934–38	651		10		
1948–52	710	59	14	4	14.8
1959–61	848	138	26	12	11.5
1969–71	1165	317	64	38	8.3
1978–80	1451	286	106	42	6.8

Source: Food and Agriculture Organization; U.S. Department of Agriculture.

With energy as with food, efforts to expand supplies eventually meet with diminishing returns. Already the most promising prospects for discovering new underground oil fields have been thoroughly investigated. Geological and seismic data indicate that new finds will be relatively meager and invariably located in more remote lands and inhospitable spots. Soviet official Gennadi Pisarevsky notes that in the USSR, for example, "over the past 15 years the average pumping distance of one ton of oil in the USSR has increased from 650 to 2,000 kilometers, by more than three times. Offshore drilling, which accounts for a substantial and growing share of the total exploration effort, can cost several times more per barrel than drilling on land."[11] At the same time, the cost of pumping oil from older fields is climbing everywhere. Secondary and tertiary recovery techniques both cost more than primary methods and yield substantially less net energy. Pisarevsky, again describing the Soviet Union, reports that "more than 10 percent of the production cost goes to maintain bed pressure: At present, 80 percent of the fuel is produced by pumping water, gas, or air into the oil layers."

Diminishing returns also govern the mining industry. From 1900 to 1970, the cost of unearthing materials generally declined as mining and extraction technologies advanced and as real energy costs declined. But as mineral reserves dwindle, lower-grade ores and less accessible deposits must be mined. Even supplies of such relatively abundant minerals as iron ore eventually give out or become more costly to mine. According to a World Bank report on the future of the iron-mining industry, "new discoveries during the last 25 years of world reserves of all grades of ore are now deemed sufficient to last at least 100 years at exponentially growing demand," but "the greatest iron resources of the world are in low-grade deposits."[12] Overall, technological advances in mineral extraction and refining cannot be counted upon to offset the added costs that mining lower-grade ores or less accessible deposits entail, particularly since both have higher energy requirements.

The capacity of the earth's ecosystem to absorb waste also brings diminishing returns. In the early stages of industrial development, removing 80 percent of the pollutants from a factory smokestack may be sufficient to avoid destruction of the environment. But later, as the volume of production and pollu tants climb, pollution control devices may have to remove 98 percent of pollutants to afford a similar level of environmental protection. Given the nature of the processes involved, the cost of removing the additional 18 percent may be far greater than the preceding 80 percent. Other things being equal, pollution control expenditures per dollar of output increase as output increases. As concerned governments restrict the discharge of wastes to protect human health and the biological systems on which human survival depends, industry will perforce return less product per dollar invested.

Investment in scientific research—long the answer when productivity lagged—may itself be experiencing diminishing returns. Within agriculture, for example, cereal hybridization and the discovery of chemical fertilizer required relatively small investments of time and money, but comparable future advances in food production may be harder to realize. In physics, splitting the atom and developing solid-state physics were landmark break-throughs, but comparable seminal gains may require the lifetime efforts of thousands of highly trained physicists.

In retrospect, Ricardo appears to have been ahead of his time. Diminishing returns were postponed by expanding geographical frontiers and advancing technology. Now the frontiers are gone and technology is not always able to offset or postpone diminishing returns. To be sensible, national economic and demographic policies must be responsive to the new Ricardian realities.

A New Source of Inflation

Inflation is usually defined as a rise in the general price level, the result of too much money chasing too few goods. In an abstract sense, a rise in the general price level does not create any particular problem. Philosopher David Hume once pointed out that if all prices were to double overnight, nothing would be changed except the amount of money people would need to carry in their pockets. In the real world, however, prices seldom rise uniformly. From a human welfare perspective, the issues are changing price relationships that affect the distribution of income and wealth and rising real prices (rising faster than the general price level) for consumer essentials such as food, fuel, and housing.

As commonly measured and reported, inflation does not cover subsistence or unpaid activities. Hence, it does not speak to the plight of the world's poorest people, the very group often most affected by environmental deterioration and resource scarcities. If inflation were measured not in monetary terms but in hours of work required to obtain a given good or service, it would reflect the additional labor required to produce food by millions of rural families whose soil is eroding or the extra hours required to gather firewood as the forests recede. Analyses of inflation measured in these terms would encompass both the subsistence and market sectors of the world economy, and thus be far more revealing of global trends.

Historically, most inflation as classically defined has been a localized phenomenon, hitting individual countries from time to time. It usually occurred when excessive demand resulted from deficit financing or from "easy money" policies. While these inflationary forces are not always easy to manage, at least they are understood reasonably well, as are the techniques for coping with them. When inflation arising from deficit financing gets out of hand, it can be curbed by reducing the deficit and slowing the rate of economic growth. If an "easy money" policy is at fault, adjusting monetary policy usually does the trick. Political leaders may have their work cut out for them persuading labor union leaders to exercise restraint in contract negotiations or convincing powerful industries to hold prices down, but at least they know what is needed.

While the misuse of monetary and fiscal policies remains a potential source of inflation, rising real prices for many essential commodities represent a newer, more intractable source of inflation. During the first seven decades of this century, the real cost of most industrial raw materials, foodstuffs, and fuels declined. Even as recently as the two-decade span from 1950 to 1970, the market price of such basic commodities as oil and wheat remained essentially unchanged.[13] Adjusted for inflation, the real prices of these two basic commodities declined markedly over this period.

Global double-digit inflation fueled by the new inflationary forces did not exist before the seventies, but the pressures that precipitated it have been building for decades. Since mid-century, world population has increased by nearly two billion and the gross world product has tripled.[14] When world population headed for four billion, inflation rates began to increase markedly. In the Organization for Economic Cooperation and Development, a group of countries that accounts for the lion's share of world economic output, the consumer price index (CPI) increased an average of 2.4 percent from 1961 to 1965. (See Table 6-2.) From 1965 to 1969, the CPI increase climbed to an average of 3.9 percent yearly.

By 1970 when the CPI climbed to 6.3 percent, the worldwide production per capita of wood, wool, and mutton was already declining, and the fish catch per person was peaking. Oil production per person peaked in 1973, and in 1974 global inflation moved into the double-digit range. In 1976, following a two-year worldwide recession, the consumer price index was still climbing by 9 percent per year. At this point, the amount of beef produced per person reached its historical peak and began to decline.

In view of these declines in production per person, it should not surprise us that during the seventies and early eighties efforts to manage inflation have been consistently less successful than in the past. Rising real costs of production are fueling the inflationary spiral as biological systems deteriorate, oil re-

Table 6–2. Annual Rate of Change in Consumer Price Index, OECD
Countries, 1961–79

Years	Change
	(percent)
1961–65	2.4
1965–69	3.9
1970	6.3
1971	4.4
1972	5.7
1973	6.8
1974	13.9
1975	11.1
1976	9.0
1977	8.2
1978	8.5
1979	10.9

Source: Organization for Economic Cooperation and Development.

quires more coaxing to get it out of the ground, readily accessible high-grade mineral reserves are used up, and little fertile, well-watered cropland remains to be brought under the plow.

Everywhere, wood is becoming more expensive as it becomes scarcer. The downturn in 1964 of world wood production per person signaled trouble for a billion and a half Third World villagers who depend on wood for fuel, and for the housing industry everywhere. In the United States, owning a home—which since frontier days has been regarded as part of the American birthright—is becoming an unattainable ideal for millions of middle-income families. According to a U.S. Council on Wage and Price Stability study, "Soaring lumber prices have been a recurring problem of increasing severity in every expansion of housing demand since the mid-sixties."[15] Until then, U.S. supplies of lumber grade timber could be easily expanded to satisfy growth in demand, but the tripling in lumber prices since 1967 indicates that this is no longer possible. Since then, lumber prices have risen more rapidly than the overall inflation index. "Over the long term," the study concluded, "the projected demand [for lumber] cannot be met by the supply of timber that will be forthcoming at currently relative prices and under current management policies." Indeed, lumber prices are expected to continue to rise for at least a decade as those born during the postwar "baby boom" establish households.

The world price of newsprint, which held remarkably steady from 1950 until 1973, has more than doubled since 1973.[16] In 1978, when prices moved above $300 a ton for the first time, the communications sector felt the reverberations. Many newspapers were forced to close or to merge, while others shifted to a tabloid format to reduce newsprint requirements, and expanded advertising space at the expense of news content. In the developing countries, the dream of universal literacy fades as the forests shrink and pulp for paper becomes dearer.

Other commodity prices are also contributing to inflation. During the seventies firewood prices have doubled or quadrupled in many locales, and in some deforested Third World communities, what goes under the pot now costs more than what goes inside it. Seafood prices, particularly those of the more palatable species, have climbed sharply. The decimated fisheries that fishermen work are even farther from home, so energy costs now register in the fish markets, especially in Japan, the Soviet Union, and other countries that depend heavily on oceanic food supplies. Beef prices have climbed sharply since 1976, when beef production levelled off, and there is no lasting price relief in prospect.

The production of food and energy appear to be moving along a rising cost curve driven by the growth in world demand. Throughout history, humanity has periodically come up against constraints, but never before has it hit so many in so many places at the same time. Now, technology no longer seems to advance fast enough to offset the diminishing returns that are setting in on so many fronts. If we continue on the current demographic path and if we rely almost exclusively on supply-side economics, ignoring the need to curb demand growth, then higher real costs and ever greater inflationary pressures may be inevitable.

Slower Economic Growth

During the fifties and the sixties, the world economy expanded by an average of 4 to 5 percent annually, but during the seventies growth fell off sharply, constrained by the earth's natural systems and resources. (See Table 6-3.) Only a handful of the smaller OPEC countries have escaped the economic slowdown. Economic expansion slowed measurably during the seventies in France, Germany, Japan, the United Kingdom, the United States, the Soviet Union, and other industrial countries. The heady 10 to 14 percent annual growth that once characterized the Japanese economy is history. Haunted by the memory of Weimar inflation, the Government of West Germany is now prepared to settle for a 3 percent annual growth or less, while recent Soviet and East European development plans set out substantially lower capital investment and growth targets.[17] Brazil, after years of 9 percent annual growth, is scaling down its goals as the economy struggles with the high cost of imported oil and with a swollen external debt.[18]

While individual countries are lowering their economic sights, an international dialogue on the causes of the changing economic outlook has been curiously lacking. The UN-spon-

Table 6-3. World Economic Growth by Decade, 1950–80

Decade	Decade Growth	Annual Rate	Annual Rate Per Capita
		(percent)	
1950–60	57	4.6	2.7
1960–70	62	5.0	3.0
1970–80	40	3.4	1.7

Source: U.S. Department of State.

sored study *The Future of the World Economy* (1977) seems
largely to ignore the fundamental changes in the global economic prospect, as do most World Bank projections.[19] As
recently as mid-1980, the World Bank was projecting economic growth in the developing countries for the eighties at
some 5.4 percent per year and for the industrial countries 3.6
percent per year—an average economic growth rate of some 4
percent annually for the world as a whole.[20]

How these rapid projected increases can be expected to
materialize when there may not be any growth at all in some
key sectors such as petroleum and fisheries is far from clear.
Capital formation, too, is likely to become more difficult as net
energy yields in the production of oil and alternative energy
sources fall. As economic growth slows, profit margins tend to
shrink, leaving less capital available for new investments. Accelerating inflation and the associated economic uncertainty
also encourage speculation in lieu of productive investment.

As economic growth slows in advanced industrial societies,
doubts are arising as to whether rapid growth is any longer
possible, much less advisable. In some advanced industrial
countries, consumer desires among the more affluent are showing early signs of satiation. Many young people in the middle
and upper income groups in the United States place less emphasis on material goods than did their parents. In Sweden, a
study by Goran Backstrand and Lars Ingelstam of the Government's Office of Future Studies asked what Swedes could possibly do with the sevenfold increase in steel output and the
tenfold increase in chemicals that a continuation of the traditional 4 to 6 percent annual economic growth rates would yield
by the end of the century.[21] Then too, political majorities in
the affluent countries are beginning to set limits on the amount
of environmental disruption they will tolerate once their essential material needs are satisfied.

On the other side of the coin, the international development
community has begun to question whether the impressive

growth rates achieved by some Third World countries have led to widespread social improvements. In the absence of any mechanism for distributing new wealth broadly, all too often income has risen while illiteracy, malnutrition, and unemployment rates have stayed the same or even increased.

Once policymakers recognize that the economic choice is often between growth and sustainability, growth is likely to subside in importance as a policy goal. Then planned obsolescence and the other tenets of the "growth at any cost" philosophy will be seen as uneconomic as well as environmentally indefensible.

Rising Unemployment

Almost all modern economies have relied heavily on economic growth to provide additional jobs, so the prospect of slower growth while the labor force is expanding unnerves policymakers. While the new policy environment is as yet ill-defined, the growth in the labor force is all too real. Its projected growth during the closing decades of this century, particularly in the less developed countries, has no precedent. The labor force in the less developed world (over 1.1 billion in 1975) is projected to increase by 780 million by the year 2000, or some 31 million per year. This contrasts with an additional 141 million jobs required in the industrial countries, or less than 6 million per year.

These additions to the labor force in the Third World are projected to come at a time when unemployment and underemployment are already at record levels. Kathleen Newland notes in a Worldwatch Paper on unemployment that these projected new entrants "will join some 50 million currently unemployed people and about 300 million who are underemployed. The figures are numbing. They are also notoriously imprecise. But even a generous allowance for error cannot blunt the challenge of finding work for more than one billion job seekers by the year 2000."[22]

According to International Labor Organization projections, the world labor force will increase by an average of 36 million per year during the final two decades of this century.[23] Productively employing this number of people each year will require vast amounts of capital and natural resources, including energy. Creating new jobs requires something for people to work with, and for the half or so of the global labor force involved in agriculture, that "something" is land.

From the age of exploration onward, Europe's unemployed moved to the frontiers of human settlement, where land could be obtained for the asking. The New World, in fact, saved Europe from overpopulation and unemployment. As long as these frontiers existed, people who wanted to work the land needed only enough capital to buy crude farm implements and seed. But now that land for settlement has become scarce or concentrated in a few hands, the frontiers of employment creation are no longer the physical frontiers.

Classical economics has it that there should never be any unemployment other than that required to give the labor force needed mobility. In the economists' perfect market, capital, land (including raw materials and energy), and labor combine in an optimum fashion. Unfortunately, market imperfections such as grossly skewed land-distribution patterns, inappropriate technologies, price fixing by large corporations, excessive wage demands by labor unions, and, in some countries, minimum wage legislation all stand in the way of realizing this ideal.

In developing countries, the concentration of land ownership militates against full employment. Where small farms are the norm, as they are in Japan or Taiwan, large numbers of people can be effectively employed in agriculture. Where the land distribution is grossly inequitable, less labor is used. Data from Colombia solidly support this point. Classifying Colombian land holdings as small farms, large crop farms, or cattle ranches, Oxford University economist Keith Griffin has found that the man/land ratio is nearly five times higher on the small farms than on the large farms and more than 13 times higher than on cattle ranches.[24]

While unions can help ensure that labor receives a fair share of the national product, excessive wage demands also serve to increase unemployment. An ILO study of Colombia reported that "the bottom third of the rural population may be no better off today than in the 1930s, and the effort by organized labor in Colombia to use collective bargaining to raise wages has seriously aggravated the situation."[25] James P. Grant, Executive Director of the United Nations International Children's Emergency Fund, states that "there will be a sizable group in the developing countries whose standard of living will be rising rapidly while unemployment is increasing, thereby sharpening the contrast between those for whom the system is working and those for whom it is not."[26] For members of labor unions in Colombia, the system is working. But for landless workers in the countryside, it is not.

Minimum-wage legislation can have a similar effect by helping to keep the unskilled or semi-skilled unemployed. While the purpose of the minimum wage—to guarantee a decent income to the poorly skilled—is laudable, some of the law's effects are not. A more satisfactory alternative might be an income protection plan that would supplement earnings and permit the unskilled to be employed at their market value, whatever it might be.

Besides these institutional contributions to unemployment, mounting population pressure is both increasing the size of the pool of unemployed and taking a heavy toll on the resources needed to create new jobs. In particular, population-induced ecological deterioration in the countryside reduces the employment prospects of those who depend directly on the soil or on other basic biological systems. Shifting cultivators, nomadic herdsmen, fishermen, and mountain dwellers, the great bulk of whom live within developing countries, all make their living close to nature. When, for example, grasslands deteriorate and the desert encroaches, nomadic herdsmen lose their livelihood. Such losses have been greatest on the broad fringe of the Sahara and on the East African plateau, in the Middle East, and in parts of northwestern Asia.

A United Nations report analyzing income distribution in the Middle East notes: "The continued deterioration in the rural environment and the natural range land zone were among the main causes responsible for the impoverishment of the nomads, pastoralists, and farmers in the arid and marginal areas."[27] One especially hard-hit class of ecological refugees includes the mountain folk of the western Himalayas, the Ethiopian highlands, and the Andes. As the soil washes down from the mountains, human settlements crumble too. Ex-farmers and their families, having lost their natural capital, are forced off the land and into the squatter settlements that encircle Third World cities.

By the same token, fishermen and those who depend indirectly on the catch have been brought to economic ruin. Members of fishing communities in the United Kingdom, the United States and in Peru have lost their jobs as their fisheries have been decimated.[28] The decimation of Peru's anchovy fishery, once the world's largest, left tens of thousands of Peruvians without productive employment.

Rapid population growth in Third World countries often has a double-edged negative effect, simultaneously increasing the number of job seekers while destroying the resources needed to create jobs. Unfortunately, political leaders and economic planners too seldom face these issues directly, though the exceptions are notable. In India, the Finance Ministry's (1980) Annual Economic Survey noted that "people seemed to wish away the menacing proportions of the population problem" and that "if unemployment is to be abolished and a reasonable standard of living is to be provided for everyone, everything possible should be done urgently to limit numbers through an intensification of family planning efforts."[29]

Since people are one of the few productive resources that poor countries have in abundance, unemployment represents a wasted resource. While countries with serious food shortages would not for a moment consider idling a large share of their productive cropland, they do follow policies that "idle" a substantial share of their productive labor force. In an age when other resources are becoming scarce, a careful review of economic policies that contribute to this waste is long overdue. In particular, the need is for programs that mobilize either seasonally or chronically idle labor to create capital resources through tree planting, small-scale hydroelectric development, or local irrigation and land-improvement activities.

Part of the vicious circle, rising unemployment also aggravates the inequalities of income-distribution. As Kathleen Newland notes, "The employment problem thus translates directly into a distribution problem because most economies allocate the fruits of production to people primarily on the basis of their employment."[30] While governments do institute transfer payments among individuals within a society, a job is still the principal means by which individuals claim their share of the national product. If unemployment and underemployment continue to increase and income distribution thereby worsens, social stresses are certain to multiply.

Social Stresses

The first manifestations of the ecological stresses and resource scarcities that emerge as population increases are physical— overgrazing, overfishing, deforestation, and soil erosion. These then translate into economic stresses—lower output, inflation, and unemployment. But, ultimately, they translate into social stresses—hunger, demoralization, forced migration, higher infant mortality, and reduced life expectancy.

Rapid population growth itself is a destabilizing influence. Rural populations that multiply 3 percent per year—or *nine-*

teenfold per century—in the Third World inevitably create pressures that push people into cities. In some countries, job seekers are pushed at great social cost across national borders in search of work. They are separated from their families, sometimes for years at a stretch, and many of those who cross borders illegally risk arrest and deportation. Many find themselves deprived of their civil rights and few have access to social services. In all too many Third World countries, the intense pressures of joblessness are the product of failed population policies.

Inflation's social consequences are just as severe. Rapid inflation can distort both economic and social values; where it prevails, speculators grow rich and savers lose ground. Because inflation can wipe out the savings of years almost overnight, retired people and others on low or fixed incomes can find themselves impoverished without warning. Inflationary stresses can also aggravate social divisions within and among societies. The ultimate threat that uncontrolled inflation imposes is the loss of confidence in social institutions.

For hundreds of millions, inflation's final payment is felt as hunger and malnutrition. For a substantial segment of humanity, the rise in food prices since the early seventies has exceeded gains in real wages. While famine was viewed largely in geographic terms before an international food distribution system developed, it is now more appropriate to view this scourge as one that hits low income groups rather than specific locales. As world food prices rise, the poorest groups in the poorest countries go without.

For those already close to the margin of survival, food price rises mean that the pangs of hunger will become sharper and that fewer infants will survive. A Catholic priest writing from Peru reports a dramatic rise in the number of emergency baptisms for infants. For 1979, he estimates that for Peru as a whole, "The number of babies who die before they learn to walk has jumped some 30 percent"—a tragic consequence of the rise in oil prices, fall-off of fishmeal production, an ineffective family planning program, and government mismanagement.[31]

The economic stresses afflicting Peru are mirrored in Ghana, where the rise in food prices exceeded the climb in the general price level by 40 percent during the seventies.[32] In Accra, a worker spends three days' wages for a kilogram of meat, one day's wages for a kilogram of fish.[33] Similar situations prevail in other hard-hit Third World countries, including northeastern Brazil, Haiti, Colombia, El Salvador, Turkey, Egypt, Ethiopia, and Bangladesh.

Often, a deteriorating food situation is brought into sharp relief by a drought, a flood, or an outbreak of crop disease. In 1975, a team from the Johns Hopkins University School of Hygiene and Public Health gathered detailed data on mortality in the District of Companiganj, in Bangladesh. Their data documented starkly what many had long suspected—that even within a poor society, the poorest suffer much more when food becomes scarce.[34]

Revealingly, death rates differed profoundly according to the victim's landowning status. The less land the family had, the less likely were all of its members to survive a food crisis; and death was a frequent visitor to that one-fourth of the population that owned no land at all. (See Table 6-4.) Those with three acres or more had a death rate only fractionally

Table 6-4. Death Rate by Size of Landholdings, Companiganj, Bangladesh, 1975

Size of Land Holding	Death Rate
(acres)	(per thousand)
None	35.8
.01–.49	28.4
.50–2.99	21.5
3.00+	12.2

Source: The Johns Hopkins University School of Hygiene and Public Health.

higher than that of a typical Western industrial society. Perhaps the most disturbing message of these figures is what they portend for the future when population growth further reduces the average size of landholdings and swells the landless population.

Scarcities of firewood, like those of food, directly affect the quality of life in the Third World. Peace Corps volunteer Paul Warpeha reports that deforestation around Andean villages near Quito forces villagers to make a full-day trip up the mountainside to reach remaining trees.[35] Such a heavy expenditure of village labor has reduced the number of hot meals to one per day.

In addition to nutrition, other social goals also disintegrate in the furnace of population growth. During the early sixties, many newly independent Third World countries established impressive health and educational goals such as compulsory primary education aimed at bringing about universal literacy. As the sixties and seventies wore on and population growth continued unchecked, however, many governments discovered that their school systems were being inundated by youngsters whom they could not accommodate, so officials quietly abandoned their goals of universal education.

Increased life expectancy, reduced infant mortality, and other social objectives embraced in happier days have also been scaled down. According to Davidson Gwatkin of the Overseas Development Council, "Demographers have been revising their mortality as well as their fertility assumptions; and their mortality revisions are as sobering as their fertility revisions are hopeful."[36] Earlier United Nations projections of average life expectancy in the Third World of 68 years by the end of the century were in 1978 reduced to 62 years. Projected declines in infant mortality have similarly been modified.

The era of rapid social progress that characterized most of the third quarter of this century appears to have ended. Without fundamentally shifting priorities in the use of the earth's resources and in social reforms, many countries will watch the prospects for sharp improvements in the living standard fade. Where population growth is most rapid, a deterioration in living conditions may result.

As social stresses multiply and begin to translate into social and political unrest, beleaguered governments often resort to treating the symptoms rather than the causes. In recent years, governments in countries such as Turkey or Peru have been paralyzed by the political unrest and friction generated by the mounting economic stresses. Where stresses intensify to this extent, the political survival of governments can replace economic progress as a goal.

Part II

The Path to Sustainability

7

Population:
A Stabilization
Timetable

The economic stresses of the eighties have their roots in environmental deterioration and resource scarcities. Testifying to the inexorable law of diminishing returns, they are anchored in eroding soils, shrinking forests, declining fisheries, deteriorating grasslands, and dwindling oil reserves. These mounting economic stresses are indicators of unsustainability, evidence that humanity cannot continue on the current path.

If civilization is to be sustained, it will have to be along another road. Effectively addressing the forces that are undermining the economy will require nothing less than a thorough reorientation of population and economic policies as well as a restructuring of economic activity. Merely to adjust monetary or fiscal policy will not do. To date, many of the remedies prescribed—such as the turn to "supply side" economics in the United States—have been directed toward the symptoms rather than the causes.

Major course corrections do not occur easily. Nor do they take place in a vacuum. Rather, they occur in response to economic and social stresses and to maturing projections of new economic realities. As inflation worsens, as unemployment climbs, as hunger and malnutrition spread, pressures to change course will intensify. Unless political leaders begin to address the causal factors, confidence in social institutions will continue to erode.

As efforts to analyze the new economic afflictions become more sophisticated, they will lead to changes in perception. One consequence of analyzing more carefully the relationship between ourselves and the natural systems and resources that support us will be the realization that population growth now affects us differently than it once did. Until a decade or so ago, population growth reduced but did not preclude gains in per capita production of such basic commodities as forest products, seafood, and petroleum. Only as world population moved toward four billion did it begin to outpace the production of the basic commodities on which humanity depends. Now, if population growth continues as projected, a decline in material living standards the world over may be unavoidable.

Among the forces that are undermining society, population growth ranks at the top. Population growth cannot continue indefinitely on a finite planet. Everyone agrees that it will eventually halt. But when? And how? Will it be because birth rates fall or because death rates climb in response to malnutrition or outright starvation? Stabilizing world population size is extraordinarily difficult and challenging, but the recent highly successful efforts by some countries to slow population growth show that even the most formidable threats to civilization are not necessarily unmanageable. In a world seemingly engulfed in pessimism, these successes are reassuring reminders that we can in fact govern our own destiny.

The Existing Projections

The official UN medium-level population projections, used by planners throughout the world, show population expanding to some 10.5 billion before eventually stabilizing a century or more hence.[1] A second set of projections, made by the World Bank and published in its World Development Report for 1980, shows world population growth stabilizing at a somewhat lower level of 9.8 billion.[2] Central to both the UN and World Bank projections is the assumption that in countries where fertility is high, it will decline as economic and social development occurs. Both also assume that all national fertility rates that are currently below the replacement level will rise to replacement by 2005. The UN and Bank projections differ in emphasis: The UN concentrates on the remainder of this century while the Bank, with its longer term planning horizon, is also concerned with the early twenty-first century.

Even under the Bank's projections, which take into account recently reported fertility declines in developing countries, the growth in store for some countries can only be described as phenomenal. India is projected to add nearly another billion people to its 1980 population before stabilizing at 1.64 billion, while neighboring Bangladesh and Pakistan are expected to increase from 89 million and 82 million at present to 314 million and 332 million. If all these countries grow as projected, the Indian subcontinent would be home to 2.3 billion people, more than the entire world population of 1940. Nigeria's population of 85 million today is projected to increase to 425 million, almost as many people as now populate all of Africa. Mexico's population would increase from 70 million to 205 million, roughly the U.S. population at present. Brazil would go from 126 million to 345 million before it stabilized a century hence. Populations of Central American countries— El Salvador, Guatemala, and Nicaragua—would triple before stabilizing.

These population projections reflect two sets of assumptions
—one explicit and one implicit. Among the explicit are the
country-by-country assumptions about future fertility levels,
sex ratios, life expectancies, and numerous other demographic
variables. If these explicit assumptions hold, then the projected
increases in world population will materialize. But population
growth does not occur in a vacuum. Current projections of
world population are based on the implicit assumption that
supplies of energy, food, and the other natural resources
needed to support human life will continue to be available.

Even apart from the difficulty of sorting out these two types
of assumptions, assessing the impact of population growth on
the earth's resources is complicated analytically because both
population growth and rising affluence exert pressure on the
earth's resources. Each does so to similar effect, and between
1950 and 1973 each accounted for roughly half of the 4 percent or so annual growth in the world demand for goods and
services. Since then, however, global economic growth has
fallen to less than 3 percent per year, and the population
component of the overall growth in global demand has become
dominant.[3]

Pressures are mounting on resources in a way that will influence future population trends. To be realistic, demographic
models need to incorporate feedback mechanisms that reflect
changing attitudes toward population size as the various ecological and economic stresses associated with continued population growth materialize. This, in turn, calls for improved
analyses and understanding of the relationship between population growth and the earth's basic human life support systems,
including energy supplies.

The Changing Backdrop

Meaningful population projections must be based on an understanding of the carrying capacity of the earth's natural biologi-

cal systems. If they are not, unrealistically large increases in numbers look feasible. As noted earlier, populations in many locales are already outgrowing their basic life-support systems and excessive demands for goods are leading to the consumption of the biological resource base and the exhaustion of soils.

With world oil production leveling off and population continuing to grow, the oil supply per person is now falling at more or less the same speed that population increases. By the same token, as the world turns from fossil energy to renewable energy sources, the area available per person to collect the solar influx either biologically or mechanically becomes a central determinant of energy-consumption levels. These upper limits posed by the collection area suggest that in the absence of an effort to halt population growth far sooner than now projected, humanity may literally lack the energy to further improve its lot.

While the recent downturns in per capita production of many essential commodities pose problems, the prospect of a downturn in per capita grain production may be the most worrisome of all. During the early fifties, the annual growth in world grain production was nearly double that of population but since then growth has been slowing. As it slowed, production's edge over population fell from 1.2 percent annually in the fifties to 0.5 percent in the seventies. (See Table 7-1.) This margin of improvement has narrowed and almost disappeared during the seventies, even with the return of idled U.S. crop-

Table 7-1. Growth in World Grain Production by Decade, Total and Per Capita, 1950–80

Decade	Decade Rate	Annual Rate	Annual Rate Per Capita
		(percent)	
1950–60	36	3.1	1.2
1960–70	32	2.8	0.8
1970–80	26	2.3	0.5

Source: U.S. Department of Agriculture.

land to production. If the growth in grain production continues to slow, it could fall below population growth, leading to a worldwide decline in per capita grain production. Indeed, in Africa, the continent with the fastest population growth ever recorded, food production has already fallen below population growth. The first continent to experience a sustained decline in food output per person, it suffered a 14 percent decline during the seventies.

Should per capita grain production begin to fall worldwide, compounding the per capita production declines of other commodities, the world's economic maladies would quickly worsen. Inflation, for example, would become far more virulent. As the U.S. Government's *Global 2000 Report* concludes, "Unless the nations of the world act quickly and decisively to change current policies, life for most of the world's people will be more difficult and more precarious in the year 2000 than it is today."[4]

As the eighties begin, population growth is not merely an obstacle to improving our lot: it may eventually make improvement impossible. If we continue to consume our biological capital and "mine" our soils then we will seal our fate as surely as did the Mayans. The demographic path we are on is untenable, inconsistent with the evolution of a sustainable society. The time has come to reject the assumption that the world's population will double over the next generation. Instead, we should establish goals for slowing population growth that are consistent not only with a sustainable society but also with continuing improvements in the human condition.

A Stabilization Timetable

Given what is now known about the carrying capacity of the earth's renewable resource systems and the pressure on remaining oil reserves, at what level should we aim to stabilize world population? A decline in the per capita fish catch could have been avoided if population had stabilized at 3.6 billion in 1970. Had it stopped growing at four billion, beef output per person might still be increasing. And had it topped off at four billion, we would have much more time to develop alternatives to oil. Unfortunately, the advantages of stabilizing population growth are matched by the difficulties of doing so.

Demographers point out that even if fertility rates were to fall immediately to replacement level, population would continue to grow for several decades in those countries with many young people. This means that if population growth is not to be slowed by rising mortality, fertility may have to drop well below replacement level in some societies, with one-child families becoming the norm.

Any abrupt reduction in the birth rate will lead to wide variations in size among age-groups. Whereas a sharp rise in the birth rate leads to an immediate rise in the dependency ratio (the proportion of nonworkers to workers), a sharp decline in the birth rate would have the reverse effect over the short run. Eventually, it would rise again as the ranks of the elderly swelled, but there would be several decades to prepare for this increase.

The great difficulty in halting population growth quickly must, of course, be weighed against the social costs of failing to do so in time to avoid the collapse of the earth's major ecological systems. The resource analyses set forth in the preceding chapters, combined with an appreciation of the difficulties in reining in population growth quickly, suggest that the sum of the social stresses on both sides might be minimized if world population growth could be brought to a halt somewhere around six billion. Adequately sustaining even six billion people would overtax some key resources, but it would be exceedingly difficult to stabilize at a lower level given the large number of young people coming into their reproductive years. Any estimate of what a reasonable stabilization level would be is, of course, necessarily subjective: While the deterioration of soils or of biological support systems can be carefully charted, so far little attempt has been made to relate the deterioration of these systems to the deterioration of the economic systems that rest on them.

Even with the comparatively modest world population increases inherent in such a goal, the per capita supply of forest products, seafood, beef, oil, and other basic commodities would undoubtedly decline further. But the prospect of bringing the decline in the renewable resources to a halt would brighten. Supporting even six billion people at acceptable consumption levels will not be possible without widespread rationing, more careful management of biological systems, stringent energy-conservation measures, materials recycling programs, and a more equitable distribution of vital resources both within and among societies. On the other hand, stabilizing world population at six billion will not require any country to do what several countries have not already done. No country would have to reduce its birth rate any more rapidly than Barbados, China, Costa Rica, and Indonesia have over the last decade.

Achieving a stable world population requires balancing births and deaths. Prior to the modern age, population stability rested upon just such an equilibrium between relatively high birth and death rates. However, with the introduction of modern medicine and sanitation, death rates dropped markedly. Long-term equilibrium in a modern society with typical "three score and ten" life expectancies is likely to occur with birth and death rates in balance at about 13 per thousand.

National death rates now range from a low of six or seven per thousand when there is a relatively young population in good health (such as in Malaysia or Sri Lanka) to a high in the twenties (such as in Ethiopia or Afghanistan).[5] The variation in birth rates is much greater—from just under 10 in West Germany and 12 in the United Kingdom to 47 in Nicaragua and 48 in Algeria.

Since fertility levels vary so widely between industrial and developing countries, they are best separated when constructing a timetable for population stabilization. In the industrial countries, where populations are already growing slowly and where per capita consumption of essential resources is disproportionately high, equilibrium will come much sooner than it will in the less developed countries.

Stabilizing our numbers at six billion will have to occur in stages, with developing countries following a slower timetable than the industrial countries. For their part, the industrial countries as a group would have to achieve a stationary population by the year 2000. In fact, several industrial countries have already reached this goal. Austria, Belgium, East Germany, Luxembourg, West Germany, Sweden, and the United Kingdom had essentially stationary populations in 1980. (See Table 7-2.) The population of West Germany, which stopped growing in 1972, is now actually declining by 80,000 per year. Most of the remaining industrial countries that have relatively modest population growth rates will likely halt growth well before the end of the century. To the extent that some industrial

Table 7-2. Countries with Essentially Stable Populations, 1980*

Country	Population	Birth Rate	Death Rate	Annual Rate of Change	Annual Change
	(millions)	(per thousand)		(percent)	(number)
Austria	7.51	11.5	11.1	−.06	− 4,506
Belgium	9.86	12.8	11.3	.15	+14,790
East Germany	16.74	14.0	13.9	.01	+ 1,674
Luxembourg	0.36	10.9	10.5	.04	+ 144
Sweden	8.29	11.8	11.1	.07	+ 5,803
United Kingdom	55.95	13.2	11.9	.13	+72,735
West Germany	61.21	10.0	11.3	−.13	−79,673
Total	159.92				+11,067

*Excludes both emigration and immigration.
Source: United Nations.

countries achieve stability ahead of schedule, others can lag accordingly without disrupting the overall timetable.

Interestingly, in the seven countries where population size is now stationary, stabilizing population was not a national goal. Rather, the decline in fertility flowed from social improvements. As levels of education and literacy rose, as employment opportunities for women expanded, as access to family planning services improved, and as abortion laws were liberalized, people chose to have fewer children. This suggests that in several European countries, population size would stabilize in short order if such pro-natalist economic policies as baby bonuses were abandoned.

For the developing world, population would have to be stabilized more gradually, taking four decades instead of two. The first step would involve reducing the average birth rate from 32 per thousand (the 1980 level) to 26 by 1990. Each decade thereafter the rate would drop by 5 until reaching 11 in 2020, roughly the same as in Austria, Sweden or West Germany today. The crude death rate would remain at the 1980 level of 12 until 1990, rather than continuing the postwar decline, largely as a result of higher food prices and severe nutritional stress. With population growth in the Third World slowing from 1.4 percent in 1990 to 1.0 percent in the year 2000, the enhanced potential for improving nutrition would permit the death rate to drop to 11, where it would stay during the remainder of the stabilization period. While some further improvement in living conditions would lower the death rate further, this would be offset by the aging of the population that follows a sustained decline in fertility.

Lowering the average birth rate in the developing countries to 26 by 1990 will require a Herculean effort, one that many observers consider impossible. But while not all countries will reach this target, others are far ahead of schedule. Birth rates in Taiwan and South Korea are now 25 or below, while those in Barbados, China, Cuba, Hong Kong, and Singapore are below 20. The keys to meeting the timetable are China and India. China, whose population accounts for one-third of the developing world, already has a birth rate of 18. India's 1980 birth rate is estimated at 34.[6] Combined, India and China have a 1980 birth rate of 24, already well below the 1990 target.

At the other end of the spectrum, more than a score of African countries have, along with relatively high death rates, extremely high birth rates of between 40 and 50 per thousand. Needless to say, a country such as Ethiopia—where the birth rate is 48—will be hard-pressed to reach the 1985 target. But if it does not check its growth soon, the famine that claimed an estimated 200,000 lives in 1974 could well return. The same applies to the string of countries across the southern fringe of the Sahara and down Africa's eastern coast.

The stabilization target proposed here for the less developed nations may well strike even seasoned population analysts as unattainable. Yet, the consequences of not meeting it make any other course almost unimaginable. Under this timetable, India, which is already struggling to feed and maintain political and economic order among its 676 million people, would end up with a population of close to one billion to provide for in 2020. Bangladesh, badly overcrowded with an estimated population of 91 million, would have to find the means of supporting an increase of over 40 percent. And Egypt, with its current population of some 42 million, would have to squeeze nearly 20 million more people into the crowded Nile Valley even if it met the proposed timetable.

Under this timetable, the substantial declines in birth rates between now and 1990 in both the industrial and the developing countries would reduce the annual world population growth to 1.1 percent in that year. (See Table 7-3.) The timetable is admittedly ambitious, but attitudes toward family size are changing and birth rates are stationary or falling almost everywhere. Should the world fall far behind the stabilization timetable, population pressures could become unbearable,

Table 7-3. A Proposed Population Stabilization Timetable

Year	World Population	Annual Growth Rate	Annual Increase
	(billions)	(percent)	(millions)
1970	3.6	1.9	69
1980	4.4	1.7	75
1990	5.0	1.1	55
2000	5.5	0.8	44
2010	5.8	0.4	23
2020	6.0	0	0

Source: Worldwatch Institute.

leading to widespread collapses of local biological life support systems. In this event, population growth would be checked by rising death rates rather than declining birth rates as scheduled in the timetable.

Thus far, much of the global decline in population is concentrated in a few of the world's most populous countries. The decline in China's birth rate between 1970 and 1980, among the most rapid of any country on record, may be family planning's greatest success story.[7] This achievement in a country where more than one-fifth of humanity resides shows what a government committed to reducing fertility can do when it attacks the population problem on several fronts simultaneously.

A second sign of hope, the decline of the U.S. population growth rate by one-third between 1970 and 1975, surprised demographers.[8] The sharp upturn in birth rates expected to occur when the children of the postwar baby boom entered their prime reproductive years has not materialized. An unanticipated drop in the marriage rate, steady growth in female employment, a sharp upturn in female enrollment in graduate and professional schools, and other social changes no doubt contributed to this turn of events.

Other populous countries making impressive strides in reducing birth rates are Japan and Indonesia, the third and fourth largest countries in Asia. The fall in the birth rate in Indonesia has come close to matching that in China—both countries attribute their success in part to their village-level focus and to widespread local participation.[9] In Japan, the late seventies decline in the birth rate reflects more than anything else the sharp fall-off in the number of women entering the reproductive years.[10]

While several West European countries now have essentially stationary populations, fertility declines in other countries are also helping to set the stage for population stabilization. Altogether, some 31 countries had a fertility level in 1980 that was at or below replacement level (the births needed for a given generation to replace itself, or roughly 2.1 births per woman). Including China, a recent addition to the list, these countries contain nearly 1.8 billion people, or roughly 40 percent of the world total.[11]

Once fertility settles at the replacement level or below, it is only a matter of time until population growth stops. How long it takes varies according to the age distribution of the society. For some, stability is only years away. For others, generations may be required to reach equilibrium. In any event, it is now clear that population size can stabilize even when stabilization is not an explicit national goal. It is also clear that replacement level fertility can be attained by countries with widely varying income levels and different cultures and religions. Available evidence, including the most recent data on fertility, suggests that world population size can stabilize at a level far lower than that projected by the United Nations or World Bank, and good sense indicates that it must.

The Family Planning Gap

Providing family planning services to all who want them is one of the most obvious ways governments can help slow population growth. Despite steady progress over the last decade in

expanding the availability of contraceptive services, much remains to be done. By even the most conservative estimates,
vast numbers are not yet served by family planning services.
According to one study based on data gathered during the
mid-seventies, close to half the world's couples have no protection from unplanned pregnancies.[12]

Data becoming available from the World Fertility Survey—
a project that is interviewing some 350,000 women from 60
countries (19 developed and 41 developing), asking them about
their childbearing practices, beliefs, and desires—begin to
show the dimensions of the family planning gap. In a detailed
analysis of Colombia, Panama, Peru, Indonesia, Korea, and Sri
Lanka, demographer Charles Westoff concludes that "the pre-
vention of unwanted births . . . would reduce fertility by one-
quarter to one-third in five of the six countries."[13]

In country after country the World Fertility Survey, the
largest social research project ever undertaken, has made it
clear that the share of married women of reproductive age who
do not want more children is large indeed. The Population
Division of the United Nations observed in a paper presented
to the World Fertility Survey conference that "there is no
doubt that the desire to cease child-bearing is surprisingly high,
ranging from 30 percent in Nepal to 72 percent in Korea."[14]
The larger the current family size, the more likely is the woman
to want to stop bearing children. The UN report further notes
that "a majority of the women with four living children in all
countries report that they do not want any more. The range
is substantial—from 52 percent in Malaysia to 92 percent in
Korea."

Even in a country as poor as Bangladesh, unfulfilled demand
for family planning services is great. In 1980, Minister of
Health and Family Planning Dr. M. A. Matin reported that
"38 percent of eligible couples have said they want to practice
birth control but only 17 percent have been reached by services."[15] What is even more surprising is that in some develop-

ing countries childlessness and the one-child family are losing their negative stigma. Results of the World Fertility Survey show that "in most countries childlessness, or even the one-child family, is clearly regarded as undesirable. But in Korea and Mexico 10 to 13 percent of women with no living children also reported that they wanted no more children. And in Peru and Colombia almost 20 percent of women with only one child stated that they wanted no more."[16]

Many studies confirm that great numbers of married women who do not want any more children nevertheless lack access to contraception.[17] As some demographers have noted, this apparent gap does not automatically translate into demand for family planning services, since some couples want no more children but lack the motivation to act on that desire. This unknown variable makes it difficult to estimate precisely the effect of the broadening availability of family planning services on fertility.

Still, where the demand for contraceptives has preceded their availability, the initial provision of family planning services has led to a sharp decline in birth rates. Such was the case in Costa Rica, where the birth rate fell from 47 per thousand in 1961 to 28 in 1973.[18] Moreover, as family planning services become available, they tend to generate additional interest and demand for services. Westoff notes that "as awareness increases so does demand."[19] In analyzing World Fertility Survey data for Mexico over time, demographer James Brackett notes that "one indication of the expansion [in family planning programs] is the fact that knowledge of family planning outlets in rural areas increased from 26 percent in 1976 to 60 percent in 1978."[20]

To be widely used, family planning services need to be readily accessible, preferably within 30 minutes travel time from the residence of the potential user. In addition, the services and contraceptive materials themselves must be either free or cheap. In explaining China's highly successful program to an American delegation, Chinese official Liu Ching-Shen said, "We practice the principle that anyone who wants birth planning can get it, and the government should pay for it."[21] Experience also indicates that the more successful family planning programs offer both males and females a wide range of family planning services and that clinic-based contraceptive services are usually less effective than community-based efforts that involve local people in setting birth rate goals, designing the program, and delivering the services. Indonesia's family planning program, described in a Worldwatch Paper on family planning by Bruce Stokes as a unique blend of government initiative and local custom, has led to an impressive drop in fertility levels.[22] On the island of Java alone 27,000 village pill and condom depots, many of them in private homes, provide ready access to contraceptive supplies.

Regardless of the efforts made to meet these criteria for success, achieving a stationary population will be painfully difficult if contraceptive services are not backed by legal abortion. With the legalization of abortion in Italy in 1978, the share of world population living in societies where abortion is readily available reached two-thirds, up from one-third a decade ago.[23] Yet, one-third of the world's women are still denied this basic public health service except on illicit terms.

Few initiatives will contribute as much to the sustainability of society as the extension of family planning services to those who desire them but lack access to them. In a world threatened by overpopulation, such an inexcusable gap should concern political leaders everywhere.

Social Improvement and Fertility

Demographers explain the relationship between social progress and fertility in terms of a three-stage demographic transition. In the first stage, social conditions are poor, both death rates and birth rates are high, and population grows little or not at all. In the second, social conditions begin to improve and death rates decline, but birth rates remain high—so population growth is rapid. In the final stage birth rates also decline, reestablishing equilibrium with death rates, and population grows slowly or not at all.

While the demographic "transition theory" has provided a useful analytical framework within which to view the relationship between social progress and changes in fertility, it has its limitations. Indeed, many fertility declines appear to be independent of any social or economic improvement. Demographer Michael Teitelbaum of the Ford Foundation believes that counting on the demographic transition to reduce fertility of its own accord is "wishful thinking," since the modest level of development that most Third World countries can aspire to will not, he says, be sufficient to stabilize population size.[24] As the data from the cross-sectional comparisons gathered in the course of the World Fertility Survey become available, they too point out some holes in the theory of demographic transition.[25]

Of all social indicators, the one that seems to correlate most closely with fertility decline is a rising level of education. Survey data from 27 study populations in the Third World show that women and men who have a primary education have fewer children than those who do not.[26] Fertility also declines when nations urbanize and when more women work outside the home. At the lower end of the social spectrum, among rural and agricultural couples, where both spouses have less than a primary education and where the woman does not work, the average number of children is 6.9.[27] At the other end of the spectrum, where both spouses have at least a primary-level education or live in an urban setting and where the woman works, the average number of children is 4.2.

The World Fertility Survey data indicate that the age of marriage is rising in most countries and that late-marrying people have fewer children. An analysis of data for 18 countries by demographer Mercedes Concepción shows that overall "the age of marriage reported by women belonging to each educational group shows a steady rise as schooling increases."[28]

Marriage age appears to be increasing in industrial as well as developing countries. In the United States, the share of never-married women among those aged 20 to 24 increased from 29 percent in 1960 to 50 percent in 1980.[29] In Denmark, where population stability may be imminent, the figure increased from 44 percent in 1970 to 59 percent in 1975.[30] In the island country of Sri Lanka, where the birth rate has declined steadily over the past two decades, the median age of marriage of women is 23.9 years, reasonably high even by international standards but particularly so for a developing country. The World Fertility Survey data for Sri Lanka indicate that the share of women aged 20 to 24 who are not married "has steadily risen from about 30 percent in 1946 to about 60 percent in 1975," almost exactly the same level as Denmark's.[31]

Expanding employment opportunities for women can also help curb birth rates. In nearly all the advanced industrial countries, rising employment for women in combination with other social and economic trends is reducing fertility. In the United States, the share of women in the prime child-bearing years who are working has climbed from two-fifths in 1960 to two-thirds in 1980.[32] Similar trends are unfolding in Europe. In the Soviet Union, 93 percent of women aged 16 to 55 are either employed or in school.[33] Soviet demographer Galina Kiseleva writes that this great increase in female employment has brought about a transformation of the whole range of women's needs, including that for children.

Although social improvements will undoubtedly continue to help reduce family size, fertility is now falling in some communities and countries where living conditions are actually deteriorating. In such places, the keys appear to be the active local participation of people in the design and implementation of their family planning program, a broad understanding of the social need to limit population size, and the widespread realization that reducing family size may be the only way out of the poverty trap.

Incentives for Smaller Families

Besides insuring ready access to family planning services and improving social conditions, governments can also use public policy to encourage smaller families. In societies where women are widely employed outside the home, maternity-leave policies can directly influence child-bearing decisions. In Singapore, women in civil service or unionized jobs get two months of paid maternity leave only for the first two children.[34]

Tax policies that limit the number of "tax deductible" children can also discourage couples from having large families.[35] As of 1973, Filipino law limits to four the number of children for whom tax deductions can be claimed. More recently, Nepal has eliminated tax deductions for children altogether. In Singapore, tax relief is granted for the first three children only. In contrast, in the United States, legislation to limit the number of tax-deductible children to two has not received the broad support needed for passage although a bill to stabilize U.S. population size through just such measures was introduced in Congress in early 1981.[36]

While in the industrial countries the rise in the marriage age is keeping birth rates down, raising the legal age of marriage in preindustrial societies can officially encourage a drop in the birth rate. In China, the officially recommended minimum age of marriage is 28 for men and 25 for women in the cities, 25 for men and 23 for women in the country.[37] Overall, though, such minimums can be difficult to enforce, and they are apparently more widely accepted in urban than in rural areas. An effort by Bangladesh's Minister of Health and Family Planning to increase the legal age of marriage from 16 was blocked at the cabinet level, while violations of India's minimum age of marriage are widespread.[38]

Other techniques used by countries to encourage small families include such incentives as preferred access to housing. Singapore, for example, gives priority access to public housing to families with no more than two children.[39]

While most countries now officially encourage family planning, China is the first to undertake national birth planning. Each year, Beijing establishes a national birth quota as an integral part of overall economic planning. Two American demographers, Deborah Oakley and the late Fred Jaffe, recently reported that commune officials "meet with their counterpart in each production brigade and transmit the target number of births for the brigade and its component teams during the coming year."[40] These quotas are then translated into birth permits, with allocations made on the basis of the couple's age and their current number of children. A newly married couple in their late twenties would be high on the eligibility list while a couple in their mid-twenties with a newborn infant might be encouraged to wait a few years before having another child.

Save for China and a few other pathbreakers, few countries have fully accepted the challenge of inculcating public understanding with the need for restricting future population growth. Yet, evidence shows that knowledge of the relationship between population size and the carrying capacity of natural systems, particularly at the national and community levels, markedly influences people's child-bearing decisions. The challenge now is to bind the family's fate to the nation's—a challenge first for governments and educators, then for individual men and women.

China's One-Child Family Program

As part of the broad policy reassessment since Mao's death, China's new leadership has looked anew at population. Analyzing the population-resource balance and the end-of-century prospect has been an unsettling experience. The handwriting on the wall appears distinctly Malthusian. China's population reached an estimated one billion in 1980.

Foreign exchange shortages are playing a key role in China's reassessment. The country's capacity to earn foreign exchange is limited, and yet China has become dependent on imported food that must be paid for in dollars. As the dimensions of the population threat have become clear, the Chinese leadership has initiated public discussion and distributed background information on the population-resource relationship. Now the Chinese know both how their national population-resource base compares with other countries and what changes are in store within China if population continues to increase.[41] In particular, the literature points out that each Chinese currently subsists on scarcely one-quarter of an acre of cropland, one of the smallest per capita allotments in the world, and that their children and grandchildren can expect to have less still if population growth continues.

Although China's birth rate has been falling and may already have reached an average of two children per couple, the leadership understands that even replacement-level fertility will not do. Like many developing countries whose birth rates were high during the fifties and sixties, China has a large number of young people who are reaching their reproductive years during the eighties. Even if these couples have only two children each, this would still add a few hundred million to the current population, an increase the Chinese no longer feel they can handle. With this in mind, the Chinese have launched a campaign to promote the one-child family. In August 1979, Vice Premier Chen Muhua, the only female of that rank, announced that the government was taking steps to check the birth rate. As well as outlining incentives for those who limit their families, Premier Chen Muhua declared that those "who insist on having several children in spite of patient attempts at persuasion and education" will be subject to "a multichild tax."[42]

Chinese-born American demographer Pi-chao Chen reports that the first of the specific measures being used to encourage one-child families in China is a direct economic one: an increase in salary of five yuan (or roughly $3.25) per month for couples with only one child who pledge to have no more.[43] (The average salary in China is $26 per month.) In addition, access to housing will also be influenced by family size. Couples who limit their families to one child are assured of at least as much housing as those with a larger family. In some cases, they may move ahead of others on the housing lists. Similarly, the only child will be given preferential consideration in both school admissions and job assignments. Even grain rations will be influenced by family size. Couples with one child will get adult grain rations for that child, while in larger families children will receive the usual smaller allotment. Finally, besides these more immediate advantages, retirement benefits enter into the picture. Couples who have only one child will be eligible for a pension equal to 80 percent of their salary at the time of retirement compared with 70 percent for the remainder of the population. Those who elect not to have any children will receive a retirement pension that equals their salary.

With this new program added to existing efforts to slow population growth, China hopes to reduce its growth rate to 0.5 percent in 1985.[44] (The U.S. rate in 1980 was 0.7 percent, excluding immigration.) Whether China will meet this ambitious goal remains to be seen, but by the end of 1979 29 percent of all the one-child families had applied for the certificates to establish their eligibility for the proffered benefits. Pi-chao Chen calculates that if China "could raise its one-child rate to 50 percent by 1985 and maintain it at that rate thereafter, the country would achieve zero population growth by the year 2003."[45]

China's plan is to halt population growth by the end of the

century at the latest. Beyond this, Beijing is now discussing a possible long-term goal of reducing its population (as is occurring inadvertently in West Germany today) to lighten the pressures on resources. Like the program to encourage the one-child family, the adoption of such a goal would represent another first in population policy.

Inflation as a Contraceptive Force

While history is of little help in judging the effect of sustained double-digit inflation on child-bearing, first-hand accounts and other indicators are revealing. In a visit to southern Senegal, Swiss demographer Pierre Pradervand found that villagers there wanted to know where they could get contraceptives, how much they cost, and how well the various devices worked.[46] Pradervand was surprised because when he visited the same village a few years earlier people had expressed little interest in family planning. Apparently, inflation had made the difference. The prices of many of the basic goods the villagers buy—kerosene, clothing, grain—had doubled within a three-year span. While the inflationary forces that are eroding the living standards of Senegalese villagers are beyond their control, they nonetheless realize that they can offset the impact of inflation by reducing the size of their families. For them, inflation has become a contraceptive force.

In Mexico, government family-planning officials were surprised to discover in 1979 that residents of even the most remote villages are eagerly awaiting the arrival of birth-planning services. Dr. Jorge Martinez Manatou, coordinator of family planning services, concludes that "because of economic pressures, the peasant is becoming aware of the need to limit the size of his family."[47]

In the United States and other advanced industrial societies, the impact of inflation may be even greater than in Third World villages. Besides coloring people's child-bearing decisions inflation may push more women onto the job market as couples attempt to protect their standard of living with two incomes. When that happens, birth rates usually decline.

In centrally planned economies, where prices are fixed, shortages at the fixed price may have the same effect as inflation does in free market economies. In the Soviet Union, for example, housing is reasonably priced but scarce. This shortage of living space, in a climate where much time is spent indoors, undoubtedly dampens the enthusiasm for children, particularly since newlyweds must sometimes wait years for an apartment of their own. In *The Russians*, Hedrick Smith cites Muscovites who commonly joke that one of the primary methods of birth control is the housing shortage.[48]

In parts of the Third World, economic stresses are leading to a rise in the age of marriage—much as they did after the potato famine hit Ireland in the nineteenth century. In Sri Lanka, rising unemployment among young men appears to be delaying marriage since parents are reluctant to allow their daughters to marry young men who cannot afford to establish independent households.[49] While inflation affects population growth primarily through its impact on child-bearing decisions at the individual level, slower economic growth may prompt governments to accelerate the adoption of national policies and programs to slow population growth.

The impact of an economic slowdown will, in most cases, be greatest in those societies where population growth is most rapid. Indeed, a fall in the economic growth rate to 2 percent per year would not pose any serious problem for West Germany or Belgium, where population growth has ceased. Incomes there would still rise by some 2 percent per year. But it could wreak havoc in Senegal or Pakistan, where population is still expanding by 3 percent or more per year. Population projections will mean little unless they take account of the effects of economic stresses on national population policies and on individual child-bearing policies. In any event, more realis-

tic projections and more awareness of the new effects of population growth are needed if that growth is to be halted in time.

A Gradual Awakening

Among those who regularly wrestle with the consequences of
population growth, the danger is clear. Former World Bank
President Robert McNamara consistently argues that world
leaders underestimate the gravity of the population threat. He
believes that "the options are closing, the easy answers are
disappearing, the hard choices are becoming more insistent."[50]
Here and there, national political leaders are beginning to share
his concern.

The initial manifestations of population pressure vary from
country to country. In Mexico, it took the form of rising
unemployment. Political leaders became alarmed when they
realized that even economic growth at an impressive 7 percent
a year simply could not create enough jobs to accommodate all
the new entrants into the labor force. Coupled with the return
to food deficit status in the seventies following the dramatic
Green Revolution gains in food production, rising unemployment induced an abrupt turnabout in Mexican population
policy. In April 1972, the government abandoned its pro-natalist stance and launched a nationwide family planning program.
In Egypt, the leadership was jolted into action when it was
calculated that the population increase in the Nile River Valley
during the period the Aswan High Dam was under construction would totally absorb the additional food production the
irrigation project would make possible.[51]

Perhaps the most surprising development in population policy has taken place in Canada, where future resource supplies
have become a matter of public discussion. Many Canadians
are disturbed by the recent loss of the traditional exportable
energy surplus, a loss that occurred as domestic needs soared.
At the same time, agricultural planners, alarmed by the sac-

rifice of the most fertile cropland to urban sprawl, fear Canada's exportable food surplus may also dwindle. A recent study by the Science Council of Canada suggests trying to limit the end-of-century population to 29 million, an inarguably modest increase over the current 22 million.[52] If such studies lead to concern in such a richly blessed country, what would similar studies prompt other, less well endowed countries to think, and more to the point, to do?

As the dimensions of the population problem grow more apparent, the more forward-looking national political leaders are responding. Recent years have brought a sharp increase in requests from developing countries for assistance in family planning. Indeed, the principal aid agencies in this field—the United Nations Fund for Population Activities, the International Planned Parenthood Federation, and the U.S. Agency for International Development—are being overwhelmed with such requests despite modest growth in their budgets. But these sensible moves are not enough in themselves. They must be augmented by those of the "laggard" nations—be they developed or developing—and by more far-reaching programs.

As world population moves toward five billion, humanity is moving into uncharted territory. The dynamics of the relationship between population size and the earth's natural resource systems are uncertain and in some respects unpredictable. If population continues to expand rapidly, living standards for substantial segments of humanity are certain to fall. Just how the sustained erosion of living standards will in turn affect family size is hard to say, but governments and individuals may well take steps to reduce population growth more quickly than has been thought possible. In any case, if population stabilization is the measure, the transition to a sustainable society has begun—albeit slowly and largely in response to enormous pressures.

8

Preserving
Our Resource
Underpinnings

Braking population growth is necessary to preserve our resource base but it is by no means sufficient. Protecting croplands will require new national initiatives in land-use planning
and erosion control throughout the world. Arresting deforestation, overgrazing, and overfishing will force us to learn to
maximize the sustainable yield, even at the expense of the
current yield. And charting a smooth transition from fossil
fuels to renewable energy will involve rigorous energy-conservation efforts.

The Mayans, the Mesopotamians, the Carthaginians—
these culturally extinct people who lived in an era when environmental tensions mounted slowly—probably did not under-

stand the forces undermining their economies. We do know what threatens us. But still lacking is the broad public awareness needed to launch an effective response. Without that understanding, the needed shifts in priorities, programs, and funds are not likely to materialize. Conversely, in the handful of nations where such understanding does exist, headway is being made against the abuses of land, forests, species, and other finite resources, and against the threat of overpopulation. The few positive national responses to each of these problems stand as models for other countries to follow.

Land-Use Planning

As population pressures mount, conflicts in land-use multiply and make plain the need for land-use planning and cropland preservation. Our present lack of well developed land-use policies is a legacy of the frontier era when fertile virgin land was available, the potential for raising cropland productivity was great, and energy was cheap. Unfortunately, countries that use land inefficiently invariably use other resources inefficiently as well. Sprawling suburbs and "leapfrog" developments not only gobble up cropland; they also make transportation and the delivery of services inefficient and wasteful of energy.

With food prices on the rise, agricultural land can no longer be treated as an inexhaustible reservoir of land for use in industrial development, urbanization, and energy production. On the contrary, cropland must be viewed as irreplaceable, a resource that is paved over, built upon, or otherwise taken out of production only in emergencies and only after public deliberation and choice. As former U.S. Assistant Secretary of Agriculture M. Rupert Cutler aptly observes, "People must fully understand the irreplaceable value of prime farm land and the ominous meaning of the war between the bulldozer and the plow."[1]

Historically, the marketplace has functioned as the arbiter

of land use. Unfortunately, though, the market does not protect cropland from competing nonfarm interests. For that, careful land-use planning is needed at the national level, the local level, or both. Whether in the form of legislation, government decrees, or such incentives as differential tax rates, the only defenses against the ultimately destructive opportunism of the marketplace are land-use planning and restrictions.

Until recently, most governments have stayed out of land-use planning. But many that have rationalized their neglect have overlooked the fact that both national and local governments shape land-use patterns—whether or not they view themselves as planning authorities. A study by the Organization for Economic Cooperation and Development (OECD) notes that "governments have long been making decisions directly bearing on the use of certain lands, such as when a motorway is to be built or when, under the heading of agricultural policy, some area is marked for irrigation."[2] Within the United States, scores of national policies and over 20 federal agencies have directly or indirectly influenced land use.[3]

The first step toward a national land-use policy is classifying land according to its productivity. This step has many precedents. The United States and Canada, for example, have agricultural land-classification schemes based on the categorization of land into seven classes. In the United Kingdom, agricultural land is divided into five grades according to its productivity. Similar systems are used in Denmark, France, Portugal, Sweden, and West Germany, while Australia and New Zealand estimate land productivity on the basis of tax returns.[4]

An OECD study comparing land-use planning internationally reports that Japan is the only country with comprehensive zoning nationwide.[5] In 1968, the entire country was divided into three land-use zones—urban, agricultural, and other. In 1974, the plan was further refined to include forests, natural parks, and nature reserves. Acutely pressed for space and land-based resources, Japan has faced the issue first, developing a highly successful model that other countries can emulate. Indeed, even though its hundred million people are crammed onto a mountainous sliver of land smaller than California, Japan produces an exportable surplus of rice, the national food staple.

In the OECD countries, where there is little opportunity for reclaiming new land, land lost to urbanization or other uses is permanently removed from agriculture. Consequently, during the sixties, Belgium, France, the Netherlands, and West Germany established national land-use guidelines, and accorded planning responsibilities to local communities.[6] Besides protecting agricultural land, such guidelines also address such issues as the control of urban sprawl and the need for both parks and urban green belts.

Among the Western industrial countries, France appears to have by far the most effective farmland preservation program. Law professor Anne Louise Strong of the University of Pennsylvania ascribes the French success to the work of local nonprofit Sociétés d'Amènagement Foncier et d'Établissement Rural (SAFERs).[7] Statutorily empowered with the right to preempt any sale of farmland, Strong observes that these local societies both "assist those who wish to remain in farming to obtain suitable land and to keep prime land from being subdivided." SAFERs were authorized in 1960 as nonprofit organizations and were empowered to buy and sell farmland. They can be organized within a single department (county) or can span several counties. As of 1981, SAFERs cover virtually all of France. Charles Little, president of the American Land Forum, reports that SAFERs purchased 2.1 million acres of land and sold 1.7 million acres between 1964 and 1975.[8] Although they buy only about 12 percent of the agricultural land up for sale, their influence is far greater. Even when not exercised, their right of preemption has an important effect on market behavior.

In some countries, including the Netherlands, land-use planning is viewed as part of a broader approach to managing all physical resources. Such a comprehensive approach involves planning not only the use of land, but also that of water and energy, so as to maximize the benefits from all.[9]

In Canada, land-use planning has been left largely to the provinces, with British Columbia providing early leadership. Despite the image of Canada as a land-rich country, the area of high-quality farmland is limited. In British Columbia, less than 5 percent of the land area is suitable for farming.[10] G. G. Runka, Chairman of the British Columbia Land Commission, indicated that it was "the scarcity of agricultural land in British Columbia and the increasing expansion of urban uses onto some of the best agricultural lands that led to provincial legislation to preserve agricultural land use for future food production."[11]

Within the United States, national land-use planning remains rather rudimentary. So far, the government has done little beyond setting aside national parks, forests, and wildlife reserves. Most zoning is local, consisting largely of restricting the use of land for commercial purposes. While efforts by states to protect agricultural land were nil before the seventies, several states have since launched programs to preserve farmland. For example, in 1972 Massachusetts established a program with an initial appropriation of $5 million to purchase "agricultural preservation restrictions."[12] This program was augmented in 1980 by the Massachusetts Farmland Trust, a parallel private initiative.[13]

After mapping, one of the first steps that states customarily take to preserve farmland is to enact differential tax-assessment laws. William J. Sallee of the U.S. Department of Agriculture describes these as "laws under which farmland is assessed for taxes on the basis of its value in agricultural use regardless of what other uses or values it might have."[14] As of early 1980, forty-six states have laws or constitutional amendments that enable local governments to assess taxes on such a basis.[15] In

New Jersey, passage of the Farmland Assessment Act of 1964 slowed the conversion of farmland to other uses and, consequently, its diversion from agricultural purposes. "If farmland in New Jersey were to be taxed at the going rate for urban and suburban residential and industrial uses," says New Jersey Secretary of Agriculture Philip Alampi, "it would be impossible to maintain agriculture as a business in the state."[16]

A second technique for preserving farmland, the purchase of development rights from farmers, surfaced in the early seventies to a warm reception. This approach involves getting two assessments for the value of land—its value for development, and its value for farming. The difference between the two, the "development rights" for the land, can be purchased from farmers by either state or local governments and held in perpetuity, regardless of how many times the land changes hands. Once the development rights of land have been purchased it can be used only for farming. The principal disadvantage of this approach is its high cost. Yet, the process is cumulative and even though it starts on a small scale, the area protected expands with time.

Zoning too can be used to prevent the conversion of farmland to nonfarm uses, though this approach is useful primarily in heavily rural communities. For example, in rural Black Hawk County in northeastern Iowa, the county zoning plan both preserves prime farmland and permits well-conceived residential development on land of lower agricultural productivity.[17] Under this plan, prime farmland is defined as land that yields the equivalent of 115 bushels or more of corn per acre. On it, all residential development is prohibited.

Of course, many countries must solve more basic problems before they can follow Black Hawk County's lead. In some— namely, in Latin America where peasants struggle to continue ruinous cultivation on mountainsides while cattle graze in the valleys—destructive land-use patterns have evolved as a result of a skewed landownership. Where prime cropland is in grass and steeply sloping hillsides that should be grass are being plowed, the key to more sensible land use hinges on a reform of these feudal land-holding systems.

No two countries or communities can approach zoning in precisely the same way; each must work out the details of programs to preserve cropland. Yet, all face the need to order priorities among competing uses. As Richard C. Collins of the University of Virginia points out, "Land-use conflicts and their resolutions represent a litmus test of national values, attitudes, and directions."[18]

Ensuring Soil Security

Halting soil erosion requires a staggering effort, one complicated by social factors. In most countries, the challenge is so vast that only a strong national political commitment and a detailed plan of action will suffice. In the United States, the Soil Conservation Service has risen to that challenge by outlining a national plan that would bring the annual loss of topsoil down to a tolerable level.[19] In addition to maintaining the conservation systems already in place, some 158 million acres, or 38 percent of the 413 million acre cropland base, need additional attention. Of this total, 17 million acres of cropland is eroding so rapidly that SCS recommends that it be withdrawn from cultivation and converted to either forest land or grass land. The remaining 141 million acres of cropland that is currently losing more than five tons of soil per year requires the adoption of some form of conservation tillage such as terracing, contour farming, strip cropping, or minimum tillage. Over the next 50 years the USDA estimates that the implementation of these programs would require $103 billion in budgetary appropriations, or roughly $2 billion per year.[20]

Apart from the heroic effort required, adopting these soil-saving measures would in many cases run counter to the immediate economic interests of farmers and consumers. The cost to farmers of adopting the needed measures will raise food production costs and prices. To the extent that severely erosion-prone land is withdrawn from crop production and converted to other uses, it will reduce food supplies and raise prices in the short run. Yet, difficult though this increase might be to accept, the alternative is to do nothing and face soaring food costs over the long term as soils deteriorate.

At this writing, the program proposed by the U.S. Department of Agriculture in 1980 has not yet been adopted but there is growing recognition of the problem. Whether it will be adopted will depend on the support of the Reagan Administration and Congressional leaders. It is the type of plan that a majority of the world's countries now need if their soils are to be stabilized.

Half a world away, Indian officials are wrestling with the same issues that trouble U.S. officials and soil scientists. Although it has three times as many people as the United States, India has a cropland base that is almost exactly the same size, roughly 350 million acres, but political support for soil conservation is miniscule. Despite the highly visible deforestation of the Himalayas, the denudation of watersheds, and the increasing frequency of crop-destroying floods, the problem is not being addressed. According to B. B. Vohra, a senior Ministry of Irrigation official, "Even at the national level, there is as yet not even a broad perspective plan for the care of the land, no exact information regarding the extent and the location of lands which require protective and ameliorative treatment, and no agency specifically charged with the responsibility for the assessment and management of our irreplaceable land and soil resources."[21]

In the Soviet Union, the loss of topsoil appears to be even greater than it is in the United States. Indeed, mounting Soviet dependence on imported food is due less to a lack of land than to low productivity. Unfortunately for Soviet consumers, few of whom are even aware of the threat, governmental support for remedial action is even weaker than in India.

In the world's semi-arid regions, soil degradation translates into desertification. While virtually every national government in the world's semi-arid regions has sponsored anti-desertification programs, most such programs have been too scattered or too weak to reverse the process. In view of this dispiriting record, successful anti-desertification programs such as Israel's are all the more deserving of emulation. Parts of the Negev Desert that suffered thousands of years of overgrazing and deforestation are once again productive and prosperous. Controlled grazing, improved dry-land farming techniques, and the adoption of innovative irrigation practices all contributed to the transformation. As uncommonly successful at mobilizing people to accomplish common goals as Israel, China too has been struggling to halt deterioration of its huge desert area. Algeria, Iran, Somalia, and Sudan are also launching large-scale environmental restoration programs aimed at halting the desert's spread and restoring productivity on debilitated land.[22]

The economic wisdom of making massive efforts to protect and enhance the productivity of the world's arid lands has been well established. According to UN estimates, the cumulative degradation of rangelands and unirrigated farmlands has cost farmers and consumers $12 billion a year—all of it paid in lost production.[23] If damage due to waterlogging and salinity is added, the yearly losses total nearly $16 billion. Fortunately, as arid-lands specialist Harold Dregne has emphasized, few of the degraded areas have passed the point of no return. In most, full productivity could return with wise management.[24] Furthermore, according to UN calculations, a worldwide anti-desertification program that invested $400 million-per-year would yield a handsome financial return.[25]

Yet, detailed studies on the economics of soil conservation for eroding soils do indicate that the short-term costs of conservation programs often exceed the short-term benefits. As the study of southern Iowa soils showed, the immediate costs to farmers of reducing soil erosion to a level that would not reduce inherent productivity would be three times as great as the benefits.[26] In these circumstances, only government's willingness to share the costs of the needed measures—terracing, contour farming, strip cropping, cover cropping, rotating crops, fallowing, and planting shelter belts—will induce farmers to fight soil erosion. In some countries, the expenditures required simply to stabilize soils will dwarf the total appropriations for agriculture. Yet, the alternative is for governments to neglect the short-term deterioration and then face long-term food scarcity as the cropland base deteriorates.

Time too is at a premium—time to lay the groundwork for such massive financial investments and time to train the people required to do the job. Because they are too leisurely, traditional approaches to financing and training will almost certainly fail. More promising is the deployment of paraprofessionals. In Third World countries, the best approach may be to train village leaders who are themselves farmers to master soil-conservation practices during the off season so that they can help design and administer local soil-conserving plans.

But even proof of the long-term profitability and necessity of conservation just isn't sufficient. While soil scientists can chart a national plan of action in detail, as they have in the United States, they cannot call forth the political support needed to fund and administer such a plan. Indeed, U.S. soil scientist R.A. Brink and his colleagues, writing in *Science*, question whether in our predominantly urban society anyone can generate needed support until the food crisis deepens.[27]

In predominantly rural societies, where most people are illiterate and hard-pressed just to survive, a lack of public interest in soil conservation stems from other roots. Farmers in many Third World villages can muster little concern about the future when their immediate survival is in question. In India, reports B. B. Vohra, "An informed public opinion cannot . . . be wished into existence overnight. A great deal of painstaking and patient work will have to be done to wipe out the backlog of ignorance, inertia, and complacency. . . ."[28]

The most important ingredient missing from unsuccessful responses to the growing menace of soil erosion is political will grounded in awareness. People know that food prices are rising, but most don't know quite why. An understanding that lost soil means lower productivity, which in turn means less and costlier food, is needed to inculcate a national soil conservation ethic. Given the necessary information, more people will understand not only the compelling environmental reasons for adopting a national conservation ethic, but also the economic payoff in implementing a program based on it.

Stabilizing Biological Systems

Efforts to protect the biological systems that support the economic system deserve to be high on humanity's political agenda. In practical terms, ensuring biological protection means devising comprehensive economic policies and plans that limit the offtake or harvest from fisheries, grasslands, and forests. But lowering consumption to a sustainable level is complicated since many resources are still held in common.

Fisheries have been particularly plagued by "the tragedy of the commons."[29] In a way, overfishing is the inexorable outcome of the unwritten law of the seas, which long held that oceanic resources belonged equally to all. Of course, this "law" served well only as long as oceanic resources exceeded the human capacity to exploit them. When overfishing first became a widespread problem, the international community tried to organize an oceanic regime with the authority to manage fisheries in society's long-term interest. Bold and innovative, this concept nevertheless eluded the political grasp of the international community. Although the threat of overfishing was already clear when the third United Nations Conference on the Law of the Sea convened in 1973, conference delegates quickly discovered that individual countries were not prepared to have their fishing rights arbitrated by an international body.

The alternative hammered out after years of negotiating is a system of Exclusive Economic Zones (EEZ): individual countries now control the waters within 200 miles of their coastlines. While this approach does cover 99 percent of the oceanic fish catch, it leaves vast stretches of water uncontrolled and contains an important loophole.[30] Merely according countries the legal authority to manage their off-shore fisheries does not ensure that those fisheries will necessarily be well managed. Indeed, even the basic step of determining the sustainable yield of a fishery and establishing annual quotas accordingly requires information and analytical expertise in marine biology, oceanography, and other disciplines that few coastal Third World countries possess. Consequently, the risk of establishing an unrealistic quota—and thus either wasting fish or destroying a fishery—is high.

If the quotas for a given species in a given fishery are set too high, disaster ensues. John Gulland, chief of the Marine Resources Service of the FAO Fisheries Department, points out that even though Antarctic whale stocks were controlled by a catch quota in the fifties, there was a lack of reliable scientific information on sustainable yields. As a result the quotas were set too high and "the Antarctic whale stock collapsed and the Antarctic whaling industry virtually disappeared."[31] Similarly, the Peruvian anchovy fishery collapse in 1972 might have been avoided had a reasonable quota been in effect.

Besides information, many countries lack the naval resources needed to enforce compliance with the quotas they have established. In some instances, efforts to prohibit fishing by other countries in the EEZs have been completely ineffectual. But even with these drawbacks, the institutional machinery for managing fisheries to maximize their sustainable yield is at last in place.

The same protein hunger that has led to overfishing has led to overgrazing. Like soil erosion and overfishing, overgrazing increases food supplies and lowers food prices in the short run, but at the expense of the long run. Moreover, the severity of overgrazing, like that of soil erosion, is greatest in Third World countries, where curative resources are limited and group ownership complicates resource management.

In many African countries, where cattle play a central economic role and where all grazing lands are held in common, effective land management is exceedingly difficult. Where livestock populations have multiplied along with human populations, as they have in the Sahelian zone countries, excessive pressures on the land have become graphically evident during recent droughts. Some communities and nomadic groups have lost all of their animals; others lost many or most. The unmet challenge in such cases is largely social and institutional. With the traditional constraints on population growth removed, nomadic and semi-nomadic societies have no means of regulating grazing to check grasslands deterioration.

The proper response to this challenge is training and empowering clan leaders to regulate grazing and migratory movements, using their knowledge of natural conditions and the advice of range-management specialists. Jeremy Swift, a British specialist in pastoral development, has proposed creating pastoral cooperatives in Somalia "to take on some of the functions of traditional pastoral society, such as the regulation of grazing, security against the loss of animals, regulation of conflicts over land use, and making investments in the land."³² Apart from introducing ecologically sound management, these cooperatives could also provide a two-way communication channel between the nomads and governments of the states they traverse.

As with many other adjustments called for in the transition to a sustainable society, ending overgrazing calls for changes in values. In many Third World societies, particularly in Africa, status and wealth are measured by the number of animals one owns. While this was once a reasonable yardstick, it is no longer appropriate where overgrazing leaves herds and flocks half-starved. Indeed, if instead the output of meat, milk, and other livestock products was the measure of success, sharply reducing the size of herds would make sense. This seeming paradox—reducing herds to increase livestock yields—is rooted in the nature of livestock metabolism. Roughly half the food a grazing animal consumes is required just for bodily maintenance and survival, another fourth is required for reproduction, and the final fourth goes into milk production, growth, and fat storage.[33] Any cutback in feeding forced by the depletion of pasture is mostly at the expense of these latter functions.

To open the way for herd-management and grazing policies that emphasize productivity over herd size, marketing systems for livestock products will have to be developed. Herders will permanently reduce the size of their herds only if they understand the need for change, have a say in decisions as change is carried out, and see in a revamped livestock-management system a genuine opportunity for a better life for themselves and their children.

Of course, most ranchers who own the grassland that supports their cattle know precisely how many cattle their land can sustain without damage and thus usually carry a number somewhat smaller than the maximum so as to allow a margin of safety for periods of drought. In the United States, most grazing land is owned by individual ranchers, so its problems are a far cry from those in Africa and the rest of the developing world. Still, much U.S. grassland is publicly owned. This land is managed by the Bureau of Land Management, which leases the grazing rights to local ranchers. But while U.S. ranching is sophisticated and U.S. ranchers are well aware of overgrazing's effects, local BLM officials often find themselves pressured by ranchers to permit grazing beyond the level that the land can sustain over the long term. Residents of the same community as the ranchers, they cannot easily resist community pressures. Consequently, well over half of the publicly owned grazing land in the United States is now deteriorating.[34]

While overgrazing occurs in both industrial and developing countries, over the past generation most deforestation has been concentrated in the Third World. In the United States, the area in forests has held steady and in some places even increased during this century as agriculture migrated westward and much of the abandoned terrain in New England, Appalachia, and the Southeast returned to forest.[35] Whether forest acreage will remain stable as those large groups born during the two decades following World War II form households and as industries and residential consumers turn to wood for fuel remains to be seen.

Elsewhere in the industrial world, continental Western Europe and Japan have also stabilized the area in forests, largely as a result of public intervention and control. But these countries have relieved the pressure on their own forests in part by greatly increasing their imports.[36] The upshot is redoubled pressure in Indonesia, Malaysia, Thailand, and other Third World countries where wood-cutting is subject to fewer restrictions.

This "go for bust" approach contrasts sharply with policies in industrial wood-exporting countries such as Finland and Sweden. As demand for forest products has outstripped the sustainable yield of Scandinavian forests, these two leading forest-products suppliers have begun to restrict the annual harvest. Finland's response has been to establish a national quota on the offtake from its shrinking forests, and Sweden may shortly follow the Finnish example.[37]

In many Third World countries, deforestation can no longer be blamed upon a lack of awareness. Instead, a lack of means for controlling wood cutting is at fault. In many cases, a handful of forest officials has the impossible task of keeping throngs of desperately poor people from scavenging for the wood they need for cooking. In others, the national need for foreign exchange, particularly to pay the oil-import bill, has poor country governments up against a wall: they will not limit the offtake from their forests if doing so means doing without oil. Controls on wood cutting do not by themselves make a forest-management policy. At the global level and over the longer term, they can be effective only if combined with other measures—paper recycling in the industrial countries, the use of more efficient wood stoves in the Third World, and, ultimately, efforts to halt population growth.

Not all programs for restoring the balance between human demands and the sustainable yield of the basic biological systems that satisfy these demands will be popular. On the demand side, programs aimed at slowing population growth and making more efficient use of resources are progressing far too slowly because they are not seen as serving the self-interest of the participants. On the supply side, governmental actions to assure a sustainable yield may raise prices of animal protein or forest products in the short run, even as they assure supplies over the long run. At the global level, overfishing, overgrazing, and deforestation all call for efforts to limit the harvest from these systems, but deforestation calls for a massive tree-planting effort as well.

Reforesting the Earth

Aside from family planning, few activities can contribute more to the evolution of a sustainable society than planting trees. As governments have come to recognize the multiple economic roles and ecological functions of forests, many have launched reforestation programs. Yet, for a number of reasons, the failures greatly outnumber the successes.

Often, the need for reforestation is recognized too late, only after protecting new plantings from fuel-hungry villagers and hungry cattle or goats has become well-nigh impossible. In some instances, inexperienced foresters plant species that are ill-adapted to local conditions. In others, the overall approach is ill-conceived, so the people involved often do not stand to benefit. One such case has been described by Erik Eckholm in *Losing Ground.*[38] In Ethiopia, a rural reforestation effort organized as a public works program was launched for the right reasons—to control soil erosion and eventually provide fuelwood supplies. Local villagers, many of them landless laborers, were paid low wages to plant trees. But whenever they were not supervised, these villagers planted the seedlings upside down to express their resentment of a feudal social structure in which the tree-planting program's ultimate benefits would accrue to the landlords.

Although the overall record is dismal, not all efforts at reforestation have fallen flat. Exciting successes in South Korea, Gujarat (one of India's western states), and China have not only kindled new hope among foresters and government planners, but have also featured innovations that may find wide use elsewhere in the world.[39]

In reforestation, South Korea has emerged as the model much as Israel has become the model for desert reclamation. Within a decade, the face of the Korean countryside has been transformed. As recently as 1970, South Korea was a barren, denuded country plagued by soil erosion. Its hillsides were eroded, and the land had lost most of its water-retention capacity. But as of 1977, some 643,000 hectares (roughly half the area in rice) had been planted to fast-growing pine trees.[40]

The keys to Korea's success have been the organization of the federally linked Village Forestry Associations and the direct participation by villagers in reforestation efforts. Through an association composed of a representative of each of its households, each participating village plants, tends, and harvests the woodlots without pay.[41] Harvested wood is distributed among households, and the proceeds from any marketable surplus are used to support other community development projects. The reforestation program's primary economic objective of producing enough firewood to satisfy the fuel needs of rural communities has been met. The economic gains are obvious to the villagers: the switch back to local wood supplies means they can now pocket the 15 percent of their income they were forced to spend on coal when firewood became scarce.

The Korean achievement is exciting. Even as ecological deterioration was reversed, a new national energy resource was created, all within a matter of years and all by combining seasonally idle labor and unused land. Capital inputs in the form of seedlings were minimal; the decisive factor was the organizational technique for mobilizing villagers.

Another community forestry success story is beginning to take shape in India in Gujarat. Several years ago the state forestry office began to see that existing forest reserves, however skillfully managed, could not begin to satisfy local firewood needs. In 1969, under the leadership of M. K. Dalvi, the government of Gujarat launched a village woodlot-development program, planting trees on roadside strips, irrigation canal banks, and other state-owned land.[42] The idea in each case was to let a nearby community take responsibility for managing the woodlots.

In an early evaluation, a state official, B. K. Jhala, reported that the "early roadside and canal bank plantations did not involve public participation to the degree that we hoped social forestry can achieve, but they nevertheless marked a critical psychological turning point. Seeing stands of trees arise on what had been desolate ground, people started to realize that forestry is possible around their communities and that trees can grow quickly."[43] Among other things, these new plantations began to alter the relationship between community residents and forestry department officials, from one of suspicion to one of cooperation.

Once local suspicions were overcome, the number of village tree plantations began to multiply. Erik Eckholm reports that within four years some 3,000 of the 18,000 Gujarati villages were participating in the program, and the number of villages involved continues to increase.[44] In 1978, nine years after the project's tentative beginnings, some 6,000 of the state's 17,000 kilometers of roadway and canals combined were lined with young trees. Each year, another 1,500 kilometers of tree plantings are to be added.[45] Within India, Gujarat leads the way in social forestry. But the model it provides serves not only for other Indian states, but other countries as well.

The story of China's forests also bears telling. Between 1949 and 1978, official figures show, China's forested area expanded from 5 percent of the country to 12.7 percent.[46] (Swedish forestry expert Reidar Persson estimates that China's forested area has increased from 30 to 60 million hectares over the last three decades.)[47] This upturn reflects China's massive mobilization of rural labor during the off season for reforestation and other efforts to reduce flooding and soil erosion, to increase the supply of firewood in rural areas, and to produce lumber for construction and industrial uses.

Governments are not alone in their efforts to reforest barren plains and denuded hillsides. The World Bank, the UN Food and Agricultural Organization, and the U.S. Agency for International Development are also involved. The World Bank, calculating both the ecological and economic costs of deforestation, now supports community-based forestry projects along with the commercial timber ventures it has traditionally backed in Third World countries. These projects are tailored to specific conditions in individual countries. In India, South Korea, and Malawi, the Bank is emphasizing firewood production through community woodlots and individual farm plantings.[48] In both India and Malawi, these investments in fire wood production have been wisely combined with a loan program for buyers of more fuel-efficient woodstoves.

In Nepal—where extensive deforestation is leading to flooding, soil erosion, and siltation downstream in the flood plains of Pakistan, India, and Bangladesh—World Bank investment in reforestation is designed to reforest the hills and arrest excessive runoff. A second objective is to create village woodlots.[49] If these prove successful, villagers would not have to substitute cow dung for scarce firewood at the expense of food production.

The Bank also supports noncommercial reforestation projects in Sahelian Africa to help halt the advance of the Sahara.[50] A loan has already been made to Niger to help expand its meager remaining forested area. Other loans earmarked for similar purposes are under consideration for Mali, Upper Volta, and other Sahelian countries.

The World Bank is supporting yet another approach in northern Turkey, where an extensive tract of valuable forest is largely inaccessible. The Bank plans to underwrite the construction of a 26,000 kilometer road network that should permit the more effective use of the forest, take the pressure off other regions, and allow for the forestation of some wasteland areas with fast-growing species.[51]

The strength of the World Bank's commitment can be seen in its long-term lending trend. Between 1968 and 1977, forestry lending increased roughly tenfold, from about $10 million to $100 million per year.[52] Another fivefold increase is slated between 1979 and 1983, by which time annual lending should reach a half billion dollars, and Bank-sponsored forestry projects should be under way in some 40 to 50 Third World countries.

With increased interest in local forestation and reforestation over the last decade, both governments and scientific organizations have begun to identify the species with the most potential in the neediest regions. Among the most promising possibilities is the plant family *Leguminosae*, which contains some 18,000 different species of legumes, only about 20 of which are widely cultivated. FAO forester Michael Arnold describes one *Leguminosae* tree shrub, *Callindar callothyrsus*, that "sprouts and coppices so vigorously that it can be harvested as early as at the end of the first year."[53] Noel Vietmeyer of the U.S.

National Academy of Sciences reports that this tree can be harvested annually for up to 15 years, providing some 35 to 65 cubic meters of wood per hectare.[54] In Java, some 30,000 hectares of this spectacularly fast-growing tree have been established in local firewood plantations.

Perhaps the most promising of the woody legumes is the *Leucaena leucocephala* or "ipil-ipil," now widely planted in the Philippines. These trees can reach the height of a three-story building in two years and a six-story building in six to eight, and they can produce 30 to 50 cubic meters of wood per hectare annually. According to Vietmeyer, one exceptionally vigorous stand in the Philippines actually produced 100 cubic meters per hectare per year, a marvel even compared to the world's fastest growing trees.[55] (A well-managed pine plantation in the temperate zone, says Vietmeyer, produces only about a tenth as much wood.) The ipil-ipil tree also fixes nitrogen, making it ideal for revegetating eroded hillsides in the tropics. Its nitrogen-rich leaves provide nutritious forage for cattle and an excellent compost for crops.

Along with these biological "discoveries," the new concepts of community forestry, agroforestry, and village woodlots are altering traditional forestry. Indeed, the World Forestry Conference held in 1978 in Jakarta may well have been a turning point for the forestry profession. At this "Forests for People" congress the FAO director general Edouard Saouma noted that while community-based forestry was "still in its infancy," it represented an important new approach to satisfying basic human needs. He also warned the international assemblage of professional foresters that the new forestry "introduces problems which are far removed from your traditional training."[56] In the past, foresters have worked largely with trees. The relatively infrequent human contact was with poachers. But with the advent of community forestry, the compelling need is to work cooperatively with all those whose interests lie in the output of forest products.

One keystone of the new forestry is making wiser use of existing forests. In the United States, for example, many forests in New England and Appalachia are not harvested at all. Nationwide, only a minor share of the forested area, much of it privately owned, is managed to maximize its yield. Both harvesting those neglected forests that are not reserves, parks, or protected wildlife habitats and maximizing sustainable yields will lessen pressure on forests elsewhere, particularly in the Third World.

The potential for agroforestry (the cultivation of trees, often on land not suitable for crops) is in some parts of the world enormous. Indian environmentalist Shankar Ranganathan estimates that some 40 to 50 million hectares of degraded land in India is suitable for agroforestry.[57] Converting this land to forests could, he contends, provide millions of jobs and sizably increase India's gross national product. Here again, such a program would combine unemployed labor and unused land, creating a productive resource.

The forces behind the annual loss of some 6,000 square miles of forest land per year, most of it in the developing countries, have already gathered considerable momentum. Encouraging signs that this trend can be arrested do crop up here and there, but overall the pressures continue to mount. However ambitious and successful reforestation projects are, they cannot in themselves restore a stable balance between people and forests. But pursued along with the use of more efficient wood stoves, the adoption of paper-recycling programs, and the spread of family planning services, they can do so.

Preserving the Web of Life

Cutting across the threats to biological systems is the potential loss of innumerable plant and animal species that help make up the web of life. In a world that now has over four billion demanding human inhabitants, preserving other forms of life is no longer a simple matter. As species specialist Norman Myers notes, "When water bodies are fouled and the atmosphere is treated as a garbage can, we can always clean up the pollution. Species extinction is final. Moreover, the impoverishment of life on earth falls not only on present society, but on all generations to come."[58]

Hunting and the discharge of toxic materials both contribute to the loss of species, but the destruction of habitats is the overriding concern at this late hour. With a biological massacre in prospect, the value of such measures as the U.S. Endangered Species Act and the establishment of parks and wildlife sanctuaries is becoming evident. Unfortunately, measures of this sort are no longer sufficient, partly because they focus more on the symptoms than on causes.

Fortunately, these limited approaches to protecting species are not the only ones at our disposal. Since the issue is more fundamental than can be addressed by a ban or quota on the killing of forms of wildlife prized by hunters, tailors, or furriers, so is the solution. Indeed, reform must be aimed at modern materialism and human reproductive habits. If human population growth continues indefinitely and if materialism is pursued beyond the point at which it bears any positive relationship to well-being, then the pending biological massacre may be unavoidable.

At the international level, some encouraging initiatives have been launched in recent years. One, the Convention on International Trade in Endangered Species of Wild Fauna and Flora, came into effect in 1975. Although confined to trade policy, it provides a significant instrument for the endangered species of animal wildlife. The key to achieving the agreement's full potential, though, is getting many countries that have not yet signed to cooperate.

As efforts to protect endangered species have evolved, it has become clear that a species-by-species approach to protection is no longer adequate. It is equally clear that we can no longer hope to save all species. Biologist Thomas Lovejoy believes that we should now make the difficult decisions that battlefield commanders do, deciding which casualties to try to save and which to abandon.[59] Since saving everything is impossible, the reasoning goes, net losses would be minimized if the species whose prospects look bleakest were left to disappear and if all available energies and resources were concentrated on the most important that remain. In any case, available resources can be more effective if they are focused on the preservation of habitats. Thus, UNESCO's decision to organize a worldwide network of ecological protectorates—"Biosphere Reserves"—in which extant species can be preserved in their native habitats is pivotal. As of mid-1978, 35 countries had committed a total of 144 areas that encompass a wide cross-section of the planet's biological diversity.[60]

As concerns over potential biological impoverishment mount, it is becoming obvious that protection programs should be focused where the richest concentrations of plant and animal life are—the tropical and subtropical regions of the developing countries. This fact has as much political as biological significance since most of the countries needing to make the greatest efforts to conserve their indigenous flora and fauna are those that can least afford to do so. In a Worldwatch Paper on endangered species, Erik Eckholm contends that "this predicament could be at least partially untangled through the international sharing of the costs of habitat protection by which wealthier nations would contribute to conservation-related expenses in poorer countries. If the world's extant species and gene pools are the priceless heritage of all humanity, then people everywhere need to share the burden of conservation according to their ability to do so."[61]

As the eighties begin, a few governments in affluent industrial countries are beginning to help the Third World countries that are attempting to develop a conservation infrastructure. In addition, the World Wildlife Fund, the International Union for the Conservation of Nature, the Nature Conservancy, the New York Zoological Society, and other private groups are providing both technical and capital assistance to countries interested in setting up wildlife preserves and parks.

These governmental and private efforts aside, responding quickly and fully to the threat of species extinction is still difficult given the lack of public understanding. Raising funds and generating publicity to save the whales or the whooping cranes is easy enough, but mobilizing support for thousands or even millions of less glamorous, though not necessarily less important, species is another proposition altogether. These broader, more comprehensive, more essential efforts do not lend themselves to sloganism. Only when economic planners and political leaders understand that biological impoverishment ultimately leads to economic impoverishment will an effective strategy evolve, one that deals with causal factors, not merely symptoms.

Beyond the Throwaway Society

The throwaway society evolved when energy was cheap, raw materials were abundant, and when far fewer people were competing for resources than do today. But, with origins in a bygone era, the days of the throwaway society are numbered. Societies that fail to adjust to this reality are likely to pay with a falling standard of living.

In modern industrial economies, materials such as metal, glass, and paper are often discarded after a single use. As a result, the world's high-grade ores are being exhausted, urban waste disposal sites are becoming scarce, and pollution is exceeding tolerance levels in many communities. At the same time, the wasteful use of materials is promoting double-digit inflation.

The throwaway society operates on the principle of planned obsolescence, a concept introduced by the automobile industry. In the industry's early years, competition led to price wars and to product improvements. Henry Ford worked diligently to perfect his Model T, permitting only those year-to-year changes that improved the car's performance and durability. Wary of frivolous change, he was thus able to lower the Model T's price from $780 to $290 over a 15-year period.[62] Left behind in this price competition, other manufacturers, led by General Motors, hit upon the idea of making annual style changes. By introducing new models each year, Detroit made those produced in earlier years appear out of fashion and less desirable.

The clothing industry, almost by definition "fashion conscious," puts even trend-enslaved Detroit to shame. Each year's collar, hemline, and lapel is calculated to make those of preceding years appear to be outmoded. By forecasting the new designs and colors for the coming season, clothing manufacturers not only shape consumer tastes and buying habits, they also dictate that millions of serviceable garments made of precious natural fibers and oil-based synthetics are retired from use for no good reason.

The appeal of convenience too has played a role in the evolution of the throwaway society. Prepared foods come packaged in aluminum ovenproof containers that can be thrown out instead of washed. Paper towels replace kitchen towels that need laundering. One novelty-crazed firm even designed a plastic throwaway camera that came loaded with film. The camera had to be returned to the manufacturer when it came time for the film to be developed. To extract the film, the manufacturer broke open the camera and then discarded it.[63]

Too often, governments have abetted industry efforts to discourage the reuse and recycling of materials. In the United States, policies adopted during the nineteenth century to encourage the development of fledgling industries have long outlived their usefulness. Mining and forest-product industries still enjoy anachronistic extraction allowances comparable to the depletion allowance the oil industry receives.[64]

Throwing away materials after a single use also means throwing away energy. Conversely, recycling materials increases an economy's energy efficiency and health. Consider a few examples of the savings possible. The energy required to recycle aluminum is only 4 percent of that required to produce it from bauxite, the original raw material, while the energy required to recycle copper is only a tenth that used to produce the original material.[65] For steel produced entirely from scrap, the saving amounts to some 47 percent. Recycling newsprint saves 23 percent of the energy embodied in the product and also reduces the pressure on forests: a ton of recycled newsprint saves a ton of wood, a dozen trees. Recycling glass containers saves 8 percent, but returnable glass containers, of course, save far more energy.

A materials-conservation policy based on recycling reduces inflationary pressures at their source. Robert Fuller, author of a Worldwatch Paper analyzing global inflationary pressures, points out that "an examination of the city dump may reveal as much about the causes of inflation as does all the theorizing of monetary analysts."[66] There, he says, one finds "innumerable signs of profligacy and waste, the debris of our affluent, consumerist, throwaway societies. The inventory ranges from junked cars and furniture to thousands of cans and bottles, the archetypal litter of modern times."

Besides curbing inflation, abandoning our throwaway mentality will also alleviate waste-disposal problems. In the United States, nearly one ton of solid waste per person is collected annually from residential, industrial, and institutional sources. At present, some 14,000 landfills and other disposal sites on some 476,000 acres are in use.[67] Yet, this Rhode Island-sized dump isn't enough. Each year, several hundred new sites must be found to absorb the ever swelling flow of waste.

Although advertising may blind us to the fact, planned obsolescence can also be fought on aesthetic grounds. Not many heirlooms will be found among the consumer durables produced today. Pride of craftsmanship has all but disappeared in the drive to produce goods that wear out or lose their appeal quickly. Many modern home appliances cannot be repaired, even though it makes no sense to scrap the whole when only a part is broken. Yet, ironically, the engineering techniques and materials needed to design superdurable consumer goods are at hand.

Once the decision is made to reuse, recycle, and repair, the problem of waste should be tackled at its source in homes, offices, and factories and at large resource-recovery centers where trash is assembled. Separating materials at their source holds many advantages. In the case of paper, it keeps soiling at a minimum. In Sweden, which has both a generous endowment of forest resources and a large forest product export industry, legislation now requires waste paper to be separated from garbage in individual homes, businesses, and offices.[68] Source separation also permits individual home owners to separate out kitchen refuse, leaves, and other organic materials for composting. A backyard compost heap both reduces the amount of garbage to be hauled away and provides a rich organic fertilizer for gardening. This in turn reduces the need to purchase costly energy-intensive chemical fertilizers. If used to produce vegetables, the compost heap may help shoppers reduce the frequency of trips to the supermarket during the growing season.

A less tangible benefit of source separation is the sense of participation that it provides individuals. As Brian Hammond writes in the *New Scientist*, "In an increasingly impersonal world in which political and economic events seem as arbitrary and unalterable as the weather, many of us feel remote from the real levers of power. At the individual level, recycling systems give us the chance to help to exercise control over at least one section of the whole complex and bewildering macroeconomy."[69]

Where source separation is not feasible, resource-recovery centers provide an alternative. Typical of these centers is one planned for Leningrad. Although the city of 4.3 million now has a facility that processes 580,000 tons of garbage per year, a new plant scheduled to be operational by 1985 will be several times larger. This alternative is not, however, without its drawbacks.[70] To be economical, such centers must be large and involve hundreds of trucks that create noise, odors, and traffic congestion.

In some of the Third World's major cities, garbage is carefully sorted by hand. In Cairo, most of the constituents of garbage are reused. As Denis Hayes wrote in a Worldwatch Paper on recycling, workers "remove tin, glass, paper, plastic, rags, and bones from the refuse and forward these materials to factories and other markets within the city. They extract about 2,000 tons of paper a month that is reprocessed into some 1,500 tons of recycled paper and cardboard. Cotton and wool rags are converted into upholstery and blankets; metals are converted into new implements; even bones are used to make such things as glue, paints, and high-grade carbon for sugar refining. Most organic wastes are fed to pigs; the rest is converted into compost."[71] In a society plagued with unemployment, this approach certainly makes more sense than the high-technology resource recovery centers used in cities in industrial countries.

Ultimately, the solution to the waste problem is to reduce the amount of materials wasted. Container legislation is one step in this direction, whether its form be mandatory deposits on returnable bottles or absolute bans on nonreturnable containers. In the United States, the Environmental Protection Agency estimates, national returnable bottle legislation would save annually some 500,000 tons of aluminum, 1.5 million tons of steel, and 5.2 million tons of glass.[72] These savings would in turn reduce by 46 million barrels the oil consumed in the US each year—by enough, that is, to equal almost eight days of oil imports at 1980 levels.

Besides cutting the volume of garbage down to size, enacting returnable bottle legislation also reduces roadside litter. Michigan, Maine, Washington and other U.S. states that have passed returnable bottle legislation all report a substantial reduction in litter.

One of the most imaginative approaches to the container problem is one being explored in Denmark, where beverage container design would be standardized with, say, five standard sizes, that would cover the range of common needs. If fruit juices, milk, beer, or even wine came in the same bottles, bottle recovery would be greatly simplified. All bottlers would draw on a common inventory of containers, changing labels or brands with the contents. If this inventory were controlled by an economy-wide computer system, transportation as well as manufacturing energy would be sharply reduced too.

In an era of costly energy, the extent to which a country recycles raw materials influences its industrial strength and competitive position in the world market. In Japan, a high-strung industrial economy that must import almost all the oil it uses, the proportion of waste materials recycled increased from 16 to 48 percent between 1974 and 1978.[73] The Japanese automobile industry has benefited particularly from Japan's recycling effort. It recycles not only indigenous scrap but also imported scrap, much of it purchased from the United States. "This year's Toyota," the quip goes, "is last year's Buick." The use of recycled metal is but one of the many components in the farsighted strategy that has enabled Japan to displace the United States as the world's leading automobile producer. In contrast, the ailing U.K. economy has made very little progress in increasing consumer waste recycling. For steel, the figure is 10 percent; for paper, an estimated 15 to 30 percent; and for glass containers, 3 percent.[74] Unlike more economically dynamic Japan, it still dumps close to 90 percent of all consumer waste into local landfills.

In East Germany, which imports two-thirds of its raw materials, the prices paid for metals, glass, and paper at the government-run recycling centers have been increased sharply to encourage recycling. In early 1980, the price of recycled newspapers was tripled, that of old books was doubled, and the price of a glass jar was increased sixfold, from 5¢ to 30¢.[75] Following the price increases, long lines formed at the country's 11,000 collection points. Now, ordinary citizens will help meet the national goal of becoming increasingly self-sufficient in raw materials and relying largely on continuously recycled raw materials rather than on imported virgin materials.

In environmentally conscious Norway, a deposit program encourages the recycling of automobiles. When a car is purchased, the buyers pay a $100 refundable deposit that they can collect along with a $100 premium at authorized resource recovery centers when the car wears out.[76] Adopted in 1978, the success of the program is making other countries take notice.

The challenge confronting governments everywhere is the same: how to maintain and improve living standards while using less energy and material resources. The details remain to be worked out, but it is clear that consumer well-being must be related more to the quality of the existing inventory of goods and less to the rate of turnover. In a sustainable society, durability and recycling replace planned obsolescence as the economy's organizing principle, and virgin materials are seen not as a primary source of material but as a supplement to the existing stock.

Conserving Energy

One key to the evolution of a sustainable society is the conservation of energy, particularly that from petroleum. Fortunately, as energy has become more costly, interest in conservation has intensified. Indeed, the progressive lowering in recent years of projected U.S. energy demand for the end of the century bears out conservation's rise from a minor household virtue to a major national economic opportunity.

Prior to the Arab oil-export embargo in 1972, projections of

U.S. energy consumption for the year 2000 ranged from a low of 124 quads (quadrillion BTUs) by energy analyst Amory Lovins to 190 quads by the Federal Power Commission. (See Table 8-1.) These figures compare with a 1979 U.S. energy consumption of 78 quads. Since 1972, estimates have been consistently lowered across the spectrum, regardless of whether the analyst's bias is toward conservation or supply expansion. By 1980, Exxon was forecasting that U.S. consumption at century's end would be only 105 quads, and one office of the Department of Energy had projected, at the low end of a set of projections, a low-energy, high-efficiency energy budget that would require only 57 quads by the year 2000, a figure 26 percent below 1979 consumption.

The potential for conserving energy in the United States is enormous, partly because the amount of waste is also enormous

Table 8-1. Downward Drift of Projected U.S. Energy Demand in 2000

Year of Forecast	Source of Projection	High Range	Low Range
		(quadrillion BTUs)	
1972	Federal Power Commission	190	
	Amory Lovins, Friends of the Earth		124
1974	Edison Electric Institute	160	
	Ford Foundation (Zero Energy Growth Scenario)		100
1976	Edison Electric Institute	140	
	Amory Lovins		75
1980	Exxon Corporation	105	
	U.S. Department of Energy (Low Energy Growth Scenario)		57

Source: Adapted from Amory Lovins and updated by Worldwatch Institute.

and partly because the United States has the technology and engineering wherewithal needed to increase the economy's energy efficiency. As the eighties began, even some of the organizations traditionally cautious about potential gains in energy efficiency had raised their sights dramatically. In 1980 the National Academy of Sciences, for example, sketched out several scenarios for U.S. energy use in 2010. In two of these consumption would range as low as 58 and 74 quads—projections that only a few years ago would have been viewed as heresy.[77]

In the United States, even such production-oriented organizations as the National Petroleum Council, Exxon, and the Petroleum Industry Research Foundation were by 1980 announcing that U.S. oil consumption had peaked in 1978 and would never again regain that level. In early 1980, the Petroleum Industry Research Foundation projected that U.S. oil consumption would drop 5 percent during the eighties and that gasoline demand would drop by 20 percent. In 1981, the National Petroleum Council was projecting an even greater decline in oil consumption of 10 percent by 1990. Even these lowered projections may prove to be on the high side.[78]

These projections for the U.S. economy indicate, among other things, that the link between the Gross National Product and energy use is not nearly as tight as once thought. Until recently, GNP and energy use had always increased in tandem, so people wrongly assumed that the two could not be disassociated. But what recent experience and some of the projections show is that it is quite possible that the Gross National Product can increase over the remainder of this century even as energy use declines.

In the United States and other industrial countries, where "thinking big" has been the norm, the potential for conserving energy is almost endless. In examining the merits of manipulating production versus manipulating conservation to achieve a satisfactory energy balance, Daniel Yergin, co-author of *Energy*

Future, notes that "it is certainly easier for the government to organize itself to do one big thing, but, alas, that is not what productive conservation is about. It involves 50,000 or 50 million things, big, medium, and little, and not in the one centralized place where the energy is produced, but in the decentralized milieu where it is consumed."[79]

While the U.S. may have the greatest potential for energy conservation, other industrial countries can also benefit from conservation programs. A summary of energy policies in the OECD countries notes that by 1985–90 some countries might be able to save more than 10 percent of the energy now consumed per unit of industrial output.[80] In the residential commercial sector 40 percent of the energy used in existing buildings could be saved through conservation measures, and well-built new buildings might well use less than half the energy of present stock. By improving automobile fuel efficiency, fuel consumption in the transport sector could be cut by 10 to 20 percent.

In the Third World, extolled in early literature on the world energy crisis as frugal because it had such low energy use per capita, the energy problem has different dimensions. But in character it is much the same—wasteful. A large share of the primary energy used in the Third World is wasted, principally in the inefficient use of fuel wood for cooking. Indeed, according to some estimates, as much as 90 percent of the energy used for cooking in the Third World is wasted. Yet, doing nothing more than shifting food from an open fire to a closed, more efficiently designed cook stove made of local materials could cut firewood use by an estimated 50 percent.[81]

In both the developing and the industrial worlds, actions to conserve energy are essentially of two kinds. The first approach is simply to carry out our present activities more efficiently. For example, if we want to heat a building to maintain a given temperature but with less energy, we insulate the building. The second approach to conserving energy is to curtail some activities—driving less for example. Intermediate cases do make up most of the opportunities at hand. For example, commuting from home to work in a bus instead of a car saves energy and, in some cases, permits travel along exactly the same route.

To affect either of these types of actions, governments have resorted to three public policy tools: information or exhortation, regulation, and financial incentives or disincentives. The first involves encouraging constructive action by providing people with the facts they need to make sensible social and financial decisions. President Carter took this approach in 1979 when he urged Americans to turn their thermostats down in the winter and turn them up during the summer.

Some of the most impressive energy savings have occurred as a result of regulations. The most publicly visible example in the United States is probably the regulatory effort to save automobile fuel. Both the fuel-efficiency standards that American automobile manufacturers must now meet and the 55 mile per hour speed limit are contributing to hefty savings in gasoline. The Japanese have also applied mandatory fuel-efficiency standards to hold down gasoline consumption.[82]

The third approach to energy conservation is the use of financial incentives or disincentives. The high tax on gasoline, exceeding a dollar a gallon in some West European countries, has effectively discouraged the purchase and manufacture of gas-guzzling automobiles. (See Table 8-2.) By the same token, the efficiency of the existing automobile fleets in the United States and Canada, where the gasoline tax is trivial by comparison, leaves much to be desired.

As energy supplies have tightened, governments have begun to set conservation goals. In some sectors, such as transportation, buildings, and household appliances, governments can set energy-efficiency standards. In the United States, the Energy Policy and Conservation Act of 1975 set a timetable for increasing the average fuel efficiency of new automobiles sold, raising the fleet average from some 14 miles per gallon in 1974

Table 8–2. Price, Including Tax, of Regular Gasoline in Selected
Countries, Early 1981

Country	Price (Tax)
	(dollars)
Brazil	2.52 (.99)
East Germany	2.65 (none)
France	2.65 (1.43)
India	2.72 (n.a.)
Japan	2.74 (1.02)
Tanzania	3.78 (n.a.)
United States	1.35 (.14)
West Germany	2.35 (1.05)

Source: Department of Energy; Central Intelligence Agency; Embassies of the German Democratic Republic, India, and Tanzania.

to 27.5 by 1985. Interestingly, the fuel efficiency of American-made cars sold in the United States, abetted by sharply higher gasoline prices, is rising well above the standard. When combined with those realized by the more fuel-efficient imported cars, the improvement is even more impressive. Other countries, including Australia, Canada, Sweden, and the United Kingdom have outlined voluntary fuel economy goals for automobiles to encourage the production of increasingly efficient cars in the eighties.[83]

With buildings, as with automobiles, thermal efficiency standards are being set in the United States. As of early 1981, Congress was debating the U.S. Department of Energy plans to issue energy-efficiency standards for buildings. But even much-needed Building Energy Performance Standards will not help the existing stock. Since on the average it takes close to a century for the building stock to turn over, large short-term gains in the thermal efficiency of buildings can be achieved only through retrofitting. Incentives for retrofitting have been offered by national programs that include grants and loans. According to the OECD 1979 Review of Energy Policies and Programs, Canada, Germany, the Netherlands, and Sweden now apply such programs at least to pre-1960 buildings and in some cases to the entire building stock.[84]

Physicists Robert H. Williams of Princeton and Marc H. Ross of the University of Michigan believe that the amount of fuel used for space heating in the United States could be cut in half if relatively simple improvements were made in buildings, innovative financing procedures were adopted, and realistic economic criteria set forth.[85] They propose an all-out campaign to increase the thermal efficiency of housing by installing storm windows, wall insulation, floor insulation, extra attic insulation, and other weatherization measures. Using life-cycle costing techniques, they calculate that many such investments are now financially attractive.

Williams and Ross also recommend that the nation's housing stock be systematically audited, and they lament that so few trained energy auditors or "house doctors" are available to take on the job. In general, these physicists contend, building owners do not have the financial information they need to make wise investments in conservation or to design an optimal housing retrofit. Since simple "hole plugging" and relatively straightforward architectural modifications are all that is needed to eliminate most substantial heat losses, taking the approach Williams and Ross recommend is essentially substituting intelligence for oil.

Energy-efficiency standards for appliances ought to be another high priority, given that refrigerators, stoves, water heaters, clothes dryers, furnaces, air conditioners, and the like account for 75 percent of all residential energy use. In the United States, preliminary standards were issued in mid-1980. At that time the Assistant Secretary of Energy Thomas Stelson estimated that applying these standards would save cumulatively the equivalent of 4.28 billion barrels of oil by 2005 if they took hold in preliminary form immediately and were fully phased in by early 1986.[86]

Critical as efficiency standards are, they represent only one small part of the conservation potential. Indeed, one reason projected U.S. energy demand has been dropping so dramatically is that the various efforts to conserve energy reinforce each other, acting as conservation "multipliers." For example, in a matter of years fuel-efficiency standards for automobiles could double the number of miles per gallon, even as carpooling expanded substantially and raised the average number of occupants in an automobile from 1.6 to 2.0. If at the same time people become more energy conscious as they establish residences and accept jobs, so that the distance from home to work declines, fuel use would decline faster still. Indeed, if increased mileage efficiency resulted in savings of 50 percent, increased automobile occupancy in savings of 20 percent, and a greater proximity to work in savings of 5 percent—all reasonable figures—automobile fuel consumption would drop by a phenomenal 62 percent. And all this without any voluntary curtailment of driving or shifts to more fuel-efficient public transport!

Residential heating and cooling is just as ripe for the efficiency multiplier effect as transportation is. For example, insulating a house to increase its thermal efficiency can reduce the heating and cooling requirements by 40 percent. Installing a day/night thermostat can reduce fuel requirements by 10 percent, and turning off the heat and air conditioning in an unused guest room, another 10 percent. Together, these reductions—none of which is at all outlandish—would reduce residential heating and cooling requirements by over half.

The potential contribution modern technology and engineering know-how can make to energy conservation has scarcely been tapped. We know, for example, that there are already standard-sized T.V. sets that use less electricity than a 60-watt light bulb does, and that some modern office buildings are so thermally efficient that interior lighting and the body heat of their occupants provide all the space heating needed. Prototypical automobiles travel 80 miles per gallon on fuel.[87] Only a few of the possibilities for energy conservation that modern technology has already made possible, these energy-savers represent the first offspring of the promising applied science of conservation and embody the hope that advanced technology can be substituted for energy.

9

Renewable Energy: Turning to the Sun

Prior to the age of fossil fuels, solar energy was humanity's sole source of heat, light, and mechanical energy. Wood was the principal fuel. Wind and water power were used to pump water, grind grain, and saw wood. Now that reserves of oil and gas are dwindling, constraints on the use of coal are growing, and nuclear power's future is in doubt, solar or "renewable" energy is making a comeback in both new and familiar forms.

New technologies and adaptations of traditional ones permit solar energy to be harnessed in innumerable ways. It can be captured directly through such devices as windmills, hydroelectric generators, rooftop collectors, photovoltaic cells, and buildings incorporating solar architecture, or indirectly through forests, fuelwood plantations, and energy crops. In addition, geothermal energy, available on such a vast scale that it can be considered renewable, holds great promise. In whatever form, these new energy sources and technologies must be developed quickly if national economies are to prosper in the post-petroleum age.

While each country's energy-development strategy must be tailored to its indigenous endowment of solar energy resources and while no two countries have precisely the same endowment, no nation is without solar potential. Some countries may end up relying heavily on a single, locally abundant form of solar energy; others may have highly diversified "solar economies." For example, Norway, Nepal, and Paraguay, all richly endowed with hydroelectric potential relative to population, could rely heavily on electricity. Heavily forested countries, in contrast, could fashion an energy strategy centered around wood. For a few countries, the United States among them, the wise course is to develop the entire panoply of renewable energy sources—wood, wind, hydro, solar collectors, livestock waste, energy crops, geothermal power, and photovoltaics.

Wood as a Fuel

Before the 1973 oil price rise, wood's share of the global energy budget was shrinking. In almost all countries, its importance was declining relative to that of other fuels, and in many countries its use was declining in absolute terms as well. In the industrial countries, wood was almost entirely abandoned as a fuel during the era of cheap oil. Within the Third World, a combination of cheap postwar oil, rapid urbanization, and deforestation diminished wood's relative importance as a fuel. Nonetheless, in many countries, it wholly dominates the energy budget.

With the surge in oil prices since 1973, wood began making a strong comeback. Used not only for cooking and heating, wood is also a suitable fuel for industrial process heat and for generating electricity. Within the developing countries, wood's many uses translate into extra pressure on local forest resources. In some, they also translate into a strong interest in wood-fuel plantations.

Within the industrial countries, particularly those with abundant forest resources, the use of wood fuel has increased dramatically since 1973. Nowhere is this more evident than in the United States, where wood has eclipsed nuclear power in the national energy budget.[1] By 1981, close to a tenth of all U.S. residences were burning wood as either a primary or secondary source of heat. An estimated eight million wood stoves and furnaces were being used for residential heating in the United States. (See Table 9-1.) The shift to wood use was most dramatic in New England, though it was plainly evident in Appalachia, the Great Lakes States, the Northwest, and other heavily wooded areas. In Vermont, New Hampshire, and Maine, 20 percent of all homes were burning wood as the primary source of heat by 1980.[2] In two-thirds of the remaining homes, wood provided a secondary source of heat. So swift, in fact, was the conversion that the revived stove- and furnace-manufacturing industry was swamped by demand.[3]

Hardhit by soaring oil costs, U.S. industries also began looking at wood as a possible alternative fuel. As of late 1979, some 150 businesses in New England—from paper producers to

Table 9-1. U.S. Sales of Residential Wood Stoves & Furnaces, 1972–80

Year	Annual Sales	Cumulative Sales
1972	160,000	160,000
1973	210,000	370,000
1974	340,000	710,000
1975	760,000	1,470,000
1976	670,000	2,140,000
1977	1,030,000	3,170,000
1978	1,200,000	4,370,000
1979	1,500,000	5,870,000
1980 (prel.)	1,100,000	6,970,000

Source: Booz, Allen & Hamilton for U.S. Department of Energy.

horticulturists—had switched from oil to wood.[4] Nationwide, the pulp and paper industry met over half of its energy needs with wood waste in 1980, up from 40 percent in 1972, the last year before the oil price hike.[5]

To the north, the Canadian government launched a $150 million five-year program in 1978 to encourage industry to burn wood wastes instead of oil or gas.[6] In Finland, where the forest-products industry dominates both the economy and exports, the government is also pressing for the greater use of wood, particularly waste wood, so as to reduce the need for imported oil.[7] In the Brazilian Amazon, U.S. billionaire Daniel Ludwig's vast Jari project was burning waste wood for heat to run its wood fiber plant and to provide electricity both for the giant industrial complex itself and for Jari's 20,000-member community of workers and families.[8]

In some tropical countries, fast-growing trees are providing industry with energy. In the Philippines, for example, wood-generated electricity figures prominently in long-term energy plans. Each year from 1981 to 1984, the National Electrification Administration plans to invest in 200 megawatts of new wood-fired capacity.[9] The electrical plants will rely on the yield of some 66,000 hectares of land planted with ipil-ipil. The Brazilian steel industry, eleventh largest in the world, smelts 40 percent of its steel with charcoal.[10] A Japanese steel producer in the Philippines is investing in plantings of ipil-ipil as a source of charcoal for fuel.[11] Other countries such as Uganda use wood to fire cement kilns.[12]

South Korea's highly successful tree planting program of the seventies had as its prime objective fuelwood production. According to Bong Won Ahn, a Seoul official who helped plan the village forestry program, "The fuel wood component of our forestry program is essentially finished. . . . By the early eighties, when increasing amounts of wood will be harvested from the new plantations, our rural fuel problems will be largely solved."[13]

Within the United States and other industrial countries, the risk associated with the wood revival is that soaring firewood demand could lead to clearcutting and to progressive deforestation of the sort that has plagued much of the Third World. The challenge is to manage forests on a sustainable-yield basis, thus ensuring a lasting supply of wood for fuel purposes, creating local employment, and increasing the forested land's commercial value.

Scores of governments are coming to see forests as among the most efficient means of converting sunlight into usable energy and of supplementing wind and other forms of solar energy that are not available at all times of the day or year. But how rapidly wood's long-term potential as fuel is realized will depend in part on how ably forests are managed. Obvious as this may seem, the implied social challenge is immense given the mounting pressures on local wood supplies. Certainly, one determinant of wood's long-term potential as a fuel will be the growth in energy plantations. While more trees are being planted than ever before, worldwide tree-planting efforts are far from being strong enough to satisfy the longer-term growth in demand.

In the years immediately ahead, the most rapid growth in the use of wood as a fuel is likely to occur in the United States and in other countries where forest growth dwarfs the current harvest. Indeed, by U.S. Office of Technology Assessment estimates, U.S. fuelwood use could multiply sevenfold without depriving the wood products industry of its raw materials.[14] Over the longer term, as deforested areas are replanted and as plantings mature and begin to yield, fuelwood growth likely will be concentrated in the Third World where energy needs are greatest.

Energy from Waste

With fuel costs escalating and combustible wastes accumulating, interest in converting waste products into usable energy is gathering force. While organic waste can be converted into useful energy by various processes, most promising are direct combustion and the conversion of such waste into alcohol, methane, or other storable fuels.

One of the world's most developed waste-to-energy programs is that for converting urban garbage to electricity. Some 20 years ago, European cities faced with waste-disposal problems began exploring the possibility of burning garbage to produce electricity. German experience in burning damp fuel, such as lignite or brown coal, made it relatively easy to adapt the lignite-burning technology to urban waste. As a result, three-fourths of the 262 plants that as of 1978 were converting urban garbage into energy are located in Europe.[15] Most of the remainder are in Japan, while only six are in service in the United States.

Munich, a model city from this perspective, derives some 12 percent of its electricity from garbage and other local wastes.[16] Some of the world's largest refuse-burning plants lie on the outskirts of Paris, where each year they burn 1.7 million tons of the city's garbage in the production of steam. That steam, which both generates electricity and heats buildings, substitutes for an estimated 480,000 barrels of imported oil each year. Not far away, near Rotterdam, the world's largest single waste-burning facility burns over a million tons of waste annually to fuel a 55-megawatt electrical generating plant.

As fuel costs escalate and as waste-disposal problems become harder to manage, more cities will likely follow the European model, turning garbage into useful energy. Already, the European firms that have pioneered and perfected the technologies for converting urban waste into electricity are aggressively marketing their plants abroad. For many urban political leaders and planners, the attraction of simultaneously reducing electrical generating costs and alleviating the garbage-disposal problem may prove irresistible.

Within industry, the extent to which combustible waste products are converted into usable energy varies widely. The forest-products industry has long made extensive use of wood wastes for fuel, in some cases to produce process steam, in others to generate electricity. As oil prices have climbed, the industry has more and more turned to wood wastes. So too, the sugar industry has channelled some of its by-products into energy production. Bagasse, the fibrous residue that remains once sugar is extracted from sugarcane, is commonly used to fuel sugar refineries. In some countries, food processors are beginning to convert such waste by-products as cheese whey, citrus wastes, and vegetable-processing wastes into fuel-grade alcohol. By U.S. Department of Energy estimates, it is now economically feasible to convert four-fifths of all such U.S. wastes into alcohol for a net gain of 500 million gallons of ethanol per year, or one-half of 1 percent of 1980 gasoline consumption.[17]

On the farm, livestock manure and other agricultural wastes represent a potentially huge and self-replenishing source of energy. Cow dung serves as fuel for cooking in deforested parts of the Third World, even as buffalo chips were once used on the American Great Plains for both cooking and heat. More novel technologies for converting livestock manure into methane on a large scale have also been developed within recent decades.

One such process involves fermenting livestock manure in an air-tight digester to produce methane, also known as natural gas. Converting livestock manure into this blend, rather than burning it directly, yields more energy and also produces a nutrient-rich sludge that can be used as a fertilizer. Before this process was developed, livestock manure could be used for fertilizer or for fuel, but not for both.

This double use of livestock manure on a large scale was pioneered in China. As early as 1974, Sichuan Province had 30,000 methane digesters in operation.[18] By the late seventies, the technology had spread throughout China's other southern provinces, and by 1978 some seven million methane digesters were in use nationwide. (See Table 9-2.) Plans, obviously ambitious, called for the completion of 20 million digesters by 1980, 70 million by 1985.

Whether or not it reaches the 1985 goal, China has already created a major source of renewable energy in the countryside. According to Dr. Wu Wen, Director of the Institute of Energy Conversion, a typical digester produces some 34 cubic feet of methane per day for seven or eight months of the year.[19] At this rate, China's potential biogas production is equivalent to 22 million tons of hard coal. Energy analyst Vaclav Smil observes that "well managed biogas production offers a clean, efficient, and—what is certainly most important—a nonexhaustible source of energy which can be tapped inexpensively to benefit indefinitely a large segment of China's population."[20]

As the Chinese have acquired experience with digesters, they have discovered ways of using local organic material other than animal wastes. This is reflected in the various recipes for combining materials that go into the digester. One widely used combination for digester loading consists of 10 percent human waste, 30 percent animal waste, 10 percent straw and grass, and 50 percent water.[21]

In the small-scale production of methane from animal waste, China is in a league all its own. Although India's vast cattle

Table 9–2. Methane Digesters in China, 1970–78

Year	Number
1970	100
1972	600
1974	120,000
1975	410,000
1977	4,300,000
1978	7,000,000

Note: Data, largely for Sichuan Province, through 1977.
Source: Derived from Soft Energy Notes, December 1979.

herd is far larger than China's, efforts to realize the biogas potential have run up against formidable social and economic barriers, holding the Indian program to a much smaller scale. By 1979, the Indian Government had financed the construction of 70,000 digesters.[22] In Europe, generators are still a novelty. In the United States, which has one of the world's largest cattle herds, if all cattle manure were fed into digesters it would yield four trillion cubic feet of methane per year, the equivalent of 18 percent of U.S. natural gas consumption.[23] This huge potential notwithstanding, U.S. attention to the technology is recent. One of the pioneers in this field is Oklahoma-based Thermonetics, Inc.[24] In the Thermonetics process, protein, as well as natural gas and fertilizer, are extracted from livestock waste. The fiber from the feedlot waste is separated out before the material enters the methane digester. This material, which contains 12 percent protein and resembles ensilage, is sold as cattle feed. After the methane is produced, the remaining effluent is dried and made into a high-protein cake marketed as a livestock feed supplement. The remaining spent slurry can be piped to local farmers and spread on the fields through their irrigation systems, thus returning the remaining nutrients to the soil.

According to researchers at the U.S. Meat Animal Research Center in Nebraska, the annual cost of recovering methane and protein from feedlot waste is $16 to $100 per head of livestock, depending upon the size of the feedlot.[25] In 1978 prices, the methane produced per animal was worth $7.10 and the protein supplement, $82.90. While this complicated process for extracting gas and protein cannot be justified economically unless the feedlot has at least a thousand head of livestock, above that threshold profitability rises with feedlot size. While such operations obviously require a sophisticated technology that a small-scale producer might find unwieldly, they do both recycle protein and generate methane. Thus in the United States, investment in this process will become increasingly attractive as protein prices rise and as natural gas prices are decontrolled. As familiarity with the methane technology spreads, producers of livestock and poultry in all countries will give the technology a close look. If the use of the small-scale Chinese version now makes economic sense, it seems likely that larger-scale models will prove profitable elsewhere.

As oil supplies dwindle, it seems clear that wastes, be they urban, industrial, or agricultural, are going to become important sources of energy. In particular, clean-burning and versatile methane can be produced from locally available materials, can conserve firewood, reduce the need for imported coal and kerosene, upgrade various vegetable, human, and animal wastes into a high-quality fertilizer, and, in the process, displace more environmentally harmful fuels. Deriving energy from waste is not only a socially attractive proposition, but an economically attractive one as well.

Planting Energy Crops

Born of the liquid fuel shortage, the concept of planting crops specifically to get energy is relatively new. The concept is simple, but not without risks. In a world where production pressures on land are already excessive, planting of energy crops on a large scale will exacerbate the situation. To the extent that energy crops divert land and other agricultural resources from food production, they will surely drive food prices upward. The challenge is to use marginal land or crop by-products that do not compete directly with food.

Liquid fuels can be derived from vegetable matter either by converting plant starches and sugars into alcohol or by extracting oils from plants naturally high in hydrocarbons. Ethanol (ethyl alcohol) has been produced from fruit and grains as an intoxicant for centuries. It can be produced directly from sugar by fermentation or indirectly from starches and cellulose that are first converted to sugar and then fermented. The basic feedstocks for ethanol production are sugar crops (such as sugarcane, sugar beets, and sweet sorghum), root crops (mainly cassava), and cereals.

Of all energy crops, sugarcane produces the highest liquid fuel yield per hectare. Even at the relatively low yields of cane prevailing in Brazil, sugarcane produces 3,630 liters of alcohol per hectare, compared with only 2,200 liters per hectare from corn in the United States.[26] Second in yield is sweet sorghum, a commercially neglected crop whose stalks can be crushed to extract the syrup from which alcohol is distilled. Although sweet sorghum is not widely grown in the United States, its potential as an energy crop appears unsurpassed since it can be grown as far as north as Minnesota. Indeed, a modest plant-breeding effort aimed at increasing yields of this "sugarcane of the temperate zone" could pay handsome dividends.

Ethanol's potential as a fuel was recognized in Brazil from the early days of the automobile. But for the decades that cheap petroleum was available, the production of alcohol fuels was miniscule, limited to that derived from molasses, a by-product of sugar manufacture. But by 1975, when Brazil's alcohol fuel program was launched, all that had changed and the country's energy goal was to become self-sufficient in auto-motive fuel—a goal whose importance was reinforced by the Iranian revolution. From 1975 to 1979, alcohol production in Brazil increased fourteenfold. (See Table 9-3.) By 1979, alcohol accounted for an estimated 17 percent of national automotive fuel consumption.[27] Most of this alcohol is blended with gaso-line but in early 1980 new cars with engines designed to run exclusively on alcohol began rolling off the assembly line.

Brazilian government officials are projecting an output of just over nine billion liters of alcohol for fuel by 1985.[28] Alcohol industry sources, far more bullish, claim production may reach 20 billion liters by 1985, enough to fuel 60 to 70 percent of the projected Brazilian fleet of 12 million automo-biles.[29]

Building a Sustainable Society

Table 9–3. Production of Ethanol for Fuel Use in Brazil, 1975–80,
with Projections to 1985

Year	Ethanol
	(billion liters)
1975	.2
1976	.2
1977	.6
1978	1.6
1979	2.9
1980	3.5
1981	4.1
1982	4.7
1983	5.7
1984	7.3
1985	9.2

Source: Carvalho *et al.*, "Future of Alcohol Fuels in Brazil," 1980.

A vast area of cropland must be planted to sugarcane to fuel the projected auto fleet.[30] While planting only 2 percent of Brazil's total land area to sugarcane would permit automotive fuel self-sufficiency, this would increase by half the 4 percent now planted to crops. Indeed, this projected sugarcane area (roughly 15 million hectares) would exceed the sugarcane area in the 65 other countries that now grow the crop.

In the United States, enthusiasm for alcohol fuel has increased in direct proportion to the rise in gasoline prices. Between March and October of 1979, a period of unprecedented gasoline price hikes, the number of service stations selling gasohol jumped from 500 to over 2,000.[31] The first major boost for the U.S. alcohol fuels program came with the Energy Act of 1978, which removed the federal gasoline tax of 4 cents on every gallon of gasohol containing 10 percent alcohol obtained from non-petroleum sources. In January 1980, the U.S. alcohol fuels program received a second big boost when the White House announced major new production goals of two billion gallons of ethanol per year by 1985—roughly 2 percent of U.S. 1980 consumption of 100 billion gallons of automotive fuel.[32]

Meeting this goal would require distilling some 20 million tons of grain, or roughly one-fifth of the U.S. exportable surplus. In the Philippines, a government-sponsored crash program to reduce oil imports by producing alcohol fuel from sugarcane has been launched. As oil prices soared in 1979, the government stepped up the "alco-gas" (gasohol) production program, doubling the 1989 goal to an estimated 244 million gallons.[33] For now, the alcohol will be derived largely from cane, though cassava (a tropical dietary staple) and sweet potatoes are also being eyed as feedstocks.

In Africa, alcohol fuels production is just taking hold. Alcohol distilleries are converting molasses, a by-product of local sugar mills, into alcohol in Zimbabwe and in Kenya. The Kenyan plant will annually convert 180,000 tons of molasses into ethanol, which will be blended with gasoline in Nairobi.[34] South Africa, the world's leading producer of liquid fuel from coal, also plans to produce alcohol from cassava and sugarcane. It intends to convert the semi-arid and sparsely vegetated Makatini Flats in Northern Zululand into cassava plantations, erecting 13 ethanol distilleries that would produce 137 million gallons of liquid fuel annually and create jobs for 2,600 people in cassava production and alcohol distillation.[35] To the extent that cassava can be grown in areas where nothing of agricultural value is being produced and with resources that would not otherwise be used to produce food, these new "oil fields" will not edge out food crops.

One way to minimize food-fuel competition is to identify undomesticated plants with a high hydrocarbon content that might serve as future fuel sources but that would be adopted to soil otherwise unfit for agriculture. Melvin Calvin of the University of California, a leader in this effort, believes that cultivating *Euphorbia lathyris*—a hydrocarbon-rich desert shrub found in Mexico and the American Southwest and well adapted to semiarid growing conditions—could year after year yield the equivalent of 6.5 barrels of oil per acre.[36] Another potentially important energy plant, the "copaiba" tree of the Amazon, can be tapped like a rubber tree, yielding a liquid that can be used unprocessed in place of diesel fuel. Less esoteric energy crops include sunflowers, soybeans, and African oil palm.

In the United States, growing uncertainty about diesel supplies for farm use has prompted North Dakota State University to initiate research on both the technology and economics of producing and using sunflower seed oil in diesel engines. Should diesel fuel prices continue to climb and thus surpass those of sunflower seed oil, corn farmers could grow enough sunflowers on just 10 percent of their land to provide all the fuel for their tractors.[37] Sunflower seed oil is easily extracted on the farm with a relatively simple mechanical crushing process, and the net energy yield is much greater than that of the alcohol fermentation processes.[38]

As with alcohol fuels, Brazil has taken the lead in the production of vegetable oil fuels. In late 1980 its National Energy Council approved a program to substitute vegetable oil for 6 percent of diesel oil consumption in 1981, increasing it to 16 percent in 1985.[39] Initially, the oils to be substituted are soybean, peanut, sunflower seed, and rapeseed, but over the longer term African palm oil is expected to figure prominently as a diesel substitute. Tentative plans call for government incentives to plant up to 50,000 hectares of African palms in the Amazon region in 1981.

Apart from such land-based energy crops as sunflowers or sugarcane are water-based energy-rich plants such as water hyacinths, kelp, and algae. Off the coast of Southern California at the Naval Undersea Center of San Diego, giant kelp is being cultivated as a possible source of methane. This project too could eventually point the way to a new source of energy, particularly if it involves developing an efficient system for mechanically harvesting water hyacinths and giant kelp.

The potential for making methane from water hyacinths, which clog irrigation canals and reservoirs, is being actively

studied by the U.S. National Aeronautics and Space Administration. One proposal calls for funneling the sewage from urban
communities into large lagoons where water hyacinths would
utilize the nutrients in the sewage as fertilizer, thus converting
an otherwise wasted resource into usable energy. Such a system
has an impressive energy-yield potential; one acre of sewage-
enriched warm water can produce several tons of water hyacinths each day, enough to yield between 3,500 and 7,000
cubic feet of methane.[40]

At present, projects involving crops suitable for use in alcohol production greatly outnumber those based on plants that
yield hydrocarbon extracts that can be used directly as fuel.
Eventually, though, both are likely to find a place in an economic system based on renewable fuels. Given the obvious
physical limits on land for energy crops, such crops are not
likely to solve the world's liquid fuel problem, but they can be
an important part of the solution.

Falling Water

For at least 2,000 years, people have been harnessing water to
do work. In 85 B.C., the Greek poet Antipater celebrated the
development of a water-powered grist mill, noting that it had
liberated Greek maidens from the arduous task of grinding
grain.[41] Once the basic mechanics of harnessing water power
were worked out, the devices spread rapidly, reaching Japan by
610 A.D.

Yet, while water wheels were used throughout the Roman
Empire and during the Middle Ages to power mills for grinding flour, sawing wood, and producing textiles, not until the
late 19th century was water power used to generate electricity.
The first central hydro-generating facility began producing
electricity in Appleton, Wisconsin in 1882.[42] It powered 350
light bulbs and set the stage for the rapid spread of hydroelectric generation throughout the world.

Most of the world's current generating capacity was developed after World War II.[43] Between 1950 and 1978, installed hydroelectric generating capacity increased ninefold, reaching 409,000 megawatts. The world's leading generator of electricity from falling water is the United States, generating 71,000 megawatts, followed by the Soviet Union with 47,000 and Canada with 40,000. Third World development efforts during the fifties and sixties included ambitious hydroelectric projects, such as the Kariba Dam in Zimbabwe (1300 megawatts), the Aswan High Dam in Egypt (2,100 megawatts), the Furnas Project in Brazil (4,000 megawatts), and the Guri Project in Venezuela (2,900 megawatts).[44]

This impressive growth notwithstanding, the world's hydropower potential is far from developed. Fully developed, it could triple, or perhaps even quadruple existing generating capacity. While a few countries such as Japan and Switzerland have little undeveloped hydroelectric potential remaining, most countries are far from this point. Brazil, for example, (currently ranked fifth in the world in hydroelectric generation) has developed only 14 percent of its hydro potential because most of the untapped capacity is located in remote reaches of the Amazon Basin.[45]

Two other countries with vast untapped hydroelectric potential are Nepal and China. Although it has never been thoroughly surveyed, the small mountainous kingdom of Nepal, where several of Asia's major rivers originate, is believed to have a hydroelectric potential equal to that of the United States and Canada combined.[46] If Nepal, whose 12 million people have an average per capita income of $120 per year, can obtain the engineering capacity and financial resources, it could convert these rivers into a major source of income, marketing the electricity in Pakistan, India, and Bangladesh. In China, source of two of Asia's largest rivers—the Yellow and the Yangtze—small-scale hydroelectric projects undertaken locally have sprung up in recent decades, but little progress has been made in harnessing the nation's large-scale hydroelectric potential. As the eighties began, China was actively exploring with Japan and the United States the potential for developing four dams on the Yellow and Yangtze that would have a combined generating capacity of 32,000 megawatts. Although an estimated investment of $30 billion would be required to pull off this venture, the dams would triple China's existing generating capacity of 14,000 megawatts.[47]

Even front-ranking hydropower producers—the United States and Canada—still have room for significant development. During the sixties, some farsighted Quebecois began to see the potential for tapping Quebec's hydropower, both for domestic use and for export to the United States. Under the leadership of provincial Premier Robert Bourassa, La Société d'Energie de la Baie James (The James Bay Energy Society) was formed as a subsidiary of Quebec Hydro to develop a 13,200 megawatt hydroelectric project by 1990.[48] Raising the $15 billion to finance the four-river project centered on the La Grande River was a formidable undertaking, but the completed project now provides cheap electricity both for Quebec and for export. In fact, Quebec Hydro made available some 1,360 megawatts of power to the New York State Power Authority from April through September of 1979—an electrical grid linkage that serves both countries well since the peak demand in Quebec comes in the winter, while air-conditioned New York City is "summer peaking."[49] Quebec could, Bourassa believes, sell electricity much as the Arabs sell oil but, he observes, this income flow could last forever whereas that from the oil under the Middle East sands will not.[50]

Within the United States, according to the Army Corps of Engineers, the current 71,000 megawatts of generating capacity (including pumped storage) could be raised dramatically if dams that do not now have power-generating facilities were equipped with them and if the hydropower output of other dams was increased to full capacity.[51] A survey of existing dams and undeveloped sites identified some 11,000 sites with a po-

tential generating capacity of 15 megawatts or more.[52] Undeveloped sites could be exploited to develop some 300,000
megawatts of power, over half of it in Alaska.

The vast untapped potential existing in such remote places
as Alaska, which is well beyond feasible transmission distance
from U.S. population centers, indicates the need to locate
energy-intensive industries near power-generating sites. Selective development of hydro sites in Alaska, so as to minimize
environmental disruption, would make it possible to shift energy-intensive industries there, thus freeing up for residential
uses the hydro-electricity these operations currently use in the
contiguous 48 states.

In the "bigger is better" world of the postwar era, small-scale
hydropower sites have been sorely neglected. A notable exception is China, where a program was launched in the mid-sixties
to develop numerous mini-hydro projects at the community
level. By 1978, some 87,000 small-scale hydropowered electric
generators were in use. (See Table 9-4.) Of this total, most are
located in the rainy provinces south of the Yangtze River and
powered by water impounded behind small earthen and rock
dams that have been constructed by seasonally unemployed
rural labor. According to energy analyst Vaclav Smil, these
small stations now account for a third of China's total hydrogeneration, providing power to run irrigation pumps, grist
mills, sawmills, and local light industries in the Chinese countryside.[53]

Table 9-4. Small-Scale Hydropowered Electric Generators in China,
1949-78

Year	Number
1949	50
1965	6,000
1971	35,000
1973	50,000
1975	60,000
1978	87,000

Source: *Soft Energy Notes*, December 1979.

Rapidly rising costs of nuclear, oil, and coal-fired electricity generation in the United States has led to a fresh look at the potential for small-scale hydroelectric projects by government at all levels, private investors and utilities. A survey undertaken in 1977 identified over 50,000 dams built for water storage, flood control, or recreational purposes that were not being used to generate electricity.[54] These sites are attractive because the water-impounding structures already exist and require only the installation of electrical generators to tap the energy in the overflow. Small and widely dispersed, such facilities do not require long distance transmission lines.

In the United States, companies are forming to develop small-scale hydroelectric sites. One such firm, started by Lawrence Gleeson in 1976, had plans by mid-1978 to develop some 20 dams in the northeastern United States.[55] According to *Business Week*, Gleeson's firm "contracts with the dam owner, develops the site, sells power to the local utility, and returns a share of revenues to the owner." Its approach is being emulated by a wide array of U.S. specialty companies, local governments, farmers, and corporate landowners now developing small-scale hydroelectric potential wherever topographically and commercially feasible.

In Europe, France is among the first countries to inventory the potential for small-scale hydrogeneration. Some 90,000 sites have been identified and, as in the United States, many landowners are beginning to view them as highly profitable investments and long-term sources of income.[56] By some reckonings, these small dams—whether in China, the United States, or France—are the oil wells of the future.

In the Third World, a U.S. AID-sponsored survey of small-scale hydroelectric potential shows the scope for development of local generating facilities is broad. Opportunities look particularly rich in the Andean countries of Latin America. Peru, for example, has thousands of developable sites in close proximity to its unelectrified Andean communities.[57]

Although the world's hydroelectric potential has yet to be

inventoried in detail, the information at hand suggests that a vast potential awaits development. The obstacles to realizing this potential are less technological than political or institutional. In some cases, difficult tradeoffs will have to be made. Case by case, it will have to be decided whether the loss of cropland or wilderness areas through inundation is defensible in view of the need for a renewable source of electricity. In remote locations, development of hydroelectric sites may await the arrival of energy-intensive industries or further advances in the efficiency of long-distance transmission. Overall, this source of renewable energy promises to become a cornerstone of a renewable society.

Harnessing the Wind

The first known device for putting the wind to work, a wind-powered water lift, was designed in Persia around 600 B.C.[58] During the twelfth century, windmills appeared in Europe, where they were used in grinding grain and pumping water. Wind-powered sailing ships were instrumental both in the European colonization of the world during the Age of Exploration and in the growth in international trade that followed.

Embodying an estimated 2 percent of the solar radiation the earth receives, the kinetic energy in the movement of air along the earth's surface is enormous.[59] Much of the economically harnessable wind energy is concentrated along coastlines and in mountain passes. Among the promising coastal sites now being considered for wind generation are the northern coast of the United Kingdom, the southern and western coasts of Australia, the Soviet Union's extensive Arctic coastline, and the Third World countries astride the trade winds belt.[60] The coastal and mountain regions of the United States are richly endowed with wind power.

The United States, Sweden, and Denmark lead the world in the development of wind power. Both Sweden and Denmark, poor in fossil fuels but rich in wind power, are investing heavily in wind research and development. With most of its electricity generated by burning oil imported from the Middle East and with strong public opposition to nuclear power, Denmark particularly is looking to harness its powerful coastal winds. The Danish Academy of Technical Services and the Niels Bohr Institute have each published reports exploring the various components of a national wind-power strategy.[61] Several small-scale wind generators have been built and connected to the electricity grid. Perhaps the single most innovative Danish effort has been the design and construction of a wind generator by a group of professors and students at the Tvind Schools. Supported by advisors from the Technical University in Copenhagen and elsewhere, this group built the world's largest wind generator between 1975 and 1978 for a modest investment of $900,000.[62] Located near the village of Ulfborg in West Jutland, it stands as a remarkable example of what local initiative can do in developing alternative energy sources.

Like Denmark, Sweden is naturally endowed with a belt of strong westerly winds. Since 1975, the Swedish government has committed substantial resources to wind generator design, to the construction of experimental models, and to "wind prospecting." Swedish scientists have outlined an ambitious plan that calls for the construction of some 3,300 large wind generators, enough to generate as much electricity as seven large nuclear reactors.[63] Many will be integrated with pumped-storage systems at existing hydro reservoirs to stabilize the flow of electricity.

In Australia, wind prospecting is a nascent art, but meteorologist Mark Diessendorf of the Commonwealth Scientific and Industrial Research Organization reports that "regions of high wind energy potential should exist around the coast of the Great Australian Bite, the southwest of Western Australia, parts of Victoria, and the west of Tasmania."[64] In coastal areas where Australian utilities burn oil or in remote communities that rely on diesel generators, wind power is already becoming economical. At many other Australian sites, wind power could be economically used now to produce electricity if existing diesel generators were used as a backup power source.

Although many countries are now seriously exploring wind power, the United States is at the leading edge. Between 1973 and 1980, the Department of Energy (DOE) spent nearly $200 million studying and developing wind turbine generators.[65] Most of that sum went to the development of large and middle-sized turbines, but roughly a quarter of the budget underwrote the development of generators of the two-to-ten kilowatt variety—machines small enough for use by individual homeowners, farmers, and ranchers.

DOE's early wind-generator prototypes were medium-sized machines designed to produce a flow of 200 kilowatts and erected at a variety of sites around the country.[66] Members of the second generation of wind turbines are much larger, mostly in the 2.0 to 2.5 megawatt range, a size that some engineers believe will be economically optimal. The next step in the DOE program will be to construct three 2.5-megawatt wind turbines in the state of Washington near the border it shares with Oregon. Each of the propeller blades of these Boeing-built prototypes will exceed in length the wingspan of a Boeing 747 jumbo jet. The machines will stand in a windy gorge of the Columbia River and feed electricity into Bonneville Power, the local utility. At full power, this cluster of three will provide enough electricity for 2,500 average American homes. (Four hundred such machines could produce as much power as a large nuclear or coal-fired generating plant.)

Besides developing prototypes on government contracts, most U.S. wind-machine companies have focused their early efforts on selling wind generators to electrical utilities. Among the exceptions is U.S. Wind Power, a 50-year old Massachusetts-based firm that proposes to sell electrical power rather than the generators themselves. The assumption is that utilities are accustomed to buying power, as they often do from each other, but not to buying new technologies. As a starter, U.S. Wind Power has signed a preliminary agreement with the California Department of Water Resources under which the company will build a 100-megawatt "wind farm" consisting of some 2,000 of the small 50-kilowatt machines.[67]

In tandem with the rising cost of power generated from nuclear and coal-fired plants, the declining cost of wind-generated electrical power is spurring the formation of new firms to exploit this promising new market.[68] After operating only a year, Wind Farms, Ltd., of San Francisco has plans to construct an 80-megawatt "wind farm" that would utilize 32 of the 2.5-megawatt windmills on 2,500 acres in Hawaii and sell its power to the local utility. Panaero, headquartered in Denver, Colorado, is following a similar tack. According to its director, the company is negotiating the sale of wind-generated power with ten electrical utilities, mostly west of the Mississippi. Recent economic analyses show that if capital investment, fuel costs, and maintenance and operating costs are all taken into account, areas with persistent high winds can produce wind-generated electricity competitively now.

Sensing this new potential, the U.S. Congress passed the Wind Energy Research, Demonstration, and Utilization Act of 1980, a bill that would provide strong market support for wind generators through 1985, by which time the industry should be mass producing wind generators. Support for the bill stems from the conviction that wind could supply 2 to 4 percent of national electrical power demand in the year 2000.[69]

As more and more countries come to understand wind power's potential and to engage in wind energy prospecting, the market for electrical wind generators could expand rapidly. The Soviet Union, which has thus far focused on small-scale wind turbines averaging roughly 10 kilowatts each, plans to generate 4,500 megawatts of electricity annually with wind by

1990. Under this plan, the number of wind generators will increase from 4,500 in 1980 to 150,000 by 1990.[70] In the United Kingdom, writes Dr. Peter Musgrove in the *New Scientist*, "North Sea wind might just join North Sea oil and gas in making a useful contribution to Britain's energy supplies."[71] Ironically, the very winds that roughen the North Sea and make oil extraction so difficult could prove to be an even more valuable long-term source of energy than oil. If capital from the valuable oil being pumped from the North Sea were invested in wind farms along the northern and western coast of the United Kingdom, this could help secure the country's long-term energy supplies even after 1983, when oil production is expected to begin declining.

A global survey of the potential for developing wind power resources led M. R. Gustavson of the Lawrence Laboratory at the University of California to a hopeful conclusion. "Should the large-scale capture of wind energy prove economically rewarding and otherwise acceptable," says Gustavson, "it has a magnificent potential."[72] Indeed, by at least one published estimate, the world's economically harnessable wind power is seven times greater than its hydropower potential. As it becomes economically attractive, this benign and relatively abundant source of renewable energy should be quickly and systematically put to use.

Tapping the Earth's Heat

Hot springs, geysers, and the molten rock that pours from erupting volcanoes all testify to the great heat within the earth. But only recently have scientists begun to assess the earth's geothermal potential. Neither solar nor fossil, the geothermal heat stored under the earth's cool outer crust is so vast relative to human needs that it is for all practical purposes a renewable resource. While a complete inventory of geothermal potential is years away, the principal geothermal belts are well known as a result of volcanic activity and available geological information.

While geothermal energy is highly visible around the Pacific rim with its frequent volcanic activity, it is a widely dispersed energy source, one that can be readily tapped wherever the earth's crust is thin. Energy analyst Louis J. Goodman and his colleagues believe that "new drilling techniques borrowed from the oil business should eventually allow the earth's awesome subterranean energy to be harnessed in large quantities, at economic costs, in most parts of the world."[73] The earth's richest geothermal resources border the Pacific Ocean in the so-called "rim of fire" that stretches from New Zealand up through New Guinea, the Philippines, Japan, Western Siberia and then down through the western United States, Mexico, Central America, and the west coast of South America.

Geothermal heat can be used either directly for residential heating or industrial processes and in greenhouses, or indirectly as electricity, depending on end-use needs and the temperature of the geothermal resource. But since geothermal energy is site-specific and cannot be readily transported except in the form of electricity, industries are likely over time to concentrate in the world's major geothermal fields, much as they are beginning to concentrate in areas rich in hydroelectric power and in heavily wooded areas.

Several countries use geothermal energy for space heating. Iceland has long relied on geothermal energy for residential heating. Indeed, 65 percent of all Icelandic homes are heated by hot water drawn from underground, and most of Iceland's fresh tomatoes, lettuce, and cucumbers are produced in geothermally heated greenhouses.[74] Two U.S. cities—Klamath Falls, Oregon, and Boise, Idaho—also rely heavily on geothermal energy for residential heating. Hungary and the Soviet Union both have extensive acreages of geothermally heated greenhouses.

Direct industrial applications of geothermal heat are just

beginning to be developed.[75] One of the first industrial firms to use it was the Tasman Pulp and Paper Company in Kawerau, New Zealand, starting in the early fifties. Tasman used geothermal heat to operate its pulp and paper plant and timber-drying kilns. In Iceland, one of the world's largest high-grade diatomaceous earth-processing plants relies entirely on geothermal heat, most of it averaging 250° C at the wellhead.

Although geothermal heat is used directly in many locations, its greatest long-term potential is in electrical generation. As of 1981, geothermal electricity is still in the early stages of development, but it is growing by leaps and bounds. Among the early leaders are the United States, Italy, New Zealand and Japan. Total capacity at the beginning of 1979 was 1,500 megawatts, the equivalent of roughly one and one-half of the largest coal or nuclear-powered generating plants. Within the United States alone, the 500 megawatts of capacity on line in 1979 is expected to reach 1,800 megawatts by 1983.[76] By that time, 3 percent of the electricity in the states with geothermally powered plants—California, Utah, Nevada, Hawaii, and New Mexico—will be geothermally produced.[77] By the end of the century, California could be drawing 25 percent of its electricity from geothermal sources.[78]

Japan's Natural Resources Research Commission estimates that the country has enough recoverable geothermal energy to provide 40,000 megawatts of electricity for 1,000 years.[79] By 1985 Japan is expected to be drawing 1,400 megawatts of electricity from geothermal sources. By the end of the century, some sources see oil-short Japan emerging as the world leader with as much as 48,000 megawatts of geothermal-electric capacity.[80] According to the Inter-Agency Geothermal Coordinating Council, the United States is projected to be second with 27,000 megawatts of installed capacity by the year 2000.[81] The Philippines, which has only lately taken its geothermal resources into account, expects to make those resources its second-ranking source of electricity by 1985 with some 700 megawatts of capacity.[82]

El Salvador, one of the first Third World countries to exploit its geothermal reserves, now obtains nearly a third of its electricity from its Ahuachapan geothermal field.[83] By 1985, it expects to be generating all of its electricity from geothermal and hydro sources. Turkey, with some 600 boiling hot springs, has a great potential for geothermal electrical generation. The Turkish Government also has ambitious plans for using geothermal energy to heat buildings and greenhouses.[84] Given the widely dispersed nature of geothermal energy (and hence broad geographic accessibility) in Turkey, it should figure heavily in the national energy budget by the end of the century.

Perhaps the most ambitious single geothermal power plant under consideration is in the Soviet Union. A study sponsored by the U.S. Department of Energy reports that "plans are under way to tap the Avashinski volcano on the Kamchatka peninsula at a depth of 3.5 km (11,500 feet) in the hope of establishing a resource which might supply a 5,000 megawatt geothermal plant for 500 years."[85]

Largely ignored during the era of cheap oil, geothermal energy development now looks relatively cheap and environmentally benign. On prime sites in the western United States, it is already generating electricity more cheaply than coal, oil, or nuclear power. In the Philippines, geothermal-generated electricity costs only one-fifth as much as that generated from oil.[86]

While geothermal energy development is not without its problems, particularly the environmental drawbacks of reinjecting underground the mineral-laden water once the heat has been extracted from it, they do not appear to be as troubling as the acid rain and carbon dioxide pollution associated with coal production or the radioactive waste-disposal problems associated with nuclear power. By the end of the century, geothermal heat promises to be the dominant source of electricity in several countries and a major entry in the global energy budget.

Rooftops as Collectors

The technology for collecting solar energy for heating purposes is one of the simplest imaginable. In essence, it consists of a glass-topped box with a dark bottom that absorbs incoming sunlight. The box traps the sunlight and converts it into heat. The glass permits light to stream through unimpeded but checks the reverse flow of energy once it is converted into heat.

A slightly more complex variation of this technology is the vacuum tube collector, now widely marketed in the United States. In this collector, a tube containing the water or other heat-absorbing liquid is situated inside a larger tube. The space between the tubes—a partial vacuum—serves as an insulator. Once the heat is trapped in either type of solar collector, it can be used to heat water, interior space, or as low-grade industrial process heat.

One salient advantage of solar collectors is independence. They can provide household energy without being hooked up to the grids through which electricity, natural gas, and other forms of energy are distributed. Another is size. Collectors can be fitted on rooftops, so their land requirements are minimal. A third selling point is invulnerability to politically inspired embargoes or other international disruptions such as those associated with oil or uranium economies.

Simplicity and these other advantages have not yet made rooftop collectors standard household features in most of the world. Interest in solar collectors heightened after World War II and the devices began to catch on in a few countries. Within the United States, for example, there were some 50,000 rooftop solar water heaters in the Miami area alone by the mid-fifties.[87] But the availability of cheap oil and natural gas all but deadened that interest in the ensuing years.

Foremost among those countries that continued to rely in part on solar energy when other nations developed petroleum-based economies is Israel. Roughly one-tenth of all Israeli households use solar energy for heating water, and the Israeli government expects the number of solar heating units to increase from 400,000 to 650,000 between 1980 and 1990.[88] Underpinning this growth is the requirement that all new public buildings incorporate solar water-heating systems and the Ministry of Energy's commitment to covering 10 percent of the costs of all new solar installations.

In the United States, as in most other countries, interest in solar collectors surged following the OPEC oil price increase in late 1973. Although sales from the fledgling industry totaled only 1.3 million square feet of collectors in 1974, over 10 million square feet were sold in 1977. (See Table 9-5.) In 1978, sales stagnated as consumers waited for the passage of the National Energy Act, which contains financial incentives for solar energy installations. In 1980, sales exceeded an estimated 19 million square feet, bringing the cumulative installed area of collectors up to nearly 66 million feet or one square foot for every three people in the United States.

During the seventies, most of the solar panels sold were used for heating water for homes and swimming pools. (A California ban on new swimming pools that used fossil fuels furthered this trend.) But as fuel costs rise, solar panels will find wider application among commercial users of low-grade heat. On-farm grain

Table 9-5. U.S. Sales of Solar Panels, 1974–80

Year	Annual	Cumulative
	(million square feet)	
1974	1.3	1.3
1975	3.7	5.0
1976	5.8	10.8
1977	10.3	21.1
1978	10.9	32.0
1979	14.3	46.3
1980	19.5	65.8

Source: U.S. Department of Energy.

dryers, car washes, restaurants, food processors—all are likely to find investments in solar collectors increasingly attractive.

Solar collectors' potential must be gauged in terms of the need for heat at low temperatures—since low-grade heat is what collectors produce. In the United States, where some 33 percent of all energy is used for heating purposes, the solar potential is commensurately large.[89] As the phased decontrol of U.S. oil and natural gas prices nears completion, this potential is likely to be increasingly appreciated. An added inducement to install solar heating devices is being provided by tax credits at both the federal and state levels. The Energy Tax Act of 1978 as amended by the Windfall Profits Act of 1980 provides through 1985 a 40 percent credit toward the first $10,000 spent on active solar equipment designed to heat water or heat or cool a home. Supplementary financial incentives, mostly in the form of tax credits, are also available in most states. California, for example, provides a tax credit of 55 percent, as long as it does not exceed $3,000, toward the cost of residential solar installations.[90] In some cases, the two types of credits are cumulative, so the consumer actually pays less than half the up-front costs of the system.

By a Department of Energy estimate made before the 1979 oil price rises and the beginning of oil-price decontrol in the United States, 1.6 million homes will be using solar water heaters by 1985 and another 300,000 would be using solar energy for space heating.[91] As of early 1981, these projections appear too conservative. Indeed, California alone expects to have 1.5 million solar installations by 1985.[92] With energy prices and public incentives increasing in the United States, rooftops may well sprout solar collectors in the eighties the way they did television antennas in the fifties.

That market hunch has two sets of adherents. While individual companies are beginning to research the profitability of manufacturing solar collectors, others are experimenting with their large-scale use. In Minneapolis, Minnesota, for example, the Honeywell Corporation has recently built an eight-story office building heated and cooled largely by solar collectors. With 106,000 square feet of floor space, the building gets 50 percent of its space heating, 80 percent of its cooling, and 100 percent of its water heating from the collectors.[93] As solar energy technologies become more cost-competitive vis-à-vis fossil fuels, more profit-minded corporations will invest heavily in them.

In France, which imports all of its oil and most of its coal, interest in solar collectors runs high. While only 20,000 solar hot water heaters were in use in 1979, France hopes to be manufacturing a half million solar water heaters per year by 1985.[94] Low-interest loans that completely cover the cost of solar collectors and their installation are expected to undergird the expanding market.

Among Asian countries, Japan is indeed the Land of the Rising Sun. As of 1980, over 1.6 million buildings were already using solar heating systems, the great majority for heating water.[95] By 1985, the Japanese government expects some 4.2 million buildings—homes, factories, and offices—will be similarly equipped. The plan is to increase this to 7.8 million buildings by 1990; to 12 million by 1995. By this latter date, 30 percent of all buildings are expected to have solar collectors on their rooftops.

As the eighties began, rooftop solar collectors contributed only marginally to the world's energy supply. But the stage is set for rapid expansion. In the United States, some 360 firms were manufacturing and marketing solar collectors in 1980.[96] As fossil fuel supplies dwindle, as energy prices rise, and as the costs of solar collectors fall with mass production, solar collectors can be expected to meet a steadily expanding share of the world's need for low-temperature heat.

Electricity from Sunlight

Electricity can be generated from sunlight in two ways. One is concentrating sunlight to generate steam; the steam is then used to drive an electrical generator, just as it is in fossil or nuclear-fired electrical generating plants. Despite a few government-sponsored solar "power towers" in the United States and southern Europe, this technology does not appear to be cost effective and is unlikely to go beyond the pilot plant stage. The second technology, the photovoltaic cell, is far less conventional.

In 1954, scientists in New Jersey's Bell Laboratories discovered that a silicon wafer could generate an electrical current when struck by sunlight.[97] Writing in *Science,* physicist Henry Kelly describes the process: "Energy in light is transferred to electrons in a semi-conductor material when a light photon collides with an atom in the material with enough energy to dislodge an electron from a fixed position in the material, giving it enough energy to move freely in the material."[98] In the photovoltaic cell, the energy that dislodges the electron is funneled into a wire leading from the cell. The direct current (DC) generated in this way can then either be converted to alternating current (AC) or, more efficiently, it can be used directly with DC-compatible appliances.

Despite the photovoltaic's latecomer status, the feasibility of the technology for special uses is no longer questioned. By the mid-sixties, photovoltaic cells were being used to power Intelsat's communications satellites. At issue is whether the cost of photovoltaic-generated electricity will fall far enough to make it broadly competitive. Costs are falling rapidly. The photovoltaic cells installed in the orbiting Skylab that was launched in 1973 cost $300 per peak-watt.[99] A small-scale purchase made by a railway in 1976 cost $45 per peak-watt of power.[100] In 1978, a large government purchase was made at $11 per peak-watt; another was made at $7 per peak-watt.[101] DOE projects that the price will fall to $2 per peak-watt by 1982, to 50 cents by 1986, and to 10 to 30 cents in the 1990s.[102]

U.S. government support for photovoltaic development in the form of research grants and large-scale procurements, along with rapid technological advances, has stirred substantial interest in photovoltaic cells in the business community. By early 1980, five U.S. companies were committed to the mass production of photovoltaic cells.[103] ARCO-Solar has made one of the heaviest investments to date. By mid-1980, the firm was putting the finishing touches on a 4,000 square-foot factory equipped with the world's first fully automatic production line for photovoltaic cells.[104] ARCO's pet project is a photovoltaic roofing material that simultaneously replaces conventional roofing and generates electricity that can be converted into alternating current for household use or (should surpluses accumulate), fed back into the local electrical grid. In Texas, Photon Power is planning to produce enough photovoltaic cells to generate five megawatts of electricity annually.[105] Using a cadmium sulfide technology, the company expects a combination of future increases in the conversion efficiency of the cells and the economies associated with large-scale production to reduce the cost per watt to perhaps as little as 10 cents by 1990.

In the United States, virtually all of the early entrants in the race to commercialize photovoltaic cells are owned partly or wholly by oil companies. ARCO Solar, for example, is a subsidiary of ARCO, which infuses its solar arm with large amounts of capital. The majority interest in Photon Power is owned by Compagnie Française de Petrol. SEF, which plans to produce photovoltaic cells commercially by 1981, is a subsidiary of Shell Oil. Exxon, which has not yet embarked on commercial production, is experimenting with the amorphous silicon technology. Elsewhere in the world electronic firms dominate the fledgling industry.[106] In West Germany, AEG Telefunken is producing 2 megawatts of photovoltaic capacity annually with a potential for going to 6 megawatts if market conditions warrant. Siemens, AEG's principal competitor, is planning an annual output of 1 megawatt and has finished design work on a photovoltaic water pump. Philips, the Dutch electronics giant, is producing photovoltaic cells in France. Although details are not available, Japan is readying for a big push in photovoltaics.

Somewhat ironically, the big potential market for photovoltaic cells may be in the hundreds of thousands of villages in the Third World that have not yet been electrified. Although it now costs more to install photovoltaic generating capacity than conventional generating capacity, the grid needed to distribute conventionally derived energy can be far more costly than the generating capacity itself. For that reason, and because photovoltaic arrays need not be large to be efficient, photovoltaic devices may already be cost-effective for villages that have modest electrical needs and no connection to a utility transmission grid.

The world's first solar-electric village is in a U.S. setting with a Third World character. In December of 1978, the village of Schuchuli, one of 53 villages on the Papago Indian Reservation in Arizona, was electrified for the first time when its photovoltaic array was turned on. When the switch was thrown in this remote, small (96 residents), and sundrenched location, it illuminated flourescent lamps that replaced the kerosene lamps and it started a small water pump that replaced a diesel-powered pump. The photovoltaic panels now produce 3.5 kilowatts of peak-watt power—enough for 47 fluorescent lights, a two-horsepower water pump, 15 small refrigerators, a sewing machine, and a communal washing machine.[107] Excess power is stored in batteries for use at night or on cloudy days.

The world's second solar electric village is in Upper Volta. There, the U.S. Agency for International Development has sponsored a 1.8-kilowatt photovoltaic generating array that produces power that villagers use to pump water and grind grain. The water pump lifts 5,000 liters per day, the most the well can supply, while the grist mill produces enough finely ground grain to meet the requirements of about 640 families.[108] In this village of 2,700 inhabitants, where farming and cattle raising are the main activities, the new power source is particularly appreciated by the village women, who have traditionally spent long hours drawing water and grinding grain by hand.

In India, the Indian Institute of Technology is designing a 10-kilowatt solar power plant. It hopes to see such plants installed in India's villages, most of which have not yet been electrified. Here, they would be used primarily to pump water, light homes, and power community radio and television receivers.[109]

Heartening as early photovoltaic applications may appear, it is difficult to say exactly how rapidly use of this energy technology will grow given the uncertain pace of technological advance. Yet, as the eighties begin, the industry is gathering speed and activities once sponsored and funded solely by government are being taken up by private enterprise. If production costs fall as projected, electricity from photovoltaic cells could become particularly important to that segment of humanity living in the hundreds of thousands of villages not yet connected to power grids.

Solar Architecture

Solar architecture was an advanced profession 2,500 years ago when the ancient Greeks practiced its principles. As Ken Butti and John Perlin report in *A Golden Thread*, Socrates himself explained the importance of building houses with a southern exposure and overhanging eaves: "In houses that look toward the south, the sun penetrates the portico in winter, while in summer the path of the sun is right over our heads and above the roof, so that there is shade." Such a design proved efficient enough to keep the houses comfortable for two-thirds of the days from November to March.[110]

The archeological remains of other ancient civilizations in North Africa, the Middle East, northern India and the southwestern United States also indicate that the principles of solar architecture were fully mastered millenia ago. Before the potential of fossil fuels was known, much less the utility of electricity, buildings had to be made warm in winter and cool in summer. Now that fossil fuel reserves are being depleted, modern civilization is rediscovering the value of solar architecture —structures with minimal fuel requirements for heating and cooling.

Passive solar design, described by one enthusiast as an energy system that has only one moving part—the sun—begins with site selection. Any given building site accentuates some local climatic features while minimizing the effect of others. Locating a house on or nearby a hilltop will usually mean more wind exposure—a spur to both summertime ventilation and wintertime heat loss. Although some sites actually afford good air movement during the summer without excessive exposure to winter winds, most entail a combination of costs and benefits, all of which need to be carefully calculated.

Building orientation can increase or decrease fuel bills by a third. In the north temperate zone, buildings should face south in order to take advantage of the wintertime sun low in the southern sky. Incorporating a roof overhang insures that the house's southern side will be shaded from the hot midday sun during the summer, while minimizing the amount of glass used on the northern side restricts heat loss. Locating living spaces on the southern side of the home, while placing closets, baths, storage rooms, entry ways, and garages on the north side also saves energy and reduces drafts. By the same token, a two-story house loses less heat than a sprawling one-story house with the same floor space. Town houses, row houses, or other structures that share common walls also lose less heat to the outdoors than free standing buildings do.

Insulation obviously plays an important role in energy architecture. A poorly insulated house that acquired one-fifth of its wintertime heat from the sun could acquire half if carefully insulated. For this reason, keeping the amount of such poor insulators as glass to a minimum on all but south-facing walls is also critical. Doing so helps minimize the heat loss in wintertime and the cooling costs when air conditioning is needed. Indeed, some new glass-walled office buildings have turned out to be extraordinarily costly to cool in the summertime since they function as giant solar collectors. As energy prices soar, the cost of cooling buildings of this design could become prohibitive, even as insulation becomes more and more economical.

These and other design features enable modern architects to better even the ancient Greeks, who designed buildings that provided two-thirds of the daytime heat they needed during winter. Advances in engineering, a better understanding of thermodynamics, and the availability of new building materials all spell exciting new possibilities in passive solar design. At the University of Saskatchewan, for instance, the Mechanical Engineering Department faculty has designed a house that is so energy-efficient that it does not pay to install a furnace. Homes built on the Saskatchewan model remain comfortable in the Canadian prairie's interminable subzero winter. What is more, they resemble in both appearance and price conventional homes in the area, and cost their residents about $40 annually to heat.[111]

The heating requirements of these carefully designed homes are so low that most of the heat needed (85 percent) comes from the occupants' bodies, the operation of electrical appliances, and from the windows on the southern exterior. This extraordinary thermal efficiency is due to several ingenious design features: double-studded walls contain 12 to 15 inches of fiberglass or cellulose insulation, the whole building (except for windows and doors) is wrapped in a "bag" of polyethylene plastic installed in the walls, and the windows (seven out of nine of which are on the south side) are double- or triple-glazed and are covered with heavy shutters at night. Also needed in a house as tightly built as this one is an air exchanger to introduce fresh air from the outside and to exhaust stagnant air once its heat is captured for reuse. (A similar technique is used to retain heat from waste water: a thrifty grey-water heat-recuperator system helps transfer the heat from hot water used for bathing, dishwashing, and laundry to the fresh water being heated.)

Needless to say, the economic appeal of such a home in the severe climate of Saskatchewan is strong. While the extra insulation, window shutters, and heat exchangers represent additional costs, the expenses can be recouped because no furnace is needed. Furthermore, an analysis of the economics of these energy-efficient homes indicates that the "high levels of insulation and passive solar design were shown to be the most cost-effective options in the life-cycle comparison—much cheaper than active solar and many times less expensive than electricity or natural gas."[112]

Overall, the annual heating bill of homes built to different building standards vary widely. Assuming the same climate, the energy-conserving Saskatchewan house described above can be heated for less than a tenth the cost of heating a house in California constructed according to the state's building code. (See Table 9-6). Similarly, a home built in Sweden according

Table 9–6. Annual Heating Costs According to Different Building Standards*

Structure or Standard	Annual Cost
	(dollars)
U.S. average house, 1978	680
French building code, 1974	500
U.S. building standards, 1978	360
Swedish building code, 1977	230
California building code, 1979	220
Townhouse with retrofit, Twin Rivers, New Jersey	95
Saskatchewan conservation house	20
Village House I, passive solar	15

*Assumes similarly-sized houses using oil heat in a similar climate.
Source: A. H. Rosenfeld et al.

to the National Building Code can be heated for less than half the cost of heating one built in France according to the French building code.

Office buildings too can be built to sharply reduce commercial energy use. The Tennessee Valley Authority is planning to construct a new five-story, energy-efficient office building in Chattanooga, Tennessee, to house some 5,000 of its employees. The transparent roof of this spacious office building will permit large amounts of sunlight to enter during the wintertime. When combined with the tight insulation and additional sources of heat from bodies, office machines, and lights, the building will require relatively little additional energy for heating purposes. In the summertime, the roof will be shaded with louvers, and the building's air-conditioning system will rely on cold water from an underground aquifer beneath the building. (This water will enter the building at 59 degrees, well below normal room temperature, and will be returned to the aquifer downstream when it reaches 70 degrees.) This system will cut air-conditioning costs by some 75 percent below those of a conventional system.[113]

The private home in Saskatchewan and the office building in Chattanooga are but two of many examples of how architectural ingenuity can substitute for the use of purchased energy. Both demonstrate dramatically the potential for substituting modern technologies for dwindling fossil fuels. Both also highlight the need for new building codes. To date, international experience indicates that the most effective and workable building codes are those that—like the mileage standards established for automobiles in the United States in 1975—emphasize standards and performance rather than specific structural requirements. These give architects and builders maximum flexibility.

Beyond formulating building codes, careful planning at the community level is a key to increasing the thermal efficiency of buildings. In West Germany, a new community being planned as a suburb of Erlangen will integrate advanced concepts of energy efficiency, including solar architecture. It will be Germany's first community to be shaped largely by energy considerations. In Davis, California, town planners discovered that wide streets were serving as heat collectors, raising the energy requirements for air conditioning within the community. They responded by making the streets narrower, by reducing on-street parking, and by substituting parking bays. This reduced the paved area of heat collection, allowed more room for trees, and thus substantially reduced Davis' air-conditioning requirements.

Solar-oriented landscaping in public places and around homes and offices can also measurably reduce buildings' energy requirements. Trees, which both provide shade and cool the air by means of evaporation through transpiration, are natural summertime air conditioners. In the wintertime, strategically located evergreens provide shelter from the wind. Temperate-zone deciduous trees that provide shade in the summertime lose their leaves in the winter, permitting the sun to shine through when it is most needed. Solar landscaping, like solar architecture, increases energy efficiency.

Overall, it is quite possible, perhaps even likely, that the world's buildings will use less energy for heating, cooling, and lighting at the end of the century than they do today. In summing up this prospect in a Worldwatch Paper on energy and architecture, Christopher Flavin observes: "Even assuming substantial growth in housing, the world's buildings may be using 25 percent less fuel and electricity in the year 2000 than they do today—an important step toward achieving a sustainable world energy economy."[114]

The Renewable Energy Potential

Wood and hydroelectric power, currently the world's leading sources of renewable energy, rank fourth and fifth in the global energy budget after oil, coal, and natural gas. Yet, despite their importance in the global energy budget, many sources of renewable energy are frequently omitted from projections of world energy use because data on their abundance and availability are not available. For example, harnessing energy with rooftop solar collectors to heat water is not a commercial transaction, so this form of solar energy does not show up in national economic accounts. Likewise, much of the world's firewood is produced and gathered in subsistence economies without ever entering the marketplace. Hundreds of cities use urban garbage to generate electricity, but there are no readily available worldwide data on the quantity of combustible waste used for this purpose.

The data in Table 9-7 represent an initial effort to document the use of renewable energy in 1980 and to project that use to the end of the century. These data show renewable energy sources collectively supplying the energy equivalent of 1.81

Table 9–7. World Consumption of Energy from Renewable Sources, 1980, with Projections to 2000*

Source	1980	1985	1990	1995	2000
	(million metric tons coal equivalent)				
Wood	1,015	1,100	1,220	1,410	1,640
Hydroelectric	600	710	850	1,020	1,200
Wind	3	5	17	90	200
Crop Residues	100	110	110	100	100
Waste—methane	4	10	30	53	90
Waste—electric & steam	10	12	15	20	25
Geothermal	13	27	52	87	140
Energy Crops	3	16	30	45	55
Solar Collectors	1	5	18	49	100
Cow Dung	57	60	60	55	45
Photovoltaics	1	1	2	20	40
Total	1,807	2,056	2,404	2,949	3,635

*Electricity from all sources calculated in terms of coal required to produce equivalent amount.
Source: Worldwatch Institute.

billion tons of coals—or some 16 percent of the global energy budget. Between 1980 and the year 2000 the use of renewable energy is expected to more than double. In addition to offsetting the impact of rising oil prices, interest in renewable energy sources is being spurred by several economic considerations. First, since renewable energy resources are largely indigenous, the outlays of foreign exchange are often nonexistent or negligible, limited to those for imported equipment or technical advice. Second, many renewable energy sources are virtually inflation proof. Once a hydroelectric dam is constructed, the cost of generating electricity remains quite stable. Similarly, a homeowner who installs a solar water heater is immune to rising utility bills for heating water.

In employment terms too, renewable energy sources are attractive. Invariably, they require less capital and create more jobs than do fossil fuels or nuclear power. In this respect, the timing of the transition from fossil fuels to renewable energy could not be more fortuitous, coming as it does when unemployment is high and record numbers of young people will be entering the job market.

Another advantage is that time lags in the development of renewable energy resources are shorter than for most other energy sources. A decision to turn to wood in a heavily forested area takes no more time than that required to purchase a wood stove or a wood-fired boiler in the case of industry. A methane generator can be built in days. A small-scale hydro facility can be constructed with seasonally unemployed labor in a matter of months. Exceptions to this short lead time include large-scale hydroelectric projects, which can take many years, and firewood plantations, which can require close to a decade before harvesting can begin. But in general, renewable resources can be developed extraordinarily rapidly, as have wood fuel in the United States, geothermal energy in the Philippines, and energy crops in Brazil.

In some cases, rapid development of a given renewable energy source requires commercial mass production of a utilization technology. For example, the key to rapid growth in wind-generated electricity will be the assembly line production of wind generators. With the first wind farm scheduled to start generating in the state of Washington in 1981 and the first assembly line-produced wind generators scheduled for production in 1982, the stage is being set for rapid growth in the exploitation of this abundant energy source.

In some cases, the technologies required to develop renewable energy resources are closely related to existing, well understood technologies. For example, the engineering and aerodynamics of wind generators are close to those employed in the aerospace industry. Similarly the knowledge of deep drilling and geology brought to bear in oil exploration and production can be easily modified for geothermal development. Indeed, oil companies frequently discover geothermal resources when drilling for oil.

Of the several renewable energy technologies, the one whose future depends most heavily on further advances is photovoltaics. Unless costs are substantially reduced, solar cells' use will be limited to special situations, mostly remote applications. But if the costs can be brought down to the levels envisaged by the U.S. Department of Energy in its photovoltaic program (50¢ per peak watt) then these cells have a vast potential, particularly where electrical grids do not exist.

Aside from the economic and security considerations, the development of renewable energy resources could also be accelerated by negative developments in the use or production of other energy sources. If the acid rain damage were to build up, coal could become an unacceptable energy source. Or, if a way is not found safely to dispose of nuclear wastes, interest in renewable energy could accelerate even faster.

The rate at which renewable resources are developed will be influenced by how quickly national governments can inventory and exploit their indigenous resources. As of 1981, only a few have devised plans that will permit a smooth transition from the use of fossil fuels to dependence on renewable sources of energy. Here, legislation and financial incentives that encourage renewable energy resource development will play an important role. One example in the United States is the Public Utilities Regulatory Policies Act of 1978, which requires utilities to buy power generated by small systems at the cost required to generate that energy from new sources. The Natural Resources Defense Council reports that "homes or businesses that generate power from renewable resources such as hydropower, biomass, wind, and from cogeneration facilities or photovoltaic equipment will be able to sell back excess power to their local utility at reasonable rates."[115]

Of course, realizing and maximizing the renewable energy potential will mean that difficult tradeoffs will have to be made. If the world's hydro potential is to become a mainstay of a sustainable economy, it may be necessary to compromise on wilderness preservation, at least enough to permit this energy source to be tapped. If Japan is to develop its vast geothermal potential, it may have to relax its restrictions on energy development in its national parks, which are situated where geothermal potential is greatest. But even in view of the need to make these trade-offs, the potential of "renewables" is promising. In many cases, an upsurge in their growth may outstrip projections and expectations simply because envisaging their potential while they are still in such an early stage of development is difficult. The return to renewable sources promises a security of energy supply unknown to the latter stages of the petroleum era.

10

The Shape of a
Sustainable Society

A sustainable society will differ from the one we now know in several respects. Population size will more or less be stationary, energy will be used far more efficiently, and the economy will be fueled largely with renewable sources of energy. As a result, people and industrial activity will be more widely dispersed, far less concentrated in urban agglomerations than they are in a petroleum-fueled society.

The transition to renewable energy will endow the global economy with a permanence that coal and oil-based societies lack. More than that, it could lead us out of an inequitable, inherently unstable international energy regime since, unlike coal and oil, solar energy is diffuse, available in many forms, and accessible to all countries.

As the switch from fossil energy to solar energy progresses, the geographic distribution of economic activity is destined to change, conforming to the location of the new energy sources. The transition to a sustainable society promises to reshape diets, the distribution of population, and modes of transportation. It seems likely to alter rural-urban relationships within countries and the competitive position of national economies in the world market. Then too, a sustainable society will require labor force skills markedly different from those of the current oil-based economy.

The Changing Global Energy Budget

The energy component of the transition to a sustainable society has two dimensions as discussed—a shift to renewable energy sources and an increase in energy efficiency. Indeed, the shift in the composition of the global energy budget during the next two decades promises to be unprecedented. Trends in the share of energy supplied by some fuels will actually be reversed. After rising for several decades, the oil share began to decline in the late seventies while the wood share began to increase, reversing a three-century decline.

Some components of the future energy budget can be projected with more confidence than others. Oil is one of the easiest to project. With oil production either remaining essentially at current levels or, perhaps more likely, declining somewhat as a strong depletion psychology emerges in key exporting countries, its share of the global energy budget seems certain to continue the decline that started in 1974. For projection purposes, it is assumed that output will decline by roughly 5 percent by 1990 and an additional 10 percent by 2000. (See Table 10-1.)

Projecting future production of natural gas is somewhat more complicated. Historically, the production of gas and oil have increased in tandem, largely because natural gas and oil

Table 10–1. World Consumption of Energy, Nonrenewable and
Renewable, 1980, with Projections to 2000*

Year	Coal	Petroleum	Natural Gas	Nuclear	Renewables	Total
			(million metric tons coal equivalent)			
1980	3,149	3,908	1,807	244	1,807	10,915
1985	3,831	3,810	1,850	445	2,056	11,992
1990	4,660	3,712	1,900	645	2,404	13,321
1995	5,145	3,526	1,875	720	2,949	14,215
2000	5,680	3,322	1,850	730	3,635	15,217

*Electricity from all sources calculated in terms of coal required to produce equivalent
amount.
Source: Worldwatch Institute.

are often found together. But now, even though more gas fields
are being developed independently, new sources will presum-
ably be offset by the decline during the eighties and nineties
of gas production at oil fields.

Coal production will increase, but probably by ever smaller
increments. In the early eighties, world coal output could expand at about 4 percent per year, with much of the additional
output being substituted for oil in electrical generating plans
and in the production of steam heat for industry. With virtually all major industrial countries systematically converting
their oil-fired electric power plants to coal, this potential for
substitution will be largely exhausted by 1985. As a result, the
growth in coal production is likely to slow to some 3 percent
yearly during the last half of the decade. Thereafter, growth in
the demand for coal will depend in part on the capacity for
converting it into liquid fuel, a capacity that is not developing
as fast as once predicted.

Two potentially severe environmental constraints may limit
growth in coal use as the end of the century approaches. The
first is pollution. Even at current levels of coal burning, acid
rain is seriously damaging both plant and marine life in the
northern hemisphere. The second is the potential rise in the
atmospheric carbon dioxide level, which could induce unacceptable climatic changes. While burning the remaining re-

serves of readily accessible oil or natural gas would probably not markedly elevate carbon dioxide levels, burning all the coal that remains would do so.

A third constraint to coal use is economic. In weaning ourselves from petroleum, it makes sense to shift directly to a renewable energy source whenever possible rather than to shift to coal as an interim fuel and then switch to "renewables" later as coal reserves dwindle. The cost savings of the one-step shift would include those for retrofitting, fuel production, fuel distribution, and end-use facilities.

And finally, coal-importing nations face supply vulnerabilities. Like oil, coal can be embargoed for political reasons. Moreover, there are fewer exporters of coal than of oil, and two of the four principal exporters—South Africa and Poland—are uncommonly vulnerable to strikes, political unrest, and other disruptions. Given the risks associated with growing dependence on coal, the pressures to shift directly to renewable energy sources are likely to reduce the growth in coal production in the nineties to 2 percent per year.

With nuclear power plagued by economic, environmental, and political problems, its development is losing momentum—witness the fact that each successive annual projection of global end-of-century nuclear generating capacity gets smaller. Unless new reactor orders are placed soon in the United States, the world's leading producer of nuclear power, the national nuclear generating capacity will be declining by the end of the century as older plants are shut down.

Over the next two decades, growth in the solar component of the global energy budget will stand out. By the year 2000, the contribution of all sources of solar energy will collectively exceed that of petroleum, though by country that share will vary widely. While a few countries have laid well defined national plans for the switch from oil to solar energy, most have not.

Among the countries moving rapidly toward a sustainable

energy economy, Brazil is emerging as an early leader. Its program—aimed at eliminating most oil imports by 1990—is centered around the development of its vast hydroelectric potential, the use of wood as a residential and industrial fuel, and its fast-advancing agriculturally based alcohol fuels programs. With a pauper's endowment of fossil fuels and a once-ambitious nuclear program in arrears, Brazil is building an industrial economy based almost entirely on renewable energy resources. To ensure success, Brazil could further exploit its hydroelectric potential by relying less on the automobile and more on electrically powered urban and inter-city rail systems. This change would reduce liquid fuel requirements and thus lessen the competition for food-producing resources between the transport and food sectors. At the same time, Brazil urgently needs to curb population growth; if it does not, the favorable resource/population endowment that gives it so many energy options will begin to shrink.

China too has moved vigorously to develop its renewable energy resources—not so much because it lacks fossil fuels, as because it lacks the transportation infrastructure, investment capital, and technologies needed to exploit them. China's efforts have centered upon the construction of small-scale hydroelectric generating systems in rural areas, the production of methane from organic wastes, and an ambitious village-reforestation program designed to ensure a long-term supply of fuelwood. Alone, none of these programs will dominate China's long-term energy picture, but together they already dominate rural energy systems. And over the longer term China can develop its as yet largely untapped large-scale hydroelectric potential.

Under the pressure of near total dependence on imported oil, the Philippine government has designed an ambitious 10-year energy program intended to reduce oil from 91 percent to 56 percent of the energy budget by 1989.[1] Although coal and nuclear power are expected to account for some 15 percent of total commercial energy use in 1989, renewable energy sources —including hydroelectric, geothermal electric, wood, agricultural wastes, timber-industry wastes, and fuel alcohol from sugarcane—could push the renewable energy share of total energy use to one-third by the end of the ten-year plan.

So far, none of the advanced industrial countries is as far along in implementing renewable energy programs as Brazil and China. Yet Sweden, almost wholly dependent on imports for oil, is considering a plan for weaning its economy from the use of fossil fuels and nuclear power by exploiting its forest resources and abundant wind-generating potential—even as total energy consumption increases by an estimated 50 percent.[2]

In 1978, President Carter announced that the United States would try to obtain 20 percent of its energy from various solar sources by the end of the century.[3] Developments since then including the 1979 oil price hike and the virtual abandonment of new reactor orders by utilities suggest that the solar share could be substantially higher. Even as conservation efforts are reducing total energy consumption, the shift to renewable energy sources is accelerating. For example, use of fuelwood for residential and industrial purposes is rising far more rapidly than projected.

As outlined in Table 10-1, the global energy budget will grow from an estimated 10.9 billion tons of coal equivalent in 1980 to 15.2 billion tons at the end of the century—an increase of 39 percent, or 1.7 percent per year. Should population increase as projected, per capita energy consumption by 2000 for the world as a whole would change little in the midst of this growth. However, if population growth should slow along the lines of the timetable proposed earlier, then per capita energy consumption could increase accordingly. If per capita energy consumption in the United States and other affluent societies continues to decline as waste is eliminated, the low-income countries would be the principal beneficiaries of effective population policies.

The critical dimension of the global energy transition is time. The challenge is to use coal to supplement dwindling oil reserves, thus buying time to develop the earth's hydroelectric and geothermal potential, to plant community woodlots, to install solar collectors, to build electric wind generators, to build the methane generators, to plant the energy crops, to develop the many other renewable energy resources, and to design a more energy efficient economic system. In this light, increasing energy efficiency should be a high priority in all countries. Perhaps the greatest contribution that the United States could make would be to apply its unmatched technological and engineering know-how to reduce its imports of oil, phasing them out by 1990. Such an act, quite possible without sacrificing growth or reducing the quality of life, would measurably reduce pressure on world oil supplies, reduce inflationary pressures worldwide, and buy additional time to make the transition.

Even while the global shift to renewable energy progresses, the world needs to go beyond elementary concepts of conservation to redesign the economic system, making it more energy efficient. Our energy-wasteful global economic system evolved when oil cost $2 a barrel, so it cannot be expected to function smoothly when the price of oil or its equivalent reaches $40 or more per barrel. As cheap oil fades into history, each economic sector will have to be redesigned. For example, in a fuel short world, societies can maintain personal mobility only if they shift to more efficient forms of transportation. Likewise, forty-dollar-a-barrel oil also means overhauling the food production system. With costly oil, steers will not be able to stay in feedlots until they are heavily layered with fat. Just as we seek more fuel-efficient transportation, so we must also find more efficient processes for converting grain into animal protein. A steer in a feedlot requires seven pounds of grain for each pound of weight gained; a modern poultry producer requires scarcely two pounds of grain to produce a pound of meat.[4] In an energy-short world, we will eat more poultry and less beef.

Pulling off the energy transition smoothly will be an absorb-
ing activity involving governments, corporations, and individuals. Some steps will be obvious and straightforward. Finding
substitutes for oil in electrical generation will be relatively easy,
for instance, since the options are so various—coal in the short
run, hydropower, wind, geothermal heat, waste, wood, and
over the longer term, photovoltaics. By contrast, the transportation sector, which is so heavily dependent on petroleum,
faces adjustments in kind as well as degree.

A Sustainable Transportation System

The overwhelming thrust in the evolution of transportation
systems since World War II has been toward growing dependence on automobiles. Within a single generation, the world's
automobile fleet increased more than sixfold, going from just
under 50 million in 1950 to some 315 million in 1980.[5] In the
Western industrial countries, the automobile shaped both the
economic system and the way of life as well, becoming the
symbol of affluence and modernization. Even the Soviet Union
began to lay plans for an automobile-centered transportation
system, imitating the industrial West. Virtually all the Third
World countries, with the notable exception of China, aspired
to the U.S. model.

By the late seventies, North America had one car for every
two people, Western Europe had one car for every three people, and Japan was well on its way to the same sort of "automo-
bility."[6] According to a 1975 international survey, the automobile accounted for 89 percent of motorized passenger transport
in North America, 78 percent in Western Europe, and 68
percent in Latin America.[7] Elsewhere in the world the automobile's place was more confined. In the Soviet Union, for example, the automobile accounted for 11 percent of passenger
miles, and buses and trains, 89 percent—the inverse of the
ratio in the United States.

The worldwide trend toward automobile-centered transportation systems met with resistance during the seventies when the world automobile fleet began to outgrow its fuel supply. When supplies became particularly tight, as they did in 1974 and 1979 following disruptions in the flow of Middle Eastern oil, the United States and some other countries instituted odd-even day purchases of gasoline.[8] Japan and Brazil closed service stations on weekends to discourage unnecessary driving and fuel use, and New Zealand adopted a carless day, with a $500 penalty for violators.[9] Sri Lanka instituted the carless Sunday.[10] In Eastern Europe, Bulgaria went further than most countries and adopted an odd-even day use of automobiles.[11] East Germany raised the price of gasoline to nearly $3 per gallon, while most West European governments raised the tax on gasoline to over $1 per gallon.[12] Singapore began restricting automobile use in the inner city.[13] In West Germany cities, pedestrian malls became commonplace.[14] In various forms, "nuisance rationing" and other restrictions on auto use indicated clearly that the automobile fleet was indeed outgrowing its source of sustenance.

With the tightening of the liquid fuels supply, the automobile faced a day of reckoning. Once it became necessary to set fuel-allocation priorities, the private automobile was invariably accorded a low position on the totem pole of priorities. Regardless of the level of economic development or of the government's ideology, countries everywhere accorded food production higher priority than cars. In deforested Third World countries where kerosene is used for cooking fuel, governments gave cooking fuel priority over automobile fuel. (In Asia, for example, the refinery mix of products now yields two-thirds as much kerosene as gasoline.)[15]

Throughout the Third World, the industrial expansion needed to undergird national economies and accommodate the enormous growth in the labor force will also be given priority over private automobiles by planners: industry will require for fuel and, to a lesser degree, for feedstock much of the oil now allocated by market forces to cars. Even with the transport sector, the automobile will be accorded a lower priority. As fuel supplies tighten and governments are forced to support the use of more fuel-efficient forms of transportation, buses and trains will invariably take precedence over automobiles. In the competition between passenger transportation, part of which is discretionary, and freight, the latter almost always gets top priority.

Yet, establishing priorities for the use of dwindling supplies of liquid fuel is not itself enough. New sources of fuel are needed. Efforts to produce liquid fuels from coal, oil shale, and agricultural commodities notwithstanding, liquid fuels are likely to become ever more scarce. Meanwhile, remaining liquid fossil fuel reserves must be used sparingly and efficiently.

Fuel efficiency in a post-petroleum world comes down in one sense to getting more passenger miles per gallon—a quest in which the automobile fares poorly compared to the alternatives. In cities, buses and trains have a potential fuel efficiency of at least 150 passenger miles per gallon. In intercity transport, buses can achieve 200 passenger miles per gallon and trains twice that much if they are fully loaded.[16] In the United States, Greyhound buses (which account for a large share of intercity bus transport) averaged 144 passenger-miles per gallon of gasoline in 1979. In contrast, the American automobile, carrying an average of 1.4 passengers, got only 24 passenger-miles per gallon.[17]

The energy performance of buses and trains is often matched in fuel efficiency by mopeds, which can travel 130 miles on a gallon of fuel. But even mopeds cannot measure up in fuel efficiency to the bicycle. Weighing less than 30 pounds, the bicycle is durable and transportable; it requires little land and can often be powered with the excess food calories consumed by its rider.

In the worldwide effort to raise the fuel efficiency of the

transportation system, the auto is destined to fare poorly even with the scheduled efficiency improvements. Closely tied to liquid fuels, the growth in automobile production roughly parallels that of oil. From 1950 to 1973, growth in production was rapid, expanding at some 5 percent per year. Since then, it has oscillated around 30 million vehicles per year. (See Table 10-2.) It is quite possible that the production of 31.3 million automobiles in 1978 represents the historical peak and that production will continue the decline occurring since then as oil reserves dwindle.

Both the design and role of the automobile and the future of the automobile industry—the world's largest manufacturing industry—will be affected by the changing oil outlook. Suppliers to the industry of steel, rubber, glass, and parts will find their markets shrinking. The automobile service sector, including dealerships, gasoline service stations, and auto repair gar-

Table 10-2. World Automobile Production, 1950–80

Year	Number of Vehicles
	(million)
1950	8.0
1960	12.3
1970	22.6
1971	26.1
1972	27.5
1973	30.0
1974	26.1
1975	25.5
1976	29.2
1977	30.5
1978	31.3
1979	30.7
1980	27.6

Source: 1950–1979: U.S. Motor Vehicle Manufacturers Association; 1980: Worldwatch Institute.

ages will all be affected. In the United States, the number of automobile dealerships and service stations has already begun to decline.[18]

Realistically, of course, there is often no feasible substitute for the automobile. Thus, improving automobile fuel efficiency deserves the industry's highest priority. As of 1981, the most efficient automobile commercially available is the diesel-fueled Volkswagen Rabbit, a 4-passenger vehicle capable of getting close to 60 miles per gallon on the highway—an impressive performance record though by no means the ultimate.[19] A British Leyland 4-passenger vehicle prototype gets 83 miles per gallon.[20]

Regardless of which other efficiency improvements are made in the transportation system, passenger and freight traffic will have to be shifted from road to rail along major transportation arteries. The need is grounded in a simple fact: steel wheels on a steel rail have an inherent efficiency that rubber-tired vehicles on a road can never match. In addition, rail vehicles can run on electricity or coal, which makes them more versatile than cars or trucks. Among other things, this last point means that those railroads in Third World countries that still use coal may not have to worry about conversion. Trolleys, street cars, and other light rail systems can play an increasingly important role throughout the world's cities. C. Kenneth Orski, a U.S. urban transportation specialist, makes a strong case for them not only because they are energy-efficient in their own right but also because their use can define corridors for high-density development and thus encourage a more rational use of both land and energy.[21]

How fast national transportation systems are restructured depends on the effectiveness of national political and industrial leadership. Countries that quickly develop more fuel-efficient transportation systems will find themselves with a competitive advantage in world markets. By the same token, those faced with increasingly costly road-centered freight and passenger transport will find themselves handicapped in international competition. One industrial country, Sweden, has gone so far as to examine a future without private automobiles. In Stockholm, the Office of Future Studies, attached to the Prime Minister's office, has recommended phasing out private automobiles.[22] To accompany this phaseout, it recommends greatly expanding and improving the public transportation system and complementing it with an expanded fleet of rental automobiles for use on special occasions.

In the United States, the use of public transportation has been rising while gasoline usage has been falling. Following a steady decline for nearly three decades after World War II, mass transit ridership has been increasing since 1973.[23] In 1979 it jumped by a record 7 percent in one year, well above the 4 percent annual rise over the five preceding years. U.S. funding for mass transit in fiscal year 1981 totalled a record $4.6 billion.[24]

Just as rises in gasoline prices give public transportation a boost, they take their toll on highway usage. In November of 1979, the U.S. Secretary of Transportation, Neil Goldschmidt, cancelled a stretch of interstate highway planned for the state of Ohio.[25] For the first time, plans to build a highway were abandoned because of the projected lack of fuel. Early pronouncements by the Reagan administration indicate that the remaining segments of the U.S. interstate highway system may not be completed because of the high cost of construction.[26]

As longstanding transportation trends are reversed, the great risk to both consumers and governments is that of over-investment. The individual who buys a new car with a typical life expectancy of 10 to 13 years makes certain assumptions about the long-term availability and price of fuel—assumptions that may no longer be warranted. Similarly, public policymakers who invest public money in highway construction risk over-investment and the waste of scarce capital.

Where national and local governments plan wisely, making

a deliberate effort to shift to more fuel-efficient transportation, it may be possible to increase personal mobility and lower passenger and freight transport costs, even as liquid fuel supplies shrink. And where leadership and planning is inept, the converse is likely to be true.

The Resurgence of Agriculture

As efforts to create a sustainable society gain momentum, agriculture seems destined to play a far more central economic role, one that derives from its additional role as energy producer. The several-fold rise in oil prices is certain to translate into higher food prices over the longer term. Higher oil prices mean higher food-production costs. But, more important, since grains, root crops, sugarcane, and oilseeds can be converted into liquid fuel, the minimum market value of agricultural commodities will become their oil-equivalent value less the cost of converting them to fuel. As the installed capacity to convert food or feed commodities to fuel expands, the oil-equivalent value of the commodities will eventually become the floor price. In effect, the distinction between the agricultural and the energy sectors will fade as the price of oil begins to set the price of food.

More broadly, land once valued solely for its food-production capacity will acquire additional value because of its energy-collection potential. In some cases, the land used for energy collection may be poorly suited to agriculture anyway, but in others energy crops may displace food crops. Addressing this point, agronomist R. Neil Sampson observes that "seldom has such a totally new set of competitive forces been unleashed on the land as those that appear on the horizon in the declining decades of the petroleum era. As America and the world search for new sources of industrial materials and fuels to replace increasingly expensive, scarce, or unreliable sources of the past, the major focus of attention has turned to agriculture."[27]

This competition, in turn, promises to alter the relationship between agriculture and the rest of the economy, giving agriculture more favorable terms of trade with industry than it had in the petroleum era. In addition, land use will intensify and land will become more valuable, while relatively more jobs will be created in the countryside and fewer in the city. For millennia, agriculture has been a source of food, feed, and fiber—the demand for which will continue to expand along with population growth and rising incomes—but now agriculture is being called upon to produce more and more of the world's energy and industrial raw materials as well. For example, under the 10-year energy plan launched in the Philippines in 1979, energy-related activities will require nearly 3.5 million hectares of land, 440,000 of which will be in agricultural zones.[28]

As these trends take hold and as the natural forests shrink, farmers will turn more and more to agro-forestry, the simultaneous production of crops and trees. They will commercially produce trees for fuel, lumber, and even forage and industrial raw materials. In this production shift, chances are that farmers will plant trees on land that is least well suited for row cropping, either because it is too steeply sloping, too arid, or not fertile enough. With the proper selection of species and appropriate management, such efforts can increase food and energy production without intensifying the competition between the two.

Besides producing energy crops for liquid fuels and trees for fuel wood, farmers will be supplying more of the world's natural gas, largely from livestock waste. While energy is not yet extracted from feedlot waste on a wide scale, more and more of the world's large feedlots are likely to follow the example set by the 100,000-head operation in Oklahoma that converts all its waste into methane.[29]

As the market for agricultural products broadens and expands, cities stand to lose some of the traditional competitive advantage conferred by their control of advanced technology and capital, much as the industrial countries with similar advantages have lost ground in their dealings with pre-industrial oil exporting countries. Increasingly, the countryside will amass its own bargaining power. Third World countries in particular face a shift in rural-urban terms of trade that will favor the cities less than at present. Since World War II, many Third World governments have used export earnings to import cheap energy and cheap food for their cities. But with these cheap imports no longer available, clearly cities will increasingly have to turn to the rural economies of their own countries.

If a sustainable society is to be created in the post-petroleum era, land everywhere will have to be used much more intensively and carefully. The need to extract the utmost from land represents the basis of a potentially productive field of research, if not a new science. Particularly in view of the need to re-examine agricultural employment opportunities in a labor-surplus economy, agricultural practices that both provide work and make cultivation sustainable must be developed.

New techniques for managing land more intensively by using more labor are beginning to emerge, principally in Asia. In the Philippines, for example, a new rice-production system is evolving in areas that have the year-round water supplies needed for continuous production.[30] A farmer with, say, four acres of land divides it into small plots in such a manner that it is all in rice continuously except during the few days between harvest and replanting. Each week another plot is harvested and replanted as part of a continuous process. With such intensive rotation, the workload is distributed evenly throughout the year. Labor is used with maximum efficiency and the land yields three or four crops of rice per year.

Even in temperate zones, the potential for more intensive cropping deserves a close look. In the United States, for example, U.S. Government programs to limit production have until recently encouraged farmers to idle cropland, but with agricultural land now becoming scarce, the need to use it more intensively could lead to some fundamental shifts in cropping patterns. For example, one way of raising the overall output of land would be to double-crop the land with a winter food grain (such as wheat) and a summer energy crop (such as sweet sorghum) or feed crop (such as soybeans). Keeping the land covered with a crop for most of the year would both increase the amount of sunlight converted into biochemical energy and reduce soil erosion. The dual use of land to produce both food and energy may become commonplace in the post-petroleum world. In the U.S. western plains, for example, land could be used both for livestock grazing and for wind farms. Land that would provide wind-generated electricity for Denver, for example, could also produce beef. Similarly, land inundated for hydroelectric generation could also be used for intensive fish farming. Forested mountain passes could be used both to produce timber and to capture wind for electrical generation.

In a society sustained by renewable resources, agriculture and agroforestry will play far more prominent roles than they do today. As the pressures to intensify land use and to create more jobs begin to multiply, so too will the pressures for land reform. Only by breaking up large holdings into small ones on which family labor can be applied intensively will it be possible to satisfy the many claims on agriculture, including that for jobs.

New Industries, New Jobs

Designing an energy-efficient economy, shifting to renewable energy sources, arresting the deterioration of the earth's cropland, and stabilizing the basic biological systems will perforce alter the structure of the global economy. New industries will emerge even as old ones fade. The composition of the labor force will change. Numerous new skills will be needed, while many existing skills will become obsolete.

Initial attention in this economic restructuring has focused on the casualties—the beleaguered automobile industry and, in particular, on unemployed assembly-line workers. Yet, some employment changes will be for the better. For example, as oil becomes too costly to use to heat water, a wholly new, labor-intensive industry engaged in the manufacture and installation of rooftop solar collectors is springing up. At the same time, rekindled interest in railroads is certain to create a boom market for railroad cars and for new locomotives. In the sustainable society equivalent of beating swords into plow shares, the Montreal-based Bombardier Corporation is shifting manufacturing capacity from snowmobiles, which are energy consuming recreational vehicles, to subway and trolley cars, which are energy efficient transportation vehicles.[31]

Already, the demand for buses and bicycles is climbing almost as rapidly as the price of oil. In West Germany and the United States, bicycles outsold automobiles in the late seventies, and in 1980, they outsold automobiles in the oil-surplus United Kingdom for the first time in at least 20 years.[32]

As the potential for modern technology to harness wind power for electrical generation becomes more widely appreciated, another new industry will appear. Some analysts see a $10 billion-a-year industry, one that would rival the current U.S. aircraft industry in size, coming into its own by 1990.[33] Among the U.S. companies that are already investing heavily in the research and development of wind generators are Bendix, Boeing, General Electric, Hamilton Standard, Lockheed, Alcoa, and Westinghouse. As distilleries begin to produce fuel-grade alcohol along with alcoholic beverages during the eighties, the number of distilleries is likely to multiply several-fold, in some situations replacing refineries as the principal source of liquid fuels.

As forests increase in importance as a source of fuel, lumber, and raw materials for industry, and as agroforestry expands throughout the world, the demand for trained foresters will soar. Those who will find employment in this new industry will range from university-trained professionals to villagers who have been given no more than a six-week course in village-woodlot management. Others will have specialized training in selective cutting to maximize long-term forest yields.

In industrial countries with underutilized forests, climbing fuel prices will also stimulate forest industries and employment. In the United States, for example, a burgeoning fuelwood industry has begun to emerge. Closely associated with the emergence of the market for wood as a primary fuel is the growth in the market for wood stoves, wood furnaces, and wood-fired industrial boilers.

In a few countries, the business potential inherent in the transition to a solar-based society is drawing the attention it deserves. In West Germany, the German Association for Solar Energy—a consortium of companies in electrical engineering, air and space heating, air conditioning, and energy supplies—estimates that domestic and export sales of solar equipment combined could add up to a $62.5 billion market by 1990.[34]

The potential for the materials recycling industry grows with each increase in the price of oil. As recycled metal, glass, and paper become the primary source of materials in key industrial sectors, replacing virgin resources, the industry is certain to grow rapidly. Eventually, as materials recycling approaches 100 percent, the recycling industry will become a major sector in its own right. Numerous studies show that using recycled materials requires less energy and less capital, but creates more jobs than does the use of virgin materials. In a sustainable society, where planned obsolescence itself becomes obsolete, the ratio of employment in repair relative to that in the production of goods will increase.

As the transition to a sustainable society gains momentum, entirely new professions and vocations will emerge as new industries form. (See Table 10-3.) Within the energy sector, efforts to harness the enormous energy potential of the wind, for example, will create a need for thousands of wind prospec-

Table 10–3. A Sampling of New and/or Expanded Employment in a
Sustainable Society

Energy auditors	A Princeton University study estimates that 200,000 are needed in the United States over the next few years to identify the profitable conservation potential in existing housing stock.
Wind prospectors	Given the enormous potential for harnessing wind power, wind prospectors may become the sustainable-society equivalent of petroleum geologists in the petroleum culture.
Agronomists	Will be in demand as agriculture becomes a source of fuel as well as food and feed.
Foresters	Needed to plan and direct reforestation (primarily in the Third World), to serve as agro-forestry advisors, and to manage forests to achieve maximum sustainable yields.
Solar architects	Scale of need for the design of energy-efficient building is such that many practicing architects will require retraining.
Biogas technicians	An estimated 200,000 trained in China during late seventies to operate methane digesters.
Family planning midwives	Needed to ensure that family planning services are available to that one-half of the world's couples currently denied them.

Source: Worldwatch Institute.

tors to evaluate local wind power potential and to select generating sites—much as petroleum geologists guided us to new
energy sources during the petroleum era. Also needed will be
biogas technicians and engineers to supervise the construction
and operation of methane generators. China already has some
200,000 trained biogas technicians, though it needs many more
if it is to reach its goal of having 70 million methane generators
operating by 1985.[35]

As agriculture comes to produce fuel along with food, feed,
and fiber, the need for skilled agronomists to raise further the
productivity of land will expand accordingly. Arresting the
excessive erosion of soil from croplands will require a worldwide

cadre of agronomists trained in soil conservation. So too, the production of energy crops will require a new breed of agronomic specialists to advise on the production of these crops and their conversion into usable forms of energy.

In northern industrial countries, the need for energy auditors to improve the energy efficiency of buildings is increasing along with the price of energy. Energy analysts Robert Williams and Marc Ross estimate that the United States alone could profitably employ 200,000 energy auditors, or "house doctors," to audit the national housing and commercial building stock over the next several years.[36] Indeed, standards are now being set by the U.S. Government for the certification of qualified energy auditors. Worldwide, rising energy costs will generate jobs for hundreds of thousands of energy auditors.

If world population is to be stabilized, the world demand for family planning workers will also escalate accordingly. In some cases, high-level medical and administrative skills will be needed. But most of the work can be done by paramedics or by village midwives whose traditional delivery skills have been supplemented with training in family planning.

As architecture is revolutionized in the transition to a sustainable society, the demand for energy architects will outstrip the available supply. To meet the demand for both energy efficiency and solar design, practicing architects will require retraining since solar design skills will be needed before a new generation of architects comes into the field.

As pressures on the earth's land resources intensify, the market for land-use planners will increase accordingly. In a world economy depending heavily on solar energy, skills in raising the efficiency of land-use patterns will hold the key to maximizing energy availability. Numerous studies show that the sustainable society will be labor-intensive, particularly with respect to energy production. The Philippine Government's ten-year energy plan that is centered on a shift from oil to renewable energy is expected to employ some 441,000 people in the construction of energy facilities and some 30,000 in their operation.[37] In the United States, a detailed comparison of two alternative energy strategies for Nassau and Suffolk counties in eastern Long Island concluded that "an energy conservation/ solar energy strategy would create about 2.2 times as much employment within the Nassau/Suffolk region as would the proposed Jamesport nuclear power plant, per million dollars of expenditure and per unit of electricity supplied."[38]

Although the transition to a sustainable society has scarcely begun, it is already beginning to claim casualties as well as to generate employment. For instance, those companies that anticipated the demand for well-engineered, fuel-efficient cars are flourishing while those that did not are paying a high price. In fact, misjudgments in the U.S. auto industry have forced it to forfeit world leadership to Japanese automakers. In the economic transformation now beginning, those governments and corporations that can anticipate the changes will fare well economically but those that insist on clinging to the past risk becoming part of it.

The Future of Urbanization

United Nations projections show urbanization trends continuing unabated over the remainder of this century. Twenty-five percent urban in 1950 and 41 percent urban in 1980, the world is expected to be over half urban by the year 2000.[39] Even though widely accepted and frequently cited, these projected trends may not materialize.

The premise that urbanization trends will continue unaltered until most of the world's population is concentrated in huge urban agglomerations rests on the assumption that food surpluses produced in the surrounding countryside or imported from abroad can sustain urban expansion, that energy will be available to underwrite the higher energy costs of urban living, and that ever more people can find productive employment in the cities. There is now reason to doubt whether any of these assumptions will hold.

For each person who moves from the countryside to the city there must be a corresponding surplus of food produced in a rural area somewhere in the world. From the first urban settlements several thousand years ago until the middle of this century cities were sustained largely, if not entirely, by the food produced in the surrounding countryside. Since then, more and more cities have come to depend on food produced in the North American countryside. Accelerating urbanization since mid-century has been closely paralleled by the vast growth in grain shipments from North America—from 14 million tons in 1950 to 131 million tons in 1980.[40] As of 1980 most of the world's cities—from Leningrad to Lagos, Mexico City to Bombay, Cairo to Tokyo—depend on North American grain shipments for at least part of their food supplies. Yet, doubt grows as to whether the recent growth in North American grain exports can be sustained much longer.

Each person who moves from the countryside to the city raises energy requirements for food in two ways. First, as the urban population increases, each person remaining in agriculture must produce an ever larger surplus, which in turn invariably requires the substitution of energy for labor. At the same time, more energy is needed to process the food and to transport it to urban areas.

Urbanization also increases the amount of energy needed to dispose of waste. In the village, organic wastes are an asset that can readily be returned to the soil as fertilizer. Recycling these nutrients lessens the energy needed for synthesizing atmospheric nitrogen and for mining and processing phosphate and potash. In smaller communities where recycling is possible, the energy efficiency of the food system is thus far greater than in large cities, where such recycling of waste is much less efficient.

Apart from the amount of energy that urbanization requires, it requires energy in certain forms, most of them relatively expensive and hard to obtain. In a solar culture, energy sources are more widely dispersed and less transportable. Third World cities of five, ten, or fifteen million people can cook with kerosene, but supplying such large agglomerations with firewood is virtually impossible. Villagers can cook with firewood from village plantations, but collecting and sending firewood to large cities can be a logistical nightmare.

As with energy and food, jobs may be harder to come by in large cities. Creating a job in urban industry requires far more capital than putting someone to work in agriculture does. In addition, establishing village firewood plantations, growing energy crops, and undertaking other activities called for in the shift to renewable energy resources will create jobs in the countryside, not in the city. For example, because sugarcane distilleries must be located within roughly five kilometers of their feedstocks, the new forms of industrial employment they offer will be in the countryside.

Unchecked, the flow of people from the countryside to the city will precipitate food and energy shortages and add to unemployment. In view of this fact, the pro-urban biases implicit in much official policy deserve attention. The two sets of forces now propelling urbanization—the push forces that undermine the lot of peasants in the countryside, and the pull forces attracting migrants to the city—have often been reinforced by government policy.

National food-price policies, for example, that rely on ceiling prices to keep food costs down for city dwellers end up discouraging domestic food production. Ultimately, such urban-oriented policies both depress employment in the countryside and increase the need to import food—a double burden many Third World countries now bear. Public investment policies heavily biased toward urban welfare also aggravate both the push and the pull forces in most developing countries. Commonly, countries with 70 percent of their populations in rural areas will allocate only 20 percent of their public sector investment to the countryside.[41] As Professor Michael Lipton of the

University of Sussex has noted, "The rural sector contains most of the poverty and most of the low-cost sources of potential advance, but the urban sector contains most of the articulateness, organization, and power. So the urban classes have been able to 'win' most of the rounds of the struggle with the countryside, but in so doing they have made the development process needlessly slow and unfair."[42]

The resource availabilities and economic trends that stimulated the massive movement from the countryside to the cities over the past quarter century are now changing. These changes may help convince governments that the time has come to abandon their urban bias. Among other facets of the changes underway, the energy transition will inevitably affect human settlements, favoring the development of relatively smaller, more widely dispersed communities, rather than the continued amassing of people in large megalopolises. In short, the optimum size of human settlements is likely to be far smaller in a sustainable society.

Simpler Life-styles among the Affluent

As the transition to a sustainable society progresses, the rich are simplifying their life-styles either because economic forces leave them no choice or because materialism has lost some of its appeal. The rise in oil prices since 1973 precipitated a massive transfer of wealth from affluent industrial countries to the preindustrial societies that export oil. Oil-importing preindustrial societies have been dealt a severe economic blow, but in absolute terms the massive shifts in wealth have been away from the affluent industrial societies. Paying for high priced oil to maintain their life-styles is draining even the most affluent oil-importing countries of their wealth. Oil-price increases during 1979 alone increased the U.S. oil import bill by $40 billion, or roughly 2 percent of the gross national product.[43] As economist Lester Thurow points out, "If the members of OPEC get an extra 2 percent of our GNP, then there is 2 percent less to be divided among Americans. Someone's income and spending has to go down."[44] The international redistribution of wealth generated by the oil price rise may be only the beginning.

As oil prices continue to rise and to drive the transition to a post-petroleum world, changes in life-styles will increasingly come to reflect more than transfers of capital. In a petroleum-based economy, energy consumption per person is usually determined largely by purchasing power. But in a solar-based economy, energy consumption per person will be determined by such factors as solar intensity, population/land ratios, and the availability of the technological know-how and investment capital needed to develop local renewable energy resources.

Early indications of this international leveling effect can be seen in the shrinking size of U.S. automobiles. Of all the symbols of American affluence and conspicuous consumption, perhaps none is stronger—or more outdated—than the over-sized American automobile with its seemingly insatiable thirst for gasoline. As Americans turn to smaller, more fuel-efficient cars and to public transportation, gasoline consumption trends have been reversed. Driving a small car has become as fashion-able as it is practical. Between 1950 and 1978, gasoline consumption per person in the United States climbed steadily, rising from 274 gallons to 521 gallons. Since 1978, however, it has fallen sharply: 1980 gasoline consumption per American is estimated at 449 gallons, 14 percent less than the 1978 peak. (See Figure 10-1.) If this decline continues, as is likely, energy-importing Third World countries will be among the principal beneficiaries of this lessened pressure on resources.

Yet another transportation trend that portends simpler life-styles among the affluent is the resurgence of the bicycle. While bicycles are widely used in the Third World countries, particularly in Asia, they had virtually disappeared as a means of transport in industrial countries by 1970. In recent years, however, as the price of gasoline has climbed, they have staged a strong comeback in North America, Western Europe, and Japan. By some estimates the number of bicycle commuters in

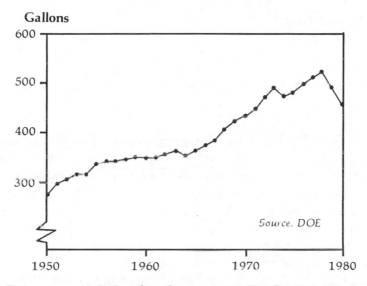

Figure 10-1. U.S. Gasoline Consumption Per Capita, 1950-80

the United States may have more than doubled since 1975, when U.S. Bureau of Census figures showed nearly half a million people riding to factory and office by bicycle every day.[45] On the eve of the transit workers' strike in New York City during the spring of 1980, Mayor Koch encouraged New Yorkers to commute by bicycle, saying, "We'd like to see New York look like Peking in the morning.[46] All indications are that the share of miles travelled by bicycle is gaining steadily in Western industrial societies.

Another harbinger of life-style change is the recent upsurge in wood fuel use in affluent countries. After a century-long decline in the use of wood as fuel in the northern tier of industrial countries, millions of families have recently returned to wood as a source of fuel.[47] In heavily wooded areas of the affluent north, industries too are turning to wood as a fuel, much as Brazilian, Thai, or Ugandan firms already have. Further larger increases appear to be in store.

In diets, too, the trend among the affluent is toward simplicity. Even though the heavy consumption of grain-fed steak, like that of gasoline, has long symbolized American affluence, beef consumption per person in the United States declined from 128 pounds in 1976 to 105 pounds in 1980, a fall of some 18 percent. (See Figure 10-2.) While U.S. beef consumption per person may fluctuate somewhat, it will likely continue to decline over the longer term.

Ironically, declines in consumption of some items among the affluent often correlate with improvements in the quality of life. The reduced consumption of fat-rich beef, for example, is in part the result of individual efforts to reduce cholesterol intake and the risk of heart disease. Similarly, supplementing automobile driving with bicycling is often as much a matter of exercise as economy.

Whether motivated by self-interest or not, consumption cutbacks by the affluent can also contribute to the welfare of the neediest. In the case of food consumption, efforts to reduce

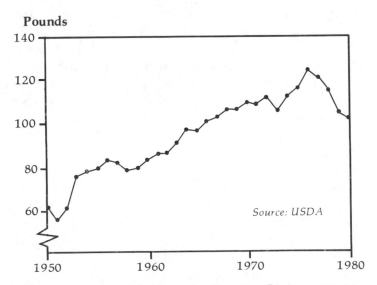

Figure 10-2. U.S. Beef Consumption Per Capita, 1950-80

the adverse effects of overconsumption—reduced life expectancy, increased susceptibility to illness, and reduced productivity—can free up resources to increase consumption among the undernourished, many of whom suffer the same symptoms.

As recycling technologies are perfected and programs developed, raw material consumption per person in affluent societies with slowly growing or stable population is also likely to decline. In a mature industrial economy that recycles materials invested in its capital stock, the consumption of virgin materials could actually fall below that in a developing country that is still accumulating its basic capital stock.

Yet another facet of life-styles likely to become much more similar among classes and nations is family size. While families are not likely to get much smaller in industrial countries where fertility levels are already below replacements levels, families in many Third World countries almost certainly will. Indeed, the average family size in Singapore and Hong Kong is now essentially the same as in Western Europe.[48] After several years of rapidly falling fertility in China, families there are now little larger than in the United States.

Clearly, the trend toward ever greater consumption on the part of the rich is weakening in some quarters and life-styles are beginning to converge in some respects. In a world where the production of energy, food, and other key commodities is no longer expanding rapidly, people in the low-income countries will be able to consume more only if the world's affluent reduce their claims by using resources more efficiently. Indeed, as long as the production of key commodities is being outpaced by population growth, the poor can consume more only if the rich consume less.

Third World Reinforcement

Until a decade ago, the conventional wisdom in international development held that the faster the industrial countries grew, the better the growth prospects for the developing countries would be. Faster growth in the industrial countries was believed to create more markets for the raw materials and the products of light industry in the Third World. Maintaining robust economic growth was thought to be the industrial countries' most important contribution to Third World development.

While this "trickle down" model of international development was plausible when resources were abundant, it is obviously inappropriate when they are scarce. If industrial countries were to continue to expand rapidly their already voracious consumption of energy and raw materials, it could deprive the Third World of the resources for development. If, as the traditional model of development holds, developing countries are closely tied to the industrial economies, poor countries cannot make economic headway unless the rich ones do. With slower growth in prospect for the industrial societies, developing-country dependence is thus ultimately an economic dead end.

Faced with this clearly untenable situation, developing countries would seem to have little choice but to decouple their economies gradually from those of the industrial countries and to concentrate instead on expanding their trade and investment ties with each other. Indeed, the reasons for expanding economic ties among Third World countries are becoming stronger—in part because they possess most of the world's exportable surplus of oil and in part because some (including India, Brazil, South Korea, Taiwan, the Ivory Coast, Mexico, and Venezuela) now have well-developed industrial sectors. An example of such a profitable relationship would be one between energy-rich Nigeria and heavily industrialized Brazil—the most populous countries on their respective continents. Similarly, India (which is trying to establish new industries) has needs complementary to those of the capital-rich oil-exporting countries around the Persian Gulf (including Iran, Kuwait, and Saudi Arabia). Among the Andean Pact countries, Venezuela

is in a position to provide both industrial leadership and investment capital to the other members.

In light of these new developments, much of the rhetoric of
Third World proponents of the New International Economic
Order is curiously out of date. Since economic growth in the
industrial countries is becoming progressively slower, efforts by
Third World countries to reinforce each other's growth would
be more effective than depending on stagnating industrial-
country markets.

In strengthening trade and investment ties with each other,
Third World countries often have one advantage over industrial countries: industrial goods designed for internal use in one
Third World country are more relevant to the needs of other
Third World countries than most products designed for use in
industrial countries. For example, two-wheel "walk-behind"
power tillers made in Taiwan are far more appropriate for
export to other Third World rice-producing countries than are
the huge tractors commonly used in North America and the
Soviet Union.

By the same token, rugged, durable buses of the sort needed
for unpaved country roads and manufactured in, say, India
would have an edge in Third World markets over those manufactured in an advanced industrial society. When Tata, an
Indian manufacturer, won a contract for the sale of 200 buses
to Ghana in competition with British and German interests in
1980, the precedent represented more than the triumph of
Indian technology. As India's High Commissioner in Ghana,
P. Alan Nazareth, observed, the deal brought to the fore "the
practical benefits of economic collaboration among developing
countries."[49] Similar opportunities for Third World lateral
trade exist in the manufacture and sale of railroad passenger
cars, freight cars, locomotives, motorized rickshas (India), bio-
mass-conversion technologies (Brazil), methane digesters and
small hydropowered electrical generators (China), and flat-
plate solar collectors (Hong Kong).

Services and technical assistance could also be exchanged bilaterally and profitably among Third World countries to a much greater extent than they are now. South Korea's exciting achievements in community forestry, for instance, deserve to be shared with other countries. Within the field of family planning, Colombia and Indonesia could share with other developing countries the organizing techniques used in their highly successful birth reduction programs. Taiwan, producing almost two crops per acre per year, leads the world in land-use intensity and could profitably exchange its know-how with other nations.[50] When these opportunities for Third World cooperation and reinforcement in industrial development, agriculture, family planning, and developing renewable energy resources are viewed against the backdrop of the vast capital surpluses now accumulating in several Third World countries, the emerging potential for Third World economic reinforcement is clear.

Greater Local Self-Reliance

From the onset of the Industrial Revolution and the time fossil fuels were first put to use, economic interdependence among countries has been deepening. Early on, differences in the rates of industrial development among countries set the stage for the profitable exchange of industrial goods for food and raw materials. Much later, the availability of cheap oil made transportation of goods over long distances relatively easy and affordable, further expanding the international trade potential.

Beginning in the mid-seventies, rising oil prices became an engine of growth for world trade as oil-importing countries, unable to quickly cut back on oil use, tried to increase exports of other commodities in order to pay their oil bills. As a result, international trade expanded rapidly and the world economy became extraordinarily interdependent as the seventies ended. International economic integration, in turn, left countries and individuals highly vulnerable to external economic and political forces.

With the transition to a sustainable society under way, the growth in international interdependence may shortly come to an end, reversing a trend that began with industrialization. With only limited access to cheap and versatile petroleum, moving bulky goods over long distances becomes increasingly prohibitive. More important, while both coal and oil are highly concentrated in a few regions, all countries have renewable energy sources in one form or another. Thus, in the solar age the amount of energy traded among countries will be only a fraction of what it was in the petroleum age. While world trade in coal has recently turned upward, the 9 percent of output crossing national borders is not likely to even remotely approach the 54 percent share of oil that enters international trade.[51]

Even as international trade patterns come to reflect declines in the amount of oil available for export, importing countries will of necessity turn inward to develop their indigenous energy resources. Developing comprehensive materials-recycling programs, for example, will enable mature industrial economies with stable populations to live largely off the indigenous raw materials embodied in their capital stock, thus reducing the need for imported virgin raw materials to a low level.

In a post-petroleum world dependent largely on renewable energy sources, industry will be located near new energy sources. Countries and localities generously endowed with energy—either hydropower, geothermal energy, wind power, or perhaps energy crops—will undoubtedly have a competitive advantage in attracting industrial investment and sustaining industrial activity. Moreover, in this world, economic self-sufficiency is likely to be greater at all levels—the family and the community as well as the nation—since many of the forces that prompt countries to reduce their dependence on external supplies of food, energy, raw materials, and even manufactured goods will also work their will on communities and individuals. Indeed, public and personal efforts to reduce consumption, especially of imports, will reinforce each other. For instance, national policies aimed at minimizing food or energy imports serve the same end as local efforts to increase food or energy production. By the same logic, by helping reduce demand for oil, bicycle commuters and transit riders are doing their part to immunize their country against disruptions in the international flow of oil.

More generally, the decline of oil as an internationally traded commodity could indirectly trigger other actions that will reduce international economic interdependence. For example, as exportable oil supplies dwindle, food-exporting countries will be tempted to convert their exportable surpluses of grain, sugar, and other foodstuffs into automotive fuel. If they do, exportable food supplies will diminish, forcing food-importing countries to increase their food self-sufficiency. Thus a decline in international trade in oil could trigger a comparable decline in international trade in food. In turn, absolute declines in international trade in these two commodities would markedly reduce overall international trade and economic interdependence.

By definition, a sustainable society is likely to be more self-reliant and less vulnerable to external forces. In some ways, a new autonomy for nations is inevitable since the complexities of managing growing interdependence have often proven too much for existing international institutions to handle. In other respects, self-reliance will come about as a result of careful planning and hard work on the part of governments and individuals working toward the same ends—against inflation and for security of supply.

From Growth to Sustainability

For governments, engineering the transition to a sustainable society may become an all-absorbing activity, one that will eclipse growth as the focus of economic policy making. As the eighties begin, there is already in evidence a subtle but unmistakable shift in investment away from that designed to achieve growth and toward that designed to ensure sustainability. This shift takes many forms, but investments in various renewable energy sources and in energy conservation as replacements for oil or natural gas and, to a lesser degree, coal are among the most numerous. Occasionally, renewable sources will supplement nonrenewable ones, but for the most part they will substitute for them, helping more to sustain than to expand the economy. Although the switch in energy sources may not expand energy output, the investment in new equipment used in the conversions will boost GNP in the short run.

Electric utilities are already investing heavily in converting existing generating capacity from oil to coal, geothermal power, hydropower (large-scale or small-scale), wind power, and in a handful of countries, wood-fired capacity. Substantial though such investments are, most are aimed not at increasing generating capacity, but at ensuring that the utility will continue to generate electricity as oil supplies dwindle. Likewise, in those countries shifting to the use of alcohol fuels, the large investment in fuel-grade distilleries to replace oil refineries will not increase the liquid fuel supply. Rather, it will help keep the arteries of transportation open as oil supplies dwindle.

Corporations the world over are investing large sums of money to insure that their operations can be sustained. For example, the Scott Paper Company, one of the world's largest manufacturers of paper products, is converting its oil-fired plant and electrical generating plant complex in Maine so that it can be fueled with wood.[52] This $65-million expenditure will not increase the Scott Paper Company's output of tissues by one box. But the company thinks the investment is justified because it will insure that output can be sustained when oil is no longer available. Worldwide, hundreds of other such investments are being made in the paper and wood-products industry.

In the aluminum industry too, plants are being relocated as part of the shift from fossil fuels to renewable energy sources. Producers of aluminum, an extraordinarily energy-intensive commodity, are attracted particularly to cheap hydroelectricity in remote areas accessible only by water. Prominent among the relocation sites are the Brazilian Amazon region, Alaska, and remote Canadian locations such as Goose Bay, Labrador.[53]

Perhaps the most dramatic early example of the shift of economic production facilities to the site of renewable energy sources is that of the aluminum industry to the Brazilian Amazon. Brazil plans to exploit the enormous hydroelectric potential of the Amazon and its tributaries for this manufacturing process while aluminum firms from the United States, Canada, the Netherlands, West Germany, and Japan are also investing in Brazil. As a direct consequence, Brazil's aluminum output has quadrupled in ten years, a pace that appears likely to continue as investment plans materialize.[54] Clearly opting for sustainability of aluminum production over growth in output per se, Japanese firms are closing their domestic fossil-fuel-based aluminum facilities as they build new plants in Brazil and elsewhere.[55]

Within the United States, where the aluminum industry depends heavily on fossil fuels, rising prices are making the cost of building additional smelters prohibitive. Yet, developing a small fraction of the vast Alaskan hydro potential could help the U.S. industry maintain its competitive position. While the gradual relocation of the international aluminum industry to sites where cheaper, renewable power sources are available will be costly, this investment is key to the evolution of a sustainable economic system since these new plants will be powered by an energy source that can, in effect, last forever.

Similar shifts in investment emphasis are occurring in Detroit. Until recently, new investment in the automobile industry was largely in new plants for expanded output. Now, however, the automobile manufacturers are committing vast sums of investment capital to the design and production of more

fuel-efficient automobiles. The associated retooling investments, the largest in the industry's history, are not intended to
expand automobile production capacity, but rather to help
insure that automobile-centered transport systems will become
efficient enough to survive as liquid fuels become scarce.

One of the earliest industrial investments in sustainability
was in pollution control mechanisms. Beginning in the early
seventies, the share of new investments going to pollution
control, as opposed to production expansion, increased steadily.
Billions of dollars were committed to minimizing the destructive effects of pollution on both the biological life support
systems and on human health. The tens of billions of dollars
invested to reduce the flow of pollutants from factories in the
seventies did not increase production of consumer goods from
these factories one iota. In effect, this was an investment in
sustainability.

In households, investment trends reflect the same philosophy that industry and governments are adopting. During the
fifties and sixties, most home-improvement loans in the United
States were for adding new rooms either for family expansion
or recreation. In the late seventies, this investment pattern
began to shift as homeowners invested more in insulation, solar
retrofitting, and other "no-growth" measures in order to reduce their requirements for purchased energy. These investments do not increase the capacity of the home, but they will
help ensure that living in the house is comfortable and affordable as energy prices climb.

The shift in emphasis from growth to sustainability is subtle,
sometimes more subconscious than conscious. But it is
nonetheless real, affecting not only progress toward a sustainable society but also the rate of economic growth. This belated
concern with sustainability is now permeating the thinking in
councils of government, in corporate boardrooms, and that of
individuals as well. This new attention to sustainability at the
expense of near-term growth may be the most important, but
analytically neglected, economic development of recent years.

II

The Means of Transition

The transition to a sustainable society will challenge the capacity of countries everywhere to change and adapt. Some adjustments will occur in response to economic forces, some in response to public policy changes, and still others as a result of voluntary changes in life-styles. Market forces will also play a central role in the adjustment process, but in many situations they will be more effective if augmented by public policy. To exploit fully the market's role in the transition, political leaders will have to learn its strengths and limitations.

These same leaders will also have to learn how better to manipulate tax policy, sometimes using it as an incentive, sometimes as a disincentive—sometimes both. Other institutional keys to the shift to a sustainable society are the more creative and responsible regulation of economic activity, and the reordering of budgetary and R&D priorities. In all, some policy instruments will have to be sharpened, some retired, and some created to fit the changing contours of circumstance and social will.

Urgency of the Transition

The scale of the transition to a sustainable society is matched by the urgency with which it must occur if major economic disruptions are to be avoided. That urgency notwithstanding, the shift to a sustainable society takes place in two stages. First, trends that the environment and the economy cannot withstand must be arrested; then they must be reversed. For example, the historical growth in dependence on oil has apparently ended; it will have been reversed if the fall in consumption between 1979 and 1980 continues. By contrast, soil erosion is worsening, and its reversal is as yet impossible to foresee. Similarly, while awareness of deforestation is spreading, concern has not yet been translated into sufficient programs and resource commitments.

The urgency of arresting and reversing unsustainable trends derives in part from the tendency of the negative trends to reinforce themselves. For instance, once forests begin to shrink under pressure of excessive demand, the process feeds on itself. When the sustainable yield threshhold is crossed, ever increasing claims are made on an ever smaller resource base which helps explain why some countries have been largely deforested within a few generations. The same negative syndrome applies to soil erosion, overgrazing, and overfishing.

Efforts to arrest and reverse ecological and economic deterioration are proceeding unevenly. Population is a case in point. While a few West European countries have already stabilized their populations, others have yet to recognize even the need

Building a Sustainable Society

for slowing population growth, much less stabilizing it. Between these extremes are those countries that have introduced family-planning services, and those countries that have adopted population stabilization as a goal but have some distance to go before achieving it. (See Table 11-1.)

An examination of the principal components of the transition shows that it has just begun. With respect to each of its

Table 11–1. Early and Advanced Stages of the Transition to a Sustainable Society

	Early Stage	Advanced Stage
Population Policy	Introduction of family planning services	Adoption of population stabilization as a social goal
Energy Consumption	Focus on saving energy	Redesign economic system to reduce energy needed
Land Use	Cropland preservation	Land-use planning
Agriculture	Produces food, feed, and fiber	Produces food, feed, fiber, and fuel
Population Distribution	Flow from countryside to cities slows	Population distribution shaped by location of renewable energy supplies
Role of Automobiles	Smaller, more fuel efficient automobiles	More sophisticated planning at community and personal level reduces need for automobiles
Energy Sources	Largely fossil fuels with limited dependence on renewable energy sources	Renewable energy sources dominate
Materials Recycling	Largely voluntary piecemeal programs	Mandatory recycling programs

Source: Worldwatch Institute.

facets, a few countries have reached the advanced stage but most are only beginning the process. Basic changes in values usually occur only incrementally, and institutions do not learn as fast as individuals. As a result, years often elapse before changes in personal values are reflected in public policies and programs.

Role of the Market

As a transitional force, the market has both strengths and weaknesses. One of its strengths is its capacity to allocate resources among various uses. In a complex, modern economic system, central planners are hard-pressed to allocate resources more efficiently or intelligently than the market does. As economist Lester Thurow points out, "Economic markets make better decisions than those made by the political process because they economize on the knowledge needed by any one individual to make good decisions."[1] Moreover, when market discipline is not imposed on production, waste occurs: resources get plowed into products that no one wants.

The functioning of a market economy rests heavily on a complex information system, one that tells the producer what consumers want. Not only can the market perform this function more precisely than a centrally planned economy, but it can also do so faster. In a perfectly competitive market economy, the failure to satisfy consumer demands shows up immediately, whereas in a centrally planned economy it may take years to adjust to consumer demand. Meanwhile, vast quantities of productive capacity and of manufacturing materials go to waste. For example, a women's shoe factory in the Soviet Union may perform quite satisfactorily according to socialist standards, meeting its production quotas year after year. But the shoes can simply pile up in a warehouse if Soviet women do not consider them stylish. Such gaps between producers and consumers in the Soviet Union contribute to a continuing inventory of unmarketable goods with a value that has been estimated at three to four billion rubles.[2]

Yet another strength of the market is its ability to substitute one commodity for another as relative abundances and scarcities shift. Concisely and unambiguously, prices tell buyers which commodities are scarce and which plentiful.

Its many "selling points" notwithstanding, however, an unregulated market economy functions better in a frontier society than it does in one that is pressing against resource limits. Where virgin resources are abundant, their use or the conditions under which they are used need not be restricted. However, when the demands of the economy begin to press against the available supplies of land, minerals, water, and waste-absorptive capacity, the market economy needs to be modified in the public's interest.

One problem with the free market is that it is no respecter of carrying capacity. Market forces can destroy fisheries, forests, grasslands, and croplands. The market has no alarm that sounds when the carrying capacity of a biological system is transgressed. Only when the system collapses and prices soar does the market "know" that anything has gone wrong. By this time, of course, the threatened resource may be irreparably damaged.

Another weakness of markets is their inability to take into account the external costs associated with various economic activities. The classic case is industrial air pollution. The polluted air emerging from the smokestacks of a steel smelter may destroy fresh water fisheries or agricultural crops for miles around. But what does the producer or the consumer care? The costs of pollution are borne by neither. They are paid instead by those who live on the leeward side of the steel plant.

In general, modern markets function far less effectively than economic textbooks suggest. Corporate concentration in key production sectors such as computer, automobile, and aerospace manufacturing reduces competition. Then too, the manipulation of public tastes and appetites through advertising distorts the market in ways that may not serve the public interest, and that sorely impede the transition to a sustainable society.

Another market pitfall is short-sightedness. In the market, day-to-day decision-making takes place with little concern for long-term perspectives. For example, even if existing farming practices contribute to excessive soil erosion and to a gradual long-term decline in the soil's inherent productivity, measures to arrest soil erosion will not be sanctioned by the market unless they pay off quickly. In a highly competitive market with narrow profit margins, adopting soil-conserving practices could lead to bankruptcy. In such a situation, only public subsidies of the needed conservation practices or regulations requiring farmers to adopt practices can serve the long-term public interest. The market cannot.

Similarly, the world oil market until recently lacked both a long term perspective and any responsiveness to the public interest, which is best served by a rate of depletion that allows a successful transition to alternative energy sources. From this perspective, OPEC was a godsend. For more than 20 years prior to the dramatic increase in oil prices in late 1973, the world's oil consumption had been expanding at some 7 percent per year.[3] Had the increase continued at this rate, it eventually would have culminated in an abrupt, traumatic transition to the post-petroleum era.

As a general matter, markets serve private not public interests. But this is particularly so with respect to land use. In American suburban communities where little land-use planning or zoning has taken place, unsightly and inefficient urban sprawl has resulted. While the land speculators have profited, often handsomely, from this lack of regulation, the community at large has been stuck with both an unwieldy system and with the higher costs of providing social services and utilities, a burden it bears in the form of higher taxes and utility rates.

Some market proponents argue that market forces can always be counted upon to bring supply and demand into balance. This point is well taken, but this alleged market strength is not an undiluted blessing. The more important question may be at what price demand and supply are brought into balance. If wheat is in short supply in the world market, the price rises, signaling to farmers the need to produce more wheat. At the same time, the rising price shrinks effective demand (that is, demand backed up by purchasing power). As the price rises and thus trims effective demand, consumption may be driven below subsistence levels. Untrammeled, market forces can lead to hunger, even famine.

While most governmental intervention in the market is in the public interest, many ill-conceived interventions have done more harm than good. For example, oil-price controls in the United States during the seventies prolonged excessive dependence on oil. Indeed, artificially low oil prices have distorted the economic system to such an extent that belated decontrol is requiring some painful adjustments. In effect, oil-price controls encouraged consumption and delayed development of the alternatives.

As worldwide pressures on natural resources and ecosystems intensify, the resulting ecological and economic stresses are likely to lead governments to intervene more in the marketplace. The worse an economy appears to perform, the greater the pressures to intervene. Here, the risk is that government will address the symptoms of the malady rather than the causes, thus aggravating the problem. For example, as growing demand forces food costs up, governments will be tempted to impose food-price controls. But such controls discourage production and further escalate food-price inflation. Needed in this case instead is a greater commitment to agricultural development and more effective family-planning programs.

As a transitional force, the market system will no doubt need the reins of public policy. Financial incentives and disincen-

tives, regulatory measures, and shifts in budgetary priorities—
these and other policy instruments will be needed if the disruptions associated with the transition are to be minimized.

Financial Carrots and Sticks

When market adjustments are not fast enough, governments
can use financial incentives and disincentives to bring about
the needed changes. These include tax deductions, subsidies,
outright grants, low-interest loans and accelerated equipment-
depreciation schedules. In centrally planned economies, they
may also take the form of wage increases, performance
bonuses, and preferred access to housing, education, or medical
care.

Financial incentives and disincentives are now being widely
employed in the effort to conserve energy, speed the shift to
renewable energy resources, and slow population growth. Tax
deductions, one of the most widely used financial incentives,
are being offered by many national governments to individuals
and businesses that invest in energy conservation or install solar
equipment. In the United States, where there are some 38,000
tax-levying authorities, many local governments are joining
Washington in offering tax relief to those who participate
actively in the energy transition. For example, Vermont has
waived property taxes on residential solar installations.[4]

Some governments use outright grants to help underwrite
the cost of transition-facilitating investments. In the United
Kingdom, for instance, the government provides £50 grants to
all homeowners who insulate their residences.[5] Subsidies for
adopting soil-conservation activities are used in some countries.
Following the Dust Bowl era of the thirties, the U.S. Department of Agriculture made direct payments to farmers who
planted winter cover crops, set up windbreaks to reduce soil
erosion, or took other soil-conservation measures.

Governments can also use low-interest or interest-free loans to encourage investments in activities that will help create a sustainable society. In Brazil, which imports nearly all of its oil, the government is providing low-interest loans for the construction of distilleries.[6] This program is designed to accelerate production of alcohol as an automotive fuel and, to a lesser degree, as a feedstock for the chemical industry. (See Table 11-2.)

Those centrally planned economies that use wage increases or bonuses to affect production can help the transition along in various ways. They may, for example, give bonuses to factory managers who reduce energy use while maintaining production or to managers of state farms who reduce soil erosion to the tolerance level. In China, couples with one child who sign a pledge not to have any more children receive an immediate wage increase of some 12 percent.[7]

In societies with a large public sector, giving preferred access to housing, education, medical care, and jobs can further social objectives. The Government of Singapore, which administers much of the new housing in this South Asian city-state, rewards small families with preferred access to housing.[8] In China, if a student is an only child and if the student's parents sign a pledge not to have any more children, he or she gets preferential consideration for admission to the better schools.[9]

On the other side of the tax coin are tax penalties. (See Table 11-3.) In densely populated Nepal, no income tax deductions for children are permitted for more than two children.[10] While the tax-paying segment of the population is small, this measure does nonetheless signal official support for small families. In Germany, a stiff tax on gasoline, originally designed to raise revenue, has recently been increased to encourage gasoline conservation.[11] Singapore has recently enacted steep auto-registration fees, up to $2,320 per vehicle, to discourage any further growth in the automobile fleet.[12] The import tax the Kenyan government imposed on automobiles imported for private use may exceed the cost of the vehicle itself.[13]

Table 11–2. A Sampling of Financial Incentives Designed to Facilitate the Transition to a Sustainable Society

Place	Incentive	Purpose
California	Zero-interest loans from utilities for house weatherization	To encourage energy conservation and eliminate need to build new power plants.
Norway	A $100 refundable deposit on new cars plus a $100 premium when old car is scrapped.	To encourage recycling and reduce steel imports.
East Germany	Prices of steel scrap doubled and of newspapers tripled at recycling centers.	To reduce imports of energy and raw materials.
China	Couples with one child who sign pledge to have no more children receive monthly bonus until child reaches 14.	To encourage smaller families and bring population growth to a halt.
United Kingdom	Homeowners eligible for grants up to £50 for installing insulation.	To conserve energy
Brazil	Low-interest loans for construction of alcohol distilleries.	To spur production of alcohol for fuel.
United States	Nonrefundable income tax credit up to $4,000 for homeowners who install solar heating equipment.	To encourage the use of solar heating systems.
Finland	Government grants and loans for remodeling that decreases energy consumption or permits the use of domestic fuels like wood and peat.	To conserve energy, increase the use of domestic fuel resources, and create new jobs.

Source: Worldwatch Institute.

Table 11–3. A Sampling of Financial Disincentives Designed to
Facilitate Transition to a Sustainable Society

Place	Disincentive	Purpose
West Germany	Gasoline tax of $1.05 per gallon.	To promote gasoline conservation.
Michigan, Maine, Connecticut, Oregon, Iowa, Vermont	Deposit on glass bottles.	To reduce litter, conserve materials, and conserve energy.
Denmark	Progressive tax on cars increasing with price of car.	To reduce steel imports by 20 to 25 percent.
China	No free education or medical care for more than two children.	To discourage large families.
New York City	Increase in fees on toll-access routes to city.	To discourage use of automobiles.
South Korea	Gasoline tax of $1.75 per gallon.	To promote gasoline conservation.

Source: Worldwatch Institute.

Another financial tool that can be either a penalty or a reward, depending on how it is used, is the deposit on purchased goods that can be recycled. In the United States, for example, some states require high deposits on beverage containers to ensure that bottles and cans (or at least the materials from which they are made) are reused or recycled.[14] Norway uses a similar approach for automobiles.[15] In both cases the purposes are the same—to reduce the use of raw materials, to conserve energy, and to reduce litter.

Change through Regulation

While market forces and financial incentives and disincentives can speed the transition to a sustainable society, regulation is the best means of making some adjustments. Where feasible, regulation may be simpler, more direct, and more easily administered than other market interventions. But while it can be a powerful tool of public policy, it requires an enforcement mechanism to be effective.

Regulation is well-suited for and widely used to increase energy efficiency, protect life-support systems, and control pollution. It is poorly adapted to the development of renewable energy sources (though here market forces and incentives are effective) and even less so to the stabilization of world population size. (For halting population growth, public education and incentives have been the most effective techniques.)

For protecting the basic biological systems, regulation is indispensable. Limiting the fish catch is an effective and widely used means of managing oceanic fisheries. If deforestation is to be arrested, tree cutting will have to be regulated and limited to a level no greater than the sustainable yields of forests allow. Where grazing areas are held in common, similar measures will have to be adopted if the grasslands are to be preserved. Saving threatened species from extinction often requires nothing short of regulation, international regulation in some cases.

Pollution control has been achieved almost exclusively through regulating the type and volume of waste discharge. All industrial countries and most non-industrial countries now regulate industrial waste discharge.

In many parts of the world, greater energy efficiency is being achieved through the adoption of mandatory fuel-efficiency standards. The United States, for example, relies heavily on such standards to increase the energy efficiency of its automobiles, appliances and, potentially, buildings. If market forces alone are trusted to increase the energy efficiency of buildings, progress is likely to be limited since energy efficiency has a long-term payoff and is not a highly visible characteristic of a building, and its investment cost puts off landlords who can easily pass along higher fuel costs to tenants. Indeed, even architects and builders have little incentive to devote much

effort to constructing energy-efficient buildings unless governments mandate building energy-performance standards. (See
Table 11-4.)

In the United States, regulations requiring automobile
manufacturers to raise vehicle fuel efficiency have helped boost
the national auto fleet's overall efficiency.[16] Since 1979, these
have been vigorously reinforced by consumers' responses to
rising gasoline prices. While the legislation got manufacturers
headed in the right direction, the combination of legislation
and market forces is raising fuel efficiency even faster than
originally planned.

Speed limits are another type of regulation designed to increase automotive fuel efficiency. Posted speed limits in most
countries have traditionally been substantially above the fuel-
efficiency optimum. But with the supply of oil tightening, most
Western industrial countries have lowered speed limits.
Within Western Europe the only major holdout is West Germany, where public resistance has cowed political leaders.[17]

The shift from oil to renewable (or at least more plentiful)
energy sources in the generation of electricity is being achieved
through a combination of market forces and regulation. In the
United States, market forces are spurring the shift from oil to
alternative fuels—most commonly, coal—at a far faster pace
than regulation alone would prompt. In Japan, the construction of any new oil-fired electrical generators has been prohibited.[18] The United States and many other countries are not
only banning the construction of new oil-fired plants; they are
also requiring that existing plants be systematically retrofitted
to use coal or some fuel other than oil.

On a much smaller scale, San Diego is one of several counties in California that have passed ordinances requiring builders to install solar hot water heaters in new houses and new
swimming pools.[19] The upshot was a great increase in the
market for solar heating equipment. While regulations affecting swimming pools would not much affect fossil fuel consump-

Table 11–4. A Sampling of Regulations Designed to Facilitate
Transition to a Sustainable Society

Place	Regulation	Goal
Tanzania	Ban on weekend driving.	To reduce gasoline consumption and oil imports.
New York City	Proposed ban on single occupant cars entering Manhattan on non-toll bridges.	To reduce air pollution and fuel consumption.
California	Ban on sales of appliances with pilot lights.	To conserve natural gas. (Pilot lights in U.S. account for 13 percent of residential gas consumption.)
Denmark	Ban on air conditioners in new houses.	To conserve energy.
United States	Fuel efficiency standards for new automobiles.	To reduce gasoline consumption of new cars between 1975 and 1985 by 50 percent.
United Kingdom	Maximum heating temperature of buildings and minimum level of insulation.	To reduce industrial and residential energy use.
Portland, Oregon	Proposed mandatory "weatherization" by 1985 of all privately owned buildings.	To conserve energy.
United States	Energy efficiency standards for household appliances	To conserve energy in residential sector.
Japan	Recommendation to raise fuel efficiency of new automobiles by 20 percent.	To conserve energy.

Source: Worldwatch Institute.

tion in many places, they will in California where there are many swimming pools and much sunshine. They also illustrate the advantages of using local regulations to facilitate the energy transition.

Setting either mandatory or voluntary regulations for controlling the temperature in buildings is already common in industrial societies. For example, France and Japan have established maximum wintertime temperatures.[20] In some countries, compliance is largely voluntary, but in France energy monitors periodically check building temperatures and issue citations to violators.

Reliance on regulation has obvious limitations. Where regulations are politically unacceptable or unenforceable, they may not work at all. Prohibiting the cultivation of land that is too steeply sloping to sustain agriculture over the long-term, for instance, may not be enforceable in countries with acute land hunger. Likewise, setting aside national parks to preserve wildlife in East Africa may not be a viable option if population growth is not slowed.

Not all societies will choose the same combination of policies to curb unsustainable trends. For example, the United States is relying heavily on fuel efficiency standards to reduce gasoline consumption, while Western Europe is using a stiff gasoline tax. Eastern European countries meanwhile use their governmental price-fixing authority to set high prices that achieve the same end. There is nothing sacred about any particular approach. Each society must select those approaches that are best suited to its own situation and needs.

Financing the Transition

Financing the transition to a sustainable society will require vast sums of investment capital, public and private. The demand for these unprecedented sums is coming at a time when capital formation is becoming more difficult, when growth is slowing and profit margins are narrowing. The hefty expenditures needed to sustain the housing stocks and transportation systems that evolved when energy was abundant and cheap, such as those in North America, will restrict savings. During this decade and the next, the capital needs of the transition will strain the capacity of governments and financial institutions. Competition for investment funds will be keen and interest rates promise to remain high.

The economic transformation required to put society on a sustainable footing will involve making heavy investments simultaneously in several sectors. Capital will be needed for building fuel-efficient mass transit systems, constructing soil-conserving terraces, installing rooftop solar collectors, and taking thousands of other steps. Once the transition is largely complete, investment requirements will fall sharply. But until then, capital will be scarce and costly.

While global expenditures on soil conservation, reforestation, and population stabilization need to be doubled, tripled, or even quadrupled in the years immediately ahead, they will be dwarfed by the massive energy-related investments. With energy, all societies will have to find a balance between investing in energy production and energy efficiency. For Third World countries, the balance must be between expenditures to produce more firewood and those to produce more fuel-efficient wood stoves. In industrial societies, the trade-off will be between producing synthetic fuels and manufacturing more fuel-efficient automobiles.

The cost-effectiveness of investing in production versus efficiency has been studied in more detail for the United States than for any other country. Independent studies by the Energy Productivity Center of the Mellon Institute, the Center for Energy and Environmental Studies at Princeton, the Harvard Business School, and the Solar Energy Research Institute all conclude that investments in energy efficiency are far more profitable than those in producing more energy.[21] Indeed, all

seem to agree that it would be economically profitable to reduce U.S. oil consumption so that oil imports could be phased
out by 1990. As Roger Sant of the Mellon Institute notes, "All
of the oil that we import is more expensive than our other
energy services options. This means that if everyone's economic self-interest were fully accommodated, we would not be
purchasing any foreign oil."[22]

The Mellon Institute projects that if every economically
sensible action were taken between now and the end of the
century vis-à-vis energy use, the typical American's needs could
be satisfied at costs well below those of 1980—even though
energy prices will increase dramatically. Sant notes that the
most attractive investments in the energy field are the "thousands of devices that improve the amount of service consumers
get for each unit of fuel or electricity used."[23] Among these
are double-paned windows, automatic fuel dampers, electronic
pilot lights, sophisticated thermostats, small units that co-gen-
erate electricity and usable heat and diesel engines in automobiles.

Study after study claims we should de-emphasize investment
in synthetic fuels, noting that they cannot compete with the
various investments in increased efficiency now and may not be
able to for years. Indeed, the cheapest energy available is that
now being wasted. An analysis by Robert H. Williams, of the
Princeton Center for Energy and Environmental Studies,
using life cycle costing techniques, shows that a house retrofitted by the National Bureau of Standards in Maryland for
$2,840 in 1978 saved 580 gallons of oil per year at a cost of only
60 cents a gallon, roughly half of the 1981 price of heating
oil.[24] According to Williams, investing $1,300 in a typical new
house in the United States to make it conform to the proposed
Building Energy Performance Standards would save 260 gallons of oil equivalent per year at a cost of 34 cents per gallon
saved.

Equally attractive returns on investments are available with home appliances.[25] For example, modest design improvements adding $100 to the purchase price of a frost-free refrigerator would save electricity at a cost of 1.6 cents per kilowatt hour, compared to current costs of about 5 cents per kilowatt hour. On average, notes Williams, it would be profitable to continue investing in technologies to raise auto-fuel efficiency over the next 15 years until on-the-road fuel economy reached 60 miles per gallon, even assuming the price of gasoline was only $1 per gallon.

Market behavior is beginning to reflect the result of the various energy analyses cited above.[26] U.S. businesses, homeowners, and government spent $8.7 billion in 1980 on energy-efficiency improvements, more than in the preceding five years combined. Energy analysts project that such expenditures could easily increase to $30 billion per year in the United States by 1985. In industry, most expenditures have been for cogenerators, fluidized-bed combustion technologies for coal, waste heat recuperators and heat pumps, more efficient heat exchangers, more efficient industrial processes, and computer-controlled energy-management systems for commercial buildings. Homeowners are investing in storm windows, insulation, and more efficient furnaces. In 1980, homeowners took advantage of tax incentives by claiming tax credits for $4 billion worth of expenditures on conservation and solar retrofitting.

Some of the technologies are long-standing, others are new. Cogeneration, a process that reuses steam produced for electrical generation as industrial process heat or for space heating, has long been used in Europe where energy has never been as cheap as in the United States. Newer to the scene is the use of computers linked to sensors to adjust heating, cooling, and lighting in buildings. This technology has become practical only with recent advances in micro-computers.

A pivot point in any effort to increase energy efficiency is the operation of utilities, which are increasingly hard pressed to raise the capital needed to construct additional electrical generating capacity. Indeed, many utilities have begun to look carefully at the alternative ways of balancing supply and demand. What they are discovering is that it is far cheaper, less risky, and more profitable to invest in programs to conserve—and particularly to reduce peak requirements—than it is to build new capacity. For example, Pacific Gas and Electric, a large utility based in San Francisco, is planning to invest $164 million in the next decade in dozens of programs designed to cut peak demand by 25 percent by the year 2000.[27] The object is to avoid having to invest several times this amount in additional generating capacity.

In Third World countries, where energy waste is far less, satisfying basic energy needs will require heavy investments in energy production. In late 1980, Ernest Stern, Senior Vice President for Operations at the World Bank, reported that the Bank would try to double its existing $13 billion authorization for energy lending for the period 1980 to 1985 to $25 billion.[28] This latter figure would represent the Bank's share of funding for energy projects that total more than $90 billion. Behind this proposal is the desire to help developing countries reduce their oil import bill, which collectively climbed from $7 billion in 1973 to roughly $50 billion in 1980. To facilitate the sharp increase in energy lending, the Bank proposed to establish a new energy affiliate, the International Energy Corporation. Evidence of the unfolding difficulties in financing the transition to a sustainable society came in early 1981, when the newly inaugurated Reagan Administration announced that it would not support creation of the proposed energy affiliate.[29]

Whether the Bank will be able to expand its energy lending along the lines envisaged by Stern remains to be seen, but at current lending levels it provides invaluable assistance in the energy transition. When the Bank committed $11 million in early 1980 to a mangrove plantation in Bangladesh, it helped assure a long-term supply of indigenous fuel there.[30] Similarly, its commitment of $125 million to a new hydroelectric project in Colombia will help put Colombia's electrical supply on a sustainable basis.[31] A $40 million loan to Kenya following earlier technical assistance from the United Nations Development Program will permit Kenya to obtain much of its additional electrical generating capacity for the eighties from geothermal sources.[32]

In countries that import oil, the option of importing energy-producing equipment will become increasingly attractive as oil becomes ever more costly. If a government can import wind generators or geothermal plants to replace oil-fired electrical power plants, for example, it can sharply reduce foreign exchange outlays. Moreover, unlike expenditures for imported oil, investment in indigenous energy resources can be made partly, and sometimes entirely, with local capital.

The issue of local investment deserves a closer look, given the goals of the transition. In contrast to investments in fossil fuels, which are largely reserved to corporations and governments, those in renewable energy resources can be made by individuals and communities. Whether by buying solar panels for water- or space-heating or planting trees for firewood or constructing a small-scale community hydroelectric facility, individuals, small firms, and local communities can participate meaningfully in the development of the renewable energy potential and thus broaden the capital base.

One of the attractions of investing in both energy efficiency and renewable energy resources is that such investments are inflation proof. Once a homeowner invests in insulation to reduce fuel needs, his vulnerability to fuel-price increases is permanently diminished. Similarly, once a solar water heater is installed, the cost of the heat it supplies throughout its lifetime is fixed. Yet, the cost of electricity, oil, and natural gas used to heat water will undoubtedly continue rising.

As investments in energy are climbing, so too are those in food production. As world population increases, the capital investment required to feed each person increases apace. With little new land to plow, virtually all future gains in food production must come from boosting output on the existing resource base. Such boosts, in turn, are posited on highly capital-intensive techniques. Even if world population were to stabilize at six billion, as earlier proposed in the stabilization timetable, vast increases in food output would still be required to satisfy minimal needs. In Asia, where half of humanity lives, future gains in food production will depend largely on heavy investments in water control and irrigation. Saburo Okita and Kimo Tahare of the Overseas Cooperative Development Fund of Japan estimate that doubling rice production in Asia over the next 15 years will require $67 billion, largely for investment in irrigation facilities.[33]

One of the most troubling investment deficits is that in efforts to control excessive soil erosion and to halt the conversion of prime cropland to nonfarm uses. Few governments have recognized this dual threat to future food supplies, much less translated such awareness into budgetary commitments. As governments become more aware of this dilemma, soil conservation programs are likely to become a major budget item. Official estimates indicate the United States needs to at least double the public contribution to cost-sharing.[34] Many Third World countries need a several-fold increase in expenditures on soil saving measures. Farmers will, of course, have to make heavy investments of their own resources in soil protection practices. But without governmental cost sharing, the world's soils will continue to deteriorate.

Public funding aimed at keeping cropland from being diverted to nonfarm uses in most of the world is at best negligible. Indeed, in late 1979 when Connecticut purchased the development rights for a farm threatened by urban sprawl it earned a news story in *The New York Times*.[35] Neighboring Massachusetts has set aside some $10 million for the purchase of agricultural preservation restrictions for farmland. Of all Western industrial countries, only France has come anywhere near investing enough to make a major difference at the national level. As the eighties begin, this sound approach to farmland protection remains the exception rather than the rule that it must become if future supplies are to be assured. With reforestation, the commitment of resources is grossly inadequate. Only a handful of Third World countries have made a solid commitment to reforestation despite the obvious imperatives to do so. In contrast, the United States, which by international standards is generously endowed with forests, committed funds to reforesting 460,000 acres in its 1981 budget.[36] The funds earmarked for this effort covered direct Forest Service commitments plus the employment in reforestation of thousands of young people in the Young Adult Conservation Corps, a youth employment and training program. Fortunately, international aid agencies are increasing sharply their investment in reforestation during the eighties. Since 1978, the U S Agency for International Development has quintupled its financial support for firewood projects.[37] World Bank support of reforestation projects for the eighties has increased some tenfold over the preceding decade.[38]

Investments aimed at stabilizing population are probably slighted most in government budgets. While most national political leaders at least acknowledge the threat of continued population growth, few governments have adequately funded either population education or family planning programs. The International Conference on Family Planning in the Eighties, meeting in Jakarta in early 1981, estimated that $3 billion will be needed annually to meet population and family planning program needs, compared with roughly $1 billion currently being spent.[39] Nationally, few governments have yet launched effective population-education programs—programs that explain the urgency of halting population growth.

By any reckoning, the transition to a sustainable society will require all the investment capital that can be mustered. Without a reduction in the $500 billion global military budget, the capital for a smooth and timely transition may not be available. Governments will be forced to weigh carefully the trade-off between reductions in military expenditures or possible declines in living standards. However unlikely a reversal of the recent trends in military expenditures may appear to be, new realities may make such a reversal mandatory. Indeed, straightening out our investment priorities so that they are aligned with new economic and social realities is one of the most basic and urgent challenges of the transition.

Reorienting R&D Programs

The systematic investment of public resources in scientific research is a relatively recent phenomenon. As recently as 1940, the U.S. was spending only $74 million annually on research.[40] But World War II brought an outpouring of public funds for scientific research, a flow that has expanded substantially since. As of 1979, global research and development was a $150 billion undertaking, employing an estimated three million scientists and engineers.

The global R&D budget is dominated today by military expenditures, much as it has been since World War II. (See Table 11-5.) Far above any other category of expenditures, the global military establishment claimed some $35 billion for the development of new weapons systems, an activity that employed close to a half million of the world's finest scientists and engineers.[41]

Ranking a distant second after military R&D was space research, roughly a third of that for the military. Although still large, its share has declined since the late sixties, when the American program that led to the moon landings culminated. Other major areas of research and development expenditures are energy, health, transportation, pollution control, and agriculture. All told, the wartime imprint on government R&D expenditures remains bold. Today, more scientists work on new

Table 11-5. The Global Research and Development Budget, 1979

Program	Share
	(percent)
Military	24
Space	8
Energy	8
Health	7
Information Processing	5
Transportation	5
Pollution Control	5
Agriculture	3
Basic Research	15
Others	20
Total	100

Source: Norman, *The God That Limps: Science and Technology in the Eighties.*

weapons systems than on new energy sources and increased food production combined.

But the role of technology in the transition to a sustainable society is a central one. A pressing and in some cases a near desperate need is that for technologies to harness locally available, renewable energy sources. Development of more energy-efficient technologies is lagging far behind the need in every major sector in the world economy. Research on farming practices that will stabilize soils is nonexistent in the countries that need it most. Investment in the breeding of plants that can capture sunlight more efficiently is trivial compared with the need for such plants, as is investment in more efficient long-distance electrical transmission techniques and the development of high-yield sweet sorghums that can be grown as temperate-zone energy crops, much as sugarcane is grown in the tropics and subtropics. So long is the list of such gaps, in fact, that the global R&D budget as it is now constructed scarcely corresponds to humanity's most pressing needs.

Yet, while progress in shifting budgetary priorities is slow, changes in the energy research budget are heartening. Data compiled by the International Energy Agency for the major

Western industrial countries (except France) and Japan, show that public expenditures on energy research, development, and demonstration (RD&D) increased from \$1.9 billion in 1974 (the first year after the Arab oil export embargo) to \$7.1 billion in 1979.[42] Even adjusted for inflation, this represented a healthy increase.

During this five-year period, expenditures for conservation increased from just over 2 percent of the energy research budget in 1974 to over 6 percent in 1979, while those for solar energy climbed from less than 1 percent to over 9 percent. (See Table 11-6.) While energy conservation and the development of renewable resources should be at the center of a long-term global energy strategy, energy research expenditures do not yet reflect this recognition. Nuclear power, principally nuclear fission, still claims the lion's share of energy research and development funds in rich and poor nations alike. Although expenditures on nuclear fission declined from 69 percent to 45 percent, this commitment is still extraordinarily large given the declining prospect of nuclear power in the United States, Germany, and other key IEA countries.

Table 11–6. Governmental Energy Research, Development, and Demonstration Expenditures of IEA Members, 1974 and 1979

Program	1974	1979
	(percent)	
Conservation	2.3	6.4
Oil & Gas	2.3	3.4
Coal	5.8	10.8
Nuclear Fission	68.7	44.6
Nuclear Fusion	8.3	10.3
Solar	0.4	9.4
Other	0.8	3.2
Supporting Technologies	11.1	11.7
Total	100	100

Source: International Energy Agency.

Of the 19 member countries of the International Energy Agency, only Sweden has been fully able to realign its energy research budget in accord with the new energy realities.[43] While IEA members as a group are allocating only 6 percent of their budget to energy conservation, Sweden is allotting 34 percent. Similarly, the community as a whole is devoting only 9 percent of its energy budget to renewable energy resources, but Sweden has increased its expenditures to 32 percent. Meanwhile, Swedish expenditures on nuclear fusion and fission combined have fallen to 19 percent.

While government expenditures on energy RD&D totaled just over $7 billion in 1979, industry's annual expenditures on energy RD&D in the larger IEA countries have reached $2.9 billion.[44] Industry RD&D expenditures on energy are roughly proportional to the industrial capacity of the member countries: the United States leads with $1.3 billion, followed by Japan with $513 million and Germany with $329 million. In some cases, the industry expenditures are part of joint government-industry projects—the construction of coal liquefaction pilot plants, for instance. In others, notably those that manufacture automobiles and household appliances, government regulations (in the form of higher energy-efficiency standards) have spurred industrial product research.

With sustainability rather than endless growth as a goal, local research acquires new importance. In the case of the development of renewable energy resources, for example, data on stream flows must be collected locally and analyzed as a basis for constructing small-scale hydroelectric generating facilities. Similarly, the growing reliance on agriculture as a source of energy and industrial raw materials will require an unprecedented commitment to local research on the selection and development of crops adapted to this need.

Overall, the R&D requirements of a sustainable society will be diverse. No easy technological fixes, no simple breakthroughs will solve the food problem or the energy problem.

Rather, many smaller technological advances and adaptations of existing technologies will guide the shift to a sustainable society. For example, the use of miniaturized computers being developed in the microprocessor industry can help us conserve other resources, primarily energy. As this new technology, which stores vast amounts of information on tiny silicon chips, continues to develop, it promises to make the economic system more efficient. Already, tiny computers are being used in some cars to achieve a more efficient fuel-combustion mix, while advances in computer and communications technology, such as including video phones, may open new possibilities for reducing travel.

In microbiology, the new possibilities raised by research on recombinant DNA may also help solve some of humanity's most pressing problems. By genetically manipulating bacteria, researchers can, in effect, reprogram the genetic bacteria or other micro-organisms to do the same things they now do better or faster or in some cases to perform entirely new tasks. For example, a bacterium developed by General Electric eats oil and could thus conceivably clear up oil spills.

With these and other prospects still awaiting full development, the overwhelming emphasis on military research in R&D budgets around the world must be called into question. As Colin Norman notes in a Worldwatch Paper on the global R&D budget, "The United States has the ability to survey virtually every square meter of the Soviet Union, yet the world's scientists have barely begun to survey the complex ecosystems of fast-disappearing tropical rainforests or the malignant spread of the world's deserts."[45] Further, says Norman, "The nuclear arsenals of the superpowers contain enough explosive power to reduce to rubble most of the cities of the globe, yet the more challenging test of providing clean, safe power for those cities has received far less scientific attention."

The global R&D budget was shaped largely by the needs of the fifties and no longer serves us well. Needed now is a wholesale restructuring, country by country, that will make the efforts of scientists responsive to the needs of the eighties and to the development of technologies that will lead us to a sustainable society. Overcoming the bureaucratic inertia and vested interests in the current configuration of expenditures is essential if the technologies needed to sustain society are to evolve.

The Role of Leadership

The greater the need for economic and social change, the greater the need for leadership to guide the process. Throughout most of history, social change was so slow as to be scarcely perceptible within a given generation. Then, an occasional lack of leadership was tolerable since the consequences unfolded so slowly. But in recent centuries and decades the pace has picked up, and during the decades of transition the pace of change promises to accelerate sharply. Leadership was never needed more than it will be in the years immediately ahead.

Leadership can be defined in many ways—political, intellectual, or spiritual, to cite a few. Most commonly, it is thought of as political, in terms of elected or appointed officials. It also consists of organizers and facilitators, those who make things happen. Barbara Ward defined leadership as "the ability to get the best out of those around you."[46]

As the world enters the eighties, facing the need for a rapid economic and social transition, there is a dearth of leadership, particularly at the national level. Among contemporary political leaders of major countries, few stand out as historic figures. It is not clear whether the facelessness of national political leaders is absolute or relative to the unprecedented demands of the transition. Canadian Prime Minister Pierre Trudeau favors the latter explanation, observing that all national political leaders appear incompetent in the face of the problems societies now face.[47] Warren G. Bennis, psychologist and former president of the University of Cincinnati, takes the other view—that the world is suffering from a paucity of leadership.[48]

Whether leaders make history or history makes leaders, the eighties and nineties will unquestionably be periods of rapid, perhaps even convulsive, economic and social change. Our success in making that change smooth, purposeful, and guided will depend largely upon the willingness and ability of leaders to educate their constituents. Their responsibility in times of rapid change is to help people understand why change is needed, why it is inevitable, and what it will look like. As Bennis notes, "Our great political leaders, such as Jefferson, Lincoln, and Wilson tried to educate the people about problems," in effect "transforming murky problems into understandable issues."[49] He believes that "a leader must get at the truth and learn how to filter the unwieldy flow of information into coherent patterns." With no understanding of the underlying causes of change, governments fail to respond to emerging problems and problems become crises.

At a time when there is a dearth of leadership at the national level a few stand out. One such leader was the late President Ziaur Rahman of Bangladesh, assassinated in an attempted coup d'etat in May 1981. Few if any countries are in more desperate need of effective leadership than Bangladesh. With some 90 million people squeezed into an area about the size of Louisiana, the country has been frequently described by development economists as an international basket case. Planning Minister Fasihuddin Mahtab sums up the desperation. "Unless we make a major breakthrough in the next five years, we are finished. With 80 percent of the people below the poverty line, we are barely floating. It is survival. The alternative is yearly famine."[50] A father of two, Zia lived quietly in the same small house he occupied when he was a military commander. He worked long, hard days, frequently going from 7:30 in the morning until past midnight. His two principal goals were bringing population growth to a halt and expanding food production. Determined to halt population growth at 100 million, he was beginning to push the one-child family, following the Chinese example.

Zia believed, quite rightly, that the key to solving Bangladesh's food problem is increased multiple cropping, which in turn depends on digging irrigation canals. In his tireless campaign to slow population growth and to expand food production, he made some 20 trips a month by helicopter to remote villages where he exhorted people to greater efforts— and scolded lazy local bureaucrats for failing to get things done. His Minister of Agriculture described him as "the chief extension agent of the Ministry of Agriculture."[51]

Progress on both the food and population fronts in Bangladesh has slowly gained momentum since Zia took over in 1976, when he transformed a military government to civilian rule. One observer noted that Zia "sometimes appears to be trying to raise his country up by sheer force of his persuasion."[52] An exemplary leader, committed to improving the lot of his people, Zia provided not only leadership for Bangladesh but inspiration for other countries as well.

At a time when effective high-level political leadership such as Zia offered is scarce, intellectual leadership is also lacking. In an essay, "The Cupboard of Ideas is Bare," journalist Bernard Nossiter describes this perplexing dilemma in challenging terms, noting that American presidents no longer view academia as the source of answers to the problems they face.[53] Few contemporary economists stand tall enough to command wide public respect, perhaps because traditional economic theory no longer explains the workings of the economy. Leading economists have difficulty explaining the mounting inflationary pressures or the declines in labor productivity.

In the face of complexity, academics all too often retreat into ideology or technique. Sociologist Daniel Bell reports that two vacancies in his department for faculty members under 45 at Harvard went unfilled in the late seventies because the screening committee could not find candidates with the needed breadth.[54] Bell noted that many of the candidates were "brilliant hotshots," but that nearly all were technicians, nothing more than computer model specialists. Faced with real world complexity, academics too often bow to the temptation to retreat into the world of computer models and the academic jargon of their discipline.

Apart from a few national political leaders, those leaders most actively promoting the transition to a sustainable society are local. One such is Michel Crepeau, former mayor of La Rochelle, France. From 1971 until his 1981 appointment as Minister of Environment in the Mitterrand cabinet, he organized and led a broad-based effort to create a model city for a sustainable society.[55] Launching a recycling program, he called meetings in local neighborhoods on the proposed program for separating and recycling trash, gaining support before the project started. Street theater was used to teach how to separate the key components of garbage—metal, paper, and plastic. Solar water heaters were installed on over 1,000 public housing apartment buildings alone, reducing the vulnerability of La Rochelle's 100,000 inhabitants to oil embargoes. The center city, which dates from the middle ages, was converted into a network of streets for pedestrians only. Because the people of La Rochelle helped design and implement these programs, voter support for Mayor Crepeau has expanded steadily. Emphasizing broad public participation, the mayor has rejected dogma and ideological approaches in favor of practical proposals that work.

In energy, too, the outstanding models are local. Within the United States, California has consistently led the country in developing renewable energy resources. Under Governor Jerry Brown's leadership, the state has moved imaginatively, using tax incentives and the authority of the Public Utility Commission to encourage the shift to solar and geothermal energy. In many cases, the goals set in California are higher than those set in Washington for the country as a whole.

In local energy development, Franklin County in rural western Massachusetts stands out. A detailed inventory of the potential both for conserving energy and for developing local renewable energy resources yielded astounding results. It showed that the county could rely heavily on available local energy resources—including existing, abandoned, and potential hydroelectric sites—and reduce its overall energy consumption by 60 percent through conservation.[56] It further determined that the county had enough potential hydroelectric generating capacity to more than satisfy any projected needs for electricity and could even market surplus power.

Above all, the Franklin County study emphasized the need for community energy planning. Mark Cherniak, codirector of the energy-management project, notes that "energy statistics must be gathered as locally as possible if they are to be of value in policy making. . . . A particular building, stream, windy hillside, or acre of woods exists in town or city and is owned by someone. The decision to develop an energy resource can only be properly made at this most local level."[57]

Once leaders such as Michel Crepeau or Mark Cherniak and his associates take the initiative and create the local models, then it becomes easier for other community leaders to innovate. The critical input is the initial vision and political leadership that get the process started.

Outstanding among those who are launching the transition to a sustainable society are the organizers and facilitators. In 1979, Thailand had 41 percent fewer pregnancies than it had five years earlier.[58] Unplanned births had dropped to a negligible level largely because of the efforts of one young man. Trained as an economist at the University of Melbourne, Mechai Viravaikya has organized the world's most innovative family planning program. He abandoned his government position in 1974 to form the community-based, nonprofit Family Planning Services. As he pointed out, "When I was in the government planning office, with my degree hanging smartly on the wall, I was director of the team that made marvelous plans for

Thailand. I saw that we were advancing economically, but all
our gains were being eaten up by overpopulation. I realized we
would have to adopt a radical new approach to this most
terrible problem."[59] As Mechai saw it, it would be necessary
"to change the Thai's puritanical view of sex, make the whole
business of how many children a family had a subject easily
discussed and thus acted upon." The techniques and innovations introduced by Mechai seem endless. School children's
games have been devised in which condoms are used as bal-
loons. Math exercises have been organized around population
growth and its effects. Sterilization of a husband or wife in a
village after they have had the desired number of children
entitles the couple to a free baby pig. (Mechai notes that this
accomplishes "two things at once, improving the diet and
popularizing birth control.") Key to Mechai's approach has
been popularizing family planning and involving people at the
grassroots levels in the program—a two-pronged effort that has
led to wide discussion of population problems and the need for
family planning in all segments of Thai society.

More than 1,000 miles to the west in India, another organ-
izer has literally transformed large rural areas. In May of 1949,
Verghese Kurien, a recent graduate of Michigan State University in mechanical engineering, arrived in Anand (a small town
north of Bombay) to work with an Indian research creamery.
Within a few years, he had organized a farmer's dairy cooperative for village milk producers, few of whom owned more than
four cows. Then he organized another, and another. As the
number of local village cooperatives multiplied, they eventually
formed unions of about 800 villages each. The typical union
now operates a fleet of milk-collection trucks, a marketing
system that extends into the big cities, and a feed-mixing mill.
It provides veterinary and extension services, including artificial insemination to upgrade local stock. Close to 30 such
unions modeled on the original Kaira Dairy Union now exist
throughout India. They involve 5.5 million milk producers, 60

percent of whom are marginal farmers or landless laborers, and supply milk both locally and to India's four largest cities— Bombay, New Delhi, Calcutta, and Madras.[60] Much of the milk moves by insulated railway tankers on fast trains, some of it traveling several hundred kilometers.

The dairy cooperatives organized by Kurien provide a reliable market for small farmers who may have only a few acres of land and only one or two cows. It also provides them with cash income from the sale of their small marketable surplus and with technical services that would not otherwise be available to most farmers. These cooperatives have increased income in rural areas and have improved nutrition in a country where dairy products are the dominant source of animal protein in the diet. The key to developing this food resource was not massive investments or foreign aid but vision and commitment—in short, leadership.

Leadership takes many forms. It may be as simple as a personal example or as profound as the influence embodied in a head of state. Princeton's Rufus Miles believes that leadership for the transition is at least as likely to be "bottom up" as "top down."[61] Everyone will have the opportunity not only to participate in the transition but to help lead it.

12

The Institutional Challenge

The role of institutions in the transition to a sustainable society is of more than passing interest. Which will hasten the process? Which will impede it? As a general matter, says social analyst Hazel Henderson, "individuals learn faster than institutions."[1] It follows that if major institutions resist change and adjustment, the prospect for a successful transition to a sustainable society will diminish.

Besides catalyzing the transition, social institutions will themselves be transformed by the changes they help bring about. Energy analyst Charles Ryan observes, "Institutions often have difficulty in adapting to other conditions than those which gave them rise."[2] Thus, churches, universities, and other

long-standing traditional social organizations may be more
sorely tried by rapid change than are the communications
media and public interest groups—organizations of much more
recent vintage. Indeed, public interest groups grew out of the
need to accelerate the transition, to overcome resistance to
change by the vested interests· Agents of change by nature,
they stand to play a major role in the transition.

Overcoming Vested Interests

At any given point in the evolution of a political economy,
some interests are served by maintaining the status quo. Individuals, industrial firms, professional associations, labor unions—independently or collectively, these interests can stand
in the way of rapid change. Similarly, it is easier for an established industry to perpetuate itself than it is for a new industry
to establish a foothold. This fact of life has plagued, for example, virtually all new industries that would provide renewable
sources of energy. Competing for government research funds
and financial incentives, these concerns have been waging an
uphill battle against entrenched energy interests, among them
the large, well established multinational oil companies and the
nuclear power industry.

Part of the problem is that government agencies that should
function as agents of change too often develop a stake in
maintaining things as they are. As an example, agencies acquire
a vested interest in the product or industry they are supposed
to monitor or regulate. When the Department of Energy was
created, it absorbed part of the Atomic Energy Commission
and AEC's mandate to promote the commercialization of nuclear power. Thus, the newly formed department took on a
strong pro-nuclear bias.

Government involvement with industries and in activities
that are not necessarily in the public interest can also be seen
in the military-industrial complex. At base, the combination of

a large government department and numerous large industrial concerns is all but unmanageable politically. Reinforcing this unconscionable agglomeration of unchecked power is the steady flow of personnel from the Department of Defense to the weapons-manufacturing industry. This so-called "revolving door" policy ensures a close working relationship, but it also impairs government's watchdog function and gives entrenched interests a sort of right of way when government contracts are issued.

At the international level, timber companies with a keen interest in clear cutting and little or no interest in its long-term ecological impacts have formed unholy alliances with short-sighted governments concerned solely with balancing international payments. Unfortunately, this combination of economic interests has frequently overridden local and global interests in sustaining the long-term productive capacity of forests.

In many cases, economic interests have steadfastly resisted the governmental regulations that are central to the evolution of a sustainable society. U.S. automobile manufacturers fought the fuel efficiency standards. The American building industry opposes passage of building energy performance standards. In most industries, companies have resisted pollution controls, even spending corporate funds to lambast them publicly.

Often, opposition to public intervention and social change has nonideological roots. For example, nuclear engineers' strong interest in the nuclear industry may have more to do with the years they have devoted to their professional training than with politics. It may be for personal rather than for political reasons that they cannot objectively assess nuclear power as an energy source. Similarly, a principal constraint on the use of paramedics in family planning in some Third World countries has been the medical associations, which have a disproportionately large political influence in countries with small educated elites.

Whatever their reasons, vested interests employ a variety of methods and techniques to maintain the status quo. Trade associations, corporations, and unions make campaign contributions, lobby, and conduct public "education" programs to advance their particular interests. Corporations often use advertising not only to promote their products, but also to justify their use and to complain about government's attempts to watch out for the consumer.

The more sophisticated corporations often justify their actions by issuing projections, commonly made public through the auspices of industry research institutes. These projections can function as self-fulfilling prophecies. If, for example, a large oil company such as Exxon publishes projections of U.S. energy production to the end of the century that accord solar energy only a sliver of the market, the media and the public get the erroneous idea that solar energy's potential is negligible. True or not, it is in Exxon's interest to have people think so.

Perhaps the most powerful of the pressure groups are those composed of a combination of interests. The Highway Trust Fund, for example, furthers the interests of automobile manufacturers, highway construction firms, and the oil companies. Its mission is making sure that tax money from the sale of gasoline is used to extend and maintain the highway system. Once established, such institutions are difficult to get rid of, no matter how anachronistic or anti-social their purpose has become.

Clearly, underestimating their power or their effectiveness is no way to put vested interests in their place. Just as clearly, public interest groups cannot do so alone. Also needed is strong political leadership, a regrettably scarce commodity, to undergird the joint efforts of public interest groups and the communications media to expose special interest violations of the public trust.

Efforts to ban throwaway beverage containers illustrate well why political leadership is needed to check corporate activities. Companies that manufacture throwaway containers have enormous financial resources at their command, as do the unions whose members work for these companies. Thus, it is left to government and public interest groups to research the issue and examine the effects of a shift to returnable containers on energy conservation, inflation, employment, and raw materials use. And even though such analyses show that society gains by switching from throw-away containers to returnable ones, the limited financial and manpower resources of public interest groups alone are not enough to overcome the efforts by the manufacturers of throwaway containers. Only when a public interest group such as Environmental Action, which in the U.S. has led the fight against disposable containers, and the communications media work together with government leaders who understand the importance of these nongovernmental efforts to educate perspective voters, can the public interest withstand "market forces."

The Role of Corporations

Modern corporations exercise enormous influence over our daily lives. They are the "dominant social invention" of the twentieth century, says economist Robert Lekachman, who observes that "the corporation occupies a place as important in our time as that of the Holy Roman Church in medieval Europe or of the monarch who ruled by reason of divine right during the sixteenth and seventeenth century heyday of mercantilism."[3] If money is power, Lekachman's assertion is almost indisputable: the world's largest multinational corporations each have gross annual sales that exceed the gross national products of scores of countries.

Unquestionably, the large multinational corporations represent concentrations of power that rival those of the weaker nation states. Also, without question, this power brings with it responsibility. As Willis Harman of SRI (formerly Stanford Research Institute) observes, "As the largest corporations begin to wield influences over human lives that are comparable

to those of governments, they face a demand that has historically been made only of government—that they assume responsibility for the welfare of those over whom they wield
power."[4]

In command of vast resources, corporations are in a position
to either facilitate or slow the transition to a sustainable society.
History proves as much. Stanley I. Fischler describes in detail
the systematic dismantling of U.S. urban streetcar systems led
by General Motors during the early postwar period.[5] In cooperation with Standard Oil, Firestone, and others who stood to
benefit from automobile sales, General Motors formed a jointly
owned subsidiary that proceeded to purchase and dismantle
privately owned urban rapid-rail transit systems. Fischler
quotes Congressional testimony by the San Francisco Mayor,
Joseph Alioto: "In all, General Motors, acting through subsidiary mass transit companies, acquired forty-six streetcar systems
in forty-five cities and converted all to smog-producing bus
operations."[6] Los Angeles Mayor Thomas Bradley was no less
emphatic: "The destruction of a system in Los Angeles with
over one thousand miles of track took place in a very calculated
fashion. The fact that a handful of giant corporations determined the form of ground transportation for the country's
three largest cities—and for a hundred other cities—should not
be easily forgotten. . . ."[7] Thus, three decades ago, these
companies nourished U.S. dependence on the automobile,
which in turn has helped deepen national dependence on imported oil.

In the seventies, even while oil prices were climbing, Detroit
continued to concentrate its energies on producing what energy analyst Amory Lovins has called "petropigs."[8] Executives
in Detroit disdainfully talked about "small cars and small
profits," helping to slow the transition to a more energy-
efficient transportation system and setting the stage for Japan's
emergence in 1980 as the world's largest automobile manufacturer.

Another commercial interest deserving of at least some opprobrium for acting counter to the public interest is the electrical utility industry. U.S. electrical utilities, long wedded to the belief that a dollar burned is a dollar earned, have until recently been hell-bent to construct new plants, spending vast amounts of capital and raising electrical power rates to recoup those expenses.

Occasionally, a firm that has exceptional leadership will break ranks and move ahead of the industry as a whole. Such has been the case with Southern California Edision, one of the largest U.S. utilities. In late 1980, William R. Gould, the chief executive officer, declared at a press conference: "It is the policy of Edison to devote our corporate resources to the accelerated development of a wide variety of future electrical power sources which are renewable rather than finite."[9] This shift in emphasis by SCE included development of 120 megawatts of wind power, 420 megawatts of geothermal, 310 megawatts of solar, and 620 megawatts of hydroelectric generation. In summing up the reasons for this major shift in emphasis, Gould said, "We are convinced that our society in general, our customers, and our company will benefit."

Corporations can bring their impressive R&D capacity to bear on the transition. Within the food sector, a new, more energy-efficient process for synthesizing atmospheric nitrogen into chemical fertilizer that was developed in 1963 by Kellogg Engineering (a subsidiary of the Wheelabrator-Frye Corporation) reduced the cost of nitrogen fertilizer by some 40 percent. Now used throughout the world, this technology has probably done as much to alleviate hunger since 1963 as any agricultural breakthrough since mid-century. It illustrates well the potentially large contributions that corporations can make to the transition.

The automobile industry's capacity to design more fuel-efficient cars or electrical utility companies' willingness to follow a more energy-efficient path are both in question when we ask what corporations can do to facilitate the transition to a sustainable society. But even more is at issue. To the extent that new techniques and technologies can play a role in the transition—be they tree-breeding techniques or the development of more energy-efficient industrial processes—companies can begin to assume social responsibilities commensurate with their size and wealth. Since a large share of the world's research and development budget is controlled by multinational corporations, their potential to develop technologies that will facilitate the transition is obvious. (See Table 12-1.)

As a starting point, corporations can help develop renewable energy sources and thus create a more energy-efficient economy by improving the energy efficiency of their own operations. Adopting new processes that increase the efficiency with which ore is refined, for example, raises the overall energy efficiency of the economy, as does developing more energy-efficient household appliances.

Even corporate administrative policies can affect the transi

Table 12–1. R&D Expenditures by Selected Countries and Corporations, 1975

Country or Corporation	Expenditure (million dollars)
WEST GERMANY	8,847
ITALY	1,656
SWEDEN	1,216
General Motors	1,114
International Business Machines	946
BELGIUM	764
Ford Motor Company	748
American Telephone and Telegraph	619
INDIA	420
SPAIN	262
International Telephone and Telegraph	219
SOUTH KOREA	127

Source: Norman, *The God That Limps: Science and Technology in the Eighties.*

tion. Many companies provide free parking for their employees, but do nothing to subsidize employees who use public transportation. Obviously, the more energy-efficient alternative would be to charge parking fees to employees who drive automobiles and to reimburse those who take public transportation. As a first step to this admittedly radical reversal, companies could begin by charging carpoolers less than those who drive alone. Already, some companies, such as the 3-M Corporation in Minnesota, have gone even further by actively promoting vanpooling for their employees.[10] The company provides financing for the vans and helps organize the van pools. Some 135 vans carrying 1,500 3-M workers daily have now replaced over 900 automobiles, saving 297,000 gallons of gasoline each year. Here, the exercise of corporate responsibility has resulted in a valuable fringe benefit for employees.

Never has the potential for making wrong turns been as great for corporate planners as it is today. The recent history of the aircraft manufacturing industry illustrates the potential for disaster. As the seventies began, major aircraft manufacturers had to decide whether to concentrate their engineering skills and investment capital in building costly, energy-inefficient supersonic transports or the more fuel-efficient jumbo jets. Those, such as the Boeing Corporation, that ended up building jumbo jets have thrived. Those European firms that opted for the supersonic transport have invested heavily in production facilities designed to produce a product for which there is no market. Similarly, among utilities, many of the companies that bought the nuclear industry's pitch and decided to "go nuclear" are now paying a high price.

In economic terms, the years ahead promise to be extraordinarily dynamic. As the transition progresses, old industries will fall by the wayside; new ones will emerge almost overnight. Those companies that understand the economic transition and plan accordingly will benefit. Those that fail to anticipate the changes in prospect may find themselves foundering.

Religions: An Ecological Theology

As the source and custodian of values, religion should be centrally involved in the transition to a sustainable society. Yet, surprisingly, few religious leaders have grasped the opportunity and responsibilities associated with the transition, and some, such as those who oppose family planning, are standing in the way of a smooth transition.

Some of the most profound thinking on the theological implications of the transition in the Christian world have come from outside the religious community. A 1967 *Science* article by historian Lynn White, "The Historical Roots of Our Ecological Crisis," which explained the current environmental crisis in terms of the Judeo-Christian ethic, has since become a classic. In the minds of many, White noted, the Biblical legacy set forth in Genesis that man was to "have dominion over the fish of the sea and over the birds of the air and over everything that moves upon the earth" has been interpreted as a license to exploit and pillage the earth's resources to serve society's interest.[11]

Of the world's major religions, Buddhism espouses values closest to those of a sustainable society. In his famous essay on Buddhist economics, E.F. Schumacher points out that modern economic systems do not distinguish between renewable and nonrenewable resources, only between cheap and expensive ones[12] But a Buddhist economist, according to Schumacher, would distinguish between nonrenewable fuels, such as coal and oil, and renewable fuels such as wood and water power. He notes that, according to Buddhist values, "non-renewable goods must be used only if they are indispensable and then only with the greatest care and the most meticulous concern for conservation." This is not to claim that Buddhist societies differ in important respects in their patterns of resource use. But this approach to resource use does at least contrast in tone with the now-outdated Christian notion of dominion.

Rufus Miles, Princeton University Professor of Public Affairs, points out that "few theologians and fewer still of the Church's hierarchies have been willing to face squarely the need to incorporate into their doctrines the imperatives and ethics of ecology."[13] In a paper for the World Council of Churches, Jørgen Randers and Donella Meadows note that in the move toward sustainability "it will be necessary to develop new ethical principles, a goal that will inevitably involve religious institutions."[14] At issue is the church's role in the social transformation that lies ahead: Will church leaders provide leadership, or will new values be formed without church participation?

Among the notable responses to this broad question was a conference convened in July 1979 by the World Council of Churches on "Faith, Science, and the Future." Held at the Massachusetts Institute of Technology, it brought together some 300 delegates from 56 countries, roughly half of them scientists and the remainder theologians and social philosophers. Reporting on the conference, Kenneth Briggs wrote that participants focused on the often destructive relationship between humanity and nature and argued that "both science and religion have fostered an attitude that encourages the dangerous exploitation of the earth and its nonhuman forms of life."[15] Accordingly, one of the most widely discussed proposals at the conference was the need for "an ecological theology." As outlined by Australian biologist Charles Birch, this new theology is based upon the rejection of a "mechanistic world view" for a "new partnership of faith and science that . . . acknowledges the unity of creation that is the oneness of nature, humanity, and God."[16]

While overall acceptance of this new dispensation has been slow in coming, some facets of the transition are receiving church support. The perils of nuclear power, the need for disarmament, the persistence of hunger, the need for simpler life-styles, the threat of overpopulation, the right of all couples to plan their families, the rationale for land distribution, and the need for social reform have all been addressed from the pulpit and have become the object of at least limited church activities.

One issue that has engendered a particularly broad response from the religious community is the threat of continuing dependence on nuclear power. The MIT conference proposed an international moratorium on the construction of nuclear power plants to encourage and allow time for "wide participation in a public debate on the risks, costs, and benefits of nuclear energy in all countries directly involved."[17] Within the United States, the National Council of Churches has also called for a moratorium on nuclear plant construction and a gradual retirement of existing plants.[18] And in 1979, the Interfaith Coalition—a network of like-minded Christians, Jews, Moslems, Hindus, and Buddhists—also called for "a halt to the use of nuclear reactors, a cessation of the production of nuclear weapons, and a ban on the mining and transport of uranium."[19] The Catholic representative in the group, Father Paul Mayer, deemed the nuclear issue "symbolic of the entire spiritual crisis of our century." With the prospect of political repression associated with the trend toward a plutonium economy in mind, Rabbi Sally Preisand explained that support for the moratorium was at the "core of Jewish tradition."

Coupled with the rejection of nuclear power has been a call for attention to the alternatives. Bishop Paul Moore, Jr., of the Episcopal Diocese of New York has called for the wider use of non-nuclear energy sources and for a simpler standard of living to conserve energy.[20] Duane Elgin and Arnold Mitchell of SRI note that "the American Friends Service Committee, long a leader in exploring a way of life of creative simplicity, defines simple living as a 'non-consumerist life-style based upon being and becoming, not having.'"[21]

Perhaps more than any other social issue, food shortages and hunger have attracted the attention of religious groups. Unfortunately, churches and church sponsored organizations more often than not focus on the symptoms of hunger rather than its cause. Among the notable exceptions is Bread for the World, an interdenominational U.S. organization with some 20,000 members. While it has lobbied for increased emergency food relief, Bread for the World has also pressed for improved aid programs to help people feed themselves and for an international food reserve to reduce instability in the world food economy.

As for population issues, few religious organizations have been at the forefront of social activism and some—among them the Catholic church and the more fundamentalist Muslim sects—can only be counted as deterrents of progress. Yet, while the official position of the Catholic church has been to oppose the use of contraceptives, this view has not been widely accepted among church members. In the United States, for example, surveys indicate that the proportion of Catholics who practice family planning differs little from that of non-Catholics.[22] Even in some countries where Catholicism has traditionally exerted a strong influence, positions are beginning to shift. Although the Irish bishops continue to oppose artificial means of birth control, they released a statement in mid-1979 indicating that "it does not necessarily follow from this that the state is bound to prohibit the distribution and sale of contraceptives."[23] Within Latin America, where the Church has been at the center of life, many of the younger, more progressive priests and nuns are actively supporting local family planning services.

One issue some churches are beginning to face head on is that of land distribution. In Latin America, the Catholic church is particularly involved in land reform, even though traditionally it has aligned itself with the landed aristocracy. In Brazil, where land ownership is concentrated among the elite and the possession of land has become the key to social standing, the land-ownership pattern has frustrated the formation of a large middle class and made social victims of small landowners and landless laborers. But whereas these disenfranchised groups have long been intimidated by the police or military (who would evict them when they settled on land), churches and unions are now siding with them in their effort to gain possession of at least enough land for a subsistence existence.[24]

A similar realignment is taking place in Central America. Guatemala and El Salvador both have pyramidal class and land-ownership structures, as did Nicaragua before its 1980 revolution. As *Washington Post* correspondent Karen de Young writes, "After years of admitted alliance with the elite, the Church has developed a conscience."[25] In Mexico, militant young priests are siding with the landless and small landholders even though the Catholic Church there has traditionally cooperated with the ruling elite. Within the church hierarchy, only a few bishops supported these militants in the mid-seventies, but by the end of the decade at least a dozen were speaking out on behalf of the repressed and others were considering a shift. A Church document issued by nine bishops from the south of Mexico, where most of the economically and socially depressed Indians live, summarizes the conflict: "Mexico is presently passing through one of the gravest crises of its history. The political system is worsening the problems of the indigenous population and the peasantry . . . the current development model is leading us to intolerable levels of violence."[26] As the suffering among the poor increases, the commitment of the Catholic Church clergy to social reform is also increasing.

The Catholic church has also taken up the issue of land reform in the United States. In Minnesota, the church has organized seminars on land ownership among farmers to discuss "Strangers and Guests," a position paper that derives its title from a statement in the book of Leviticus. "Land," the passage reads," must not be sold in perpetuity, for the land belongs to Me, and to Me you are only strangers and guests."[27] This document is not only critical of absentee ownership. It also urges farmers to limit the size of their holdings to their needs. Invoking Jeffersonian values, these church-led discussions emphasize the value of rural living and of the family farm, and they focus on the higher productivity of smaller farms and the need to limit consumption to essential needs.

On the subject of endangered species, religious leaders have been noticeably silent. Yet the Biblical passages describing the flood and the Old Testament God's instruction to Noah that not a single species was to be sacrificed call for a different response. Noah recognized no distinction between species of obvious economic value and the others. For modern-day Christian theologians, the challenge is to update this original instruction, bringing it to bear on the destruction of species and their habitats by continuing population growth and the needless pursuit of profit.

If church leaders choose to help shape values that are consistent with a sustainable society, they have ample opportunity. From the pulpit, ministers can discuss the need for Christian stewardship in terms of limiting family size, simplifying lifestyles, and recycling raw materials. They can outline the dangers of pollution and the threat that soil erosion and cropland conversion pose to future food supplies. To practice what they preach, they could even establish car pools for those attending weekly services and other special meetings.

Many social institutions have time horizons so short that they are irrelevant to some of humanity's most pressing problems. The ultimate importance of religious institutions' role in the transition rests in part on the church's ability to compensate for that shortsightedness. If, for example, political institutions and business organizations too frequently focus on the immediate future, the need is all the stronger for religious groups to think beyond the politicians' terms of elected office and beyond annual profit and loss statements.

As the world moves from the age of growth to the age of scarcity, Christian theologians are being forced to rethink and reapply Christian values. In many cases, this means a reexamination of the interpretations of earlier Biblical admonitions, such as the commandment to mankind to "have dominion . . . over everything that moves upon the earth." Jeremy Rifkin, author of *The Emerging Order: God in an Age of Scarcity*, points out that " 'dominion,' which Christian theology for so long has used to justify peoples' unrestrained pillage and exploitation of the natural world, is suddenly and dramatically being reinterpreted. Now, according to the new definition of dominion God's first instruction to the human race is to serve as steward and protector over all of His creation."[28]

Many Christian scholars now argue that anything that exploits or harms God's creation is both sinful and disrespectful —a far cry from the materialist view of recent centuries. Rifkin observes that "as we run out of the precious stock of nonrenewable resources that allowed humans to catapult into the vast expanses of the industrial age, the Protestant Reformation doctrine that provided that theological spark to keep the giant engines running is itself nearly spent."[29] Rifkin also invites Christians and others with social consciences to consider the symbiotic relationship between Protestant Reformation theology and capitalism. "The Protestant Reformation was a driving force behind the economic expansion of the West. Capitalist development, in turn, helped institutionalize the so-called Protestant ethic as a world view." With this understanding, we may now be ready to replace materialism with a "Christian conservation ethic," one designed to accommodate the new realities.

While many religious groups are rethinking the meaning of the scriptures or putting their faith to the test of reality by actively working for a sustainable society, there is still strong resistance to necessary change in some Christian and Islamic sects. Within the United States, the Moral Majority is drumming up support for values that are incompatible with a sustainable society—materialism and opposition to sex education. Paralleling this resurgence of fundamentalism in North America is a resurgence of Islamic fundamentalism in the Middle East. In Iran, the Ayatollah Khomeini is trying to deny political equality for women and is calling for a more aggressive posture in international affairs, a hark back to Islam's early days of "the sword or the Koran."

Fortunately, these two fundamentalist examples are not at all representative of most Christians or Moslems. In a time of turmoil, many of the genuine intellectual leaders within the established religious community are beginning to wrestle with the difficult moral issues imbedded in the quest for a society that will endure. Whether they can move quickly enough to provide the leadership traditionally expected of them remains to be seen.

Universities: Getting Involved

Since universities engage in both research and education, they can play a key role in the transition to a sustainable society. While some new knowledge will be needed, the overriding need is to bring existing knowledge to bear in practical ways on the transition. Using their research capacities to aid local governments and citizens' groups in land-use planning, materials recycling, energy conservation, and the development of local renewable resources are but a few examples of what colleges and universities can do to answer the proverbial call for academic relevance.

A scattering of exciting examples attests to what educational institutions can do to prepare us for the future and to prepare a better future. As noted earlier, the University of Saskatchewan's Department of Mechanical Engineering in Canada has designed energy-efficient homes.[30] Quite possibly, these new homes—so energy-efficient that they do not need furnaces—will help revolutionize residential construction in the temperate latitudes. In the United States, the Harvard Business School embarked in 1972 on an energy research project to outline an energy strategy for the United States. The product of their efforts, *Energy Future*, demonstrated convincingly that the principal components of an energy strategy for the United States should be conservation and the development of renewable energy resources.[31] A highly readable book that made the best seller list, *Energy Future* surprised many because its hardheaded economic analysis culminated in essentially the same conclusion that many environmentalists and advocates of renewable resources had already reached.

Another impressive example of academic mobilization to facilitate the transition exists in the Netherlands. In Amsterdam, scientific research shops have been organized by university scientists and students for the benefit of environmental groups and neighborhood associations.[32] A committee of 24 advisors, consisting of faculty members, students, and representatives of citizens' groups, regularly evaluates requests for assistance. Approved projects get assigned to one of the 50 university-affiliated scientists who have volunteered their services. Following Amsterdam's lead, groups are now being organized in other Dutch cities. With some government support, these participatory research efforts are helping citizens' groups that are eager to see a sustainable society emerge but that lack the scientific skills and research capability needed to take concrete steps.

A few U.S. schools are also getting involved in local efforts to create a sustainable society. In Davis, California, for example, professors and graduate students analyzed ways to make local homes more energy-efficient. Though they were architects with little knowledge of the local climate, they decided to research and formulate a new building code. Eventually adopted by the city council, the code they devised reduces by half the energy used for heating and cooling in a typical house and yet does not significantly increase construction costs.[33]

If universities are to be centrally involved in the transition, many will need to restructure their curricula. In some cases, this will require shifts in training—fewer nuclear physicists, for example, and more meteorological engineers. As needs become clearer, universities may also need to create new fields of study. Syracuse University's president, Melvin Eggers, notes that U.S. colleges and universities produce petroleum, mining and nuclear engineers but precious few energy engineers who can advise on an overall energy strategy.[34]

Along with restructuring course content, universities must also find new ways to present material. Education is presently geared toward younger full-time students, but structural economic changes that are inherent in the transition will stimulate an unprecedented demand for adult education, part-time education, and "off-hours" learning activities on weekends, in retreat settings, or in other concentrated formats that are compatible with work or child-rearing.

One early response to the educational needs of adults is the television-based school, the prototype for which is the Open University in the United Kingdom. Instead of living on campus and attending classes, students follow their lectures by television, question their tutors by telephone, and both submit their assignments and receive curriculum materials and teachers' instructions by mail. Lectures are offered at all hours, permitting workers to arrange their studies around their jobs.[35]

The Open University is particularly attractive because its course designers are less tradition-bound than most, cutting across disciplines as well as through the boundaries between the arts and sciences. One such course, "Control of Technology," addresses the question of how to manage technology to better satisfy human needs. Open University instructor Walter Patterson indicates that those who take this course are expected to write a policy report on a real issue, one that can "serve as a basis for active participation in the issue by a specific interest group."[36] Projects proposed by students range from "increasing information available to the public on the use and effects of food additives" for the consumers' association to "a feasibility study of a recycling enterprise in 'Inner London' for a Labour Party branch."

China, too, has turned to television as a method of adult education. In Peking, a "television university" has an enrollment of some 20,000. Through this program, plus "factory-run colleges" and "spare-time universities," some 69 million people are involved in a vast experiment in adult education.[37] The flexibility and size of this system helps explain how China can train quickly 200,000 specialists in methane generation or to expand its small-scale hydroelectric generating capacity by several thousand installations per year.

The older and returning students who make use of new educational opportunities will include not only those who pursue established interests but also those who want "retraining," either because they were left stranded as certain industries became obsolete or because new fields appeal to them. For example, retraining programs can help the hundreds of thousands of auto assembly line workers who face unemployment find work on assembly lines producing wind generators, solar collectors, and photovoltaic cells. As part of such a retraining effort, courses could cover retrofitting buildings to reduce commercial energy requirements or organizing firewood plantations, orchards, gardens, and local farmers' markets. In complementary "transitional" programs, agricultural colleges and universities could offer courses on the use of solar energy on the farm, woodland management, solar economics, or the integration of food, feed, and fuel production. Local utility officials might take an introductory course in the economics and engineering of wind power. These are but a sampling from the syllabus the "transitional" university will offer.

To universities, the chance to be on the frontier of economic and social change cannot help but be invigorating. As economist Robert Heilbroner has said, young people who are bored with the existing educational establishment may "feel differently if they are offered an opportunity to work in research and development that has as its aim the renewal and reconstitution of this planet as a human habitat."[38] This opportunity to take on the problems of the real world also enables universities to restructure their research programs and reverse the recent trends toward specialization and the fragmentation of disciplines. The specialized research so essential to advancing the frontiers of knowledge should not be abandoned, but research on issues of use to policy-makers and communities should be increased. Within a more flexible institutional framework, special projects, institutes, or centers can be created specifically to address and to integrate issues associated with the transition. One such effort is the Center for Energy and Environmental Studies at Princeton University, which has within just a few years produced several studies that are being used by policy makers at both the national and local level.

The demands of the transition are in a sense demands upon our educational systems. Clearly, universities need to undertake more public policy-related research, to innovate with adult education, and to consider themselves as participants in social evolution as well as tradition bearers. Whether retraining workers or introducing new perspectives and courses, universities will have an opportunity to play a broader, more comprehensive role than they have in the past.

Public Interest Groups

If vested interests do not manage to slow or distort the transition to a sustainable society, the thousands of public interest or citizen action groups now addressing the key issues will deserve much of the credit. The engine driving the process of social change, these groups—local or global, single-issue or multi-issue—have emerged to fill a gap left between the profit-making private sector and government.

The roots of the environmental public interest movement

trace to the wildlife preservation groups launched in the United States around the turn of the century. Among these are the Sierra Club (1892), the National Audubon Society (1905), the Izaak Walton League (1922), the Wilderness Society (1935), and the National Wildlife Federation (1936). But the issues addressed by public interest groups now embrace every facet of the transition, including cropland preservation, the stabilization of world population, the conservation of energy, the preservation of threatened species, the recycling of waste products, the control of pollution, and the simplification of life-styles. Most groups concentrate their energies on research, public education, and the lobbying of both elected and appointed public officials. Some U.S. groups, such as the Natural Resources Defense Council and the Environmental Defense Fund, also engage in extensive litigation on behalf of environmental interests.

Exactly how many citizen action groups operate at any particular time no one knows. There are an estimated 10,000 to 15,000 in the United States, most of them fitting into the broad categories of environmental, consumer, or neighborhood groups.[39] In Europe, there are up to 15,000 citizen action groups in West Germany alone.[40] Keeping tabs is difficult because groups come and go as issues surface and recede. One group may be protesting the site selected for a nuclear generating station, while another group may focus on the need for an auto-free pedestrian mall in a downtown area. Some organizations, such as the World Wildlife Fund, are international in scope, while others have spawned similar organizations around the world. Friends of the Earth, once exclusively a U.S. group, now has affiliates in 23 countries, including developing countries such as El Salvador and Thailand. National groups have been formed in several Third World countries to tackle environmental problems just in their own areas. The Environmental Protection Society of Penang, made up of concerned Malaysians in all walks of life, is helping focus attention on national and local threats ranging from river pollution to deforestation. And in Porto Alegre, Brazil, several hundred activists launched Acão Democrática Feminina Gaucha to look at the wholesale destruction of Brazil's soils and rich forests by unhaltered commercial interests, as well as other pressing environmental issues.

In the United States, the allocation of resources devoted to various activities does not do justice to present-day needs. Wildlife preservation, the cornerstone of the public interest movement's origins, still commands a disproportionately large share of funds, educational efforts, and lobbying activities while solar energy, cropland preservation, and other newer issues are underattended. One way of remedying this imbalance is to broaden the interests of traditional wildlife-oriented groups. The appointment of Russell Peterson, formerly chairman of the U.S. Council on Environmental Quality, as president of the Audubon Society signals one such effort. Commenting on this appointment, Bayard Webster writes in the *New York Times* that "the National Audubon Society, long known for its activities in research in the conservation of bird life, is about to change its feathered image to one that relates more directly to the major scientific, social, and environmental problems that plague the world today."[41] Webster also noted that under Peterson the 400,000-member organization is planning both to double its scientific staff and to become more involved with problems related to population, energy, radiation, toxic chemicals, and natural resources.

Aside from the shifts in focus within the traditional wildlife groups there are changes afoot in some long-standing professional organizations that now recognize the need to help create a sustainable society. Typical of these is the Soil Conservation Society of America. A. D. Latornell of Canada, its president, recently stated that "the Society must become more active politically, not in a partisan sense, but in the matter of issues."[42] Another society member, Melvin Davis, administrator of the Soil Conservation Service, added that "the days of complacency about our croplands are over . . . we have the moral and ethical responsibility to avoid waste of our best farm and rangelands for short-term economic gains.[43]

As the eighties begin, an incredibly diverse array of citizen action groups has emerged, ranging from the mass transit movement in Paris to the hug-the-trees movement in the Himalayan foothills. The French group was born in 1970 when Parisian authorities announced a 16 percent increase in transit fares, which would be followed by a 14 percent boost the next year. In protest, the group took to the streets on three occasions, numbering an estimated 20,000 to 100,000 each time.[44] While the Cartel, a political action coalition dedicated to reversing the 1970 fare increase, failed to realize its immediate goal, it did begin to influence transportation policy. Most notably, it got the Paris Metro Authority to introduce the *carte orange*, a monthly transit pass that gives its holder the right to unlimited travel on buses, the metro, and the suburban trains within the greater Paris area. This pass has proven exceedingly popular and is credited with shifting some 70,000 daily trips from automobiles to public transport. Also as a direct result of the Cartel's work, some 120 local *comités des usagers* have banded together into the Fédération des Usagers des Transports.

Three years later and half a world away, another citizen protest movement took shape. Known as the Chipko Andolan or the "hug-the-trees" movement, and founded by Chandi Prasad Bhatt in northern India in 1973, this grass-roots effort has profoundly influenced government forest policy. Before Bhatt organized the group, the central government customarily auctioned off the cutting rights to publicly owned forest lands to timber merchants. Villagers were upset because the deforestation borne of carelessness and abuse was leading to excessive erosion and landslides in the Himalayan foothills, to increasingly destructive flooding on the plains below, and to a loss of local jobs in forest industries. In addition, local people derived little benefit from the cutting of the trees in their own community.

Failing in their effort to elicit any response from the central government, villagers took matters into their own hands. Whenever the timber merchants entered the local communities, people literally gathered about the trees and hugged them, thus preventing their felling. During the years since 1973, the Chipko movement has spread throughout northern India. More important, it has forced the central government to revise forest policies to benefit local communities. In addition, the Chipko movement has sparked extensive voluntary reforestation efforts that are often superior to those designed by the government.

The origins of these citizens' protest movements are often similar. According to Cynthia Whitehead of the Washington-based Conservation Foundation, citizens' initiatives reflect not only growing concerns about the environment and resentment of bureaucracies but also "deep rooted feelings of impotence and helplessness against powerful government and business."[45] Whether or not these citizens' organizations can bring about the needed changes quickly enough to avoid ecological collapse and social breakdown is not yet known. One thing, however, is certain: they have become a permanent part of the political landscape.

More than a decade of intensive effort by environmental groups has yielded impressive results. For example, a coalition of U.S. environmental organizations led to the withdrawal of Congressional support for the supersonic air transport. Without such opposition, the United States might have found itself in the sorry company of the Anglo-French consortium and the Soviets, whose ill-conceived ventures in supersonic transport wasted billions of taxpayer dollars and failed to produce a single sale to a commercial airline.

Another major achievement of citizen protest groups has been the public reassessment of nuclear power. Until public interest groups challenged the feasibility of this energy source, governments were committing countries to nuclear power while withholding much of the information essential to an objective assessment. Now attempts to open more nuclear facilities are being questioned and blocked as local and national environmental groups publicize the issues and the facts, mobilizing the public. In West Germany, for example, grass-roots political activists have brought nuclear power development to a halt.

Some groups have turned their attention to alternative energy sources. In Washington, D.C., the Solar Lobby was formed in late 1977 under the leadership of Denis Hayes to represent the public interest in the development and use of renewable energy resources. By May 3, 1978, the Solar Lobby had organized Sun Day and had launched a national public education program in solar energy. Within two years the Lobby had over 30,000 members prodding reluctant bureaucrats to develop a variety of renewable energy options as quickly as possible.[46]

Environmental and consumer groups have also played a key role in shifting U.S. electrical utilities to a least-cost path. In California, for example, the Pacific Gas and Electric Company was planning to build ten new coal or nuclear power plants until a court suit by the Environmental Defense Fund provided an opportunity for EDF economist Zack Willey to analyze the utility's plans. His analysis, based on PG&E's own data, demonstrated not only that nine of the ten proposed plants could be replaced by utility investment in solar equipment and insulation at a lower cost to consumers, but also that taking this alternative approach would earn the utility higher profits.[47] As a result of the EDF analysis in California, which brought to the fore the changing economics within the utility industry, utilities elsewhere in the United States are reassessing their long-term plans.

On the population front, family planning associations

around the world have been struggling since Margaret Sanger's day to ensure all women access to birth control information and services. One key group in these lobbying efforts has been the Population Crisis Committee, which fought for a specialized UN agency to focus on the population threat. Under the leadership of General William Draper, the Committee lobbied governments everywhere to create the United Nations Fund for Population Activities. The spectacular growth in the UNFPA under Rafael Salas, director of the Fund from its inception, represents one of the United Nation's great success stories. Were General Draper alive he would be impressed with the scope and the scale of UNFPA activities, ranging from a major project to help China conduct its 1980 census with the aid of computers to the provision of contraceptives for Egypt's family planning program.

The faster society has to change, the greater the need for public interest groups to spur the change. In a world of strongly vested interests, public interest groups provide a counterbalance. Often more responsive than government or business to the needs of the poor or the powerless, they can move quickly. Whether in an educational or activist role, they are in many ways the engine that is powering the transition.

The Communications Media

If the transition is to occur rapidly enough to minimize severe economic dislocation, the communications media must play a major role. Their task will be to disseminate information on the need for change as well as ideas on how to make the various adjustments that sustainability calls for. They will be the vehicles for the education and re-education of adults and the purveyors of the concepts vital to a sustainable society: energy efficiency, biological carrying capacity, and replacement-level fertility.

Books stand to play a vital role in the transition since they contain the basic analyses of issues on which the print and electronic media rely. The emergence of the modern environmental movement itself dates to the publication in 1962 of Rachel Carson's classic *Silent Spring*.[48] This book created a widespread awareness of the potential threat of toxic chemicals to life, and its publication led directly to new laws regulating the use of toxic materials, especially pesticides.

Good books on important global issues get translated and published throughout the world. At least a half million copies of the English edition of *The Limits to Growth* are in print, for example, and it is available in about 30 languages, with over two million copies in circulation.[49] This Club of Rome study, which challenged the notion that rapid industrial growth could continue indefinitely, served as the focus of a debate that continues nearly a decade later. Similarly, U.K. economist E. F. Schumacher's *Small is Beautiful*, which questioned whether bigger is necessarily better, received a worldwide distribution when it made the best seller list, and altered the way people think about technology and the economies of scale.[50] Occasionally, an article can have as much impact as an important book. *Soft Energy Paths*, by physicist Amory Lovins, which first appeared as an article in the October 1976 issue of *Foreign Affairs*, profoundly influenced thinking on the desirable direction of future energy development.

Periodicals of all sorts, whether daily newspapers, magazines, journals or newsletters, can help inform the decisions and shape the policies that lead to a sustainable society. Newspaper editors attuned to the issues have unique access to information and unique responsibilities related to that access. By running guest articles and opinion pieces, editors can both provide a forum for a reasoned public exchange of contrasting views and exploit the knowledge and expertise of those who do not regularly write for newspapers. In fact, leading newspapers are relying less on syndicated columnists and more on solicited or contributed pieces to fill their op-ed pages. Magazines and journals can also facilitate the transition. In Washington, D.C., *Science,* a weekly magazine designed for the educated reader, provides a continuous flow of articles by eminent researchers. One of its major contributions is that the magazine deals with "cutting edge" issues, such as soil erosion and alternative energy sources. Widely read in the international scientific community, *Science* has a global influence.

One interesting indicator of the move toward sustainability is the recent appearance of specialized periodicals on various aspects of the transition. In the United States, *Solar Age* has quickly become the dominant magazine in the field of renewable energy, with a circulation that reached 40,000 in 1980 and was expanding rapidly. *Famille et Développement,* a magazine published in Dakar for distribution throughout French-speaking West Africa, is a good example of the role that can be played by the new periodicals. It deals with issues surrounding the family, and one of its most widely read features, a question-and-answer page on sexuality and sexual problems, introduces readers to family-planning practices and contraceptive technology. Filling an obvious need in countries where people are starved for information on human sexuality, this innovative journal quickly acquired a broad readership. Beyond these specialized periodicals, a number of American magazines that try to deal with the range of life-styles in a sustainable society have appeared on the newsstands over the last few years. With names like *New Age, Sustenance, New Roots, Living Alternatives,* and *Mother Earth News,* they seem to have tapped a growing market for information on how to live simply. The commercial success of magazines like *Solar Age, Famille et Développement,* and the others bears witness to the role periodicals can play during the transition.

Periodicals need not be commercially available to wield influence, however. The newsletters and magazines of some key public interest groups have become important sources of information for policymakers. *Soft Energy Notes,* for example, provides high-quality summaries of major research reports on renewable energy sources. Published by Friends of the Earth in San Francisco, both its coverage and circulation are worldwide. *People,* published by the International Planned Parenthood Federation from its London headquarters, is well known as a key source of current information on international population matters.

Also vital in the rapid dissemination of information that can speed the transition will be the wire services, which link the print and electronic media throughout much of the world. Although originally designed for use by newspapers, they also now provide much of the material for electronic news broadcasting. The principal wire services are Associated Press (AP), United Press International (UPI), Reuters, Agence France-Presse (AFP), German News Agency (DPA), and the Spanish News Service (EFE). In recent years, a Third World news agency Inter-Press Service (IPS) has been added to this list. "Over the wire" news of a newly discovered carcinogen or a new technology for converting sunlight into usable energy can now encircle the globe within 24 hours.

Television and radio have become important sources of information throughout the world. Radio is by far the more widespread medium. Indeed, radio is accessible to people almost everywhere: An investment of a few dollars in a transistor permits isolated Third World villagers to tap into the international information network, becoming part of what Marshall McLuhan dubbed the "global village."[51] Since television can transmit pictures as well as words, its impact can be greater than radio. Besides presenting news, television documentaries or specials can with great force present problems and ideas that lead to action. Within the United States, a CBS documentary shown in the mid-sixties profoundly influenced the future shape of public food-assistance programs. "Hunger in America" raised public awareness of the persistence of malnutrition in an affluent society and it led to a shift in budgetary priorities in Washington.

Both television and radio have the capacity to disseminate

information quickly at the international level and skills at the local level. If, for example, a documentary showing the development of small-scale hydroelectric power in China were shown in North America or in Europe, it could sharply accelerate development of this new energy source in the West. Used in literacy instruction, agricultural improvement programs, and family-planning campaigns, television can compensate for a lack of teachers, teaching materials, and time.

Unfortunately, communications hardware is much more developed than the software in most parts of the world, and a lack of good programming constrains the full exploitation of new technologies. Yet, some governments have learned how to use television and radio effectively for educational purposes. In Costa Rica, where 46 percent of all family-planning expenditures are devoted to education and information services, radio is credited with some of the nation's success in reducing the birth rate by 40 percent since 1960.[52] A nationally broadcast daily radio program, *Dialogo*, is believed to reach one-seventh of Costa Rica's 2.1 million people, including villagers in remote rural areas.

A successful transition to a sustainable society will require the most massive adult-education program ever launched. This, in turn, will shift part of the responsibility for education from the formal educational system to the communications media. For better or worse, the educators of the future will include newspaper and magazine editors, radio newscasters, and TV producers of news and documentary programs. These professionals may not be prepared for their new role, and they may not wish to assume it, but circumstances leave them little choice.

13

Changing Values
and Shifting Priorities

Values are the key to the evolution of a sustainable society not
only because they influence behavior but also because they
determine a society's priorities and thus its ability to survive.
"Values," says environmentalist Tom Bender, "are really a
complex and compact repository of survival wisdom—an ex-
pression of those feelings, attitudes, actions, and relationships
that we have found to be most essential to our well-being."[1]
Over time, values change as circumstances change. If they did
not, society would not long endure.

Perhaps some among the now extinct Mayans recognized
that the foundation of their society's strength was eroding with
the soil from their fields. But their value system did not adapt

in time to turn the new information into new values, priorities, and programs. Will ours—now that we know that we too are on an unsustainable course?

Before us now is the opportunity to adjust our values according to our changing perceptions of our world and our place in it. Of necessity, the path to sustainability will be littered with cast-off values. Materialism, planned obsolescence, and a desire for large families will not survive the transition. But they will not leave a void. Frugality, a desire for a harmonious relationship with nature, and other values compatible with a sustainable society will take their place.

Values in Transition

In many industrial countries, and in those parts of developing countries that can afford to emulate them, materialism appears to have supplanted more profound social ethics—those posited on survival, personal growth, and ecological harmony. The danger is that the acquisition of material goods will eventually cease to bear any direct relationship to human need. The ultimate goal of survival is suborned by that of consumption. (See Table 13–1.) Individual identity becomes equated with the accumulation of material possessions; social progress, with the growth of the GNP. Indeed, in affluent nations, the quality of life becomes confused with an ever-expanding consumption of goods and services.

None of the political philosophies dominant today embraces the values essential to a sustainable society. Indeed, as scientist Bruce Murray noted in an address to theologians, "Capitalism and Marxism have one thing very much in common: they both presume that man's fundamental needs are material."[2] Murray believes that for this reason both fall short. Whether capitalist or socialist, materialism is neither sustainable nor satisfying over the long term. The survival of civilization depends on pragmatic, not ideological, responses to the forces now undermining it.

Table 13-1. Value Contrasts in Pretransitional and Transitional
Societies

	Pretransitional	Transitional
Organizing Principle of Economy	Materialism	Sustainability
Nature of Product	Planned obsolescence; throwaway mentality	Durability, high quality engineering and design
Relationship to Nature	Domination of nature	Harmony with nature
Scale	Bigger is better	Smaller has a place too
Speed	Let's go faster	Where are we going?
Specialization	Key to efficiency	Increases dependency, leads to boring work
Determinants of Status	Material possessions	Personal development, social contribution
Childbearing	Taken for granted, virtually automatic	Optional; to be given serious thought

Source: Worldwatch Institute.

Ironically, some of the values that have contributed to human survival over the last few million years, such as acquisitiveness and the desire for many children, are precisely those that now threaten survival. Acquisitiveness, a peculiarly human trait, may have served society well in earlier times when the margin of survival was thin. Continuous childbearing throughout the reproductive life-span was also undoubtedly a key factor in the survival of the species. But now circumstances are changing and as they do, so must values.

The challenge to materialism is scarcely new. Historian Arnold Toynbee notes that while Jesus, Buddha, Lao-Tse, and other spiritual guides disagreed about many things, they all agreed on the emptiness of materialism as an ethical precept. They all believed that "the pursuit of material wealth is a wrong aim," and that "we should aim only at the minimum wealth needed to maintain life; and our main aim should be spiritual. They all said with one voice that if we made material wealth our paramount aim, this would lead to disaster. They all spoke in favor of unselfishness and of love for other people as the key to happiness and to success in human affairs."[3]

The displacement of spiritual goals by the drive to accumulate wealth has its origins in the belief that man is separate from nature, and its master. Carried to extremes, this attitude has led to the abuse of natural systems and resources. It has blinded economic planners to the need to acknowledge nature's carrying capacity and degenerated into license in corporate decision-making. Yet only when this ultimately self-destructive belief is overturned and, as social analyst Willis Harman puts its, man is seen as an "integral part of the natural world, hence inseparable from its governing processes and laws," will "a sense of the total community of man and responsibility for the fate of the planet" mesh with self-interest and the "interests of fellow man and of future generations."[4]

If we begin to see ourselves as "an integral part of the natural world" instead of apart from it, then many complex issues will quickly resolve themselves. For instance, some public debate is focused on whether an environmental ethic is desirable. In fact, it is not optional. Without an environmental ethic that preserves the biological and agronomic underpinnings of society, civilization will collapse.

A world that now has over four billion human inhabitants desperately needs a land ethic, a new reverence for land, and a better understanding of the need to use carefully a resource that is too often taken for granted. Civilization cannot survive a continuing erosion of the cropland base or the endless conversion of prime farmland to nonfarm uses. Agronomist R. Neil Sampson observes that "if land and land use are to be a battleground, then facts, trends and ideas must be the major weapons. The new land ethic must be a product of education and social evolution."

Over the last century, changing conditions in the industrial countries, particularly the decline in infant mortality, have altered attitudes towards family size, and as values have changed, birth rates have fallen. With 90 percent of all babies born in the world now surviving to adulthood, stabilizing world population will require an acceleration of that process in many countries.[5] As with other values, the key to spurring changes in attitudes toward family size is information. In China, this has taken the form of a population-education campaign based on data on reduced infant mortality and on careful calculations of such things as the amount of cropland per Chinese today compared to what it will be a generation or two hence if birth rates are not sharply reduced. A similar educational effort is being launched in Bangladesh.

At the individual level, value changes are translating into shifts in public policies and governmental priorities. For example, greater investment by governments in more energy-efficient public transportation reflects a desire to maintain personal mobility even as liquid fuel supplies dwindle. Mandatory investment in pollution controls to protect biological systems and human health represents a shift from the "growth at any cost" school of thought.

Changing values are leading not only to changes in individual behavior and to shifts in public priorities but also to changes in corporate decision-making as well. As noted earlier, some corporate managers have consciously sacrificed growth in output in order to ensure the sustainability of their enterprises. More often than not such shifts reflect perceived self-interest rather than a deliberately adopted social consciousness, but the result is the same in either case.

At a more personal level, corporate behavior also reflects a change in values. During the sixties and much of the seventies, U.S. corporations often moved promising young executives from one location to another as a result of promotions or as part of executive-training programs, with little thought of the personal consequences. The end result was a highly skilled executive with a family life that was often in ruins. Children grew up rootless and without long-standing friendships. As the social cost of such policies became apparent, more and more employees declined promotions in favor of a more stable family life and a strengthened sense of community. This same awareness of social costs has led to a growing reluctance to relocate corporate headquarters for strategic reasons. The *Wall Street Journal* reports that a marked slowdown in corporate headquarter shifts has occurred because "companies are examining more closely the supposed benefits of moving their headquarters and weighing them more critically against the costs." This is but one of many indications that the pursuit of materialism is beginning to recede somewhat in the face of a wide reassessment of values.[6]

Voluntary Simplicity

One alternative to materialism is what is often described as voluntary simplicity. By definition, it is an option only for those who are affluent, whether in the industrial countries or the Third World. Put simply, to practice voluntary simplicity is to acquire goods only to satisfy basic needs and to seek a high satisfaction in personal development, in human relationships, in intellectual and spiritual growth.

Adherents of voluntary simplicity, those who content themselves with no more than they need, can now be found in significant numbers in most Western industrial societies and in some other societies as well. Deliberately abandoning the frenetic pursuit of material goods in favor of a simpler life-style, they are involved in recycling, home gardening, biking to work, and the rebellion against conspicuous consumption and planned obsolescence.

Various public opinion surveys indicate that Americans are aware of the need to simplify life-styles.[7] A 1976 Roper poll found that over half of all Americans believe that it will be

necessary to "cut way back" on consumption to conserve resources and keep the economy strong. An earlier Harris poll
had found that 92 percent of Americans were willing to eliminate annual model changes in automobiles if doing so would
reduce consumption of raw materials. A similar percentage was
willing to dispense with annual fashion changes in clothing.

Those who are voluntarily simplifying their life-styles are
found largely among the middle and upper income groups in
the United States and northwestern Europe, particularly in
Scandinavia.[8] Within the United States, the Stanford Research Institute estimates that some four to five million adult
Americans practice the philosophy of "less is more," and an
additional eight to ten million Americans have accepted at
least some of its tenets. In Norway, a poll revealed that 74
percent of those interviewed "would prefer a simple life with
no more than essentials to a high income and many material
benefits if these have to be obtained through increased stress."

The desire to acquire material goods beyond basic needs may
imply personal insecurity. Conversely, those who have voluntarily abandoned materialism tend to be better educated, more
independent, and more successful than those who continue to
cling to the shopworn creed. At any rate, voluntary simplicity
is clearly more than a fad. As one observer notes, "Its roots
reach far too deeply into the needs and ideals of people everywhere to be regarded as a transitory response to a passing
societal condition."[9] Most important, it permits the development of the inner self when outer growth is no longer possible.

Perhaps more than any other ethic, voluntary simplicity
reconciles the needs of the person, the community, the economy, and the environment. It is a response to the emptiness
of materialism. It answers questions posed by resource scarcities, ecological stresses, and mounting inflationary pressures.
Practiced by significant portions of society, it may also relieve
alienation and assuage the international conflicts associated
with competition for scarce resources.

Conspicuous Frugality

In a society where wealth and material possessions confer status, consumption that is excessive and highly visible communicates that status to others. But where frugality and the careful use of resources are valued, conspicuous frugality also carries a message. Among young people, particularly those in the upper middle class in Western industrial societies, conspicuous frugality is political as well as economic. In opting for frugality, whether manifested by less formal clothing, simpler dietary habits, or altered modes of transportation, it has become possible to align personal choice with a common cause. At a time when values are shifting rapidly, this alignment is welcome indeed, particularly since many people have not yet recognized, much less come to grips with, the need for such a shift.

Of course, some changes are obvious. Throughout much of the postwar period, for instance, the relationship between the size of one's automobile and one's status was more or less direct —the larger the car, the higher the status. In recent years, however, the mention of the purchase of a new car almost invariably leads to a discussion of its fuel efficiency. For many, the more fuel efficient the vehicle, the greater its value as a status symbol. In an earlier period the focus would have been on the car's speed, power, and extra amenities.

Closely related to conspicuous frugality is what might be described as conspicuous self-reliance. In the revival of home gardening, bicycling between home and work, and interest in reducing heating fuel use is the opportunity to substitute ingenuity for money and the more enjoyable forms of labor for stressful activities. Here, too, new status accrues to those who most dramatically reduce their heating bills by installing insulation, resetting thermostats, or deciding not to live in the largest home they can possibly afford.

What looks to be the coming of wisdom at the household

level seems to have an international counterpart. Now, when Western political leaders gather at summit conferences, they sound a bit like homeowners as they talk about reducing national energy consumption. In fact, among the nations that consume the most energy, the competition is to see who can become the most efficient, the most frugal. In the 1980 election campaign, President Carter boasted of the one-third reduction in U.S. oil imports that took place during his administration—a far cry from President Nixon's belief that Americans should be proud of their high energy consumption —and industrial nations are now challenging each other to reduce national per capita energy consumption.

Political leaders may practice conspicuous frugality as a means of setting an example for government employees. When Jerry Brown was elected governor of California, he declined to move into the mansion that had been built by his predecessor, choosing instead to live in a modest apartment. He also opted for a small automobile in place of the customary large limousine. In so doing, he indicated to all California civil servants that they were expected to use tax payers' money with care and frugality.

In Tanzania, President Julius Nyerere followed a similar strategy when oil was in short supply in 1979 when he urged his cabinet members to commute to work on bicycles in order to conserve gasoline.[10] While bicycle commuting by a handful of cabinet members would not itself save much oil, it would underline the need to conserve gasoline for the populace at large.

Already, changing values are being commercialized. While this is unsettling for those who embrace conspicuous frugality as a means of rescuing spiritual life from the suffocating influence of commercialism, at least appeals to these new values indicate how widely accepted they have become. For example, an advertisement for an imported sports car with high fuel efficiency ends with the line, "It's getting downright embarrassing to be seen driving those gas guzzlers."[11] As commercialization of the new values proceeds, an additional set of energies is harnessed to assist the transition.

Equity: The Two Dimensions

In the transition to a sustainable society, questions of equity take on new importance. As the overriding emphasis on growth gives way to a greater emphasis on sustainability, evading the issue of the distribution of wealth both within and among societies grows increasingly difficult. Meanwhile, the extraordinary claims on the earth's resources by our generation are escalating, raising the question of intergenerational equity.

As long as national economies were expanding steadily, the affluent and powerful could always rationalize that since the economic pie was expanding, everyone would eventually get more. But as the growth in the production of material goods and services slows, or even levels off and declines, the distribution issue must be viewed against a new backdrop, one unfamiliar to our generation. With the economic pie no longer expanding, it becomes more difficult to dodge the question of how the pie is being distributed.

As world population moved from three billion to four billion and beyond, the production of many essential commodities fell behind population growth. When the production of a particular commodity is not expanding more rapidly than population, if some of us consume more, others must necessarily consume less. While this has occurred locally in the past, our generation has yet to come to grips with global scarcities since throughout our lifetimes the overall production of virtually all major commodities has expanded faster than population.

With this change in production potential, pressure to formulate economic and social policies with basic human needs in mind will no doubt increase, even though formulating acceptable policies in this context is far more complex and politically difficult than it was with the old growth approach and its underlying theory that a rising tide raised all ships. As economist Herman Daly perceptively observes, turning our focus to meeting basic human needs will "make fewer demands on our environmental resources, but much greater demands on our moral resources."[12]

The sweeping adjustments involved in the transition will be more easily made in socially cohesive societies—societies, that is, in which a culture is shared and wealth and opportunity are broadly distributed. Experience indicates that most people are willing to make adjustments if they are convinced that the need to do so is real and that others are doing their part. By the same logic, societies in which the richest fifth of the population has an income level 20 times as great as the poorest fifth can expect transitional adjustments to be painful, if not violent.

Social cohesion is bound to increase if materialism is gradually abandoned as a social and personal goal among the affluent. Indeed, setting our sights on what Carter Henderson describes as *enough* rather than *more* both reduces pressures on natural systems and resources and increases our ability to act in concert at crucial moments.[13] If the shift among the world's affluent away from material acquisitions to personal development gains in force, then the differences in material consumption levels will steadily diminish.

Even while wrestling with the issue of equity among ourselves, we are now faced with the issue of intergenerational equity. In many ways equity among generations is more difficult to deal with because generations yet to come are not represented in the bargaining over resources. All too many of our generation have adopted consumption patterns that reflect little concern for future generations. To paraphrase a UN report, we have not inherited the earth from our fathers; we are borrowing it from our children.[14]

The danger that our generation will consume so much of the earth's resource base that little will be left to sustain our grandchildren is a matter of rising concern within scientific and other communities. A National Academy of Sciences study on energy reports that "we are exhausting fossil fuels, ruining soil fertility, unbalancing ecosystems, and distorting human values and institutions in the greatest energy-spending spree of all times, at the expense of future generations."[15] Willis Harman underlines this danger, pointing out that existing techniques of economic analysis are not adequate for evaluating the future. He urges a shift "from discounting the future by economic logic toward direct involvement with the welfare of future generations."[16] This theme is also taken up by system analysts Jørgen Randers and Donella Meadows, who observe that "western man's personal and social values evolved in the context of an apparently infinite world where obtaining more of everything today was not inconsistent with having more tomorrow as well. Thus, his ethical system is poorly suited for guiding him in a period when short-term gains often entail long-term sacrifices and vice versa."[17] Obviously, the same holds true for non-Westerners who have embraced the materialist creed.

Some societies have begun to consider the welfare of future generations in contemporary decision-making. While concern with the exhaustion of fossil fuel reserves has led to efforts to conserve energy in many industrial societies, China is beginning to consider intergenerational equity in population and childbearing policy. Government documents and public discussions stress the fact that whereas parents traditionally have had children to ensure their own security in old age, from now on having too many children will undermine the quality of life for future generations. As noted earlier, by projecting man-land ratios over the next generation, Chinese leaders help prospective parents understand the implications of their childbearing decisions for their children and grandchildren.

In considering actions that would facilitate the development of preindustrial societies and further the transition to a sustainable society, concern with international and intergenerational equities intersect. According to the National Academy of Sciences energy study, "Countries that begin their development processes later than others will be enormously disadvantaged by the earlier squandering of fossil fuels and a higher general level of prices."[18] This in mind, a strong case can be made that dwindling oil reserves should be saved for societies that are still struggling at the subsistence levels. With preferential access to the remaining oil, they would be better able to satisfy basic human needs, particularly in such key areas as food production.

Apart from the depletion of oil reserves, the current production of radioactive waste poses a serious threat to intergenerational equity. To our children and theirs, for generations, the carcinogenic by-products of our seemingly insatiable appetite for energy will be an economic burden and a threat to health. Whatever the unique problems of successive ages turn out to be, they will be *in addition* to this dark legacy.

The issues of equity confronting our generation, both international and intergenerational, appear to be far more complex than those faced by any preceding generation. Although international inequities in wealth grew rapidly with the onset of industrialization, much of the absolute gap in wealth among societies has developed only since World War II. Where intergenerational inequity is concerned, earlier generations did, in some situations, deprive succeeding generations of forests or soils, but none had the potential for doing so on a global scale. Our generation is the first to have the potential for inadvertently altering global climate or for creating a radioactive wasteland that will affect generations to come.

Redefining National Security

As national governments begin to focus more explicitly on the transition, many will find traditional concepts of national security challenged. Since World War II, "national security" has acquired an overwhelmingly military character. Underlying this definition is the assumption that principal security threats come from other countries. Yet, the threats to security may now arise less from the relationship of nation to nation and more from the relationship of humanity to nature. For many countries, desert encroachment or soil erosion may do more to undermine national survival than invading armies could.

Even though rapid population growth can destroy a country's ecological system and social structure more effectively than a foreign adversary ever could, national government expenditures on population education and family planning fail to reflect this fact. Countries spend large sums on tanks and planes to defend their territorial sovereignty, but little or nothing to protect the topsoil on which their livelihood depends. National defense establishments are useless against these new threats. Neither bloated military budgets nor highly sophisticated weapons systems can halt the deforestation or solve the firewood crisis now affecting so many Third World countries.

The erosion of soils, the deterioration of the earth's basic biological systems, and the depletion of oil reserves now threaten the security of countries everywhere. Ecological stresses and resource scarcities have already given rise to economic stresses—inflation, unemployment, capital scarcity, and monetary instability. Ultimately, these economic stresses will translate into social unrest and political instability.

Regrettably, nonmilitary threats to a nation's security are much less clearly defined than military ones. Because the processes that ultimately lead to the collapse of biological systems are gradual and cumulative, they are too seldom given much thought until they pass a critical threshold and disaster strikes. For this reason, it is easier for government councils of developing countries to justify expenditures for the latest model jet fighters than for family planning, which could alleviate the population pressures that are leading to the deterioration of their croplands.

If military threats are considered in isolation, the military strength of adversaries or potential adversaries can be measured in terms of the number of men under arms and the number and effectiveness of tanks, planes, and other military equipment. For the superpowers, strength is also measured in nuclear warheads and delivery missiles. Given the desire always to be stronger than one's opponent, those fashioning the military budget can argue precisely and convincingly for a heavy commitment of public resources to weapons.

Unfortunately, few governments are capable of weighing traditional military threats against those of ecological and economic origin. In part, this is due to an information gap. While reams of data cross the desks of national political leaders and their advisers, little of it has to do with the health of the earth's ecosystem. Indeed, we have only recently begun to perceive the consequences of ecological insecurity, much less measure and monitor them.

Assessing and understanding these new threats to national security will challenge the information-gathering and analytical skills of governments. While intelligence agencies are organized to alert political leaders to potential military threats, there is no counterpart network for warning of the collapse of a biological system. Nations must begin to build such networks and to find people who can draw on many disciplines to analyze the information they provide. At present, few individuals are trained to assess a diversity of threats, much less to translate such an assessment into policies for allocating public resources in a way that maximizes national security.

By focusing on military threats to security, governments not only deflect attention from less obvious and more dangerous threats. They may also make an effective response to new, nonmilitary threats more difficult. The military can absorb the budgetary resources, management skills, and scientific talent that are needed to respond effectively to the emerging nonmilitary threats, and few countries have enough investment capital available both to finance the arms race and to transform their petroleum-based economy to a solar-based one. Ultimately, continuing to spend heavily on new weapons systems rather than on new energy systems may itself become a threat to the security of nations. Ironically, as Isaac Asimov has pointed out, the world may no longer have enough oil to wage a large-scale conventional war.[19] There may no longer be enough liquid fuel to operate both tanks and tractors.

For governments everywhere, the economic slack is disappearing, the choices are narrowing. A vast amount of scientific talent is needed to develop the energy resources to replace oil, to devise resource-management techniques that will protect the earth's biological systems, and to develop agricultural practices that will protect soils. The all-out mobilization that these circumstances call for entails, among other things, shifting part of the world's scientific talent now employed in the military sector to the energy sector.

Apart from the heavy claim it represents on public resources, the continuing exorbitant investment in armaments contributes to suspicion and distrust among nations. In such a psychological climate, addressing shared threats to the security of nations becomes next to impossible. Conversely, reducing military expenditures would likely lead to a more cooperative attitude among national governments, especially if the superpowers took the initiative.

In the late twentieth century, the key to national security is sustainability. If the biological underpinnings of the global economic system cannot be secured, and if new energy sources and systems are not in place as the oil wells begin to go dry, then economic disruptions and breakdowns are inevitable. In effect, the traditional military concept of "national security" is growing ever less adequate as nonmilitary threats grow more formidable. The purpose of national security deliberations should not be to maximize military strength, but to maximize national security.

A New Economic Yardstick

As sustainability becomes the goal of economic policy and planning, the debate that was launched in 1972 with the publication of *The Limits to Growth* will fade. The choice between growth or no growth will come to seem less relevant than that between one way of sustaining ourselves and another.

As a sustainable economic system evolves, the recognized inadequacies of the existing system of national economic accounting based on the Gross National Product as the yardstick of progress will become even more evident. In particular, the shift from planned obsolescence to durability as an economic goal will call for a new indicator of economic progress. Central to this redefinition will be economist Kenneth Boulding's observation that "it is stocks of goods that contribute to human wellbeing while flows contribute to Gross National Product."[20] With the existing national accounting systems, the production of shoddy goods that have to be replaced or repaired frequently raises the GNP, whereas a modest additional investment in high-quality engineering that greatly extends the lifetime of products could actually lower the GNP.

Therefore, the shift from the use of oil and other nonrenewable energy sources to the use of renewable energy sources also calls for a new technique for measuring economic progress. Should, for instance, the United States shift from electrical water heaters to solar water heaters within a given year, the GNP would decline abruptly the following year because nobody would be paying electrical utility bills for water heating. While both electrical and solar water heaters require initial capital investments, using an electrical water heater also means paying a monthly bill, whereas use of the solar water heater entails no fuel costs. Thus, other things being equal, an overnight switch from electrical to solar water heaters would reduce the GNP even though the quantity of hot water supplied to consumers could remain unchanged or even increase. More generally, the development and use of renewable energy sources cannot be properly valued using a tool as crude as the GNP. Constructing a building that incorporates the basic principles of energy architecture will help lower the GNP over time, for instance, while constructing a poorly designed and energy-inefficient one will raise the GNP. Similarly, adopting a sensible set of building energy performance standards could simultaneously lead to a lower GNP and a higher standard of living.

As the nature of the shift from growth to sustainability becomes clear, the current emphasis placed on such key indicators of progress as economic growth and labor productivity will come to look increasingly suspect. Neither of these indicators measures progress toward a sustainable economic system, which should now be the dominant goal of economic policy. More relevant indicators of economic health might be growth in the share of national energy use derived from renewable sources or the progress toward achieving a stationary population. (See Table 13-2.) Indeed, a case can be made that one reason for the rather dismal global economic performance in recent years is that the existing set of economic indicators no longer adequately measures what governments, industries, and individuals are attempting or achieving, even if inadvertently.

Another weakness of the GNP as the measure of well-being is that as it rises, its correlation with human welfare weakens and sometimes becomes negative. For example, levels of grain consumption have traditionally been used as an indicator of diet quality. But it is now becoming clear that in many countries per capita grain consumption, in the form of grain and products derived from grain, has risen to the point where further increases indicate an unhealthy diet, one that is too rich in animal fats and alcohol. By the same token, high levels of energy use may be excessive, inviting people to eliminate exercise altogether.

Table 13-2. Selected Indicators of Progress Toward A Sustainable
Economy

Subject	Indicator	Goal
Energy	Share of Energy From Renewable Resources	A Sustainable Energy Supply
Population	Rate of Population Growth	A Stationary Population
Raw Materials	Share Being Recycled	Recycling of All Materials
Cropland	Rate of Soil Erosion	A Secure Food Supply
Forests	Ratio of Harvest to Sustainable Yield	Preserve Resource Base
Fisheries	Ratio of Catch to Sustainable Yield	Preserve Resource Base

Source: Worldwatch Institute.

The need to overhaul our economic accounting system has
long been plain. For years, the Overseas Development Council
has been using a physical quality of life index (PQLI) based on
three social indicators—life expectancy, infant mortality, and
literacy—as an alternative to per capita GNP.[21] But the need
for even more sophisticated indicators that at least indirectly
measure the equity of income distribution, as well as the average level of income, takes on a new urgency in light of the
emerging resource squeeze.

As pressures on resources mount, the need to distinguish
between basic needs and luxuries will increase. For some
one who has a single crust of bread, a second crust of bread is
of immeasurable value. Indeed, it may represent the difference between surviving and starving to death. For someone
with a loaf of bread, however, an additional crust of bread is
of marginal value. Indeed, if that person is already over-
weight, an additional crust of bread may be detrimental to
health.

One of the most basic needs, of course, is that for food. In its recent analysis of internal economic conditions and citizen well-being, Bangladesh has begun to define poverty not in terms of per capita income, but in terms of caloric intake. In 1980, it reported that 85 percent of the population was living below the poverty line, defined as 2,122 calories per day, and 54 percent below the extreme poverty line of 1,885 calories.[22] Of these extremely poor groups, half were either landless or had less than one acre of land.

At the other end of the international economic spectrum, countries faced with a reduction in oil supplies are attempting to determine exactly what constitutes a luxury. In the midst of a public debate on gasoline tax policy, the *Frankfurter Rundschau* recently editorialized: "If the future is somehow to be secure from an energy point of view, driving to the bakery to get rolls must be universally viewed as a luxury."[23] The editorial writer argued that repealing the vehicle tax and boosting the gasoline tax would ensure that "he who drives to the bakery will pay a premium for his indulgence." Public debates on issues of this sort will occur repeatedly in countries everywhere in the years ahead.

Such debates underline the need for clearer thinking and better measurement devices. It is clear that after a point, economic growth and well-being are not closely correlated at the individual level. Just as it has become necessary to abandon the long-held belief that economic growth is directly predicated on growth in energy consumption, so now it may be time to realize that the assumed relationship between human well-being and the traditional economic yardstick, growth in the Gross National Product, needs to be reexamined. Apart from the amount of growth are the important questions of its nature and of the distribution of its benefits.

Existing monetary measurements of inflation are also inadequate since for a substantial share of humanity, most basic needs are for subsistence rather than marketed goods. Using only monetary measurements of inflation obscures the increase

in effort required to satisfy basic needs in the subsistence segment of the world economy. An African farmer who must work
harder and harder to produce enough food for his family as his
plot of land deteriorates finds the efforts required to satisfy
those food needs being continually inflated though they are not
monetized. Likewise, those women and children who gather
much of the firewood for the nearly 1.3 billion people in the
Third World for whom wood is the principal fuel find they
must spend ever more hours to satisfy those needs as the forests
recede from the villages.[24]

A Sense of Excitement

Taking part in the creation of a sustainable society will be
an extraordinarily satisfying experience, bringing a sense of
excitement that our immediate forebears engaged in the
building of fossil fuel-based societies did not have. In effect,
we have embarked on a shared adventure, the building of a
society that has the potential to be an enduring one. This
awareness could begin to permeate almost everything we do,
imbuing it with a sense of excitement—one that derives in part
from the scale of the undertaking, which has no precedent, as
well as from full knowledge of the risks and consequences of
failure.

We know what needs to be done to create a sustainable
society. Each of the actions that most countries must take has
already been taken by a few. Several industrial societies have
already brought their population growth to a halt. Some countries have moved with commendable speed to develop one or
more of the various solar energy sources. Within less than a
decade, wood has regained a prominent position in the energy
budget of the United States and South Korea. Countries as
different as Sweden and Brazil are evolving national energy
strategies based almost entirely on the use of renewable energy
sources. Birth rates in a number of Third World countries have

dropped impressively while energy efficiency in the industrial societies has increased markedly since 1978.

Those who believe that the quality of life would improve with programs aimed at lowering energy use look forward to a decline in energy use among the affluent. Microbiologist and social critic René Dubos, for example, believes that such a decline in the highly industrialized parts of the world would bring with it "improvements in physical and mental health, sounder agricultural practices based on ecological principles, architectural styles more interesting because they are better adapted to local conditions, and policies of rural and urban planning that would favor a revival of community spirit—and of course a less disturbed global ecology."[25]

To the extent that the transition does bring civilization and nature into harmony, it could unleash a torrent of initiatives and innovations in science and the arts. With the human spirit unleashed, we may even find that many problems will be solved more quickly than we anticipate. Contemporary problems seem seamless, interconnected, and thus difficult to address in isolation. But this seamlessness has another side. If progress is made on some fronts, it is likely to translate into progress on many others. For example, recycling materials will simultaneously save energy, reduce pollution, and lessen inflationary pressures. Substituting bicycles for automobiles will save energy, reduce air pollution, reduce traffic congestion, and improve health. Making progress in reforestation will provide a future source of energy and raw materials, reduce flooding, reduce soil erosion, and help arrest the rise in levels of atmospheric carbon dioxide.

In *Muddling Toward Frugality*, Warren Johnson writes that in the move toward sustainability "we will regain a degree of stability that will permit the deepening of culture and the enrichment of lives lived simply."[26] The transition from an unsustainable society to a sustainable one will lead to materially different life-styles. In the former, life-styles are centered more around the pursuits of self-interest and gratification, but in the latter they will be infused with a sense of action and of common purpose.

If our attitude toward nature changes, as it must if a sustainable society is to evolve, we may find our attitudes toward each other altered too. In effect, the value changes that lead to a more harmonious relationship with nature may also lead to a more harmonious relationship with each other. If we abandon our exploitative relationship with nature, we may be less inclined to exploit each other. At the international level, we may begin to see that the real threat to the long-term security of nations and of civilization itself lies less in military conflict than in the unsustainability of society as it is currently organized.

Already, shifts in public policies, investment patterns, and life-styles are signaling that the transition has begun. Governments, businesses, and individuals are using resources more efficiently and less wastefully. Around the world at least some elements of simple living are being embraced by the affluent. Each new hydroelectric generator, each new decline in the national birth rate, each new community garden brings humanity closer to a sustainable society. Collectively, millions of small initiatives will bring forth a society that can endure. At first the changes are slow, but they are cumulative and they are accelerating. Mutually reinforcing trends may move us toward a sustainable society much more quickly than now seems likely.

The prospect of creating a sustainable society is an exciting undertaking, one capable of commanding fully our loyalties and our energies. Every person, every organization, and government at every level will have a role to play. Be it Third World villagers combining energies to organize a local firewood plantation or affluent suburbanites organizing a comprehensive materials recycling program, every effort can make a difference.

Achieving a sustainable society will not be possible without a massive reordering of priorities. This in turn depends on political action by individuals and by public interest groups;

much of it may come from the bottom rather than the top. If we fail, it will not be because we did not know what needed to be done. Unlike the Mayans, we know what must be done. What we will soon discover is whether we have the vision and the will to do it.

Notes

Chapter 1. Introduction

1. E. S. Deevey et al., "Mayan Urbanism: Impact on a Tropical Karst Environment," *Science*, October 19, 1979.
2. Ibid.
3. Thorkild Jacobsen and Robert M. Adams, "Salt and Silt in Ancient Mesopotamian Agriculture," *Science*, November 21, 1958.
4. U. S. Department of Agriculture (USDA), Foreign Agricultural Service, "Reference Tables on Wheat, Corn and Coarse Grains Supply-Distribution for Individual Countries," *Foreign Agriculture Circular* FG-4-81, January 28, 1981, and "Reference Tables on Rice Supply-Utilization for Individual Countries," *Foreign Agriculture Circular* FG-38-80, December 19, 1980.

5. United Nations (UN), Department of International Economic and Social Affairs, *World Population Trends and Prospects by Country 1950– 2000: Summary Report of the 1978 Assessment* (New York: 1979).

6. Lower estimate found in UN Conference on Desertification, "Economic and Financial Aspects of the Plan of Action to Combat Desertification," Nairobi, August 29–September 9, 1977; upper estimate based on author's analysis of more recent data for the US, the USSR, Africa, and other regions.

7. National Agricultural Lands Study, co-chaired by USDA and the Council on Environmental Quality, *Soil Degradation: Effects on Agricultural Productivity*, Interim Report No. 4 (Washington, D.C.: November 1980).

8. Organization for Economic Cooperation and Development, *Land Use Policies and Agriculture* (Paris: 1976).

9. Population Reference Bureau, Washington, D.C., private communication, April 2, 1981.

10. U. S. Central Intelligence Agency, National Foreign Assessment Center, *International Energy Statistical Review*, March 31, 1981.

Chapter 2. Eroding the Base of Civilization

1. U.S. Department of Agriculture (USDA), Agricultural Stabilization and Conservation Service, Washington, D.C., private communication, February 5, 1980.

2. USDA, Agricultural Stabilization and Conservation Service, private communication, February 5, 1980; USDA, Foreign Agricultural Service, "USSR: Agricultural Situation," American Embassy, Moscow, unpublished report, February 18, 1977; USDA, Foreign Agricultural Service, "Reference Tables on Wheat, Corn, and Total Coarse Grains Supply-Distribution for Individual Countries," *Foreign Agriculture Circular* FG-7-77, July 1977, and "Reference Tables on Rice Supply-Utilization for Individual Countries," *Foreign Agriculture Circular* FG-38-80, December 19, 1980.

3. National Agricultural Lands Study (NALS), co-chaired by USDA and the Council on Environmental Quality, *Soil Degradation: Effects on Agricultural Productivity*, Interim Report No. 4 (Washington, D.C.: November 1980). For an excellent discussion of the issues raised by the relationship between increasing grain exports and soil erosion, see Lauren Soth, "The Grain Export Boom: Should It Be Tamed?," *Foreign Affairs*, Spring 1981.

4. Iowa Experiment Station, "Our Thinning Soil," *Research for a Better Iowa*, February 1977.

5. USDA, *Soil and Water Resources Conservation Act (RCA) Summary*

of *Appraisal, Parts 1 and 11*, and *Program Report, Review Draft, 1980* (Washington, D.C.: 1980).

6. Ibid.

7. B. F. Kosov et al., "The Gullying Hazard in the Midland Region of the USSR in Conjunction with Economic Development," *Soviet Geography*, March 1977.

8. Ye. F. Zorina, B. F. Kosov, and S. D. Prokhorova, "The Role of the Human Factor in the Development of the Gullying in the Steppe and Wooded Steppe of the European USSR," *Soviet Geography*, January 1977.

9. Thane Gustafson, "Transforming Soviet Agriculture: Brezhnev's Gamble on Land Improvement," *Public Policy*, Summer 1977.

10. C. L. Watson, Letter to the Editor, *Search*, April 1980.

11. Report from United States Embassy, Jakarta, March 1976.

12. U.S. Agency for International Development (AID), "Fiscal Year 1980 Budget Proposal for Pakistan," Washington, D.C., 1978.

13. *Master Plan for Power Development and Supply* (Kathmandu, Nepal: His Majesty's Government, with Nippon Koei Company, 1970).

14. AID, "Fiscal Year 1980 Budget Proposal for Ethiopia," Washington, D.C., 1978.

15. Lecture given by John Hanks, Director of the Institute of Natural Resources, Pietemaritzburg, Republic of South Africa, in Washington, D.C., July 3, 1980.

16. United Nations (UN) Conference on Desertification, "Economic and Financial Aspects of the Plan of Action to Combat Desertification," Nairobi, August 29–September 9, 1977.

17. David Pimentel et al., "Land Degradation: Effects on Food and Energy Resources," *Science*, October 8, 1976.

18. Paul Rosenberg, Russell Knutsen, and Lacy Harmon, "Predicting the Effects of Soil Depletion from Erosion," *Journal of Soil and Water Conservation*, May/June 1980.

19. J. Kent Mitchell, John C. Brach, and Earl R. Swanson, "Costs and Benefits of Terraces for Erosion Control," *Journal of Soil and Water Conservation*, September/October 1980.

20. UN Conference on Desertification, *Desertification: An Overview*, Nairobi, August 29–September 9, 1977.

21. H. F. Lamprey, "Report on the Desert Encroachment Reconnaisance in Northern Sudan, 21 October to 10 November 1975," Nairobi, undated.

22. J. Vasconcelos Sobrinho, "O Deserto Brasileiro," Universidad Federal Rural de Pernambuco, Recife, 1974; J. Vasconcelos Sobrinho, "Problematica Ecológia do Rio São Francisco," Universidad Federal Rural

de Pernambuco, Recife, 1971; Cesar F. Vergelin, "Water Erosion in the Carcarena Watershed: An Economic Study," Dissertation, University of Wisconsin, Madison, 1971.

23. Ibrahim Nahal, "Some Aspects of Desertification and their Socio-Economic Effects in the ECWA Region," presented to the UN Conference on Desertification by the Economic Commission for Western Asia, Nairobi, August 29–September 9, 1977.

24. USDA, Economics, Statistics, and Cooperatives Service, Washington, D.C., unpublished data.

25. UN Conference on Desertification, "Economic and Financial Aspects."

26. UN Conference on Desertification, "Synthesis of Case Studies of Desertification," Nairobi, August 29–September 9, 1977.

27. Arizona Water Commission, *Inventory of Resource and Uses,* State of Arizona, July 1975.

28. Kenneth B. Young and Jerry M. Coomer, *Effects of Natural Gas Price Increases on Texas High Plains Irrigation, 1976–2025,* Agricultural Report No. 448 (Washington, D.C.: USDA, Economics, Statistics, and Cooperatives Service, February 1980).

29. Helen N. Ingram, Nancy K. Laney, and John R. McCain, *A Policy Approach to Political Representation: Lessons from the Four Corners States* (Baltimore, Maryland: for Resources for the Future, by Johns Hopkins University Press, 1980).

30. Neal Jensen, "Limits to Growth in World Food Production," *Science,* July 28, 1978.

31. USDA, *R.C.A. Summary, Review Draft, 1980;* NALS, *Final Report 1981* (Washington, D.C.: January 17, 1981).

32. M. Rupert Cutler, "The Peril of Vanishing Farmlands," *New York Times,* July 1, 1980.

33. Quoted in Cutler, "The Peril of Vanishing Farmlands."

34. Organization for Economic Cooperation and Development, *Land Use Policies and Agriculture* (Paris: 1976).

35. Philip M. Hauser and Robert W. Gardner, "Urban Future: Trends and Prospects," background document prepared for the International Conference on Population and the Urban Future, Rome, Italy, September 1–4, 1980.

36. Food and Agriculture Organisation of the UN, *FAO Production Yearbook, 1978* (Rome: 1979).

37. Science Council of Canada, *Population, Technology and Resources* (Ottawa, Ont., Canada: July 1976).

38. Akef Quazi, "Village Overspill," *Mazingira,* No. 6, 1978.

39. *Country Report of the Indian Government to the UN Conference on Human Settlements* (Vancouver, B.C., Canada: June 1976).

40. Alva Erisman, "China: Agriculture in the Seventies," in U.S. Congress, Joint Economic Committee, *China: A Reassessment of the Economy*, Committee Print (Washington, D.C.: July 10, 1975).

41. Dwight Perkins, "Constraints Influencing China's Agricultural Performance," in *China: A Reassessment of the Economy.*

42. Janet M. Smith, David Ostendorf, and Mike Schechtman, "Who's Mining the Farm?," Illinois South Project, Herrin, Ill., Summer 1978.

43. Letter to Bert Lance, Director, Office of Management and Budget, from Norman A. Berg, Soil Conservation Service, USDA, Washington, D.C., March 18, 1977.

44. Ibid.

45. Jack Doyle, "Debunking Madison Avenue," *Environmental Action*, February 25, 1978.

46. Cutler, "The Peril of Vanishing Farmlands."

47. USDA, *R.C.A. Summary, Review Draft 1980;* NALS., *Final Report 1981.*

48. Nigel J. H. Smith, *Rainforest Corridors: The Transamazon Colonization Scheme* (Berkeley, Calif.: University of California Press, 1981).

Chapter 3. Biological Systems Under Pressure

1. Council on Environmental Quality (CEQ) and U.S. Department of State, *The Global 2000 Report to the President* (Washington, D.C.: July 1980); see also Reidar Persson, "The Need for a Continuous Assessment of the Forestry Resources of the World," presented to the Eighth World Forestry Congress, Jakarta, October 16–28, 1978.

2. Adrian Sommer, "Attempt at an Assessment of the World's Tropical Forests," *Unasylva*, Vol. 28, Nos. 112/113, 1976.

3. Lester R. Brown, *World Population Trends: Signs of Hope, Signs of Stress*, Worldwatch Paper 8 (Washington, D.C.: Worldwatch Institute, October 1976).

4. R. Murali Manohar, "Deforestation in Himalayan Region Cause of India's Worst Flood," *World Environment Report*, November 6, 1978.

5. Associated Press, "Death Toll in India Flooding," *Washington Star*, September 6, 1980.

6. U.S. Agency for International Development *Environmental and Natural Resource Management in Developing Countries: A Report to Congress* (Washington, D.C.: February 1979).

7. Ian Steele, "Central America Fights a Battle of Soil Erosion," *Christian Science Monitor*, March 29, 1977.

8. Dr. Frank Wadsworth, "Deforestation—Death to the Panama Canal," in *Proceedings of the U.S. Strategy Conference on Tropical Deforesta-*

tion, June 12–14, 1978 (Washington, D.C.: U.S. Department of State, Office of Environmental Affairs, October 1978).

9. Erik Eckholm, *Planting for the Future: Forestry for Human Needs,* Worldwatch Paper 26 (Washington, D.C.: Worldwatch Institute, February 1979).

10. Food and Agriculture Organization (FAO) of the United Nations, *Yearbook of Fishery Statistics,* annual volumes 1950–1978 (Rome: 1951–1979).

11. FAO, *Yearbook of Fishery Statistics;* FAO, *Fishery Commodities 1978* (Rome: 1979).

12. United States Department of Agriculture (USDA), Economics, Statistics and Cooperatives Service, private communication, March 5, 1981.

13. D. H. Cushing, "Stocks and Shares," *Nature,* November 25, 1976.

14. FAO, *Yearbook of Fishery Statistics: Catches and Landings,* annual volumes 1973, 1978 (Rome: 1974, 1979).

15. Discussion of decline of catches in Gulf of Thailand by Edward Goldberg and Sidney Holt, in "Whither Oceans and Seas?," presented at the Second International Conference on Environmental Future, Reykjavik, June 5–11, 1977. Decreased catches in China described in report discussed by Fox Butterfield in "Peking Reports It, Too, Has a Problem with Inflation," *New York Times,* May 2, 1980.

16. FAO, *World Fisheries and the Law of the Sea* (Rome: 1979).

17. FAO, "Fishery Commodity Situation and Outlook 1979/80," *FAO Fisheries Circular 729,* May 1980.

18. CEQ, *Global 2000.*

19. Ibid.

20. CEQ, *Environmental Quality,* Tenth Annual Report (Washington, D.C.: December 1979); Ben A. Franklin, "Chesapeake Bay Pollution Fight Pits Oyster Against Automobile," *New York Times,* April 27, 1980.

21. "Extinction Seen Possible for France's Oyster Crop," *Wall Street Journal,* September 26, 1979.

22. Dr. David Tolmazin, "Black Sea—Dead Sea?," *New Scientist,* December 6, 1979.

23. FAO, *World Fisheries and the Law of the Sea.*

24. Carl. J. Sinderman, "Aquatic Animal Protein Food Resources—Actual and Potential," presented to Congressional Roundtable on World Food and Population, Washington, D.C., June 26, 1979.

25. FAO, *FAO Production Yearbook 1978* (Rome: 1979).

26. Harlow J. Hodgson, "Forage Crops," *Scientific American,* February 1976.

27. R. E. McDowell, *Ruminant Products: More than Meat and Milk* (Morrilton, Arkansas: Winrock International, September 1977).
28. FAO data, cited in N.S. Ramaswamy, "Report on Draught Animal Power as a Source of Renewable Energy, prepared for FAO, draft copy, January 1981.
29. Hodgson, "Forage Crops."
30. USDA, Foreign Agricultural Service, "Reference Tables on Wheat, Corn and Total Coarse Grain Supply-Distribution for Individual Countries," *Foreign Agriculture Circular* FG-4-81, January 28, 1981.
31. International Monetary Fund, *International Financial Statistics*, April 1981.
32. Hodgson, "Forage Crops."
33. See "Summary and Conclusions" of H. A. Fitzhugh et al., *The Role of Ruminants in Support of Man* (Morrilton, Arkansas: Winrock International, April 1978).
34. Author's estimate based on data from FAO, *FAO Production Yearbook*, 1952–1977 (Rome: 1953–1978).
35. Ibrahim Nahal, "Some Aspects of Desertification and Their Socio-Economic Effects on the ECWA Region," presented to the UN Conference on Desertification by the Economic Commission for Western Asia, Nairobi, August 29–September 9, 1977.
36. Ibid.
37. CEQ, *Environmental Quality*, Sixth Annual Report (Washington, D.C.: December 1975).
38. Data supplied by Bureau of Indian Affairs. The zone discussed was until recently open for joint use by Navajos and Hopis, but in fact was used almost entirely by Navajos. The area has now been divided between the tribes, and Navajos living in the Hopi sections are to be relocated.
39. Coquimbo Region Case Study summarized in UN Conference on Desertification, "Synthesis of Case Studies of Desertification," Nairobi, August 29–September 9, 1977.
40. U.S. Department of the Interior, Bureau of Land Management, *Desertification in the U.S.: Status and Issues*, Working Review Draft, June 1980.
41. Philip M. Fearnside, "Cattle Yield Prediction for the Transamazon Highway of Brazil," *Interciencia*, July/August 1979.
42. FAO, *FAO Production Yearbook*, annual volumes 1952–1979.
43. See Table II, "Estimates of Total Ocean Yields of Aquatic Animals," in R. van Cleve, "Factors Determining the Maximum Possible Fish Catch" in *New Protein Foods, Vol. 3* (New York: Academic Press, 1978).

44. CEQ, *Global 2000.*
45. USDA, *Agricultural Statistics 1962* (Washington, D.C.: Government Printing Office, 1963).
46. FAO, *1977 Annual Fertilizer Review* (Rome: 1978).
47. CEQ, *Global 2000.*
48. Enzo Grilly, Barbara Agnostini, and Maria Welvaars, *The World Rubber Economy: Structure, Changes, Prospects* (Washington, D.C.: The World Bank/FAO, 1978).
49. "Materials 1980," *Modern Plastics,* January 1980.

Chapter 4. Twilight of the Age of Oil

1. United Nations Department of International Economic and Social Affairs, *World Energy Supplies, 1950–1974; World Energy Supplies, 1973–1978* (New York: 1976, 1979).
2. Ibid.
3. Estimates of oil reserves in article by Larry Auldridge, "World Oil Flow Slumps, Reserves Up," *Oil and Gas Journal,* Worldwide Issue, December 29, 1980. Author's projections for consumption.
4. UN, *World Energy Supplies.*
5. Ibid.
6. See Lester Brown, *Resource Trends and Population Policy,* Worldwatch Paper 29 (Washington, D.C.: Worldwatch Institute, May 1979).
7. Dr. Herbert Block, *The Planetary Product* (Washington, D.C.: U.S. Department of State, Bureau of Public Affairs, October 1979).
8. Motor Vehicle Manufacturers Association of the United States. (MVMA), Detroit, Michigan, private communication, April 22, 1980.
9. MVMA, *Motor Vehicle Facts and Figures, 1979* (Detroit: 1979).
10. Marcus Franda, "Alternative Energies and the Renewal of India," *Common Ground,* Winter 1978.
11. Biographical information on Perez Alphonso in Stan Steiner, "The Man Who Invented OPEC—to Conserve Energy," *Washington Post,* September 23, 1979.
12. All quotes from Alphonso in Steiner, "The Man Who Invented OPEC."
13. Ibid.
14. International Monetary Fund, *International Financial Statistics Yearbook* (Washington, D.C.: 1979).
15. M. King Hubbert, "Energy Resources," in *Resources and Man,* Committee on Resources and Man, National Academy of Sciences, National Research Council (San Francisco: for the National Academy of Sciences by W.H. Freeman and Co., 1969).
16. David M. Root and Emil B. Attanasi, "World Petroleum Availability,"

presented at 37th Annual Technical Conference, Society of Plastics Engineers, New Orleans, May 7–10, 1979.

17. Hubbert, "Energy Resources"; Root and Attanasi, "World Petroleum Availability"; projections by Exxon, Petroleum Economics Limited, and Walter Levy, petroleum consultant. For an excellent discussion of oil prospects, see Walter Levy, "Oil Policy and OPEC Development Prospects," *Foreign Affairs*, Winter 1978/79.
18. "Exploration Rises as Gushers Grow Scarce," *Journal of Commerce*, July 9, 1979; Craig R. Whitney, "Soviet Oil Expert Warns of Reliance on Old Fields," *New York Times*, February 13, 1980.
19. *International Petroleum Encyclopedia 1980* (Tulsa, Ok.: PennWell Publishing Co., 1980).
20. Council on Environmental Quality (CEQ) and U.S. Department of State, *The Global 2000 Report to the President* (Washington, D.C.: July 1980).
21. Youssef M. Ibrahim, "Behind Iran's Revolution: Too Much Spending, Too Soon," *New York Times*, February 4, 1979.
22. Alan Riding, "Mexico's Oil Won't Solve All the Problems," *New York Times*, February 4, 1979.
23. Quoted in Riding, "Mexico's Oil Won't Solve All the Problems."
24. *International Petroleum Encyclopedia 1980*, and *Oil & Gas Journal*, Worldwide Issue, 1980.
25. "CIA· Global Oil Supply Outlook Poor," *Oil & Gas Journal*, September 3, 1979.
26. Typical projections are those of Exxon, Petroleum Economics Limited, and Walter Levy.
27. *Oil & Gas Journal*, Worldwide Issue, 1980. (See also Table 4–1.)
28. Atomic Industrial Forum, "Double Digit Growth Characterizes 1980 Nuclear Programs Abroad," *INFO News Release*, Washington, D.C., March 13, 1981, and "Nuclear Power Plants in the U.S., December 31, 1980," *INFO*, attached to "The Nuclear Industry in 1980: A Rocky Road to Recovery," *INFO News Release*, January 19, 1981.
29. Quoted in *Energy Finance Week*, September 10, 1975.
30. Charles Komanoff, *Power Plant Cost Escalation: Nuclear and Coal Capital Costs, Regulation and Economics* (New York: Komanoff Energy Associates, 1981).
31. Edward A. Gargan, "Indian Point Shutdown to Last Several Weeks at Minimum, State Power Authority Says," *New York Times*, February 2, 1981.
32. Amory B. Lovins and L. Hunter Lovins, *Energy/War—Breaking the Nuclear Link* (San Francisco: Friends of the Earth, 1980).
33. "Heat Wave Zooms Peak 6.6%, Long-Term Trend is Still Down,"

from the 31st Annual Electrical Industry Forecast, *Electrical World*, September 15, 1980.

34. Bradley Graham, "Bonn's Orderly Rule is Ruffled by Opponents of Atomic Power," *Washington Post,* February 15, 1981.

35. Eric Bourne, "Austria's Nuclear 'White Elephant'," *Christian Science Monitor,* November 7, 1978.

36. International Energy Agency, *Energy Policies and Programmes of IEA Countries, 1979 Review* (Paris: Organisation for Economic Co-operation and Development, 1980).

37. Information on Eastern Europe and USSR in Dr. P. Feuz, "Nuclear Power in Eastern Europe," Parts I and II, *Energy in Countries With Planned Economies* (Berne, Switzerland), April and May, 1980.

38. "Mexico and Venezuela Gear Up, Brazil Slows Down Nuclear Power Efforts," *Latin American Energy Report,* January 29, 1981; Eduardo Lachica and Jerry Landauer, "Korea May Pare Nuclear Program, Analysts Suggest," *Wall Street Journal,* January 21, 1981.

39. *Nuclear Engineering International,* Supplement, July 1980.

40. "35,000 Protest Plan for a German Dump," *New York Times,* April 1, 1979.

41. Vera Rich, "Czech Closure," *Nature,* August 28, 1980.

42. Gus Speth, "A Mandate from the Future: Nuclear Wastes and the Public Trust," speech to the American Association for the Advancement of Science, Houston, Texas, January 5, 1979.

43. "What Does It Cost to Dispose of an Old Nuclear Plant?," *Business Week,* December 25, 1978.

44. Irvin Molotsky, "House Approves Nuclear Cleanup at New York Site," *New York Times,* September 16, 1980.

45. "Nuclear Waste Kills an Investment," *Business Week,* March 17, 1980.

46. U.S. Department of Housing and Urban Development, Federal Insurance Administration, copy of a sensitivity analysis of the Price Anderson Act as it applies to the Three Mile Island Nuclear incident, prepared in April 1979.

47. Federal Insurance Administration, sensitivity analysis of the Price Anderson Act; Keiki Kehoe, *Unavailable at Any Price* (Washington, D.C.: Environmental Policy Center, 1980).

48. Victor Gilinsky, "Plutonium, Proliferation, and Policy," *Technology Review,* February 1977.

49. Quoted in Gilinsky, "Plutonium, Proliferation, and Policy."

50. "Student Designs $2,000 Atomic Bomb," *New York Times,* October 9, 1976.

51. Ann Thrupp, "Danger: Nuclear Terrorism," *Worldwatch Feature Service,* November 28, 1980.

52. Quoted in "Nobel Scientist Says Experts Know of No Safe N-Disposal," *Albuquerque Journal,* September 28, 1979.
53. J. Goldenberg, "Brazil: Energy Options and Current Outlook," *Science,* April 14, 1978.
54. "Soviet Scientists See Potential Nuclear Power Problems," *New York Times,* October 15, 1979; "Nuclear Safety: An Unusual Debate in the Soviet Press," *World Business Weekly,* January 14, 1980.
55. UN, *World Energy Supplies,* and author's estimates for 1980.
56. U.S. Department of Energy, Energy Information Administration, *Monthly Energy Review,* April 1981.
57. Vaclav Smil, "China's Energetics: A System Analysis," in U.S. Congress, Joint Economic Committee, *The Chinese Economy Post-Mao,* Volume I, Committee Print (Washington, D.C.: November 9, 1978).
58. UN, Department of International Economic and Social Affairs, Statistical Office, *1979 Yearbook of World Energy Statistics* (New York: 1981).
59. Edward D. Griffith and Alan N. Clarke, "World Coal Production," *Scientific American,* January 1979.
60. Ibid.
61. UN, *World Energy Supplies, 1973–1978.*
62. J. M. Bradley, "Coal Looms Ever Larger in West Germany's Energy Plans," *Journal of Commerce,* April 10, 1980.
63. Geoffrey Murray, "Japanese Scurrying to Get Out of Oil," *Christian Science Monitor,* September 12, 1980.
64. "West Germany Plans to Enrich the World's Coal," *World Business Weekly,* November 10, 1980.
65. World Coal Study, *Coal, Bridge to the Future,* Carroll L. Wilson, Project Director (Cambridge, Mass.: Ballinger, 1980).
66. Great Lakes Science Advisory, *Annual Report to the Joint Commission* (Windsor, Ont.: July 1979).
67. CEQ, *Global 2000.*
68. Survey by New York State Bureau of Fisheries, described in Philip J. Hilts, "Acid Rain, Snow Said to Kill 50% of High-Altitude Adirondack Lakes," *Washington Post,* January 6, 1981.
69. National Agricultural Lands Study, co-chaired by U. S. Department of Agriculture and CEQ, *Soil Degradation: Effects on Agricultural Productivity,* Interim Report No. 4 (Washington, D.C.: November 1980).
70. Ibid.

Chapter 5. The Changing Food Prospect

1. U.S. Department of Agriculture (USDA), Foreign Agricultural Service, "Reference Tables on Wheat, Corn and Coarse Grains Supply—Dis-

tribution for Individual Countries," *Foreign Agriculture Circular* FG-4-81, January 28, 1981; and "Reference Tables on Rice Supply—Utilization for Individual Countries," *Foreign Agriculture Circular* FG-38-80, December 19, 1980.

2. USDA, "Reference Tables on Wheat, Corn and Coarse Grains Supply-Distribution for Individual Countries," *Foreign Agriculture Circular* FG-7-77, July 1977, and FG-4-81, January 28, 1981.

3. The International Food Policy Research Institute, *Food Needs of Developing Countries: Projections of Production and Consumption to 1990*, Research Report 3 (Washington, D.C.: December 1977).

4. F. Kenneth Hare, "Climate and Agriculture: The Uncertain Future," *Journal of Soil and Water Conservation*, May/June 1980.

5. "A System to Provide Early Warning of Drought in Developing Countries," *Weather and Climate Report* (Washington, D.C.: Nautilus Press, February 1981).

6. Lester R. Brown, *The Politics and Responsibility of the North American Breadbasket*, Worldwatch Paper 2 (Washington, D.C.: Worldwatch Institute, October 1975).

7. Lester R. Brown, *World Population Trends: Signs of Hope, Signs of Stress*, Worldwatch Paper 8 (Washington, D.C.: Worldwatch Institute, October 1976).

8. Ibid.

9. Dr. Michael C. Latham, "The U.S. Role in African Development with Special Reference to the Sahel," *World Hunger, Health, and Refugee Problems*, record of the U.S. Senate Committee on Labor and Public Welfare Meeting, June 10–11, 1975.

10. Jack Shepherd, *The Politics of Starvation* (Washington, D.C.: Carnegie Endowment for International Peace, 1975).

11. USDA, Economics, Statistics, and Cooperative Service, Washington, D.C., private communication, August 22, 1978.

12. Kenneth Grant, "Erosion in 1973–74: The Record and the Challenge," *Journal of Soil and Water Conservation*, January/February 1975.

13. Figures through 1970 from *Soviet Statistical Handbook* (Moscow: date unknown); more recent figures are from *Agriculture in the USSR*, 1971–77 (Moscow: date unknown) and *The National Economy of the USSR* (annual) (Moscow: various issues).

14. Wouter Tims, *Nigeria: Options for Long-Term Development* (Baltimore: for the World Bank, Johns Hopkins University Press, 1974).

15. Each of these studies is cited in the National Agricultural Lands Study, cochaired by USDA and the Council on Environmental Quality, *Soil*

Degradation: Effects on Agricultural Productivity, Interim Report No. 4 (Washington D.C.: November 1980).

16. L. M. Thompson, "Weather Variability, Climatic Change, and Grain Production," *Science*, May 9, 1975.

17. Neal Jensen, "Limits to Growth in World Food Production," *Science*, July 28, 1978.

18. USDA, "Reference Tables on Wheat, Corn and Coarse Grains" FG-4-81 and "Reference Tables on Rice Supply" FG-38-80.

19. Ibid.

20. USDA, "Reference Tables on Wheat, Corn and Coarse Grains" FG-4-81, and "Reference Tables on Rice Supply" FG-38-80; USDA Foreign Agricultural Service, "World Livestock Numbers, Slaughter, Red Meat Production, Consumption and Trade 1977–81," *Foreign Agriculture Circular* FLM-2-81, February 1981; "Poultry and Egg Statistics Selected Countries, 1964–79", *Foreign Agriculture Circular* FPE-3-80, July 1980.

21. World soybean harvests 1950–63 estimated by author on basis of data from USDA Foreign Agricultural Service; harvests 1964–1980 from USDA Foreign Agricultural Service, private communication, March 10, 1980.

22. USDA Foreign Agricultural Service, "World Oilseeds Situation and Outlook and U.S. Oilseed Trade," *Foreign Agriculture Circular*, FOP-3-81, February 1981.

23. Lester R. Brown, *Food or Fuel: New Competition for the World's Cropland*, Worldwatch Paper 35 (Washington, D.C.: Worldwatch Institute, March 1980).

24. Brown, *Food or Fuel*, and Fred M. Sanderson, "Gasohol: Boon or Blunder?" *The Brookings Bulletin*, Winter 1980.

25. Author's estimates of cropland use based on 1980 fuel alcohol consumption in Brazil of 3.5 billion liters, and U.S. fuel alcohol sales estimated by Bureau of Alcohol, Tobacco and Firearms at 100 million gallons a year (including imports); Philippine "alcogas" in "Sweet Hopes", *Asiaweek*, September 26, 1980.

Chapter 6. Emerging Economic and Social Stresses

1. Dr. Herbert Block, *The Planetary Product* (Washington, D.C.: U.S. Department of State, Bureau of Public Affairs, October 1979).

2. Willis W. Harman, *An Incomplete Guide to the Future* (Stanford, California: Stanford Alumni Association, 1976).

3. Lori Ann Thrupp, *Deforestation, Agricultural Development and Cattle Expansion in Costa Rica*, unpublished Honors thesis submitted to

Human Biology Program and Latin American Studies, Stanford University, May 1, 1980.

4. Thane Gustafson, "Transforming Soviet Agriculture: Brezhnev's Gamble on Land Improvement," *Public Policy,* Summer 1977.

5. Council on Environmental Quality, *Environmental Quality,* Tenth Annual Report (Washington, D.C.: December 1979).

6. David Ricardo, *Principles of Political Economy and Taxation* (1817).

7. "A Land Use Policy for Canada," *Agrologist,* Autumn 1975.

8. Leslie T. C. Kuo, *The Technical Transformation of Agriculture in Communist China* (New York: Praeger, 1972).

9. U.S. Department of Agriculture (USDA), Economics, Statistics and Cooperative Service, Washington, D.C., unpublished data.

10. Food and Agriculture Organization (FAO) of the United Nations, *Yearbook of Fishery Statistics—Catches and Landings* (Rome: 1979); Organization for Economic Cooperation and Development (OECD), *Review of Fisheries in OECD Member Countries,* 1975 (Paris: 1976).

11. Gennadi Pisarevsky, "The Search for Oil", *Soviet Life,* May 1980.

12. World Bank, *The International Market for Iron Ore: Review and Outlook,* Working Paper No. 160 (Washington, D.C.: August 1973).

13. International Monetary Fund (IMF), *International Financial Statistics Yearbook* (Washington, D.C., 1979).

14. UN Department of International Economic and Social Affairs, *World Population Trends and Prospects by Country, 1950–2000: Summary Report of the 1978 Assessment* (New York: 1979); Block, *The Planetary Product.*

15. Barry Bosworth, "Testimony Before the Senate Committee on Banking, Housing, and Urban Affairs," Hearings, October 21, 1977.

16. IMF, *International Financial Statistics.*

17. Abraham Bergson, "The Soviet Economic Slowdown," *Challenge,* January/February 1978; R. W. Apple, "Soviet Goals: No New Priorities" *New York Times,* February 8, 1981; Eric Bourne, "Will Poland be Catalyst for Big Changes in East Europe?," *Christian Science Monitor,* January 6, 1981.

18. Edward Schumacher, "Brazil Reins in Its Economy," *New York Times,* December 8, 1980.

19. Wassily Leontief et al., *The Future of the World Economy* (New York: Oxford University Press, 1977).

20. World Bank, *World Development Report 1980* (New York: for the World Bank by Oxford University Press, 1980).

21. Goran Backstrand and Lars Ingelstam, "Should We Put Limits on Consumption?" *The Futurist,* June 1977.

22. Kathleen Newland, *Global Employment and Economic Justice: The Policy Challenge,* Worldwatch Paper 28 (Washington, D.C.: Worldwatch Institute, April 1979).

23. International Labor Office (ILO), *ILO Labor Force Estimates and Projections, 1950–2000* Second Edition, Vol. 5, World Summary (Geneva: 1977) summarized in ILO Information, Vol. 6, No. 3, 1978.

24. Keith Griffin, *The Green Revolution: An Economic Analysis* (Geneva: UN Research Institute for Social Development, 1972).

25. ILO, *Towards Full Employment* (Geneva, 1970).

26. James P. Grant, *Economic and Business Outlook for the Developing Countries in the 1970's,* Development Issues Paper No. 1 (Washington, D.C.: Overseas Development Council, 1970).

27. Ibrahim Nahal, "Some Aspects of Desertification and their Socio-Economic Effects in the ECWA Region," presented to the UN Conference on Desertification by the Economic Commission for Western Asia, 1977.

28. Christopher Huhne, "Empty Nets and Angry Fishermen," *The Guardian Weekly,* March 23, 1980.

29. Kasturi Rangan, "India Sees Slowdown, Rise in Unemployment," *New York Times,* February 24, 1979.

30. Newland, *Global Employment and Economic Justice.*

31. Jose Carrizo, "Peru's Babies Are Dying," *New York Times,* August 24, 1979.

32. Robert Fuller, *Inflation: The Rising Cost of Living on a Small Planet,* Worldwatch Paper 34 (Washington, D.C.: Worldwatch Institute, January 1980).

33. "Trees Go, Kalabule Stays," *The Economist,* September 8, 1979.

34. Dr. Colin McCord, "The Companiganj Project," presented at the annual meeting of American Public Health Association, Miami Beach, Florida, October 17–21, 1976.

35. Presentation at Worldwatch Institute, 1978.

36. Davidson Gwatkin, "The Sad News About the Death Rate," *Washington Post,* December 2, 1978.

Chapter 7. Population: A Stabilization Timetable

1. United Nations (UN), Department of Economic and Social Affairs, *World Population Trends and Prospects by Country 1950–2000: Summary Report of the 1978 Assessment* (New York: 1979).

2. World Bank, *World Development Report 1980* (New York: Oxford University Press, 1980).

3. UN, *World Population Trends and Prospects;* Dr. Herbert Block, *The*

Planetary Product (Washington, D.C.: U.S. Department of State, Bureau of Public Affairs, October 1979).

4. Council on Environmental Quality (CEQ) and U.S. Department of State, *The Global 2000 Report to the President* (Washington, D.C.: July 1980).

5. Birth rates and death rates from 1980 World Population Data Sheet of the Population Reference Bureau (Washington, D.C.).

6. Ibid.

7. Population Reference Bureau, private communication, April 2, 1981.

8. U.S. Department of Commerce, Bureau of the Census, *Statistical Abstract of the United States* (Washington, D.C.: September 1979).

9. The Draper Fund of the Population Crisis Committee, *Birth Planning in China*, Draper Fund Report No. 8 (Washington, D.C.: March 1980); Kenneth Whiting, "Family Planning in Indonesia," *Washington Post*, November 12, 1978.

10. UN Department of International Economic and Social Affairs, *Monthly Bulletin of Statistics*, July 1975 and February 1981.

11. Author's calculations based on data from the Population Reference Bureau.

12. Bruce Stokes, *Filling the Family Planning Gap*, Worldwatch Paper 12 (Washington, D.C.: Worldwatch Institute, May 1977).

13. Charles L. Westoff, "Unwanted Fertility in Six Developing Countries," presented at Substantive Findings Session No. 11, World Fertility Survey Conference, London, July 7–11, 1980.

14. UN Population Division, "Selected Factors Affecting Fertility and Fertility Preferences in Developing Countries: Evidence from the First Fifteen WFS Country Reports," presented at Substantive Findings Session No. 3, World Fertility Survey Conference, London, July 7–11, 1980.

15. Michael T. Kaufman, "Fertile Bangladesh Nurtures Birth Control Program," *New York Times*, July 26, 1980.

16. UN Population Division, "Selected Factors Affecting Fertility".

17. James W. Brackett, "The Role of Family Planning Availability and Accessibility in Family Planning Use in Developing Countries," presented to the World Fertility Survey Conference, London, July 7–11, 1980.

18. Deirdre Wulf, "Costa Rica Leads Latin America's Fertility Decline Partly Because of National Program's Rural Impact," *Family Planning Perspectives*, Vol. 4, No. 3, Fall 1978.

19. Quoted in Jeremy Cherfas, "The World Fertility Survey Conference: Population Bomb Revisited," *Science 80*, November 1980.

20. Brackett, "The Role of Family Planning Availability and Accessibility."

21. Leo Goodstadt, "Official Targets, Data, and Policies for China's Population Growth: An Assessment," *Population and Development Review,* June 1978.

22. Stokes, *Filling the Family Planning Gap.*

23 Population Crisis Committee, "World Abortion Trends," *Population,* April 1979; Lester R. Brown and Kathleen Newland, "Abortion Liberalization: A Worldwide Trend," Worldwatch Institute, Washington, D.C., February 1976.

24. Quoted in Cherfas, "The World Fertility Survey Conference."

25. Ibid.

26. Germán Rodríguez and John Cleland, "Socio-Economic Determinants of Marital Fertility in Twenty Countries: A Multivariate Analysis," presented at Substantive Findings Session No. 5, World Fertility Survey Conference, London, July 7-11, 1980.

27. Ibid.

28. Mercedes B. Concepción, "Family Formation and Contraception in Selected Developing Countries: Policy Implications of WFS Findings," presented at Plenary Session No. 3, World Fertility Survey Conference, London, July 7-11, 1980.

29. U.S. Department of Labor, Bureau of Labor Statistics, *Marital and Family Characteristics of Workers,* Special Labor Force Report No. 13 (Washington, D.C.: March 1960) and unpublished data from the Bureau of Labor Statistics.

30. Charles Westoff, "Some Speculations on the Future of Marriage and Fertility," *Family Planning Perspectives,* March/April 1978.

31. "Decline in Sri Lankan Fertility is Due to Later Marriage, Sterilization and Traditional Methods," *International Family Planning Perspectives and Digest,* Fall 1978.

32. U.S. Department of Labor, *Marital and Family Characteristics of Workers,* and unpublished data from the Bureau of Labor Statistics.

33. Galina Kiselva, "USSR Working Women Prefer Small Families," *International Family Planning Perspectives and Digest,* Summer 1978.

34. Dorothy L. Nortman and Ellen Hofstatter, *Population and Family Planning Programs,* ninth edition (New York: Population Council, 1978).

35. Information on tax policies in the Philippines, Nepal, and Singapore in Nortman and Hofstatter, *Population and Family Planning Programs.*

36. Introduced by Representative Richard L. Ottinger. See "Legislation to Establish Population Policy," *Congressional Record,* Vol. 127, No. 9, January 19, 1981.

37. Pi-chao Chen quoted in *Birth Planning in China,* Draper Fund Report No. 8.

38. Kaufman, "Fertile Bangladesh Nurtures Birth Control Program."

39. Nortman and Hofstatter, *Population and Family Planning Programs.*
40. Frederick Jaffe and Deborah Oakley, "Observations on Birth Planning in China," *Family Planning Perspectives,* March/April 1978.
41. See, for example, Chen Muhua, "Birth Planning in China," *International Family Planning Perspectives,* September 1979.
42. Ibid.
43. Pi-chao Chen, Wayne State University, private communication, August 10, 1979.
44. Pi-chao Chen, introduction to article by Chen Muhua, "Birth Planning in China."
45. Pi-chao Chen, "Three in Ten Chinese Couples with One Child Apply for Certificates Pledging They Will Have No More," *International Family Planning Perspectives,* June 1980.
46. Pierre Pradervand, then editor of *Famille et Développement,* private communication at Conference on Developments and Trends in World Population, London, November 1978.
47. Alan Riding, "Mexico's Birth Control Effort Catching On," *New York Times,* April 28, 1979.
48. Hedrick Smith, *The Russians* (New York: Quadrangle/The New York Times Book Co., 1976).
49. C. Stephen Baldwin, "Policies and Realities of Delayed Marriage, the Cases of Tunisia, Sri Lanka, Malaysia and Bangladesh," *PRB Report,* Population Reference Bureau, September 1977.
50. Quotes in Associated Press report, "Action Urged on Birth Rates," *Washington Post,* October 2, 1979.
51. Paper prepared by Roushdi el Heneidi for a population conference held in Cairo, United Nations Fund for Population Activities, New York, 1979.
52. Science Council of Canada, *Population, Technology and Resources* (Ottawa, Ont., Canada: July 1976).

Chapter 8. Preserving Our Resource Underpinnings

1. M. Rupert Cutler, "The Peril of Vanishing Farmlands," *New York Times,* July 1, 1980.
2. Organization for Economic Cooperation and Development (OECD), *Land Use Policies and Agriculture* (Paris: 1976).
3. National Agricultural Lands Study, co-chaired by U.S. Department of Agriculture (USDA) and the Council on Environmental Quality (CEQ), *Final Report 1981* (Washington, D.C.: January 17, 1981).
4. OECD, *Land Use Policies.*
5. Ibid.

6. Ibid.
7. Quoted in Charles E. Little, "Farmland Conservancies: A Middle-ground Approach to Agricultural Land Preservation," *Journal of Soil and Water Conservation*, September/October 1980.
8. Ibid.
9. OECD, *Land Use Policies.*
10. G.G. Runka, "British Columbia's Agricultural Land Preservation Program," in *Land Use: Tough Choices in Today's Society* (Ankeny, Iowa: Soil and Conservation Society of America, 1977).
11. Ibid.
12. Little, "Farmland Conservancies."
13. Ibid.
14. William J. Sallee, "Land, Water and the Environment," presented to the Capon Springs Conference No. 4, on Population, Resources, Food, and Environment, February 1980.
15. Ibid.
16. Phillip Alampi, "New Jersey's Agricultural Preserve Demonstration Program," in *Land Use: Tough Choices in Today's Society* (Akeny, Iowa: Soil Conservation Society of America, 1977).
17. Janice M. Clark, "Agricultural Zoning in Black Hawk County, Iowa," in *Land Use: Tough Choices in Today's Society* (Ankeny, Iowa: Soil Conservation Society of America, 1977).
18. Richard Collins, "Agricultural Land Preservation in a Land Use Perspective," *Journal of Soil and Water Conservation*, September/October 1976.
19. USDA, *Soil and Water Resources Conservation Act (RCA), Summary of Appraisal, Parts I and II, and Program Report, Review Draft 1980* (Washington, D.C.: 1980).
20. Ibid.
21. Quoted by B. B. Vohra, Secretary to the Government of India, Department of Petroleum in "Managing India's Land and Water Resources," August 1978.
22. Erik Eckholm and Lester R. Brown, *Spreading Deserts—The Hand of Man*, Worldwatch Paper 13 (Washington, D.C.: Worldwatch Institute, August 1977).
23. UN Conference on Desertification, "Economic and Financial Aspects of the Plan of Action to Combat Desertification," Nairobi, August 29–September 9, 1977.
24. Harold E. Dregne, "Desertification: Symptom of a Crisis," in Patricia Paylore and Richard A. Haney, eds., *Desertification: Process, Problems, Perspectives* (Tucson: University of Arizona, September 1976).

25. UN, "Economic and Financial Aspects of the Plan of Action to Combat Desertification."
26. Paul Rosenberry, Russell Knutson, and Lacy Harmon, "Predicting the Effects of Soil Depletion from Erosion," *Journal of Soil and Water Conservation,* May/June 1980.
27. R. A. Brink, J. W. Densmore, and G. A. Hill, "Soil Deterioration and the Growing World Demands on Food," *Science,* August 12, 1977.
28. Vohra, "Managing India's Land and Water Resources."
29. W. F. Lloyd, *Two Lectures on the Checks to Population* (Oxford, England, 1833), reprinted in part in Garrett Hardin, ed., *Population, Evolution, and Birth Control* (San Francisco: W. H. Freeman and Company, 1969).
30. Food and Agriculture Organization (FAO) of the United Nations, *World Fisheries and the Law of the Sea* (Rome: 1979).
31. John A. Gulland, "The New Ocean Regime, Winners and Losers," *Ceres,* July/August 1979.
32. Jeremy Swift, "Pastoral Development in Somalia: Herding Cooperatives as a Strategy Against Desertification and Famine," in Michael H. Glantz, ed., *Desertification: Environmental Degradation In and Around Arid Lands* (Boulder, Colo.: Westview Press, 1977).
33. Eckholm and Brown, *Spreading Deserts—The Hand of Man.*
34. CEQ, *Environmental Quality,* Sixth Annual Report (Washington, D.C.: December 1975).
35. Philip M. Raup, "Competition for Land and the Future of American Agriculture," presented to the Conservation Foundation Conference, Washington, D.C., July 14, 1980.
36. Erik Eckholm, *Losing Ground: Environmental Stress and World Food Prospects* (New York: W. W. Norton and Co., 1976).
37. John E. Høsteland, "Maintaining Resource Use at Sustainable Levels," presented to the Dartmouth Symposium on Renewable Resources, Holderness, New Hampshire, July 9–13, 1978.
38. Eckholm, *Losing Ground.*
39. Erik Eckholm, *Planting for the Future: Forestry for Human Needs,* Worldwatch Paper 26 (Washington, D.C.: Worldwatch Institute, February 1979).
40. Ibid.
41. Ibid.
42. Ibid.
43. B. K. Jhala, "Social Forestry in Gujarat," mimeographed, Ahmedabad, India, 1978.
44. Eckholm, *Planting for the Future.*

45. Jhala, "Social Forestry in Gujarat."
46. Robert Taylor, "Afforestation and Fuelwood in China," *Development Digest,* October 1979.
47. Reidar Persson, "World Forest Resources and Trends," *Development Digest,* October 1979.
48. John Spears and Montague Yudelman, "Forests in Development," *Finance and Development,* December 1979.
49. Ibid.
50. Ibid.
51. Ibid.
52. Ibid.
53. Michael Arnold, "A Habitat for More than Just Trees," *Ceres,* September/October 1979.
54. Noel D. Vietmeyer, "A Front Line Against Deforestation," *Ceres,* September/October 1979.
55. Ibid.
56. Edouard Saouma, "Statement by the Director-General of FAO," presented to the Eighth World Forestry Congress, Jakarta, Indonesia, October 16–28, 1978.
57. Shankar Ranganathan, *Agro Forestry: Employment for Millions* (Bombay, India: Tola Press, November 1979).
58. Norman Myers, *The Sinking Ark* (New York: Pergamon Press, 1979).
59. Thomas Lovejoy, "We Must Decide Which Species Will Go Forever," *Smithsonian,* July 1976.
60. Erik Eckholm, *Disappearing Species: The Social Challenge,* Worldwatch Paper 22 (Washington, D.C.: Worldwatch Institute, July 1978).
61. Ibid.
62. Denis Hayes, *Repairs, Reuse, Recycling—First Steps Toward a Sustainable Society,* Worldwatch Paper 23 (Washington, D.C.: Worldwatch Institute, September 1978).
63. The Lure Camera, described by David Gibson, Eastman Kodak Patent Museum, Rochester, N.Y., private communication, June 3, 1981; see also "Pop Photo Snap Shots," *Popular Photography,* March 1976.
64. Resource Conservation Committee, *Choices for Conservation* (Washington, D.C.: U.S. Environmental Protection Agency, July 1979).
65. Hayes, *Repairs, Reuse, Recycling.*
66. Robert Fuller, "Bottling Up Inflation," Worldwatch Feature Service, February 29, 1980.
67. USDA, *Our Land and Water Resources: Current and Prospective Supplies and Uses* (Washington, D.C.: 1976).

68. Robin Bidwell and Karen Raymond, "Resource Recovery in Europe," *National Center for Resource Recovery Bulletin,* Winter 1977.
69. Brian Hammond, "Recycling Begins at Home," *New Scientist,* July 17, 1975.
70. "Spectrum," *Environment,* June 1976.
71. Hayes, *Repairs, Reuse, Recycling.*
72. Environmental Protection Agency, *Fourth Resource Recovery and Waste Reduction Report to Congress* (Washington, D.C.: 1977).
73. "Ring of Confidence for Japanese Recycling," *New Scientist,* January 24, 1980.
74. Christine Thomas, "Whatever Happened to Recycling," *New Scientist,* May 17, 1979.
75. "East Germans Profit on a Craving for Scrap," *New York Times,* April 7, 1980.
76. "Norway's New Car Junking Program is a Success," *World Environment Report,* July 16, 1979.
77. Study of Nuclear and Alternative Energy Systems, *Alternative Energy Demand Futures to 2010; The Report of the Demand and Conservation Panel to the Committee on Nuclear and Alternative Energy Systems, National Research Council* (Washington, D.C.: National Academy of Sciences, 1979).
78. Petroleum Industry Research Foundation, "Oil in the U.S. Energy Perspective . . . a Forecast to 1990," (New York) May 1980; National Petroleum Council, *Refinery Flexibility,* December 1980 and Joan Cassidy, NPC, private communication, June 24, 1981.
79. Daniel Yergin, "Conservation: The Key Energy Source," in Robert Stobaugh and Daniel Yergin, eds., *Energy Future: Report of the Energy Project at the Harvard Business School* (New York: Random House, 1979).
80. International Energy Agency (IEA), *Energy Policies and Programmes of IEA Countries,* 1979 Review (Paris: OECD., 1980).
81. J.E.M. Arnold, "Wood Energy and Rural Communities," in *Natural Resources Forum 3* (New York: United Nations, 1979). See also A. Makhijani and A. Poole, *Energy and Agriculture in the Third World* (Cambridge, Mass.: Ballinger, 1975).
82. IEA, *Energy Policies and Programmes.*
83. Ibid.
84. Ibid.
85. Robert H. Williams and Marc H. Ross, "Drilling for Oil and Gas in Our Houses," *Technology Review,* March/April 1980.
86. Edward Roby, "New Appliance Energy-Use Guide Offered," *Washington Post,* June 21, 1980.

87. Rushworth Kidder, "Will New, 83 m.p.g. Car Save Britain's King of the Road?," *Christian Science Monitor,* September 16, 1980, and photograph of GM prototype and short description, "86 Miles Per Gallon," in *Canadian Renewable Energy News,* January 2, 1981; Tony Grey, "U.S. Two-seater Cars May Weigh as Little as 1,200 Pounds and Get 80 Miles Per Gallon," *Christian Science Monitor,* October 15, 1980.

Chapter 9. Renewable Energy: Turning to the Sun

1. Amory B. Lovins and L. Hunter Lovins, *Energy/War—Breaking the Nuclear Link* (San Francisco: Friends of the Earth, 1980).

2. "Making the Most of Burning Wood," *New York Times,* November 6, 1980.

3. Edwin McDowell, "A Glow on Wood Furnaces," *New York Times,* November 11, 1979.

4. "Use of Wood as a Fuel Has Risen Sharply Since 1973," *New York Times,* May 20, 1979.

5. Stephen Grover, "Heaps of Scrap Bark Take on Great Value as Cost of Oil Spurts," *New York Times,* January 30, 1979; "Use of Wood as Fuel Has Risen Sharply Since 1973."

6. James B. Brook, "Chips are Down in Industry's Gamble on Wood Power," *New York Times,* October 21, 1979.

7. Vera Rich, "Finland Turns to Wood and Peat for Energy," *Nature,* April 5, 1979.

8. Gary S. Hartshorn, letter to Peter B. Martin, September, 1979, mimeograph from Institute of Current World Affairs.

9. Philippine Ministry of Energy, *Ten-Year Energy Program, 1980–1989* (Manila: 1980).

10. Nigel Smith, *Wood: An Ancient Fuel with a New Future,* Worldwatch Paper 42 (Washington, D.C.: Worldwatch Institute, January 1981).

11. William Knowland, letter to Peter B. Martin, August 21, 1979, mimeograph from Institute of Current World Affairs; Michael Benge, U.S. Agency for International Development, private communication, May 10, 1981.

12. Smith, *Wood: An Ancient Fuel with a New Future.*

13. Quoted by Erik Eckholm, *Planting for the Future: Forestry for Human Needs,* Worldwatch Paper 26 (Washington, D.C.: Worldwatch Institute, February 1979).

14. U.S. Congress, Office of Technology Assessment, *Energy From Biological Processes* (Washington, D.C.: July 1980).

15. Walter Sullivan, "Parley is Told of European Gains from Burning Waste and Garbage," *New York Times,* May 11, 1978.

16. Ibid.

17. U.S. Department of Energy (DOE), *The Report of the Alcohol Fuels Policy Review* (Washington, D.C.: June 1979).
18. Vaclav Smil, "Biogas Production in China," *Development Digest,* July 1979.
19. Dr. Wu Wen, "Biogas Utilization in China," presented to Bio-Energy '80 World Congress and Exposition, Atlanta, Georgia, April 21–24, 1980.
20. Smil, "Biogas Production in China."
21. Ibid.
22. E. Ariane Van Buren, "Biogas Beyond China: First International Training Program for Developing Countries," *Ambio,* Vol. IX, No. 1, 1980.
23. Joanne Omang, "Barnyard a Rich Source of Fuel," *Washington Post,* November 7, 1977.
24. Ronald D. James, Vice President, Thermonetics, Inc. (Oklahoma City), private communication, May 18, 1981.
25. A. G. Hashimoto, Y. R. Chen, and R. L. Prior, "Methane and Protein from Animal Feedlot Wastes," *Journal of Soil and Water Conservation,* January/February 1979.
26. Lester R. Brown, *Food or Fuel: New Competition for the World's Cropland,* Worldwatch Paper 35 (Washington, D.C.: Worldwatch Institute, March 1980).
27. Brazilian Ministry of Industry and Commerce, "The Brazilian Alcohol Program," mimeograph from the Brazilian Embassy, Washington, D.C., 1980. For historical and projected fuel alcohol production, see A. V. Carvalho, Jr., E. Rechtschaffen, and L. Goldstein, Jr., "Future of Alcohol Fuels Programs in Brazil," submitted to the Second Miami International Conference on Alternative Energy Sources, Miami Beach, Fla., Dec. 10–13, 1979, revised 1980, available from Centro de Tecnologia Promon, Rio de Janeiro; Cesar Cals, Minister of Mines & Energy, "The Brazilian Energetic Policy," 1979, available from the Brazilian Embassy, Washington, D.C.; and data from the National Petroleum Council and Petrobras in Fred J. Bastle, "Fermentation Alcohol as Fuel—Latin America," consultant's report to U.S. Department of Energy, Office of Consumer Affairs, Washington, D.C.
28. Brazilian Ministry of Industry and Commerce, "The Brazilian Alcohol Program."
29. "Alcohol Production Goals, Programs Explained to U.S. Congress by Brazilian Diplomat," *Solar Energy Intelligence Report,* September 17, 1979.
30. Brazilian Embassy, "Brazil Today," Washington, D.C., September 21, 1979. Data on Brazilian cropland and world sugarcane area in Food and

Agriculture Organization of the United Nations (UN), *FAO Production Yearbook 1977* (Rome: 1978).

31. Earl Butz, "U.S. Farmers Mount Gasohol Bandwagon," *Journal of Commerce,* November 14, 1979.

32. DOE Energy Information Administration (EIA), *Monthly Energy Review,* March 1981.

33. "R P Reshapes Energy Program for 1980," *Filipino Reporter,* January 11–17, 1980; Dr. Perfecto Guerrero, private communication, February 14, 1980.

34. "Kenya Builds New Gasohol Plant," *Financial Times* (London), January 15, 1980.

35. "South Africa's 'Oil Field': Ethanol from Cassava Plants," *World Environment Report,* July 16, 1979.

36. Melvin Calvin and Genevieve Calvin, "Fuel from Plants," *New York Times,* August 11, 1979; "Unlike Money, Diesel Fuel Grows on Trees," *Science,* October 26, 1979.

37. "In Africa," *World Environment Report,* August 27, 1979.

38. "An In-depth Look at Farm Fuel Alternatives," *Power Farming Magazine* (Australia), February 1980.

39. U.S. Department of Agriculture, Foreign Agricultural Service, "Weekly Roundup of World Production and Trade," *FAS Release,* November 26, 1980.

40. National Aeronautics and Space Administration (NASA), "NASA and Water Hyacinths," (pamphlet). For further information on NASA research on water hyacinths, see B.C. Wolverton and Rebecca C. McDonald, "Energy from Aquatic Plant Wastewater Treatment Systems," NASA Technical Memorandum, September 1979, and B.C. Wolverton and Rebecca C. McDonald, "Vascular Plants for Water Pollution Control and Renewable Sources of Energy," presented at Bio-Energy '80 Conference, Atlanta, Georgia, April 21–24, 1980.

41. *The New Encyclopaedia Britannica,* fifteenth edition (Chicago: Encyclopaedia Britannica, Inc., 1976).

42. James R. Hanchey, "National Hydropower Study," in *Hydropower: A National Energy Resource,* proceedings of the 1979 Engineering Foundation Conference, Eastern Maryland, March 11–16, 1979.

43. UN Department of International Economic and Social Affairs, *World Energy Supplies, 1950–1974* (New York: 1976); UN Department of International Economic and Social Affairs, *World Energy Supplies, 1973–1978* (New York: 1979).

44. Capacity for Kariba and Aswan from T. W. Mermel, "Major Dams of the World," *Water Power and Dam Construction* (London), November 1979; Furnas described in "Energy Profile of Brazil," *Energy Inter-*

national, September 1976; Guri in Eric Jeffs, "Hydro to be Main Power Source for Venezuela," *Energy International,* June 1980.

45. Cissy Wallace, "Brazil Moves Towards Energy Self-Sufficiency," *Soft Energy Notes,* April 1980.

46. Richard Critchfield, "Nepal: Majestic Mountains, Snowcapped Riches," *Christian Science Monitor,* November 1, 1978.

47. Henry Scott-Stokes, "China Enlists Japanese Advisers in $30 Billion Dam Construction," *New York Times,* February 9, 1979; "An American Edge in China's Hydro Plans," *Business Week,* September 17, 1979; UN Department of International Economic and Social Affairs, Statistical Office, *1979 Yearbook of World Energy Statistics* (New York: 1981).

48. Andrews H. Malcolm, "Quebec Unleashing a Hydro Giant," *New York Times,* December 13, 1978; Clayton Jones, "Quebec Turns Water Into Gold," *Christian Science Monitor,* July 3, 1980.

49. Henry Giniger, "Quebec Power Project Opens to Joy and Debate," *New York Times,* October 29, 1979.

50. Ibid.

51. Capacity in "Reviewing Low–level and Small Hydro: 1," *Electrical World,* July 15, 1980.

52. U.S. Army Corps of Engineers, *Preliminary Inventory of Hydropower Resources,* Vol. I (Ft. Belvoir, Va.: July 1979) and R. J. McDonald, *Estimate of the National Hydroelectric Power Potential at Existing Dams* (U.S. Army Corps of Engineers, July 1977), cited in Solar Energy Research Institute, *Report on Building a Sustainable Future,* Volume II, Appendix C (Washington, D.C.: U.S. House of Representatives, Committee on Energy and Commerce, Committee Print, April 1981).

53. Vaclav Smil, "China's Energetics: A System Analysis," in U.S. Congress, Joint Economic Committee, *The Chinese Economy Post-Mao,* Volume 1, Committee Print (Washington, D.C.: November 9, 1978).

54. Hanchey, "National Hydropower Study."

55. "Small-Hydro Power Starts a Comeback," *Business Week,* March 20, 1978.

56. Andreas Freund, "Mini Home Hydroelectric Plant Marketed in France at $7,800," *New York Times,* May 15, 1978.

57. Philip F. Palmedo and Pamela Baldwin, "The Contribution of Renewable Resources and Energy Conservation as Alternatives to Oil in Developing Countries," prepared for U.S. Agency for International Development, Office of Energy, Development Support Bureau, February 6, 1980.

58. *The New Encyclopaedia Britannica.*
59. M. R. Gustavson, "Limits to Wind Power Utilization," *Science,* April 6, 1979.
60. Dr. Peter Musgrove, "Windmills Change Direction," *New Scientist,* December 9, 1976; Mark Diesendorf, "Recent Scandinavian R&D in Wind Electric Power: Implications for Australia," *Search,* May 1979; "Soviets Set Wind-Power Goal," *Christian Science Monitor,* April 26, 1979.
61. Diesendorf, "Recent Scandinavian R&D in Wind Electric Power."
62. R. W. Apple, Jr., "Danish Schools Promote 'Windmill Power'," *New York Times,* July 29, 1978.
63. Diesendorf, "Recent Scandinavian R&D in Wind Electric Power."
64. Ibid.
65. Volta Torrey, "Blowing Up More Kilowatts from Wind," *Technology Review,* February 1980; R. Jeffrey Smith, "Wind Power Excites Utility Interest," *Science,* February 15, 1980.
66. Torrey, "Blowing Up More Kilowatts from Wind."
67. Burt Solomon, "Windmills Move into the Market," *Energy Daily,* March 27, 1980.
68. Ibid.
69. "Wind Power Excites Utility Interest," *Science,* February 15, 1980.
70. "Soviets Set Wind-Power Goal."
71. Musgrove, "Windmills Change Direction."
72. Gustavson, "Limits to Wind Power Utilization."
73. Louis J. Goodman et al., "Tapping the Earth's Powering Inferno," *East-West Perspectives* (Honolulu), Winter 1980.
74. Joseph Kestin et al., eds., "Sourcebook on the Production of Electricity from Geothermal Energy," U. S. Department of Energy, Washington, D.C., August 1980; Vasel Roberts, "Geothermal Energy," in Peter Auer, ed., *Advances in Energy Systems and Technology,* Volume 1 (New York: Academic Press, 1978).
75. Information on industrial applications in Roberts, "Geothermal Energy."
76. Kestin et al., "Sourcebook on the Production of Electricity."
77. Ibid.
78. Interagency Geothermal Coordinating Council, *Geothermal Energy Research Development and Demonstration Program, Fourth Annual Report* (Washington, D.C.: U.S. Department of Energy, June 1980).
79. Goodman et al., "Tapping the Earth's Powering Inferno."
80. Kestin et al., "Sourcebook on the Production of Electricity."

81. Interagency Geothermal Coordinating Council, *Geothermal Energy.*
82. Goodman et al., "Tapping the Earth's Powering Inferno."
83. Kestin et al., "Sourcebook on the Production of Electricity."
84. Ibid.
85. Ibid.
86. "Pacific's Ring of Fire Spews Geothermal Electric Power," *Christian Science Monitor,* September 18, 1980.
87. Denis Hayes, *Rays of Hope: The Transition to a Post-Petroleum World* (New York: W. W. Norton & Co., 1977).
88. Abe Rabinovich, "More than One in Ten Israelis Heat With Solar Energy Units," *World Environment Report,* March 24, 1980.
89. Organization for Economic Co-operation and Development, *Energy Balances of OECD Countries* (Paris: 1978).
90. U.S. General Accounting Office, *Commercializing Solar Heating: A National Strategy Needed* (Washington, D.C.: July 20, 1979).
91. Ibid.
92. "California Leads Nation in Solar Development," *Washington Star,* March 3, 1979.
93. "Nation's Largest Solar System," *Journal of Commerce,* November 30, 1978.
94. George F. W. Telfer, "France Bares Solar Power Muscle," *Journal of Commerce,* March 12, 1979.
95. A. E. Cullison, "Japan to Launch Solar Heat Drive," *Journal of Commerce,* August 8, 1979.
96. DOE, Energy Information Administration, *Solar Collector Manufacturing Activity, July through December 1980* (Washington, D.C.: March 1981).
97. Henry W. Kendall and Steven W. Nadis, eds., *Energy Strategies: Toward A Solar Future* (Cambridge, Mass.: Ballinger, 1980).
98. Henry Kelly, "Photovoltaic Power Systems: A Tour Through the Alternatives," *Science,* February 10, 1978.
99. Edwin McDowell, "Solarville, Ariz: Down to $7 a Watt," *New York Times,* June 24, 1979.
100. "Southern Railways Utilizes Solar Energy," *Journal of Commerce,* July 24, 1979.
101. McDowell, "Solarville, Ariz."; Kelly, "Photovoltaic Power Systems."
102. Kelly, "Photovoltaic Power Systems."
103. "The Commercial Hunt of the Sun," *The Economist,* February 9, 1980.

104. "The Commercial Hunt of the Sun"; Anthony J. Parisi, "Arco Pays $25 Million to Speed Solar Plan," *New York Times*, January 16, 1980.

105. "The Commercial Hunt of the Sun."

106. "Siemens Moves into P.V. Cell Production," *European Energy Report* (London), February 20, 1981.

107. McDowell, "Solarville, Ariz."; Louis Rosenblum et al., *Photovoltaic Power Systems for Rural Areas of Developing Countries*, NASA Technical Memorandum 79097 available from the National Technical Information Service (Cleveland, Ohio: National Aeronautics and Space Administration, 1979).

108. Rosenblum et al., *Photovoltaic Power Systems for Rural Areas of Developing Countries.*

109. "India Developing Solar Power for Rural Electricity," *New York Times*, May 11, 1979.

110. Ken Butti and John Perlin, *A Golden Thread: 2500 Years of Solar Architecture and Technology* (New York: Van Nostrand Reinhold and Co., 1980).

111. Barbara Miller, "Super-Insulated Houses Slash Energy Use," *Appropriate Technology Times*, Spring 1980.

112. Ibid.

113. Robert M. Press, "A Building Design That Cuts Energy Costs by 70 Percent," *Christian Science Monitor*, July 24, 1979.

114. Christopher Flavin, *Energy and Architecture: The Solar and Conservation Potential*, Worldwatch Paper 40 (Washington, D.C.: Worldwatch Institute, November 1980).

115. "Plugging into Renewable Resources–NRDC Leads the Way," *NRDC News*, Spring 1981.

Chapter 10. The Shape of a Sustainable Society

1 Philippine Ministry of Energy, *Ten Year Energy Program, 1980-1989* (Manila: 1980).

2 Thomas B. Johansson and Peter Steen, *Solar Sweden—An Outline to a Renewable Energy System* (Stockholm: Secretariat for Future Studies, 1978); for short summary see Thomas B. Johansson and Peter Steen, "Solar Sweden," *The Bulletin of the Atomic Scientists*, October 1979.

3. "Solar Energy Programs and Goal for Year 2000 are Proposed by Carter," *Wall Street Journal*, June 21, 1979.

4. U. S. Department of Agriculture (USDA), *Agricultural Statistics, 1980* (Washington, D.C.: Government Printing Office, 1980).

5. Motor Vehicle Manufacturers Association of the United States, Inc.

(MVMA), Detroit, Michigan, private communications, April 22 and May 7, 1981.

6. MVMA, *Motor Vehicle Facts and Figures, 1979* (Detroit, Mich.: 1979).

7. Robert U. Ayres, for Oak Ridge National Laboratory, *Worldwide Transportation/Energy Demand Forecast: 1975-2000* (Springfield, Va.: National Technical Information Service, 1978).

8. Joel Kotkin, "Odd-Even System Eases California's Gasoline Lines," *Washington Post,* June 19, 1979; Judith Cummings, "Two More States Add Odd-Even Gas Sales," *New York Times,* June 28, 1979.

9. "Sunday Closing Working in Japan," *Washington Star,* June 6, 1979; Brazilian information based on visit to Brazil by author, July 1-9, 1979; information on New Zealand from David Barber, Washington correspondent of the New Zealand Press Association, private communication, March 13, 1980.

10. Manik de Silva, "Sri Lanka's Gas Conservation Plan has Serious Side Effects," *World Environment Report,* June 16, 1980.

11. "Bulgaria Bans Cars on Certain Days," *Journal of Commerce,* May 23, 1979.

12. "The Most Spoiled Communists in World," *U.S. News and World Report,* August 20, 1979.

13. Peter L. Watson and Edward P. Holland, *Relieving Traffic Congestion: The Singapore Area License Scheme,* World Bank Staff Working Paper No. 281 (Washington, D.C.: World Bank, June 1978).

14. Neil Peirce, "Learning from Europe's Cities," *Transatlantic Perspectives,* June 1979. For a description see Cynthia Whitehead, "Taming Automobiles in Neighborhoods," *Transatlantic Perspectives,* September 1980.

15. U.S. Department of Energy, "International Petroleum Annual 1977," Washington, D.C., June 1, 1979.

16. Lester R. Brown, Christopher Flavin, and Colin Norman, *Running on Empty: The Future of the Automobile in an Oil-Short World* (New York: W. W. Norton & Co., 1979).

17. Information on Greyhound buses and U.S. automobiles in "The Most Fuel Efficient Way to Travel: Intercity Bus," Greyhound pamphlet, 1980.

18. "The Rub in Gasoline Retailing," *Business Week,* May 4, 1981.

19. Charles E. Dole, "Diesel Cars Lure the Fuel-Thrifty Buyer," *Christian Science Monitor,* October 26, 1979.

20. Rushworth Kidder, "Will New, 83 m.p.g. Car Save Britain's King of the Road?," *Christian Science Monitor,* September 16, 1980.

21. C. Kenneth Orski, "Transportation Planning as if People Mattered," *Practicing Planner,* March 1979.

22. "No More Private Cars?," *Christian Science Monitor,* August 5, 1975; Goran Backstrand and Lars Ingelstam, "Should We Put Limits on Consumption?," *The Futurist,* June 1977.
23. John Neff, American Public Transit Association, private communication, February 14, 1980.
24. U. S. Department of Transportation, Urban Mass Transportation Administration, private communication, April 21, 1981.
25. "Energy Cited in Curtailing Ohio Highway," *Washington Post,* December 1, 1979.
26. Edward Hudson, "Uncertainty Looms Over New Projects on the Uncompleted Interstate System," *New York Times,* January 19, 1981.
27. R. Neil Sampson, "Energy: New Kinds of Competition for Land," presented to the 35th Annual Meeting of the Soil Conservation Society of America, Dearborn, Michigan, August 6, 1980.
28. Philippine Ministry of Energy, *Ten Year Energy Program.*
29. Ronald D. James, Vice President, Thermonetics, Inc., Oklahoma City, private communication, May 18, 1981.
30. Y. Morooka, R. W. Herdt, and L. D. Haws, *An Analysis of the Labor-Intensive Continuous Rice Production System at IRRI,* IRRI Research Paper Series No. 29 (Manila: May 1979).
31. "Bombadier: Making a Second Leap from Snowmobiles to Mass Transit," *Business Week,* February 23, 1981.
32. Elizabeth Pond, "Will Germans Use Their Bikes?," *Christian Science Monitor,* November 8, 1977; "Pedal Power," *The Economist,* July 19, 1980.
33. "Blowing Hard," *The Economist,* February 9, 1980.
34. Jess Lukomski, "Germans Bullish on Solar Energy," *Journal of Commerce,* July 1, 1980.
35. E. Ariane Van Buren, "Biogas Beyond China: First International Training Program for Developing Countries," *Ambio,* Vol. IX, No. 1, 1980.
36. Robert H. Williams and Marc H. Ross, "Drilling for Oil and Gas in Our Houses," *Technology Review,* March/April 1980.
37. Philippine Ministry of Energy, *Ten Year Energy Program.*
38. Council on Economic Priorities, *Jobs and Energy: The Employment and Economic Impacts of Nuclear Power, Conservation, and Other Energy Options* (New York: 1979).
39. Bertrand Renaud, "World Urbanization Trends," *International Review* (Toronto, Canada), Vol. 1, Issue 4, no date. See also Bertrand Renaud, *National Urbanization Policies in Developing Countries,* World Bank Staff Working Paper No. 347 (Washington, D.C.: World Bank, July 1979).

40. Figures for 1950 quoted from *Agricultural Statistics, 1952,* in private communication with USDA April 22, 1981; 1980 figure from Table 5-2, Chapter 5.
41. Michael Lipton, "Urban Bias and Food Policy in Poor Countries," *Food Policy,* November 1975.
42. Michael Lipton, "Urban Bias: Or Why Rural People Stay Poor," *People* (London), Vol. 3, No. 2, 1976.
43. Lester C. Thurow, "Inflation: We Have Met the Enemy . . . ," *New York Times,* National Economic Survey, January 6, 1980.
44. Ibid.
45. Bill Wilkinson, Bicycle Manufacturers Association, private communication, May 21, 1981; census figures in U.S. Department of Transportation, *Bicycle Transportation for Energy Conservation* (Washington, D.C.: April 1980).
46. Robin Herman, "Bike Riders Gearing for Transit Strike," *New York Times,* March 26, 1980.
47. Nigel Smith. *Wood: An Ancient Fuel with a New Future,* Worldwatch Paper 42 (Washington, D.C.: Worldwatch Institute, January 1981).
48. Family size in these countries averages two children per couple (based on data from the 1980 World Population Data Sheet of the Population Reference Bureau (PRB), and from a private communication with PRB on October 28, 1981), establishing a range of total fertility rates for these countries from 2.3 in Hong Kong to 1.6 in Western Europe.
49. Pranay B. Gupte, "Ghana Moves to Rebuild Transport System," *New York Times,* October 2, 1980.
50. Dana G. Dalrymple, *Survey of Multiple Cropping in Less Developed Nations* (Washington, D.C.: USDA, Foreign Agricultural Service, October 1971).
51. United Nations, Department of International Economic and Social Affairs, Statistical Office, *1979 Yearbook of World Energy Statistics* (New York: 1981).
52. James D. Stocker, Vice-President, Scott Paper Company, Philadelphia, Pennsylvania, private communication, October 29, 1979.
53. "For Aluminum, A Shift Overseas," *Business Week,* December 8, 1980; Henry Giniger, "A Dispute Over Power Escalates," *New York Times,* November 22, 1980. For a good example of the energy supply problems of the aluminum industry, see Dan Morgan, "Aluminum Industry at Center of Northwest's Energy Fight," *Washington Post,* October 29, 1981.
54. Warren Hoge, "Brazil Taps Amazon Aluminum," *New York Times,* September 29, 1980.

55. "Boosting Aluminum Output to Join the Giants," *Business Week,* September 24, 1979; Henry Kamm, "Dam Project Brings Little Gain for Sumatra's People," *New York Times,* October 2, 1980.

Chapter 11. The Means of Transition

1. Lester C. Thurow, review of *Knowledge and Decisions* by Thomas Sewell, *New Republic,* June 28, 1980.
2. Gertrude E. Schroeder, "The Soviet Economy on a Treadmill of Reforms," in U.S. Congress Joint Economic Committee, *Soviet Economy in a Time of Change,* Vol. I, Committee Print (Washington, D.C.: October 10, 1979).
3. United Nations (UN) Department of International Economic and Social Affairs, *World Energy Supplies, 1950–1975* (New York: 1976).
4. Act 226, enacted by Vermont State Legislature in 1976, authorizes the towns of Vermont to exempt investments associated with solar energy facilities from personal property tax, according to Dennis Meadows, private communication, May 7, 1981.
5. David Howell, "Conservation Key to Energy Policy," *Journal of Commerce,* September 21, 1979.
6. Brazilian Embassy, "Brazil Today," Washington, D.C., September 21, 1979; Luiz Felipe P. Lampreia, "The Brazilian Experience in Alcohol Fuels," presented in Chicago, May 1–2, 1980, available from the Brazilian Embassy, Washington, D.C.
7. Pi-chao Chen, Wayne State University, private communication, August 10, 1979.
8. Dorothy L. Nortman and Ellen Hofstatter, *Population and Family Programs,* ninth edition (New York: Population Council, 1978).
9. Pi-chao Chen, introduction to article by Chen Muhua, "Birth Planning in China," *International Family Planning Perspectives,* September 1979.
10. Nortman and Hofstatter, *Population and Family Planning Programs.*
11. "West Germans Debate Gasoline Tax Hike," *The Socioeconomic Newsletter,* Institute for Socioeconomic Studies, White Plains, N.Y., January 1981.
12. "Driving Out of Singapore," *Asiaweek,* March 7, 1980.
13. Richard Leger, "Oil Price Surge Clobbers Less-Developed Nations Such as Kenya and Cuts Their Living Standards," *Wall Street Journal,* May 30, 1979.
14. George B. Merry, "New 'Bottle Bills' Face Crucial Tests in Months Ahead," *Christian Science Monitor,* January 27, 1981.
15. "Norway's New Car Junking Program Is a Success," *World Environment Report,* July 18, 1979.

16. See discussion in Lester R. Brown, Christopher Flavin, and Colin Norman, *Running on Empty: The Future of the Automobile in an Oil-Short World* (New York: W. W. Norton & Co., 1979).

17. John Vinocur, "For West Germans, Speeding Means More Than Oil," *New York Times,* July 1, 1979.

18. A. E. Cullison, "Japan To Double Coal Energy," *Journal of Commerce,* May 25, 1979.

19. Mike Sloop, San Diego Energy Office, private communication, May 20, 1980.

20. Henry Scott Stokes, "Japan Will Dim Lights in Conservation Step," *New York Times,* January 10, 1980; French Embassy, Washington, D.C., private communication, June 2, 1981.

21. Roger Sant, *The Least-Cost Energy Strategy: Minimizing Consumer Cost through Competition* (Pittsburgh, Pa.; Carnegie Mellon University Press, 1979); Marc H. Ross and Robert H. Williams, *Our Energy: Regaining Control* (New York: McGraw-Hill, 1981); Robert Stobaugh and Daniel Yergin, eds., *Energy Future: Report of the Energy Project at the Harvard Business School* (New York: Random House, 1979); Solar Energy Research Institute, *Report on Building a Sustainable Future* (Washington, D.C.: U.S. House of Representatives, Committee on Energy and Commerce, Committee Print, April 1981).

22. Roger W. Sant, "Good News for Consumers," *The Energy Consumer,* U.S. Department of Energy, January 1981.

23. Ibid.

24. Robert H. Williams, "The Federal Government's Role in a Market Oriented Fuel Conservation Strategy," Testimony before the U.S. House of Representatives, Energy Conservation and Power Subcommittee of the Committee on Energy and Commerce, February 24, 1981.

25. Ibid.

26. Information on U.S. conservation expenditures in "Energy Conservation: Spawning a Billion-Dollar Business," *Business Week,* April 6, 1981.

27. "A High-Risk Era for the Utilities," *Business Week,* February 23, 1981.

28. "World Bank Plans Larger Energy Lending Scheme," *Oil and Gas Journal,* November 17, 1980.

29. See Colin Norman "U.S. Derails Energy Plan for Third World," *Science,* April 3, 1981.

30. "IDA Assists Afforestation Project in Bangladesh," IDA News Release No. 80/96, World Bank, June 12, 1980.

31. "World Bank Lends $125 Million for Expanding Electricity in Medellin, Colombia," News Release No. 80/118, World Bank, June 12, 1980.

32. "World Bank Provides $40 Million to Kenya for Geothermal Power," News Release No. 80/48, World Bank, January 24, 1980.

33. Saburo Okita and Kimo Tahare, *Doubling Rice Production in Asia* (Tokyo: Overseas Cooperative Development Fund, 1976).

34. U.S. Department of Agriculture, *Soil and Water Resources Conservation Act, Summary of Appraisal, Parts I and II, and Program Report, Review Draft, 1980* (Washington, D.C.: 1980).

35. Robert E. Tomasson, "Connecticut Pays $252,000 to Preserve Man's Farm," *New York Times*, December 15, 1979.

36. Executive Office of the President of the United States, Office of Management and Budget, *The Budget of the United States Government, Fiscal Year 1981* (Washington, D.C.: Government Printing Office, January 1980).

37. U.S. Agency for International Development, *Agency Congressional Presentation F.Y. 1982* as amended for the Reagan Budget (Washington, D.C.: March 1981).

38. John Spears and Montague Yudelman, "Forests in Development," *Finance and Development*, December 1979.

39. "The Jakarta Statement," issued by International Conference on Family Planning in the 80's, held in Jakarta, Indonesia, April 26–30, 1981.

40. Daniel S. Greenberg, *The Politics of Pure Science* (New York: New American Library, 1967).

41. Colin Norman, *Knowledge and Power: The Global Research and Development Budget*, Worldwatch Paper 31 (Washington, D.C.: Worldwatch Institute, July 1979).

42. International Energy Agency, *Energy Research, Development and Demonstration in IEA Countries, 1979 Review of Programmes* (Paris: 1980). See also Colin Norman, *The God That Limps: Science and Technology in the Eighties* (New York, W.W. Norton and Co: forthcoming).

43. Ibid.

44. Ibid.

45. Norman, *Knowledge and Power.*

46. Personal communication at the World Food Conference sponsored by the UN Food and Agriculture Organization, Rome, 1974.

47. Joseph Kraft, "A Talk With Trudeau," *Washington Post*, May 17, 1977.

48. Warren G. Bennis, "Where Have All the Leaders Gone?," *Technology Review*, March/April 1977.

49. Ibid.

50. "Critical Moment in Bangladesh," *People*, (London), Vol. 7, No. 4, 1980.

51. Stuart Auerbach, "President Zia Has Reputation as 'Bangladesh's No. 1 Motivator'," *Washington Post,* March 28, 1981.
52. Stuart Auerbach, "Bangladesh, at Age 10, Sees Itself in Reach of Self-Sufficiency in Food," *Washington Post,* March 28, 1981.
53. Bernard D. Nossiter, " 'The Cupboard of Ideas is Bare'," *Washington Post,* May 20, 1979.
54. Ibid.
55. Jim Browning, "Trash Recycling Makes It a Nicer Place to Live," *Christian Science Monitor,* January 3, 1979.
56. Mark Cherniak, "What One Country is Doing to Earn Energy Freedom," *Christian Science Monitor,* December 17, 1979.
57. Ibid.
58. Marie Ridder, "Births and the Nation," *Washington Post,* November 11, 1979.
59. Ibid.
60. Richard M. Harley, "Man with a Plan: How India Can Feed Its Hungry," *Christian Science Monitor,* August 8, 1978; George Dorsey, "Milk and Justice," *Ceres,* November/December 1978.
61. Quoted in Charles D. Pierce, "Who Owns the Future?," *EPA Journal,* October 1980.

Chapter 12. The Institutional Challenge

1. Hazel Henderson, address to the World Future Society Conference, Toronto, Canada, July 20–24, 1980.
2. Charles Ryan, "Energy and Social Change," in Dennis Meadows, ed., *Alternatives to Growth–II* (Cambridge, Mass.: Ballinger, forthcoming).
3. Robert Lekachman, "A Cure for Corporate Neurosis," *Saturday Review,* January 21, 1978.
4. Willis W. Harman, "The Coming Transformation," *The Futurist,* April 1977.
5. Stanley I. Fischler, *Moving Millions: An Inside Look at Mass Transit* (New York: Harper and Row, 1979).
6. Ibid.
7. Ibid.
8. Amory B. Lovins, L. Hunter Lovins, and Leonard Ross, "Nuclear Power and Nuclear Bombs," *Foreign Affairs,* Summer 1980.
9. "Edison Announces Major Policy Shift to Renewable Energy Sources," press release, Southern California Edison, October 17, 1980.
10. Ben A. Franklin, "Commuters in Vans Get Special Treatment," *New York Times,* February 10, 1980.
11. Lynn White, "The Historical Roots of Our Ecological Crisis," *Science,* March 10, 1967.

12. E. F. Schumacher, *Small is Beautiful: Economics as if People Mattered* (New York: Harper and Row, 1973).

13. Rufus Miles, Jr., *Awakening from the American Dream: The Social and Political Limits to Growth* (New York: Universe Books, 1976).

14. Jørgen Randers and Donella H. Meadows, "The Carrying Capacity of Our Global Environment: A Look at the Ethical Alternatives," in Dennis Meadows and Donella H. Meadows, eds., *Toward Global Equilibrium* (Cambridge, Mass.: M.I.T. Press, 1973).

15. Kenneth A. Briggs, "Theologians Weigh Links to Scientists," *New York Times*, July 15, 1979.

16. Ibid.

17. Kenneth A. Briggs, "Scientists and Theologians in Call for a Joint Effort to End Discord," *New York Times*, July 25, 1979.

18. National Council of Churches, private communication, April 14, 1981.

19. Kenneth A. Briggs, "Religious Coalition Calls for a Halt to Nuclear Power and Arms Race," *New York Times*, May 3, 1979.

20. Ibid.

21. Duane S. Elgin and Arnold Mitchell, "Voluntary Simplicity: Lifestyle of the Future?," *The Futurist*, August 1977.

22. Jane Brody, "Fewer Catholics Said to Meet Church Rule on Birth Control," *New York Times*, September 26, 1977.

23. Kenneth A. Briggs, "Ireland's Catholic Church, Facing Resistance to Authority, Seeks a New Role in Society," *New York Times*, July 15, 1979.

24. Warren Hoge, "Brazilians Battle Over Land, With Church Backing Poor," *New York Times*, March 4, 1980.

25. Karen DeYoung, "Catholic Church, Military Draw Battle Lines in El Salvador," *Washington Post*, May 22, 1977.

26. Marlise Simons, "Militant Clergy Side with the Poor, Spur Unrest in Mexico," *Washington Post*, April 5, 1978.

27. George Vecsey, "Catholic Church Backing Debates on Land Reform," *New York Times*, July 22, 1979.

28. Jeremy Rifkin, "Theology and Scarcity," *New York Times*, December 30, 1979.

29. Ibid.

30. Barbara Miller, "Super-Insulated Houses Slash Energy Use," *Appropriate Technology Times*, Spring 1980.

31. Robert Stobaugh and Daniel Yergin, eds., *Energy Future: Report of the Energy Project at the Harvard Business School* (New York: Random House, 1979).

32. "The University and the Third System," *IFDA Dossier 12*, International Foundation for Development Alternatives, October 1979.

33. David Talbot, "Conservatopia, U.S.A.," *Mother Jones*, August 1979.
34. Melvin A. Eggers, "Where Education is Losing Touch," *Business Week*, September 15, 1975.
35. Walter C. Patterson, "The Open University Tackles Control of Technology," *The Bulletin of the Atomic Scientists*, March 1980.
36. Ibid.
37. John Merrow, "Adult Courses in China: A Leap Forward for Millions," *New York Times*, September 9, 1979.
38. Robert L. Heilbroner, "Priorities for the Seventies," *Current*, March 1970.
39. "Survey Eyes Income of Ecology Groups," *Journal of Commerce*, October 17, 1978.
40. Neal R. Peirce, "Grass-Roots Protests on German Soil," *Washington Post*, August 22, 1977.
41. Bayard Webster, "Audubon Group Plans Science Effort," *New York Times*, May 22, 1979.
42. A. D. Latornell, "Resources for Food and Living: Will There be Enough?," *Journal of Soil and Water Conservation*, September/October 1978.
43. Ibid.
44. "Parisians Lobby for Improved Transit Service," *Transatlantic Perspectives*, March 1980.
45. Quoted in Peirce, "Grass-Roots Protests on German Soil."
46. Ralph Mongeluzo, Solar Lobby, Washington, D.C., private communication, April 29, 1981.
47. "Alternative Energy Systems for Pacific Gas and Electric Company: An Economic Analysis," prepared testimony of W.R.Z. Willey, Staff Economist, Environmental Defense Fund (San Francisco), 1978.
48. Rachel Carson, *Silent Spring* (Boston: Houghton Mifflin, 1962).
49. Donella H. Meadows et al., *The Limits to Growth* (New York: Universe Books, 1972).
50. Schumacher, *Small is Beautiful.*
51. See Herbert Marshall McLuhan, *The Gutenberg Galaxy: The Making of Typographic Man* (Toronto, Canada: University of Toronto Press, 1962) and *Understanding Media: The Extensions of Man* (New York: McGraw-Hill, 1964).
52. Deirdre Wulf, "Costa Rica Leads Latin America's Fertility Decline Partly Because of National Program's Rural Impact," *Family Planning Perspectives*, Fall 1978.

Chapter 13. Changing Values and Shifting Priorities

1. Tom Bender, "Why We Need to Get Poor Quick," *The Futurist,* August 1977.
2. Bruce Murray, "Prophet of Tomorrow's Redirected Technology," *Christian Science Monitor,* November 3, 1976.
3. Duane S. Elgin and Arnold Mitchell, "Voluntary Simplicity: Lifestyle of the Future?," *The Futurist,* August 1977.
4. Willis W. Harman, "The Coming Transformation," *The Futurist,* April 1977.
5. 1980 World Population Data Sheet of the Population Reference Bureau (Washington, D.C.).
6. John A. Prestbo, "Companies Turn More Reluctant to Move Corporate Headquarters," *Wall Street Journal,* January 16, 1981.
7. Harris and Roper polls in Elgin and Mitchell, "Voluntary Simplicity."
8. Stanford Research Institute estimates and Norwegian poll results from Elgin and Mitchell, "Voluntary Simplicity."
9. Ibid.
10. "Tanzanian Suggests Riding Bikes," *Washington Post,* August 22, 1979.
11. Volkswagen advertisement.
12. Herman E. Daly, in *The Patient Earth,* John Harte and Robert Socolow, eds., (New York: Holt, Rinehart and Winston, 1971), quoted in Jørgen Randers and Donella Meadows, "The Carrying Capacity of Our Global Environment: A Look at the Ethical Alternatives," in Dennis Meadows and Donella Meadows, eds., *Toward Global Equilibrium* (Cambridge, Mass: M.I.T. Press, 1973).
13. Carter Henderson, "The Frugality Phenomenon," *The Bulletin of the Atomic Scientists,* May 1978.
14. United Nations Environment Programme, *Annual Review 1978* (Nairobi, Kenya: 1980).
15. National Academy of Sciences (NAS), *Energy Choices in a Democratic Society,* Study of Nuclear and Alternative Energy Systems, Supporting Paper 7 (Washington, D.C.: 1980).
16. Willis W. Harman, "The Energy-Environment Dilemma," *EPA Journal,* November/December 1979.
17. Randers and Meadows, "The Carrying Capacity of Our Global Environment."
18. NAS, *Energy Choices in a Democratic Society.*
19. "Dr. Asimov: The Future is No Fun," *Washington Star,* April 27, 1975.

20. NAS, *Energy Choices in a Democratic Society.*
21. Overseas Development Council, *The United States and World Development: Agenda 1977* (New York: Praeger Publishers, 1977).
22. "Critical Moment in Bangladesh," *People* (London), Vol. 7, No. 4, 1980.
23. "West Germans Debate Gasoline Tax Hike," *The Socioeconomic Newsletter,* Institute for Socioeconomic Studies, White Plains, N.Y., January 1981.
24. David Hughart, *Prospects for Traditional and Non-Conventional Energy Sources in Developing Countries,* World Bank Staff Working Paper No. 346 (Washington, D.C. World Bank, July 1979).
25. René Dubos, "Less Energy, Better Life," *New York Times,* January 7, 1975.
26. Warren Johnson, *Muddling Toward Frugality* (San Francisco: Sierra Club Books, 1978).

Acknowledgments

Anyone who undertakes a work of the scope of this book incurs many debts. Outstanding among these is my debt to Pamela Shaw, who worked with me from the book's inception to its completion. Measured by the calendar and the clock, it was a full year. Pamela helped not only with the data gathering but also with the analysis. Our regular discusssions and her critique of the drafts as they evolved contributed to the shape of the book, making it in no small part hers as well as mine.

Kathleen Courrier brought her superb literary and editorial skills to bear on the manuscript in the later stages. In tightening and sharpening the prose, she helped clarify my own thinking. Beyond this, Kathy's intimate knowledge of some of the issues permitted her to make substantive contributions as well. You and I are both heavily indebted to her.

My secretary, Elizabeth Arnault, learned from experience that there are several drafts between the initial dictated draft and the final one. She typed, and retyped, and retyped . . . with only an occasional bemused smile. On numerous occasions Blondeen Gravely and Oretta Tarkhani helped with the typing as the drafts evolved. Patti Adams and Laurie Willingham quite willingly helped with proofreading. The other officers of the Worldwatch Institute—Felix Gorrell, treasurer, and Blondeen Gravely, secretary and assistant treasurer—lightened my managerial and administrative responsibilities, freeing up more time to work on the book.

Within the Institute, my colleagues Daniel Deudney, Christopher Flavin, Kathleen Newland, Colin Norman, Nigel Smith, Linda Starke, Bruce Stokes, Ann Thrupp, and Paige Tolbert all reviewed the manuscript. Of this group, Kathleen, Linda, Bruce, and Ann reviewed two different drafts. In addition to substantive comments, Linda Starke, editor of the Worldwatch Papers, suggested some exceedingly helpful improvements in the book's structure.

In addition to the in-house reviewers, nearly a score of readers from outside the Institute improved the manuscript with their suggestions. Among those who gave generously of their time were George Brockway, Erik Eckholm, Gail Finsterbush, Peter Freeman, Robert Gillespie, Garrett Hardin, Maureen Hinkle, Judith Jacobsen, Sander Levin, Dennis Meadows, Andrew Rice, Rick Roney, Roger Sant, Neil Schaller, and Jyoti Singh. Among this group, Gail set a record of sorts by reading three drafts.

I must acknowledge an intellectual debt to the many who have helped shape my thinking and, in turn, this book. Prominent among them are Gerald Barney, Norman Borlaug, Kenneth Boulding, Herman Daly, Rene Dubos, Erik Eckholm, Anne and Paul Erhlich, Jose Goldemberg, Willis Harman,

Denis Hayes, Robert Heilbroner, Hazel Henderson, M. King Hubbert, Warren Johnson, Thomas Lovejoy, Amory Lovins, Dennis and Donella Meadows, Rufus Miles, Norman Myers, Russell Peterson, David Pimentel, R. Neil Sampson, Roger Sant, E. F. Schumacher, Robert Stobaugh, Lester Thurow, B.B. Vohra, Frank von Hippel, Barbara Ward, Robert Williams, and Daniel Yergin. In attempting to embrace such a broad range of issues—economic, environmental, technological, social, and political—one necessarily must stand on the shoulders of others. In recognizing this, I also acknowledge that this list is by no means complete.

Since this book has benefited greatly from the research environment at the Worldwatch Institute, I am indebted to those who provide funding and direction for the Institute. Special recognition for the early funding is due to the Rockefeller Brothers Fund, particularly William Dietel. It was the Fund that provided the large start-up grant for the Institute's first three years. Other early funders included the Charles F. Kettering Foundation and Robert O. Anderson. At the international level, the UN Fund for Population Activities, which provided funding for this book, and the UN Environment Program have supported Worldwatch since its early days. Foundations that provide general support on an ongoing basis include Edna McConnell Clark, Geraldine R. Dodge, William and Flora Hewlett, Andrew W. Mellon, Edward John Noble, and the Rockefeller Brothers Fund. The George Gund Foundation provides project support on a regular basis.

Overall direction of the Institute comes from an international Board of Directors drawn from all walks of life; Charles M. Cargille (United States), Carlo M. Cipolla (Italy), Edward S. Cornish (United States), Mahbub ul Haq (Pakistan), Hazel Henderson (United States), Anne-Marie Holenstein (Switzerland), Abd-El Rahman Khane (Algeria), Larry Minear (United States), Andrew E. Rice (United States), Walter Orr Roberts (United States), Rafael M. Sales (Philippines), and Lynne G.

Stitt (United States). In addition to overall guidance, members of the Board also assist with the dissemination of the research product. Orville Freeman chairs the Board, drawing upon his wealth of management experience as three-term governor of Minnesota and as U.S. Secretary of Agriculture during the Kennedy and Johnson administrations.

When it began in early 1975, the Institute was something of an experiment, an effort to see whether a small team of analysts with a global orientation and representing no particular discipline could provide crisp, useful analyses of the important issues confronting leaders everywhere. Experience since then has shown not only that this is possible but also that there is a strong commercial demand for policy-oriented research. Income from sales of Worldwatch Papers, book royalties, and honoraria for articles and talks has increased each year since the Institute began. As of 1981, an earned income of nearly a thousand dollars a day covers just over half of total budgetary expenditures. Although the complimentary distribution of Worldwatch Papers and books to key people in some 122 countries is extensive, it is dwarfed by the commercial sales. For example, the Institute's income is fueled by royalties from some 72 publishing contracts for the first six books. There are over 100,000 copies in print of the most widely translated Worldwatch Papers. Worldwatch publications have appeared in some 26 languages ranging from Arabic, Spanish, and Russian to Tamil and Thai.

As of this writing in 1981 the Institute is no longer an experiment. It provides an ideal setting for doing the kind of research and writing embodied in this book. My thanks to all —funders, directors, and staff—who helped make it possible.

Index